Valuing People and Technology in the Workplace:

Ethical Implications and Imperatives for Success

Claretha Hughes
University of Arkansas, USA

A volume in the Advances in
Human Resources Management
and Organizational Development
(AHRMOD) Book Series

Published in the United States of America by
IGI Global
Business Science Reference (an imprint of IGI Global)
701 E. Chocolate Avenue
Hershey PA, USA 17033
Tel: 717-533-8845
Fax: 717-533-8661
E-mail: cust@igi-global.com
Web site: http://www.igi-global.com

Library of Congress Cataloging-in-Publication Data

Names: Hughes, Claretha, 1969- author.
Title: Valuing people and technology in the workplace : ethical
  implications and imperatives for success / by Claretha Hughes.
Description: Hershey, PA : Business Science Reference, [2023] | Includes
  bibliographical references and index. | Summary: "This book explores and
  further develops the five values of people and technology development
  through the enhanced seven-point Hughes Value Creation Model for
  Organizational Competitive Advantage. The original five-point model was
  derived over 20 years of personal experience within high-performance
  manufacturing industries, academia, and consulting. The original model
  depicted opportunities for examining the similarities between technology
  development and human resource development and how these similarities
  could be used for value creation within organizations. The model
  provided a starting point to determine the extent to which location,
  use, maintenance, modification, and time value creation may be obtained
  from integrating technology development and human resource development
  from the cognitive, behavioral, and cultural philosophical perspectives
  (Hughes, 2010, 2012)"-- Provided by publisher.
Identifiers: LCCN 2022043262 (print) | LCCN 2022043263 (ebook) | ISBN
  9781668453216 (hardcover) | ISBN 9781668453223 (paperback) | ISBN
  9781668453230 (ebook)
Subjects: LCSH: Personnel management. | Corporate culture. |
  Employees--Effect of technological innovations on. | Technological
  innovations--Management.
Classification: LCC HF5549 .H78136 2023 (print) | LCC HF5549 (ebook) |
  DDC 658.3--dc23/eng/20220930
LC record available at https://lccn.loc.gov/2022043262
LC ebook record available at https://lccn.loc.gov/2022043263

This book is published in the IGI Global book series Advances in Human Resources Management and Organizational Development (AHRMOD) (ISSN: 2327-3372; eISSN: 2327-3380)

British Cataloguing in Publication Data
A Cataloguing in Publication record for this book is available from the British Library.

For electronic access to this publication, please contact: eresources@igi-global.com.

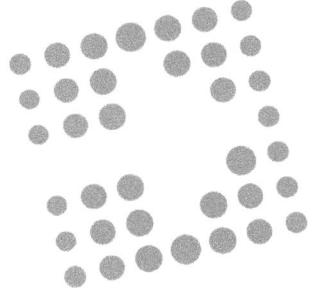

Advances in Human Resources Management and Organizational Development (AHRMOD) Book Series

ISSN:2327-3372
EISSN:2327-3380

Editor-in-Chief: Patricia Ordóñez de Pablos Universidad de Oviedo, Spain

MISSION

A solid foundation is essential to the development and success of any organization and can be accomplished through the effective and careful management of an organization's human capital. Research in human resources management and organizational development is necessary in providing business leaders with the tools and methodologies which will assist in the development and maintenance of their organizational structure.

The **Advances in Human Resources Management and Organizational Development (AHRMOD) Book Series** aims to publish the latest research on all aspects of human resources as well as the latest methodologies, tools, and theories regarding organizational development and sustainability. The **AHRMOD Book Series** intends to provide business professionals, managers, researchers, and students with the necessary resources to effectively develop and implement organizational strategies.

COVERAGE

- Executive Compensation
- Employee Benefits
- Employee Communications
- Personnel Retention
- Skills Management
- Workplace Discrimination
- Training and Development
- Performance Improvement
- Talent Identification and Management
- Employee Relations

IGI Global is currently accepting manuscripts for publication within this series. To submit a proposal for a volume in this series, please contact our Acquisition Editors at Acquisitions@igi-global.com or visit: http://www.igi-global.com/publish/.

Titles in this Series

For a list of additional titles in this series, please visit:
www.igi-global.com/book-series/advances-human-resources-management-organizational/73670

Developing Diversity, Equity, and Inclusion Policies for Promoting Employee Sustainability and Well-Being
Sónia P. Gonçalves (ISCSP, Universidade de Lisboa, Portugal) Paula Cristina Nunes Figueiredo (Universidade Lusófona, Portugal) Eduardo Luis Soares Tomé (ULHT, Universidade Lusófona, Portugal) and José Baptista (ISCSP, Universidade de Lisboa, Portugal)
Business Science Reference • © 2023 • 330pp • H/C (ISBN: 9781668441817) • US $240.00

Talent Acquisition and Retention Strategies in Global Startups
Neetima Agarwal (Symbiosis International University, India) Leo Paul Dana (Kingston University, UK) and Sujata Khandai (Amity University, India)
Business Science Reference • © 2023 • 305pp • H/C (ISBN: 9781668475140) • US $250.00

Female Entrepreneurship as a Driving Force of Economic Growth and Social Change
Ana Dias Daniel (Universidade de Aveiro, Portugal) and Cristina Fernandes (Universidade da Beira Interior, Portugal)
Business Science Reference • © 2023 • 320pp • H/C (ISBN: 9781668476697) • US $250.00

Strategic Human Resource Management in the Hospitality Industry A Digitalized Economic Paradigm
Kannapat Kankaew (Suan Sunandha Rajabhat University, Thailand)
Business Science Reference • © 2023 • 309pp • H/C (ISBN: 9781668474945) • US $250.00

Corporate Sustainability as a Tool for Improving Economic, Social, and Environmental Performance
Bartolomé Marco-Lajara (University of Alicante, Spain) Javier Martínez-Falcó (University of Alicante, Spain & Stellenbosch University, South Africa) and Luis A. Millán-Tudela (University of Alicante, Spain)
Business Science Reference • © 2023 • 337pp • H/C (ISBN: 9781668474228) • US $250.00

For an entire list of titles in this series, please visit:
www.igi-global.com/book-series/advances-human-resources-management-organizational/73670

701 East Chocolate Avenue, Hershey, PA 17033, USA
Tel: 717-533-8845 x100 • Fax: 717-533-8661
E-Mail: cust@igi-global.com • www.igi-global.com

To the memories of the late Eugene "Rooster" Hughes, Sr. and the late Eugene "Bo" Hughes, Jr.

Table of Contents

Preface

This book explains how philosophy, ethics, and systems theory influences the five values of people and technology development. Increasing this books' breadth and usefulness to the reader was needed as technology's use has exploded and many employees are being left behind during the COVID-19 pandemic. The subtitle of this book: *Ethical Implications and Imperatives for Success,* provides and expands on ethical, moral, and philosophical concepts in the context of human resource development (HRD) (Hughes, 2019). The COVID-19 pandemic is mentioned because of its impact on several of the concepts in this book.

The three main areas that are included to explain how philosophy, ethics, and systems theory relate to the five values are the three philosophical perspectives, diversity intelligence, and the workforce inter-personnel diversity talent management system. The ideas around philosophy are explained in the cognitive, behavioral, and cultural philosophical perspectives. The concepts of diversity intelligence and the workforce inter-personnel diversity talent management system were derived from the ideas in the previous *Valuing People and Technology in the Workplace* book (Hughes, 2012) and published in their own books (Hughes, 2016, 2018). The goal of this book is to explain these concepts and how they interact with each other in a single publication. The case study used to create and test the people as technology concept is highlighted for the reader. More frequent mentions of the ethical implications of decisions regarding people and technology in the workplace; increased emphasis on the importance of considering philosophical aspects of organization development initiatives; and a stronger discussion of implications for human resource development professionals, practitioners, and scholars are provided.

ORGANIZATION OF THE BOOK

The book is organized into 9 chapters. A brief description of each of the chapters follows:

Chapter 1 identifies six existing challenges in the management of people and technology within the global workplace. This chapter provides a brief introduction and synopsis of the purpose of work. It questions where organization value resides and introduces six challenges for leaders to consider. (1) The ethical people and technology development intention of management and leadership. (2) The ethical ways that managers and leaders value people and technology in the workplace. (3) The ethical impact of organization development initiatives that align people and technology within the workplace. (4) The role of the cognitive, behavioral and/or cultural philosophical perspectives of organizations and its ethical effect on people and technology. (5) How ethical leaders can understand and use diversity intelligence® (DQ) to ethically value all employees in the workplace. (6) The ethical implications and imperatives for managers and leaders to be successful integrating people and technology in the workplace.

Chapter 2 discusses philosophy and organizations and establishes the need to understand organizations and the philosophical perspectives from which organizations develop their organization development for performance. The author contends that the cognitive, behavioral, and/ or cultural philosophical perspectives are present within all organizations and can influence the productivity gains and competitive advantage of organizations. All organizations operate primarily from one of three philosophical perspectives or a combination thereof. The three philosophical perspectives are cognitive, behavioral, and cultural. An organization's core values, strategies, and/or frames originate from its cognitive, behavioral, and /or cultural philosophical perspective. The chapter focused on explaining cognitive, behavioral, and cultural philosophical perspectives of organizations and ethical implications.

Chapter 3 discusses ways that technology and people are central to the success of modern organizations. This chapter explains the creation of the people as technology concept and provides a synopsis of the case from which the concept originated and was developed. Enhancements for PT concept are discussed along with ways that education and training of employees increases organizational opportunities for success. The chapter also provides details of how the COVID-19 pandemic forced changes that highlighted the need for better people and technology interactions.

Chapter 4 provides an overview of the people as technology (PT) model and the five common values between people and technology. Location value represents power of position, power to generate revenue, power to leverage resources, and power to serve as a catalyst for change. Use value is a created value as leaders learn to create more value through effective use of employee skills and abilities within the workplace. Use value relates to the quality factor in a worker's productivity. Employee maintenance value is expressed through a combination of training and development, motivation, and health and wellness (Hughes, 2012). Modification value of people looks at how employees grow and change through activities that employees use for self-development including education. Time value is often directed but not measured accurately relative to cost for the organization or the individual. The COVID-19 pandemic made it abundantly apparent that employees are indeed the most important asset in organizations and understanding their values matters.

Chapter 5 describes the people as technology (PT) concept and the complex relationships of technology development and people development within organizations. Systems theory is a foundational theory of human resource development. This chapter describes how the PT concept relates to systems theory in the context of HRD. Implications for how ethical and unethical behavior influences organizational systems are provided. Comparison of the five values of people and technology development to six themes of high technology development, the six major factors to determine knowledge-worker productivity, and the disruption of the worldwide, COVID -19 pandemic is included. It also examines the similarities and contrasts between each value as it relates to both people and technology. The author suggests that there seems to be reluctance from organizations to fully commit the same resources for people values as they do for technology values.

Chapter 6 discusses workers' unique characteristics that contribute to their location, use, maintenance, modification, and time value. The exponential capability that exists within these values and the diversity that everyone possesses bring extensive opportunities for organizations. However, organizations must be able to recognize and leverage each person's contribution through diversity intelligence® (DQ) for added success, provides a description of diversity intelligence® (DQ), and explains how it is integral to *Hughes HRD Value Creation Model*. It also describes how DQ has the potential to impact talent development and management. The ethical implications and imperatives of leaders not being diversity intelligent is explained. It also explores how the five values can be used to expand performance and workforce inter-personnel diversity. It also explains how workforce inter-personnel diversity can be used as a talent management system. Once leaders are diversity intelligent, they will then be capable of understanding the organizations' workforce inter-personnel diversity which looks at the differences of each individual employee.

Chapter 7 provides content to help HRD scholars, professionals, and practitioners better understand the need for strategic human resource development (SHRD) The struggle of comparing people to technology and respectfully integrating people and technology in the workplace continues to be debated to the detriment of individual and organizational success. The COVID-19 pandemic revealed how far behind HRD scholars, professionals, and practitioners are when needed to integrate and enhance the relationship between people and technology in the workplace (Hughes, 2021).

Chapter 8 describes the need to align organization development (OD) initiatives with the philosophical perspectives of the organization. Cognitive philosophical perspective organizations should use cognitive OD initiatives within its organizational culture to develop people and technology within the workplace. The cognitive OD initiatives that are most popular in today's workplace are teaching, learning, procedures and processes, and motivation. Organizations that operate within the behavioral philosophical perspective often focus more on the technological impact within the workplace environment rather than employee role. The ethical and legal implications of behavioral OD initiatives are important. Cultural OD initiatives are influenced by both the internal culture of the organization and the external culture within which the organization operates. Ethical employees, ethical workplace environments, and ethical use of technology are also discussed.

Chapter 9 provides a detailed description of the seven-point *Hughes Human Resource Development (HRD) Value Creation Model* draws on many fields of study including psychology, education, human resource management, human resource development, strategic technology management, management, and engineering. All these fields intersect within the workplace, primarily through people and technology development. Understanding the links between people and technology development and value creation allows organizations to extend their competitive advantage in ways not previously considered. This model represents a comprehensive, theoretical, yet operational model that can be used to explain and illustrate value for organizations. It is robust, clear, easy to follow, and fills organizational needs. Users of this model should keep ethics foremost in their minds as they seek to integrate people and technology in the workplace.

Claretha Hughes
University of Arkansas, USA

REFERENCES

Hughes, C. (2012). *Valuing people and technology in the workplace: A competitive advantage framework.* IGI Global. doi:10.4018/978-1-4666-0240-3

Hughes, C. (2016). *Diversity intelligence: Integrating diversity intelligence alongside intellectual, emotional, and cultural intelligence for leadership and career development.* Palgrave MacMillan Publications. doi:10.1057/978-1-137-52683-0

Hughes, C. (2018). *Workforce inter-personnel diversity: The power to influence human productivity and career development.* Springer International Publishing.

Hughes, C. (2019). *Ethical and legal issues in human resource development: Evolving roles and emerging trends.* Springer International Publishing. doi:10.1007/978-3-319-99528-1

Acknowledgment

All glory to God for the gift of knowledge that He has provided me and the many people that He has placed in my life.

I would like to thank my daughter, Karla R. Banks, who was extremely supportive in numerous ways; especially enduring throughout the time it took for me to complete the first version of this book. Without Karla's mature, independent spirit and personality, this project would have been much more difficult to complete.

I would like to thank my parents, the late Mr. Eugene and Mrs. Rosa M. Hughes who supported and encouraged my interests throughout my life. I would like to especially thank my mother for continuously keeping my family and me in her prayers, and for doing everything within her power to make her children's lives better. I would like to thank all of my brothers and sisters who have always provided their support: Richard A. Hughes, John H. Hughes, Jerome Hughes, Jimmie L. Hughes, Terry W. Hughes, Bernice Hughes, Levern M. Hughes, Alfonso Hughes, Margaret A. McFadden, and Roselind L. Hughes. Their families have also been very supportive.

I would like to specifically thank Dr. Samuel Winchester for his support of this idea from its inception over 28 years ago, during completion of my master's degree, and at present. I would like to offer special recognition to Dr. Patrick A. O'Reilly for reading the initial theory paper and providing feedback for its evolution into this book and to Dr. Bobbie T. Biggs for reviewing the model upon its initial development. Thank you to Dr. Barbara Hinton for being the first to say, "Write up your work".

Thank you to all the anonymous, external reviewers for all the insightful feedback they provided during the writing of this book.

Extraordinary thanks Dr. David Robertson, Dr. Mary Ford, Dr. Merlin J. Augustine, and Sheila King for behaving like family, their friendship, and for reading the book when asked and providing sincere feedback for improvement.

Special thanks to Tim Franklin and Joseph Augustine for their brotherly support.

Thank you to the late Tamara D. McCutcheon for being a lifelong friend who was always seeking to understand the next innovation and motivating others to follow her lead. Technology and people were always at the forefront of her lifelong, continuous learning efforts.

Last but not least, I would like to thank the Reverend Lorenzo Jones, Jr. for all the love, being a prayer warrior, and a calming presence in the midst of life's challenges.

Section 1
Introduction and People as Technology Concept

Chapter 1

Six Ethical Challenges of Valuing People and Technology in the Workplace:
An Introduction

ABSTRACT

This chapter provides a brief introduction and synopsis of the purpose of work. It questions where organization value resides and introduces six challenges for leaders to consider: (1) The ethical people and technology development intention of management and leadership. (2) The ethical ways that managers and leaders value people and technology in the workplace. (3) The ethical impact of organization development initiatives that align people and technology within the workplace. (4) The role of the cognitive, behavioral and/or cultural philosophical perspectives of organizations and its ethical effect on people and technology. (5) How ethical leaders can understand and use diversity intelligence® (DQ) to ethically value all employees in the workplace. (6) The ethical implications and imperatives for managers and leaders to be successful integrating people and technology in the workplace.

INTRODUCTION

Work, in all its forms, has been required of humans since the beginning of time. It has been defined by many, understood to mean different things to

DOI: 10.4018/978-1-6684-5321-6.ch001

everyone, and its value to the individual and society remains a heated debate. The discussions around work are grounded in philosophy and how well those who explain work are understood by those receiving the explanation. Different societies have different perspectives about how much work should be required of individuals. These perspectives create divisions within communities and between countries as money has emerged as a central focus of work. Altruistic work is misunderstood, at times, if no monetary value is assigned to the work.

THE PURPOSE OF WORK

Philosophically, what is the purpose of work? What is the difference between work and employment? What has been philosophy's influence on work. There is no work without philosophies about work. Those who do no work even have a philosophy about work which is to do no work. What is the meaning of work to those who choose not to work? Is it the same as those who choose to work? When work is to be done, there is typically people and technology. So, how people and those who expect the employee to perform the work think about work matters. Do leaders think about their people or technology more? Is technology, philosophically, more important than people in the workplace.

People as Technology (PT) (Hughes, 2010) matches the development of people to the deliberate methods organizational leaders and managers use to introduce and integrate new innovations and technologies into organizations. The PT concept is a proactive, strategic method to introduce, develop, and integrate employees into organizations. Applying the PT concept requires leaders and managers to think of employees similarly and as positively as they think of technology. Technology in the context of this book includes all technology within organizations.

People are considered the most valuable asset within an organization. Yet, many employees do not feel valued by their employers. This is very evident with the quiet quitting phenomenon that has been highlighted during the COVID-19 pandemic (Formica & Sfodera, 2022; Lord, 2022). There has always been quiet quitting within organizations but not to the extent that is evident during the COVID-19 pandemic. Employees who are quiet quitting do not believe that organizations value them enough to appreciate any extra efforts, so they only perform the bare minimum that their job requires. Several questions remain to be answered by organization leaders including:

1. How do leaders show employees that they are valuable to and valued by the organization?
2. What is the best location value of an employee to the organization for the employee to exemplify use, maintenance, and modification values?
3. How does the organization best utilize the time value of an employee?

These questions are highlighted and heightened across many organizations during the worldwide, COVID-19 pandemic. There have been numerous methods used and trillions of dollars invested in organization development initiatives to try and leverage the effectiveness of people and technology to increase productivity and competitive advantage (Friedman, 1970; Hughes et al., 2019; NAECBSS, 1991; Saxena, 2014; Singh et al., 2021). In today's highly technological, globalized economy, it is essential that human resource development (HRD) professionals, practitioners, and researchers understand that people and technology are intertwined within most operations (Colbert et al., 2016; Hughes et al., 2019; Mital & Pennathur, 2004; Murray et al., 2021; Singh et al., 2022); yet their separate values are not clearly known (Hughes, 2012; Vial, 2019).

Kozlowski and Salas (2010) stated that "There are few or no comprehensive frameworks that help us understand how, why, and when particular individual differences are likely to promote learning" (p.4). The objective and mission of this book is to help organizational leaders understand better ways that they can value people in comparable ways to how they value technology. Leaders should not treat people like they treat technology but should understand their personal intentions and continue to explore ways to engage their follower when developing organizational strategies to enhance productivity. They should also consider all the ethical implications when making people and technology decisions. All ethical decisions are usually accompanied by challenges.

Six Ethical Challenges of Valuing People and Technology

There are six ethical challenges for leaders to consider as they seek to value all their followers:

1. The ethical people and technology development intention of management and leadership.

The ethical people and technology development intention of management and leadership within organizations effects productivity standards and goals of the organization (Drucker, 1999). Leaders and managers must communicate their intention of what needs to be done for the organization to be successful. Productivity occurs through and with the effective performance of people and technology, and answers to the questions below can provide insight into the intentions of managers and leaders.

a. How do leaders and managers ethically value the productivity people and technology?
b. What are the ethical ways to better value the location, use, maintenance, modification, and time of people and technology in the workplace?
c. To what extent can organization development initiatives be ethically enhanced by better understanding of the value of people and technology?

2. The ethical ways that managers and leaders value people and technology in the workplace.

Ethical practices that managers and leaders use when valuing people and technology in the workplace must be understood as organizations seek to continuously adjust to workplace changes. Continuous changes and unforeseen disruptions require leaders and managers to understand how to ethically adjust and adapt to change to increase the organizations' competitiveness and success (Hughes, 2019; Jundt et al., 2015; Rogers, 2003; Schein, 1988; van den Heuvel et al., 2013, 2020; Welch, 2005). Having a strategy to develop employees in the workplace (High, 1991) is essential but these strategies must be embedded with moral and ethical consideration of employee needs. The strategy should also address the value of the employee within the workplace. Leaders and managers could examine the ethics of assessing themselves. How do they truly examine themselves before assessing their employees and technology?

3. The ethical impact of organization development initiatives that align people and technology within the workplace.

The ethical effect of organization development initiatives that align people and technology provides managers and leaders the chance to clearly identify and develop initiatives that specifically address targeted organizational needs and goals. Often emphasis is placed on the systems within organizations and not enough attention is given to how to value people and why they are the most important asset to the organization. Many organization leaders and managers work hard to incorporate new people and new technology but should ensure that all people and technology are integrated within their organizations. The need to value all employees became distinct during the COVID-19 pandemic when essential workers were finally acknowledged.

4. The role of the cognitive, behavioral and/or cultural philosophical perspectives of organizations and its ethical effect on people and technology.

Understanding the role of the cognitive, behavioral and/or cultural philosophical perspectives of organizations and valuing people within these philosophical contexts is paramount to creating competitive advantage for organizations. Increasing employee motivation and their alignment within the organization's philosophical perspective (cognitively, behaviorally, and/or culturally) is important to determining organization development initiatives.

From a cognitive perspective, human behavior cannot be understood "without studying the internal mental and perceptual processes of specific individuals" (Gall et al., 2007, p. 492). Employees' cognitive perception of their location, use, maintenance, modification, and time value within the organization can help organization leaders better develop teaching, learning, and motivational procedures and processes (Hughes, 2012). Schmidt, et al. (1986) found that cognitive ability was the single most important cause of job performance. Organizations with a cognitive philosophical perspective are seeking to strengthen and improve employee job performance.

Skinner's (1957) operant conditioning with three basic assumptions about learning was the beginning of the behaviorist tradition in organizations. The three basic assumptions are:

1. Observable behavior, rather than internal mental events or verbal reconstruction of events, should be the focus of study.
2. Behavior should be studied in terms of its simplest elements, i.e., specific stimuli and specific responses.
3. The process of learning is behavioral change. That is a particular response becomes associated with the occurrence of a particular stimulus. (Gredler, 2009, p. 37)

As organization leaders better understand employees' location, use, maintenance, modification, and time value to an organization from the behaviorist philosophical and & Sutton, 2004).

The cognitive, behavioral, and cultural philosophical perspectives are important for developing an operational definition of the value of employees and technology to organizations. The five values of peoples and technology (location, use, maintenance, modification, and time) is suggested as one way to provide accurate and definitive measures of employee value.

1. Location Value: Technology (i.e., capital expense, engineering expertise, infrastructure changes) and People (i.e., cohesiveness in assigned environment, organizational culture, career development)
2. Use Value: Technology (often, it is known, upfront, how a piece of equipment is to be used before purchasing, process control, strategic planning) and People (i.e., selection strategy, person-job fit, job analysis)
3. Maintenance Value: Technology (i.e., preventive maintenance systems and processes, investment in new tools) and People (i.e., training and development, motivation)
4. Modification Value: Technology (i.e., upgrades, slight modification, investment to ensure value is derived from this piece of equipment) and People (i.e., growth and change, job enrichment, organization development)
5. Time Value: Technology (i.e., life span of equipment, depreciation of equipment expense) and People (i.e., time to perform work, length of time in position, downsizing/rightsizing). (Hughes, 2012, p. xxii)

5. How ethical leaders can understand and use diversity intelligence® (DQ) to ethically value all employees in the workplace.

Hughes defined DQ as "the capability of individuals to recognize the value of workplace diversity and to use this information to guide thinking and behavior" (Hughes & Brown, 2018). Leaders should be able to self-assess themselves and their capabilities. They should recognize the ethics of their power of position and personal power to effect change. In 2014 Hughes began to use the term DQ and develop concepts about DQ (Hughes, 2014). When I began to think about measures for the five values, I realized that it would be impossible for leaders to measure the five values in each of their employees if they marginalized and ignored some of them because of their biases against and unethical treatment of some employees who were different than them. Therefore, I defined DQ in the context of the federal protected class laws and mandates that organizations operating under U.S. federal laws were already required to adhere to. If they are already required to follow these laws, why is it that not all employees are being treated fairly in the workplace? Why are all employees not valued? DQ eliminates the excuses leaders have previously used to marginalize and discriminate against employees. Discrimination is unethical and immoral.

6. The ethical implications and imperatives for managers and leaders to be successful integrating people and technology in the workplace.

Ethics has become more and more important as organizations begin to better integrate people and technology in the workplace. The line between ethics and morals is very thin and very easy to cross. Managers and leaders must be careful to not allow the technology to become unethical as it attempts to be smarter than the humans who wrote its algorithms. There are many examples of instances where organizations have had to pivot and reassess how they are using technology and what they are allowing it to do. Some of those examples are shared within this book. The ethical implications of managers' and leaders' actions are imperative to the success of organizations and can only be tempered through organization policies and enforcement of those policies, and local, state, and federal laws and mandates such as Sarbanes Oxley.

These six key challenges are critical to the success of organizations who depend upon their people. Two challenges for HRD professionals, practitioners, and researchers are, 1) Provid[ing] training that meets the operational needs of the organization; and 2) Ensuring the individual employee receives personalized training for the purpose of performance improvement and self-fulfillment (Hatala & Gumm, 2006, p. 229), can be overcome by using the *Hughes HRD Value Creation Model*.

From a technology perspective technology developers must be cognizant of how and when their technology is to be used within organizations and society. With the onset of artificial intelligence (AI), machine learning, and other 21st century technologies, technology developers must consider the ethical implications of the usages of their technologies (Heilinger, 2022; Jobin et al., 2019). Organization leaders and managers should consider whether using the new age technologies are beneficial for not only their organizations but also their people (Wilson, 2019). Technology developers can also use the *Hughes HRD Value Creation Model* to better understand how their technologies align within organizations.

FUTURE RESEARCH DIRECTIONS

The idea of valuing people and technology in the workplace has become a matter of urgent consideration since the onset of the COVID-19 pandemic in 2019. As the COVID-19 pandemic is still here in 2023, organizations have had to undergo rapid changes and become flexible to their people. They have had to truly begin to examine how they value their people in similar ways to how they value technology. There has emerged the idea of Industry 5.0 where the integration of people and technology is beginning to be examined in mutually beneficial ways. The ethical challenges introduced in this chapter can be a research starting point for ethically integrating people and technology in the workplace.

CONCLUSION

The goal of organizations is to be successful within their markets. Welch (2005) stated that "Winning companies and the people who works for them are the engine of a healthy economy, and in providing the revenues for government, they are the foundation of a free and democratic society" (p. 4). Revenue is easily measured and appreciated; however, the relationship between the contribution of the people who perform the work to the generation of revenue is unclear. What is the definition of a healthy economy in the context of the workers? How exactly do the people's work create the foundation of a free and democratic society? In what way do the people who create this revenue for the government benefit from a free and democratic society and do all workers truly benefit? How much time does it take workers to benefit? Cost, quality, and service are central to the competition that exists between business competitors and businesses compete using both people and technology. Therefore, people and technology's value can be measured based on cost, quality, and service that are provided to the business and its customers.

Historically competition between technology and people within the workplace has been frowned upon by humanist scholars. Researchers who support strategic technology management (Betz, 1993; Kerr et al., 2013; Phaal et al., 2012; Snell & Dean, 1992) believe value is created through technology development while those in human resource management and economics (Becker, 1962, 1964; Black & Lynch, 1996; Blundell et al., 1999; Lepak & Snell, 1999, 2002; Ployhart & Moliterno, 2011; Polyhart et al.,

2014; Schultz, 1961; Sweetland, 1996) believe it is created through human capital investment. This debate continues today as new technologies such as artificial intelligence (AI) and machine learning have emerged. Human and computer interaction is also being studied more alongside the traditional examination of strategic technology management, strategic human resource management, and human resource development. Integration of these areas of research provide rich new ideas to organizations for better implementation of people and technology development initiatives. Equating the key connections between technology development and people development can enhance the interactions that occur between people and technology in the workplace. This book provides insights and an updated comprehensive framework that can be used to develop and design case studies and other research studies to better that could measure the identified five values that people, technology, and leadership strategy can provide to organizations.

COVID-19 ETHICAL IMPACT MINI CASE STUDY

People and technology during the COVID-19 became a central discussion within many workplaces. When businesses throughout the world were forced to shut down, employers were forced to consider technology alternatives for the work previously done by employees. In many instances AI, robot, or drone technologies were chosen to replace tasks that people typically completed. Robots and drones were used to deliver food and supplies. AI chatbots and other technologies were used to respond to telephones and operate computer equipment remotely. A debate arose around essential workers whose tasks simply could not be replaced by technology which essentially sparked Industry 5.0. Some questions for further discussion of this case are:

1. Should organizations have waited until employees were able to return to work instead of using technology to replace their tasks?
2. To what extent were robots and drones safe and reliable for use around food and supplies?
3. Why should industry 5.0 become the norm within workplaces?
4. Was it ethical to risk the lives of employees because they were deemed to be essential workers?

REFERENCES

Becker, G. S. (1962). Investment in human capital: A theoretical analysis. *Journal of Political Economy*, *70*(5, Part 2), 9–49. doi:10.1086/258724

Becker, G. S. (1964). *Human capital: A theoretical and empirical analysis, with special reference to education* (3rd ed.). University of Chicago Press.

Betz, F. (1993). *Strategic technology management*. McGraw-Hill.

Black, S. E., & Lynch, L. M. (1996). Human-capital investments and productivity. *The American Economic Review*, *86*(2), 263–267.

Blundell, R., Dearden, L., Meghir, C., & Sianesi, B. (1999). Human capital investment: The returns from education and training to the individual, the firm and the economy. *Fiscal Studies*, *20*(1), 1–23. doi:10.1111/j.1475-5890.1999. tb00001.x

Bolman, L. G., & Deal, T. E. (2008). *Reframing organizations: Artistry, choice, and leadership* (4th ed.). Jossey-Bass.

Colbert, A., Yee, N., & George, G. (2016). The digital workforce and the workplace of the future. *Academy of Management Journal*, *59*(3), 731–739. doi:10.5465/amj.2016.4003

Drucker, P. F. (1999). Knowledge-worker productivity: The biggest challenge. *California Management Review*, *41*(2), 79–94. doi:10.2307/41165987

Formica, S., & Sfodera, F. (2022). The great resignation and quiet quitting paradigm shifts: An overview of current situation and future research directions. *Journal of Hospitality Marketing & Management*, *31*(8), 899–907. doi:10.1 080/19368623.2022.2136601

Freidman, M. (1970, September 13). The social responsibility of business is to increase its profits. *The New York Times Magazine*, 32-33.

Gall, M. D., Gall, J. P., & Borg, W. R. (2007). *Educational research: An introduction* (8th ed.). Pearson.

Gredler, M. E. (2009). *Learning and instruction: Theory into practice* (6th ed.). Pearson Education, Inc.

Hatala, J.-P., & Gumm, J. C. (2006). Managing organizational cultural influences during the implementation of competency-based training. *Advances in Developing Human Resources, 8*(2), 229–246. doi:10.1177/1523422305286154

Heilinger, J.-C. (2022). The ethics of AI ethics. A constructive critique. *Philosophy & Technology, 35*(3), 61. doi:10.100713347-022-00557-9

High, J. C. (1991). Achieving excellence through people, technology, and teamwork. In NAECBSS (Ed.), People and technology in the workplace. The National Academies Press.

Hughes, C. (2010). People as technology conceptual model: Towards a new value creation paradigm for strategic human resource development. *Human Resource Development Review, 9*(1), 48–71. doi:10.1177/1534484309353561

Hughes, C. (2012). *Valuing people and technology in the workplace: A competitive advantage framework.* IGI Global. doi:10.4018/978-1-4666-0240-3

Hughes, C. (2014). *American Black women and interpersonal leadership styles.* Sense Publishers. doi:10.1007/978-94-6209-878-7

Hughes, C. (2019). *Ethical and legal issues in human resource development: Evolving roles and emerging trends.* Springer International Publishing. doi:10.1007/978-3-319-99528-1

Hughes, C., Robert, L., Frady, K., & Arroyos, A. (2019). *Managing technology and middle and low skilled employees: Advances for economic regeneration.* Emerald Publishing. doi:10.1108/9781789730777

Jobin, A., Ienca, M., & Vayena, E. (2019). The global landscape of AI ethics guidelines. *Nature Machine Intelligence, 1*(9), 389–399. doi:10.103842256-019-0088-2

Jundt, D. K., Shoss, M. K., & Huang, J. L. (2015). Individual adaptive performance in organizations: A review. *Journal of Organizational Behavior, 36*(S1), S53–S71. doi:10.1002/job.1955

Kerr, C., Farrukh, C., Phaal, R., & Probert, D. (2013). Key principles for developing industrially relevant strategic technology management toolkits. *Technological Forecasting and Social Change, 80*(6), 1050–1070. doi:10.1016/j.techfore.2012.09.006

Kontoghiorghes, C. (2004). Reconceptualizing the learning transfer conceptual framework: Empirical validation of a new systemic model. *International Journal of Training and Development*, *8*(3), 210–221. doi:10.1111/j.1360-3736.2004.00209.x

Kozlowski, S. W. J., & Salas, E. (Eds.). (2010). *Learning, training, and development in organizations*. Routledge.

Leng, J., Sha, W., Wang, B., Zheng, P., Zhuang, C., Liu, Q., Wuest, T., Mourtzis, D., & Wang, L. (2022). Industry 5.0: Prospect and retrospect. *Journal of Manufacturing Systems*, *65*, 279–295. doi:10.1016/j.jmsy.2022.09.017

Lepak, D. P., & Snell, S. A. (1999). The human resource architecture: Toward a theory of human capital allocation and development. *Academy of Management Review*, *24*(1), 31–48. doi:10.2307/259035

Lepak, D. P., & Snell, S. A. (2002). Examining the human resource architecture: The relationships among human capital, employment, and human resource configurations. *Journal of Management*, *28*(4), 517–543. doi:10.1177/014920630202800403

Mintzberg, H. (1998). Covert leadership: Notes on managing professionals. Knowledge workers respond to inspiration, not supervision. *Harvard Business Review*, *76*(6), 140–147. PMID:10187244

Mital, A., & Pennathur, A. (2004). Advanced technologies and humans in manufacturing workplaces: An interdependent relationship. *International Journal of Industrial Ergonomics*, *33*(4), 295–313. doi:10.1016/j.ergon.2003.10.002

Murray, A., Rhymer, J. E. N., & Sirmon, D. G. (2021). Humans and technology: Forms of conjoined agency in organizations. *Academy of Management Review*, *46*(3), 552–571. doi:10.5465/amr.2019.0186

National Academy of Engineering and Commission on Behavioral and Social Sciences and Education (NAECBSS). (1991). *People and technology in the workplace*. The National Academies Press.

Pfeffer, J. (1994). *Competitive advantage through people: Unleashing the power of the workforce*. Harvard Business School Press. doi:10.2307/41165742

Pfeffer, J., & Sutton, R. I. (2006). Evidence-based management. *Harvard Business Review*, *84*(1), 62–75. PMID:16447370

Phaal, R., Kerr, C., Oughton, D., & Probert, D. (2012). Towards a modular toolkit for strategic technology management. *International Journal of Technology Intelligence and Planning, 8*(2), 161–181. doi:10.1504/IJTIP.2012.048475

Ployhart, R. E., & Moliterno, T. P. (2011). Emergence of the human capital resource: A multilevel model. *Academy of Management Review, 36*(1), 127–150. doi:10.5465/amr.2009.0318

Ployhart, R. E., Nyberg, A. J., Reilly, G., & Maltarich, M. A. (2014). *Human capital is dead.*Ployhart, R. E., Nyberg, A. J., Reilly, G., & Maltarich, M. A. (2014, February). long live human capital resources! *Journal of Management, 40*(2), 371–398. doi:10.1177/0149206313512152

Rogers, E. M. (2003). *Diffusion of innovations* (5th ed.). The Free Press.

Saxena, A. (2014). Workforce diversity: A key to improve productivity. *Procedia Economics and Finance, 11,* 76–85. doi:10.1016/S2212-5671(14)00178-6

Schein, E. H. (1988). Organizational socialization and the profession of management. *Sloan Management Review, 30*(1), 53–65.

Schmidt, F., Hunter, J., & Outerbridge, A. (1986). Impact of job experience and ability on job knowledge, work sample performance, and supervisory ratings of job performance. *The Journal of Applied Psychology, 71*(3), 432–439. doi:10.1037/0021-9010.71.3.432

Schultz, T. W. (1961). Investment in human capital. *The American Economic Review, 51*(1), 1–17.

Singh, R. K., Agrawal, S., & Modgil, S. (2021). Developing human capital 4.0 in emerging economies: An industry 4.0 perspective. *International Journal of Manpower, 43*(2), 286–309. doi:10.1108/IJM-03-2021-0159

Skinner, B. F. (1957). *Verbal learning.* Appleton-Century-Crofts., doi:10.1037/11256-000

Snell, S. A., & Dean, J. W. (1992). Integrated manufacturing and human resource management: A human capital perspective. *Academy of Management Journal, 35*(3), 467–504. doi:10.2307/256484

Sweetland, S. R. (1996). Human capital theory: Foundations of a field of inquiry. *Review of Educational Research, 66*(3), 341–359. doi:10.3102/00346543066003341 van den Heuvel, M., Demerouti, E., Bakker, A. B., Hetland, J., & Schaufeli, W. B. (2020). How do employees adapt to organizational change? The role of meaning-making and work engagement. *The Spanish Journal of Psychology*, *23*(e56), 1–16. doi:10.1017/SJP.2020.55 PMID:33345770

van den Heuvel, M., Demerouti, E., Bakker, A. B., & Schaufeli, W. B. (2013). Adapting to change: The value of change information and meaning-making. *Journal of Vocational Behavior*, *83*(1), 11–21. doi:10.1016/j.jvb.2013.02.004

Vial, G. (2019). Understanding digital transformation: A review and a research agenda. *The Journal of Strategic Information Systems*, *28*(2), 118–144. doi:10.1016/j.jsis.2019.01.003

Welch, J. (2005). *Winning*. HarperCollins.

Wilson, J., & Daugherty, P. (2019). Creating the symbiotic AI workforce of the future. *MIT Sloan Management Review*, *61*(1), 1–4. https://www.proquest.com/scholarly-journals/creating-symbiotic-ai-workforce-future/docview/2315489026/se-2

Chapter 2
Philosophical Perspectives of Organizations and Ethical Implications

ABSTRACT

This chapter discusses philosophy and organizations. All organizations operate primarily from one of three philosophical perspectives or a combination thereof. The three philosophical perspectives are cognitive, behavioral, and cultural. An organization's core values, strategies, and/or frames originate from its cognitive, behavioral, and/or cultural philosophical perspective. The chapter focuses on explaining cognitive, behavioral, and cultural philosophical perspectives of organizations and ethical implications.

INTRODUCTION

Within this book the term organization is used to represent business (for profit and not for profit), establishment, foundation, society, association, and institution. Swanson & Holton (2001) described organizations as "human-made entities that rely on human expertise in order to establish and achieve their goals" (p.10). Bush (1987) defined an institution as a "set of socially prescribed patterns of correlated behavior" (p. 1076) and noted that correlated behavior consisted of two key tenets; behavior within an institution is not random but purposeful and correlated, and values are the "correlators." Therefore, behavior is influenced by values.

DOI: 10.4018/978-1-6684-5321-6.ch002

All organizations operate within philosophical perspectives and philosophical perspectives consist of core values (Collins & Porras, 1994), strategies (Drucker, 2008), and frames (Bolman & Deal, 2008). Organizations operate primarily from cognitive, behavioral, or cultural philosophical perspectives or a combination thereof. The three philosophical perspectives are. An organization's core values, strategies, and/or frames originate from the cognitive, behavioral, and/or cultural philosophical perspectives.

BACKGROUND

What is Philosophy?

Philosophy has been defined as the love of wisdom by the Greek. Wisdom is a combination of knowledge and experience. Philosophy is not alternative facts. Jaspers (1951) indicated that there is no escape from philosophy and that it is only whether philosophy is conscious or not, good or bad, muddled or clear. He also advised that anyone who rejects philosophy is himself unconsciously practicing a philosophy. The field of philosophy has many branches including ontology, epistemology, and axiology. Within these branches are philosophical questions such as:

1. What is the nature of reality? This is the concern of ontology where the nature of being is examined and it looks at how individuals see the world.
2. What is the nature of knowledge and knowing? This is the concern of epistemology which encompasses the theory of knowledge and what individuals think and know about the world.
3. What is value, valuable and valued? This is the concern of axiology and how individuals determine the kinds of things that are valuable in the world.

HRD scholars have written about philosophical aspects of HRD (Hughes et al. 2019a; Kuchinke, 1999; Ruona & Lynham 2004; Ruona & Roth, 2000) but none have provided specific philosophies of HRD. Schein (2010) questioned whether organization development (OD) was considered science, technology, or philosophy. Stewart in podcast discussions on philosophy and HRD with Short (2022), Hughes, and Chuang, proposed the idea that there are three current philosophies of HRD related to answers to the fundamental question

Table 1. Philosophical Perspectives, HRD Philosophies, and the Five Values

Organizational Philosophical Perspectives	HRD Philosophies	Five Values
Cognitive	Learning	Use, Maintenance, Modification
Behavioral	Performance	Location, Use, Maintenance, Modification
Cultural	Critical HRD	Use, Time

of: What is the purpose of HRD? The three philosophies are performance, learning, and critical HRD. A short description is provided below:

1. Performance philosophy - purpose of HRD is to improve organizational and, in relation to national HRD, country performance. Effectiveness is measured by economic and financial indicators/metrics, e.g., gross domestic product at country level and profit or ROI at organisational level. (Another assumption is causal relationships between individual performance, organizational performance and country performance)
2. Learning philosophy - purpose of HRD is to promote and facilitate development of individuals to enable personal growth, improve life chances and support self-actualization. HRD in this view is in and of itself a 'good' thing in moral terms. Effectiveness of HRD is measured by impact on and benefits for individuals' personal growth.
3. Critical HRD philosophy -purpose of HRD is to question and challenge existing power structures in social relations, including those operating in organisations, to contribute to and facilitate increased equality and diversity in organizations, and inclusion for marginalized groups in both organizations and society. Effectiveness is measured in changes in power relations within organizations and society.

These philosophies align with the cognitive, behavioral, and cultural philosophical perspectives that *Hughes's HRD Value Creation Model* identifies within organizations.

Stewart also suggested the following table of how the HRD Philosophies relate to the ontology, epistemology, and axiology branches of philosophy.

Philosophy involves continuous questioning, and as organizations seek to value people and technology in the workplace, they must continuously question how and why they do what they do. HR and HRD scholars, professionals,

Table 2. Three HRD Philosophies Applied to Branches of Philosophy

HRD PHILOSOPHIES	ONTOLOGY	EPISTEMOLOGY	AXIOLOGY
Performance	Realism	Positivism	Utilitarian - greatest good
Learning	Idealist	Interpretivism	Deontological- rule based
Critical HRD	Critical realism	Pragmatism	Virtue ethics -virtues=good person, vices=bad person

and practitioners have their own philosophies about talent (Meyers & van Woerkom, 2014; Meyers et al., 2013, 2020).

Philosophy is foundational to learning and knowledge, and the field of HRD is predicated on learning and knowledge which influences the three pillars of training and development, career development, and organization development. Within these three pillars of HRD are interactions between and among people. Each person has a philosophy or philosophical thoughts and questions in a search for truth and understanding. New people bring new thoughts and ideas into organizations. HRD scholars, professionals, and practitioners must engage with all these individuals and their philosophies. Therefore, HRD philosophy is based on numerous theories as Stewart suggests above.

Organizations and theories that define or explain human behavior within organizations have been the focus of research studies in fields including sociology, business, and HRD. Common methods and theories that have been derived include organization theory, institutional theory, organization development, and organizational design.

Organization and Institutional Theory

Barnard (1938) originated organization theory and defined organization as "Formal organization is that kind of cooperation among men [*sic*] that is conscious, deliberate, [and] purposeful" (p.4). He suggested that the organizational system could make up for the limitations of the cognitive ability of men. One area of organizational theory that is of interest is the organization- environment relationship (Tushman & Anderson, 1986) where they found that technology change affects organizational environments. Hinings and Greenwood (2002) trace the history of organization theory, from its emergence from sociologist Weber (1964) to its migration to business discipline.

Selznick (1949) expanded Barnard's (1938) work and presented institutional theory. Selznick suggested to leaders that an organization's distinctive character needed defining and defending. His view also led to strategic decision-making and the creation of organizational cultures (Scott, 1987). Institutional theory examines the processes by which social structures, including schemas, rules, norms, and routines become reliable guidelines for social behavior (Glynn & D'Aunno, 2023). It questions how these elements are created, diffused, adopted, and adapted over space and time; and how they fall into decline and disuse (Scott, 2004). Scott (1987) described institutionalization as

the social process by which individuals come to accept a shared definition of reality – a conception whose validity is seen as independent of the ac- tor's own views or actions but is taken for granted as defining the 'way things are' and/or the 'way things are to be done.' (p. 496)

Perhaps this definition of institutionalization best illustrates the link between HRD and institutional theory. HRD, through the lens of institutional theory, becomes the operational arm by which the "shared definition of reality" is expanded throughout the organization. To be competitive today, especially in developed countries, organizations deal with employees who are engaged in their career (Hirschi et al., 2014). Drucker (1999) referred to them as knowledge workers.

Organization Development and Design

Organization development has been defined by many, and involves the principles, processes, and performance within organizations (Burnes & Cooke, 2012; Cummings & Worley, 2005; Egan, 2002; Hamlin et al., 2009; McLagan, 1989; McLean, 2006; McLean & McLean, 2001). This author would replace principles with cognitive, behavioral, and/or cultural philosophical perspectives, processes with technology, and performance with people to describe and expand the definition of organizational development. From what philosophical perspective are organizations introducing its principles? To what extent do organization processes depend upon technology? To what extent does its performance depend on the operation of technological processes and the action of its people?

McLean (2006) broadly described organization development as:

... any process or activity, based on the behavioral sciences, that, either initially or over a long term, has the potential to develop in an organization set- ting enhanced knowledge, expertise, productivity, satisfaction, income, interpersonal relationships, and other desired outcomes, whether for interpersonal or group/team gain or for the benefit of an organization, community, region, or, ultimately, the whole of humanity. (p. 9)

McLean provided a comprehensive definition related to the process. A process is not implemented without people and/or technology and most often requires the action of both.

Organizations want to remain and enhance its competitiveness. Ultimately, this may benefit the society within which it operates, but it must first develop its technology and its people (Aragón-Sánchez et al., 2003; Hughes et al., 2019b; Kerr et al., 2013; Lee & Bruvold, 2003; Maidique & Hayes, 1984; Phaal et al., 2012; Swanson & Holton, 2001; Young & Choi, 2014). The seven-point *Hughes HRD Value Creation Model* will assist HRD professionals, practitioners, and researchers as they seek to improve organization development practices.

Although organizational design historically meant organizational structure, "it means an alignment of structure, management processes, information systems, reward systems, people, and other features of the organization with business strategy" (Galbraith and Lawler, 1993, p. 2). The organizational design must occur with an understanding of the philosophical perspective(s) within which it is being implemented. Misalignment with the philosophical perspective(s) can cause difficulties during mergers and acquisitions. Many mergers and acquisitions are not successful because of a misalignment between the cultural, behavioral, or cognitive philosophical perspectives of the organizations that are being combined or the leaders of the changes. Looking only at the structure and the finances of the organizations can cause leaders to miss the underlying operational principles of organizations including sensemaking (Turner et al., 2023; Weick et al., 2005). By including philosophical perspective(s) as part of the design, leaders can make better initial decisions when an alignment does not make sense. Taylor and Van Every (2000) defined sensemaking as "a way station on the road to a consensually constructed, coordinated system of action" (p. 275).

Organizations are entities that embrace change and succeed through the effective performance of people and technology. Understanding the dynamics of the relationship between and influences of the relationship of people and technology within organizations is essential to their competitive advantage.

If values are "correlators" (Bush, 1987) of an organization, organizations can use the five values of people and technology development to better correlate their efforts toward success.

COGNITIVE, BEHAVIORAL, AND CULTURAL PHILOSOPHICAL PERSPECTIVES

The cognitive, behavioral, and cultural philosophical perspectives are three foundational support phenomena when integrated into organization design can help support and establish the accurate value of employees and technology. More emphasis may need to be dedicated to employees because in most organizations, technology value is already an integral part of their value chain and measurement procedures. "Organizational design is not only the process of creating a structure, but it also includes alignment of management functions, information systems, human resources, and other elements within that structure" (Olson, 2002, p. 82). Recognizing these philosophical perspectives will require a paradigm shift for organizations.

Typically, organizations determine their vision, missions and goals based on an identified or perceived need within the marketplace and/or society. After determining the need or problem to be solved and deciding to develop ways of solving the problem, the organization's leaders will develop and implement their strategy to resolve the problem. The context within which this strategy implementation occurs often becomes the secondary focus. This author suggests that the context become the primary or equal focus alongside the problem identification so that strategies can be more effectively implemented. Before or simultaneously with the development of the vision, mission, and goal, organizations should determine the philosophical perspective within which it is operating. They must first understand the cognitive, behavioral, and cultural philosophical perspectives. Historically, due to the influences of Skinner (1957), Taylor (1911), Deming (1982), and Juran (1989) among others, the American workplace has operated from the behavioral philosophical perspective.

Cognitive Philosophical and Theoretical Perspective

Cognitive psychology and theory began with the works of Bruner et al. (1956) and Miller (1956) and evolved through the contributions of Ausubel (1960),

Ausubel and Youssef (1963), Neisser (1967), and Jenkins (1974). Bruning et al. (2011) related cognitive psychology to teaching and learning using the following eight themes:

1. Learning is a constructive, not a receptive, process.
2. Mental frameworks organize memory and guide thought.
3. Extended practice is needed to develop cognitive skills.
4. Development of self-awareness and self- regulation is critical to cognitive growth.
5. Motivation and beliefs are integral to cognition.
6. Social interaction is fundamental to cognitive development.
7. Knowledge, strategies, and expertise are contextual.
8. A cognitive approach to teaching implies new approaches to assessment. (pp. 5-8)

These themes are prevalent in consulting firms, educational institutions, and legal firms where the cognitive philosophical perspective is dominant (Hughes, 2012). The cognitive philosophical perspective is essential within organizations that value the knowledge assets of its employees. Historically the cognitive ability of employees was not valued (Pfeffer, 1994; Welch, 2005). Cognitive theorists believed that a complete view of human behavior cannot be understood "without studying the internal mental and perceptual processes of specific individuals" (Gall et al., 2007, p. 492). Cognitive researchers believe that human behavior is preceded by the formation of an attitude (Murphy, 1989). Attitudes can be positive, negative, neutral, or ambivalent and all employees' attitudes fall within these four categories or a combination thereof. Employees' attitudes are how they develop intentions towards workplace (Jago & Vroom, 1978) and ethical behaviors.

Behavioral Philosophical and Theoretical Perspective

The behaviorist's theoretical perspective began with Thorndike's (1898, 1911) instrumental conditioning and the law of effect. Using the law of effect researchers rewarded individuals who behaved the way they wanted them to behave. Watson (1913) introduced the behaviorist tradition to America along with the concept of nurture over nature, and the absence of choice for the individual. Behaviorism, "the study of learning in humans and animals as understood through behavior rather than thoughts and feelings" (Martinez, 2010, p. 6), originated with Pavlov (1927) and evolved with Skinner (1957).

The following three basic assumptions about learning are directly associated with behaviorism:

1. Observable behavior, rather than internal mental events or verbal reconstruction of events, should be the focus of study.
2. Behavior should be studied in terms of its simplest elements, i.e., specific stimuli and specific responses.
3. The process of learning is behavioral change. That is a particular response becomes as- sociated with the occurrence of a particular stimulus. (Gredler, 2009, p.37)

Both Pavlov, with classical and Skinner with operant conditioning placed very little emphasis on the mental capacity of the individual. The ethical implications of the lack of emphasis on the cognitive ability of workers remain an issue of concern in organizations. Employees want their mental and emotional needs to be acknowledged by their organizations. The mental and emotional health of employees are central to avoiding employee burnout on the job (Sultana et al., 2020).

Behaviorism was challenged by Tolman (1932), Chomsky (1959) and Bandura et al. (1961). Tolman used the idea of purposive and neo behaviorism to suggest that goals and purpose inspired action. Chomsky (1959) argued against stimulus-response-reinforcement and revealed that the ability to learn language was already embedded in the brain's structure; thus. inspiring the nativism movement within psychology. Bandura et al. introduced social learning theory, showed that individuals can learn by observing and imitating the behavior of others, and introduced the cognitive concept of self-efficacy which refers to a person's sense of his or her own. The ethics of accepting the thoughts of others as opposed to forcing a desired behavior through coercion remains relevant to individual value and success at work.

American manufacturing workplaces used Pavlov's (1927) behaviorist ideas presented as scientific management by Taylor (1911). There remains strong evidence in many workplaces that behaviorism is the dominant management style as employees push back against workplace treatment and seek to be valued at work. Drucker (1999) and others have challenge scientific management using knowledge management instead. Martinez (2010) suggested that there are strategies to promote learning using behaviorist theory. He was looking for ways to focus on the positive aspects of behaviorist theory. Ethical treatment and valuing of employees demand that organization leaders look for solutions to positively impact the teaching and learning of employees.

Cultural Philosophical Perspective

John Dewey (1910) found that elements within social life influences consciousness. Vygotsky (1979), using cultural-historical theory, suggested that the social setting influenced cognitive development. Dewey and Vygotsky's works ultimately led to the formation of the field of cultural psychology which studies the influence of culture, tradition, and social practices on the psyche. Bandura et al.'s (1961) social learning theory revealed how individuals adjusted to what they observed within their social environments. The desire to understand the culture of organizations evolved from cultural psychology and the impact of work environment was examined to better understand employee performance (Bliese et al., 2017; Kanfer et al., 2017; Schneider et al, 2017). Subsequently, it was discovered that ethical environments impact employee performance (Hijal-Moghrabi, 2017; Kuenzi et al., 2020; Meyers, 2004; Steele, 2018).

Schein (1984) described organizational culture as

The pattern of basic assumptions that a given group has invented, discovered, or developed in learning to cope with its problems of external adaptation and internal integration, and that have worked well enough to be considered valid, and, therefore, to be taught to new members as the correct way to perceive, think, and feel in relation to those problems. (p. 3)

He found that culture

(1) is always in the process of formation and change; (2) tends to cover all aspects of human functioning; (3) is learned around the major issues of external adaptation and internal integration; and (4) is ultimately embodied as an interrelated, patterned set of basic assumptions that deal with ultimate issues, such as the nature of humanity, human relationships, time, space, and the nature of reality and truth itself. (p. 14)

The organization's culture effects the way employees feel about their integration into the work environment which ultimately affects their performance. Employees' intrinsic and extrinsic motivation are influenced by the work environment. Knowing this, leaders should ethically examine how they use this information when making decisions about employees. Leaders have power over the work environment and employees.

Cultural researchers study the relationships that mediate experiences and realities with the contextualist/realist investigation of historical, social, and political structures of power (Gall et al., 2007). Organizations have historical, social, and political structures of power that influence employee performance (Bolman & Deal, 2008; Jo & Park, 2016; Kontoghiorghes, 2004; Loi et al., 2012; Pfeffer, 1994; & Pfeffer & Sutton, 2006; Zaleznik, 2004). Therefore, leaders should be ethical in how they make decisions within their historical, social, and political power structure. Organizations should ensure that their embedded values are ethical. Historical unethical mistreatment of employees cannot be sustained as a part of the organization's culture. Bush (1987) identified two types of values: ceremonial and instrumental. He stated that ceremonial values "provide the standard of judgment for invidious distinctions, which prescribe status, differential privileges, and master-servant relationships, and warrant the exercise of power by one social class over another (p. 1080)." Organizations have ceremonial values which lead some employees to view themselves as less than their managers and leaders. The socio-economic structure within organizations exists because of pay differentiation. This specific cultural difference within the workplace can be easily fixed by using ethics to eliminate pay discrimination against minorities and women.

Bush (1987) defined instrumental values as "the standard of judgment by which tools and skills are employed in the application of evidently warranted knowledge to the problem-solving process of the community" (p. 1080). He noted that these values were not unchangeable and could evolve with time. Instrumental values could be defined as organizational competencies (Hughes, 2012). Regardless of whether the competency is job-specific or a universal competency to the organization, it seems consistent with the instrumental values concept.

Issues, Controversies, Problems

Organization leaders do not clearly acknowledge their organization's philosophical perspective. This is revealed when leaders introduce new methods and procedures that are in direct contrast to their dominant philosophical perspective. Organizations operate from the cognitive, behavioral, and/or cultural philosophical perspectives and should be included in the organizational design. When employees at all levels understand the organization's philosophical perspective, better strategic planning, and decision making becomes the norm. More than one philosophical perspective is usually found within organizations and the combinations of philosophical perspectives can be beneficial to organizations. Organization leaders can better align people, technology, and organization development initiatives within philosophical perspectives.

FUTURE RESEARCH DIRECTIONS

Scholars should consider interviewing business founders and/or owners to discuss their organizations' philosophical persperspectives. Leaders and managers can also be interviewed or surveyed to examine their understanding of their organizations' philosophical perspectives. Understanding the premise of developing organizations around well defined philosophical perspectives could help future entrepreneurs and business owners as they seek to establish organizations that align with their business strategies.

CONCLUSION

Hughes's (2010) PT conceptual model's five key values (location, use, maintenance, modification, and time) allow for equivalence in worth analysis between the significance of HRD and technology development to the organization as management makes economic and strategic decisions regarding people and technology within the organization (Vroom, 1973). Incorporating the PT model into management strategy and practice will contribute to competitive advantage (Espedal, 2005; Hughes, 2012; Pfeffer, 1994). Understanding employees' location, use, maintenance, modification, and time value to an organization from the cognitive, behavioral, and/ or cultural philosophical perspectives can lead to better management and leadership practices within organizations.

Organizations can continuously gain a competitive advantage in the marketplace by strategically designing organizational vision, mission, and goals within a philosophical perspective that is known to all within the organization. Some organizations clearly do this, but many that do not. For example, Alphabet (formerly Google) is an organization where employees are immersed in a strong cultural environment and know that the cultural philosophical perspective is dominant. Alphabet's culture is fundamental to its success, but its employees operate with cognitive strength. It is an innovative, technical company where the culture stimulates the cognitive strength of its employees. It also allows employees to think and operate freely to initiate new ways of mining Internet search data.

In some organizations, it is unknown to employees if they are operating from the cognitive, behavioral, or cultural philosophical perspective, or if they may more readily accept these new strategies to the detriment of their organization's goals. They may look at the immediate needs and not the long-term implications of the decision (Gale, 1980). The ability of organizations to integrate and value people and technology in the workplace is a critical need for the viability of the organization. The philosophical perspective within which the organization operates should determine the type of people they hire and the type of technology that they introduce. Without organization design and change strategies within which the cognitive, behavioral and cultural philosophical perspectives are understood, improper decisions may be made. Some questions for future research to examine these issues include:

1. How do organizations determine their dominant operating philosophical perspective?
2. To what extent is their dominant philosophical perspective impacting their development of employees and technology?

Proper integration of people and technology requires direct planning that is objective and aligns with organizational needs. Clearly understanding organizations and the philosophical perspectives from which organizations develop their initiatives for performance is essential if managers want to remain competitive. The cognitive, behavioral, and/or cultural philosophical perspective(s) is present within all organizations and can influence the productivity gains and competitive advantage of the organization. Integrating these philosophical perspectives at the organization design stage provides a fundamental grounding for the vision, mission, and goals of the entity. It also helps as potential employees seek to work for organizations where their personal ethical concerns are considered or aligned.

Table 3 provides some suggested ways that stakeholders can examine some of the ethical implications of the three philosophical perspectives and associated initiatives.

Table 3. Philosophical Perspectives and Initiatives and Ethical Questions and Implications

Philosophical Perspectives and Initiatives	Ethical Questions and Implications
Cognitive • Teaching • Learning • Procedures and Processes • Motivations	• How are employees trained and educated? • Which employees are selected for training and development? • How are employees selected for training and development? • Is the training and education content ethical and ethically delivered? • Do all employees have access to the training and education? • How ethical policies, processes, and procedures are taught and implemented. • How all employees are valued and treated in the workplace. • Which organization development (OD) initiatives are chosen and why?
Behavioral • Impact of Technology on the Work Environment • Employee Behavior within Organizational Culture	• What are the ethical implications of replacing people with technology? • How is explainable artificial intelligence (AI) working to avoid AI ethical concerns? • How are employees introduced to technological changes? • How are technological change decisions made? • Are employees judged more harshly for mistakes than technology? • How is employee morale affected by technological changes? • How is the interaction between people and technology managed and understood? • How do organizations move away from a toxic behavior only work environment?
Cultural • Embedded in Environment • Adoption of Cultural Norms, • Leadership by Inspiration, • Evidence Based Management	• Is the culture embedded in the workplace environment and ethical culture? • How do organization leaders change an embedded unethical culture? • How does organization leaders change the adoption of unethical cultural norms? • What happens when leadership by inspiration is successfully led by an unethical leader using unethical behavior, policies, and procedures? • How does one ensure that the evidence in evidence-based management is ethical evidence? • What happens when bad data is used to produce unethical evidence? • How do organizations embed ethics into the organizational environment?

COVID-19 ETHICAL IMPACT MINI CASE STUDY

The disruption brought forth by the COVID-19 worldwide pandemic did not immediately allow organizations to contemplate their philosophical perspectives. In the reactionary mode of leaders and managers, the philosophical perspectives were revealed through their actions and ultimately their treatment of employees. With employees dying because of exposure to the COVID-19 virus at work and the lack of healthcare available to employees who became ill from the COVID-19 and other strains of the virus, organization leaders and managers were making organization altering decisions. Some of these decisions required that new policies be developed and implemented, and updates made to existing policies. Rapid discussions and change processes occurred and included remote work policies, health insurance policy changes, sick leave policies, more enforcement of Americans with Disabilities policy, among others. Some ethical questions to consider include:

1. To what extent were ethical impact on employee rights considered during the development or update of organizational policies?
2. Were employees involved in the ethical decision-making process when the changes directly affected their work roles?
3. Was the location value of the employee considered in the context of remote work and sick leave from an ethical perspective?

REFERENCES

Aragón-Sánchez, A., Barba-Aragón, I., & Sanz-Valle, R. (2003). Effects of training on business results. *International Journal of Human Resource Management*, *14*(6), 956–980. doi:10.1080/0958519032000106164

Ausubel, D. P. (1960). The use of advance organizers in the learning and retention of meaningful verbal material. *Journal of Educational Psychology*, *51*(5), 267–272. doi:10.1037/h0046669

Ausubel, D. P., & Youseff, M. (1963). Role of discriminability in meaningful parallel learning. *Journal of Educational Psychology*, *54*(6), 331–336. doi:10.1037/h0042767

Bandura, A., Ross, D., & Ross, S. A. (1961). Transmission of aggression through imitation of aggressive models. *Journal of Abnormal and Social Psychology*, *63*(3), 575–582. doi:10.1037/h0045925 PMID:13864605

Barnard, C. (1938). *The functions of the executive*. Harvard University Press.

Bliese, P. D., Edwards, J. R., & Sonnentag, S. (2017). Stress and well-being at work: A century of empirical trends reflecting theoretical and societal influences. *The Journal of Applied Psychology*, *102*(3), 389–402. doi:10.1037/apl0000109 PMID:28125263

Bolman, L. G., & Deal, T. E. (2008). *Reframing organizations: Artistry, choice, and leadership* (4th ed.). Jossey-Bass.

Bruner, J. S., Goodnow, J. J., & Austin, G. A. (1956). *A study of thinking*. Wiley.

Bruning, R. H., Schrawg, J., & Norby, M. M. (2011). *Cognitive psychology and instruction* (5th ed.). Pearson.

Burnes, B., & Cooke, B. (2012). The past, present and future of organization development: Taking the long view. *Human Relations*, *65*(11), 1395–1429. doi:10.1177/0018726712450058

Bush, P. D. (1987). The theory of institutional change. *Journal of Economic Issues*, *21*(3), 1075–1116. doi:10.1080/00213624.1987.11504697

Chomsky, N., & Skinner, B. F. (1959). A review of B. F. Skinner's "verbal behavior.". *Language*, *35*(1), 26–58. doi:10.2307/411334

Collins, J., & Porras, J. (1994). *Built to last*. HarperBusiness.

Cummings, T. G., & Worley, C. G. (2005). Organizational development and change (8th ed.). South-Western/Thomson.

Deming, W. E. (1982). *Out of the crisis*. MIT Center for Advanced Engineering Study.

Dewey, J. (1910). *How we think*. D. C. Heath & Co., doi:10.1037/10903-000

Drucker, P. F. (1999). Knowledge-worker productivity: The biggest challenge. *California Management Review*, *41*(2), 79–94. doi:10.2307/41165987

Drucker, P. F. (2008). *Management* (rev. ed.). HarperCollins.

Egan, T. M. (2002). Organization development: An examination of definitions and dependent variables. *Organization Development Journal*, *20*(2), 59–70.

Espedal, B. (2005). Management development: Using internal or external resources in developing core competence. *Human Resource Development Review*, *4*(2), 136–158. doi:10.1177/1534484305276217

Galbraith, J. R., & Lawler, E. E. (1993). *Organizing for the future: The new logic for managing complex organizations*. Jossey-Bass.

Gale, B. T. (1980). Can more capital buy higher productivity? *Harvard Business Review*, *58*(4), 78–86.

Gall, M. D., Gall, J. P., & Borg, W. R. (2007). *Educational research: An introduction* (8th ed.). Pearson.

Glynn, M. A., & D'Aunno, T. (2023). An intellectual history of institutional theory: Looking back to move forward. *The Academy of Management Annals, 17*(1), 301–330. doi:10.5465/annals.2020.0341

Gredler, M. E. (2009). *Learning and instruction: Theory into practice* (6th ed.). Pearson Education, Inc.

Hamlin, R. G., Ellinger, A. D., & Beattie, R. S. (2009). Toward a profession of coaching? A definitional examination of 'coaching', 'organization development', and 'human resource development'. *International Journal of Evidence Based Coaching and Mentoring, 7*(1), 13–38.

Hijal-Moghrabi, I., Sabharwal, M., & Berman, E. M. (2017). The importance of ethical environment to organizational performance in employment at will states. *Administration & Society, 49*(9), 1346–1374. doi:10.1177/0095399715581043

Hinings, C. R., & Greenwood, R. (2002). Disconnects and consequences in organization theory? *Administrative Science Quarterly, 47*, 411–421. doi:10.2307/3094844

Hirschi, A., Freund, P. A., & Herrmann, A. (2014). The career engagement scale: Development and validation of a measure of proactive career behaviors. *Journal of Career Assessment, 22*(4), 575–594. doi:10.1177/1069072713514813

Hughes, C. (2010). "People as technology" conceptual model: Towards a new value creation paradigm for strategic human resource development. *Human Resource Development Review, 9*(1), 48–71. doi:10.1177/1534484309353561

Hughes, C. (2012). *Valuing people and technology in the workplace: A competitive advantage framework*. IGI Global. doi:10.4018/978-1-4666-0240-3

Hughes, C., Gosney, M. W., & Sims, C. M. (2019a). Influencing people and technology using human resource development (HRD) philosophy. In Advanced Methodologies and Technologies in Business Operations and Management (pp. 854-866). IGI Global.

Hughes, C., Robert, L., Frady, K., & Arroyos, A. (2019b). *Managing technology and middle and low skilled employees: Advances for economic regeneration*. Emerald Publishing. doi:10.1108/9781789730777

Jago, A. G., & Vroom, V. H. (1978). Predicting leader behavior from a measure of behavioral intent. *Academy of Management Journal, 21*, 715–721. doi:10.2307/255711

Jaspers, K. (1951). The way to wisdom. (trans. Manheim R.). Yale.

Jenkins, J. J. (1974). Remember that old theory of memory? Well, forget it! *The American Psychologist, 25*(11), 785–795. doi:10.1037/h0037399

Jo, S. J., & Park, S. (2016). Critical review on power in organization: Empowerment in human resource development. *European Journal of Training and Development, 40*(6), 390–406. doi:10.1108/EJTD-01-2016-0005

Juran, J. M. (1989). *Juran on leadership for quality.* The Free Press.

Kanfer, R., Frese, M., & Johnson, R. E. (2017). Motivation related to work: A century of progress. *The Journal of Applied Psychology, 102*(3), 338–355. doi:10.1037/apl0000133 PMID:28150980

Kerr, C., Farrukh, C., Phaal, R., & Probert, D. (2013). Key principles for developing industrially relevant strategic technology management toolkits. *Technological Forecasting and Social Change, 80*(6), 1050–1070. doi:10.1016/j.techfore.2012.09.006

Kontoghiorghes, C. (2004). Reconceptualizing the learning transfer conceptual framework: Empirical validation of a new systemic model. *International Journal of Training and Development, 8*(3), 210–221. doi:10.1111/j.1360-3736.2004.00209.x

Kuchinke, P. K. (1999). Philosophical foundations of human resource development. *Annual Meeting of the Association for Career and Technical Education.* ACTE.

Kuenzi, M., Mayer, D. M., & Greenbaum, R. L. (2020). Creating an ethical organizational environment: The relationship between ethical leadership, ethical organizational climate, and unethical behavior. *Personnel Psychology, 73*(1), 43–71. doi:10.1111/peps.12356

Lee, C. H., & Bruvold, N. T. (2003). Creating value for employees: Investment in employee development. *International Journal of Human Resource Management, 14*(6), 981–1000. doi:10.1080/0958519032000106173

Loi, R., Lam, L. W., & Chan, K. W. (2012). Coping with job insecurity: The role of procedural justice, ethical leadership and power distance orientation. *Journal of Business Ethics, 108*(3), 361–372. doi:10.100710551-011-1095-3

Maidique, M. A., & Hayes, R. H. (1984). The art of high-technology management. *Sloan Management Review, 25*(2), 17–31.

Martinez, M. E. (2010). *Learning and cognition: The design of the mind.* Pearson.

McLagan, P. (1989). *Models for HRD practice.* American Society for Training and Development.

McLean, G. N. (2006). *Organization development.* Berrett-Koehler.

McLean, G. N., & McLean, L. D. (2001). If we can't define HRD in one country, how can we define it in an international context? *Human Resource Development International, 4*(3), 313–326. doi:10.1080/13678860110059339

Meyers, C. (2004). Institutional culture and individual behavior: Creating an ethical environment. *Science and Engineering Ethics, 10*(2), 269–276. doi:10.100711948-004-0022-8 PMID:15152852

Meyers, M. C., & van Woerkom, M. (2014). The influence of underlying philosophies on talent management: Theory, implications for practice, and research agenda. *Journal of World Business, 49*(2), 192–203. doi:10.1016/j.jwb.2013.11.003

Meyers, M. C., van Woerkom, M., & Dries, N. (2013). Talent – Innate or acquired? Theoretical considerations and their implications for talent management. *Human Resource Management Review, 23*(4), 305–321. doi:10.1016/j.hrmr.2013.05.003

Meyers, M. C., van Woerkom, M., Paauwe, J., & Dries, N. (2020). HR managers' talent philosophies: Prevalence and relationships with perceived talent management practices. *International Journal of Human Resource Management, 31*(4), 562–588. doi:10.1080/09585192.2019.1579747

Miller, G. A. (1956). The magical number seven, plus-or-minus two: Some limits on our capacity for processing information. *Psychological Review, 63*(2), 81–97. doi:10.1037/h0043158 PMID:13310704

Murphy, K. R. (1989). Is the relationship between cognitive ability and job performance stable over time? *Human Performance*, 2(3), 183–200. doi:10.120715327043hup0203_3

Neisser, U. (1967). *Cognitive psychology*. Appleton-Century-Crofts.

Olson, G. P. (2002). Organizing for the future. In J. L. Pierce & J. W. Newstrom (Eds.), *The manager's bookshelf: A mosaic of contemporary views* (6th ed.). Prentice Hall.

Pavlov, I. P. (1927). *Conditioned reflexes*. Routledge and Kegan Paul.

Pfeffer, J. (1994). *Competitive advantage through people: Unleashing the power of the workforce*. Harvard Business School Press. doi:10.2307/41165742

Pfeffer, J., & Sutton, R. I. (2006). Evidence-based management. *Harvard Business Review*, 84(1), 62–75. PMID:16447370

Phaal, R., Kerr, C., Oughton, D., & Probert, D. (2012). Towards a modular toolkit for strategic technology management. *International Journal of Technology Intelligence and Planning*, 8(2), 161–181. doi:10.1504/IJTIP.2012.048475

Ruona, W. E., & Lynham, S. A. (2004). A philosophical framework for thought and practice in human resource development. *Human Resource Development International*, 7(2), 151–164. doi:10.1080/13678860310001630665

Ruona, W. E. A., & Roth, G. (Eds.). (2000). Philosophical foundations of human resource development practice. Advance in Developing Human Resources, 2(3), 49-73.

Schein, E. H. (1984). Coming to a new awareness of organizational culture. *Sloan Management Review*, 25(2), 3–16.

Schein, E. H. (2010). Organization development: Science, technology or philosophy? In Coghlan D., Shani A. B. (Rami) (eds). Fundamentals of organization development (Vol. 1, pp. 91-100). Sage.

Schneider, B., González-Romá, V., Ostroff, C., & West, M. A. (2017). Organizational climate and culture: Reflections on the history of the constructs in the Journal of Applied Psychology. *The Journal of Applied Psychology*, 102(3), 468–482. doi:10.1037/apl0000090 PMID:28125256

Scott, W. R. (1987). The adolescence of institutional theory. *Administrative Science Quarterly*, 32(4), 493–511. doi:10.2307/2392880

Scott, W. R. (2004). Institutional theory. In G. Ritzer (Ed.), *Encyclopedia of social theory* (pp. 408–414). Sage.

Selznick, P. (1949). *TVA and the grass roots: A study of politics and organization.* University of California Press.

Short, D. C. (Host). (2022). HRD and philosophy [Audio podcast episode]. In *Human Resource Development Masterclass.* Academy of Human Resource Development. https://www. ahrd.org/general/custom.asp?page=HRD-Masterclass -Podcast-Series

Skinner, B. F. (1957). *Verbal learning.* Appleton-Century-Crofts., doi:10.1037/11256-000

Steele, T. (2018). Toxicity in the work environment: Retaining staff members of color at a predominantly White institution. *The College Student Affairs Journal, 36*(1), 109–123. doi:10.1353/csj.2018.0007

Sultana, A., Sharma, R., Hossain, M. M., Bhattacharya, S., & Purohit, N. (2020). Burnout among healthcare providers during COVID-19: Challenges and evidence-based interventions. *Indian Journal of Medical Ethics, 5*(4), 308–311. doi:10.20529/IJME.2020.73 PMID:34018959

Swanson, R. A., & Holton, E. F. (2001). *Foundation of human resource development.* Berrett-Koehler Publishers.

Taylor, F. W. (1911). *The principles of scientific management.* Harper & Row.

Taylor, J. R., & Van Every, E. J. (2000). *The emergent organization: Communication as its site and surface.* Erlbaum.

Thorndike, E. L. (1898). Animal intelligence: An experimental study of the associate processes in animals. *Psychological Review Monograph Supplement, 2*(4), 1–8. doi:10.1037/10780-000

Thorndike, E. L. (1911). *Animal intelligence.* Macmillan.

Tolman, E. C. (1932). *Purposive behavior in animals and men.* Century.

Tushman, M. L., & Anderson, P. (1986). Technological discontinuities and organizational environments. *Administrative Science Quarterly, 31*(3), 439–465. doi:10.2307/2392832

Vroom, V. H. (1973). A new look at managerial decision making. *Organizational Dynamics, 1*(4), 66–80. doi:10.1016/S0090-2616(73)80024-5

Vygotsky, L. S. (1979). Consciousness as a problem in the psychology of behavior. *Soviet Psychology, 176*(4), 3-35. (Original work published 1924).

Watson, J. B. (1913). Psychology as the behaviorist sees it. *Psychological Review, 20*(2), 157–177. doi:10.1037/h0074428

Weber, M. (1964). *The theory of social and eco- nomic organization.* Free Press.

Weick, K. E., Sutcliffe, K. M., & Obstfeld, D. (2005). Organizing and the process of sensemaking. *Organization Science, 16*(4), 409–421. doi:10.1287/orsc.1050.0133

Welch, J. (2005). *Winning.* Collins.

Young, S. S., & Choi, J. N. (2014). Do organizations spend wisely on employees? Effects of training and development investments on learning and innovation in organizations. *Journal of Organizational Behavior, 35*(3), 393–412. doi:10.1002/job.1897 PMID:25598576

Zaleznik, A. (2004). Managers and leaders: Are they different? *Harvard Business Review, 82*(1), 1–11. PMID:14723179

Chapter 3
Creation of the People as Technology Theoretical Concept

ABSTRACT

Technology and people are central to the success of modern organizations. This chapter explains the creation of the people as technology (PT) concept by providing a synopsis of the case from which the concept originated. Enhancements for the PT concept are discussed along with ways that education and training of employees increases organizational opportunities for success. The chapter also provides details of ways that the COVID-19 pandemic impact forced changes in organizational policies and procedures and emphasized the need for better people and technology interactions.

INTRODUCTION

Technology for many individuals has become synonymous with computer technology. The personal computer and now smart phones brought computer technology into the homes and hands of billions of people, worldwide. The evolution of mobile and other digital and smart technologies has expanded the way individuals think about computer and other technologies. Technology extends well-beyond computers and is not limited to computer technology in this book. This book targets human resource development (HRD), human resource management (HRM), computer technology, technology development,

DOI: 10.4018/978-1-6684-5321-6.ch003

and information technology (IT) professionals, practitioners, and scholars; business and industry managers and leaders; and corporate executives herein after referred to as stakeholders. Technology appears to be valued more than people, and there is a perceived need for more technology and less people in some US and global organizations (Heinrich & Witko, 2021; Rajecki, 2022; Spring et al., 2022). Therefore, stakeholders should better understand the interactions between people and technology in organizations (Murray et al., 2021) and the ethical implications. Decisions that are made regarding both people and technology have ethical implications associated with location, use, maintenance, modification, and time values.

BACKGROUND

In capitalist societies money is central to practically all interactions when goods and services are involved. Without a monetary value, goods and services are deemed to be less valuable. Despite the end of slavery in civilized societies, people and their capabilities are still monetized. Although slaves were never paid, they were sold and exchanged for their knowledge, skills, and abilities (KSAs) to perform work needed by their owners. While not equating workers to slaves, the construct still exists in workplaces today. Employees' and technology's value are measured by their KSAs. Hoskisson et al. (2008) stated that value was being "measure[d] by a product's performance characteristics and by its attributes for which customers are willing to pay" (p. 101). Can we then say that people performance is based upon their personal characteristics and their attributes that the organization is willing to pay for (Hughes, 2012)?

Value is often equated with money in organizations, but what truly is money? The monetary value of things has been continuously debated (Friedman, 1994; Marx, 1906). The exchange value or purchasing power of money is foundational within a capitalist society. How is value of people and technology relative to the competitive advantage of an organization? People value is more difficult to define and describe than some technology value in the workplace; yet the workplace is inefficient without both values. AI and other emerging technologies became prominent during Industry 4.0 (Klingenberg et al., 2022). AI and machine learning have become difficult technologies to define and describe so explainable AI (Arrieta et al., 2020) has become an area of study for researchers. It seems that the more computer programmers seek to make technology that relates to people functionality, the more complex and indescribable its application becomes. They are also seeking to understand how to make AI more ethical (Formosa & Ryan, 2021).

People Value

Researchers, professionals, and practitioners have sought to define the value of people to an organization for centuries without clearly identifiable success (Jasson & Govender, 2017; Phillips, 2003). They are even using machine learning to assist with determining the value of talent (Loyarte-López & García-Olaizola, 2022). Compensation and benefits departments pay employees what they are deemed worth to the organizations, but many employees feel underpaid and underappreciated within the workplace (Adams, 1963; De Clercq et al., 2023; Freedman, 1978; Leventhal & Whiteside, 1973; Loewenberg, 2015; Prause & Mujtaba, 2015; Saulnier & Frank, 2019; Sliter & Boyd, 2014). These feelings have only escalated during the COVID-19 pandemic, especially among healthcare and childcare workers (Tarrant & Nagasawa, 2020), and teachers, as the labor force continues to learn the value of their contributions to their organizations. Prior to the COVID-19 pandemic, many workers may not have been as aware of how the work they performed directly impacts their organization or society. Seeing the immediate use of products that they produce helps reveal their contributions' value. They also see the immediate earnings that their organizations reap from their work and know that they are being underpaid and undervalued. Essential workers are seeking more for their value to the organization (Siegmann, 2020).

Numerous organizations spend money, yearly, on commissioned satisfaction surveys to evaluate the satisfaction or dissatisfaction level of their employees (Judge, 2017). Based on the survey results, they try to make necessary changes to accommodate employees. Employees expect organizations to know their value upon hiring, yet upfront analysis has not clearly revealed that organizations or employees understand an employee's value. In the US this is common among employees because salaries for jobs are confidential. There is a movement to end this practice and force organizations to reveal the salary of jobs on the job postings. Some employees even feel that they do not belong within the organization (Rego et al., 2009; Wadors, 2016; Wilson, 2012). So, how are those employees expected to know their value? Some organizational leaders view employees as one-dimensional and seeks employees who meet open position criteria. They then seek to motivate or encourage the employee to come and meet the position requirements.

Sometimes this works and organizations have employees who remains with the organization until retirement, but this happens less frequently than in the past.

Employees are multidimensional (Hughes, 2018; Ramsey, 1986; Sackett et al. 2017) and their needs must be met through collaborative effort between the employees, leaders, and managers. Stewart (1997) argued that knowledge, an intangible entity, is bought and sold and Schein (1988) suggested that an unless employee adjusts to the norms of the organization, the employee is worthless. The value of an employee may be unclear and unknown, but it is known when an employee holds no value for the organization. Orr (1996) contended that

Millions of people go to work each day to do things that almost no one but themselves understands but which large numbers of people believe they know enough about to set policy offer advice, or redesign. Work has become invisible. (p. xi)

Work becomes invisible when organization leaders lose focus on the people that are doing the work and are using technology such as AI and machine learning instead.

Technology Value

Technology was introduced in organizations to increase and augment human performance. The focus on productivity was introduced by Taylor's (1911) introduction of scientific management and he advocated for the elimination of the human element within the workplace. Taylor's view was that organizations could best create wealth by having the machines do all the work and to make more with less. Taylor's ideas are still evident today in many organizations through the fourth industrial revolution's emphasis on reengineering, artificial intelligence, and machine learning (Champy & Hammer, 1993; Kolbjørnsrud et al., 2016; Klingenberg et al., 2022; Morgan, 2019; Pokrovskaia et al., 2018; Ransbotham et al., 2017; Shukla et al., 2017; Vergne, 2020). Organizations are viewed from the perspective of machines more so than as human systems; implying that technology is more valuable to the organization than its people (Pereira et al., 2023).

Technology in this book refers to any useful method of performing a work task that is completed without human intervention or through human initiation. Based on this definition technology could be a robot or robotic machines such as self- propelled forklifts or tow motors, computers, and equipment control panels or controllers among many others. Technology also includes artificial intelligence (AI), digital technology, machine learning, and other concepts are at the forefront of the fourth industrial revolution (Schwab, 2016) yet, explainable AI has emerged because the human factor is still needed to explain what AI's intents are from an ethical perspective. Technology innovations are automatically attributed with perceived value. Drucker (1999) noted that "the most valuable asset in the 20th-century company was its production equipment" (p.79). The emergence of steam engine provided faster distribution of goods through railroad transportation. The Internet has provided global communication, extensive business development, Alphabet (Google), Meta, (Facebook), and social media. The computer created billions of dollars for companies such as Microsoft, Intel, Hewlett-Packard, and Dell; supporting the proposition that technology has value.

Valuing Both People and Technology

How do we value employee abilities in ways that benefit the employees and the organization? Why is it that employees feel exploited and undervalued in the workplace? Orr (1996) stated that

In the past, those who ran organizations were familiar with production processes. They often designed the process and had even done the work themselves. Today, organizations are so complex that it is difficult for those in charge to have experienced the organization's work firsthand. Moreover, managers are often hired from the outside, and their experience frequently lies in completely different industries. (p. xi)

The legal system and organization policies are used to keep employees under control. Employees are sued by consumers if the employee makes a mistake; yet these same consumers cannot sue technology. The maker(s) of the technology may be sued which still takes us back to people. There are government regulations, unions, and corporate policies which are designed to try and create amenable relationships between the organization and the employee. Laws and policies were created to protect employee from exploitation by their employers. Employment-at-will laws exist and permit the employee and the organization to part ways as they deem appropriate (Hijal-Moghrabi et al., 2017; Koy et al., 1987; Malos, 1998).

To adjust to legal constraints, some organizations have chosen to relocate their businesses to areas with minimum employment standards and laws, whether within or outside the US. Some organizations have chosen to reduce the number of employees and increase the amount of technology which leads to the contention that is least discussed within the business press (that was until the great recession): The choice to invest in technology as opposed to people. Despite the vast numbers of unemployed people in 2010 for example, businesses still earned 1.66 trillion in profit; the most in 60 years of government records. Productivity and revenue generation did not suffer too much without the millions of former employees. Even amid the worldwide, COVID-19 pandemic, corporate profits in the United States were USD 2.42 trillion in the first quarter of 2022, from a record USD 2.53 trillion reached in the previous period. Some organizations were pondering whether they should even rehire more workers or rely on technology while others were experiencing a labor shortage as workers resign or retire during the Great Resignation (Sull et al., 2022) and some employees are quietly quitting (Formica & Sfodera, 2022; Lord, 2022; Melin & Egkolfopoulou, 2021; Wen et al., 2023; Zenger & Folkman, 2022). People and technology are the foundation of organizations (Becker, 1964 & 1993; Betz, 1993; Carrig & Wright, 2006; Hughes et al., 2019; Jacobs, 1989; Martelli, 1998; Pfeffer, 1994), but the degree to which one has more value than the other is undecided. There are multiple competing opinions regarding the value of people versus the value of technology (Baldi & Trigeorgis, 2020; Morgan & Liker, 2020).

Issues, Controversies, Problems

Drucker (1999) stated:

The most important, and indeed the truly unique, contribution of management in the 20th century was the fifty-fold increase in the productivity of the manual worker in manufacturing. The most important contribution management needs to make in the 21st century is similarly to increase the productivity of knowledge work and knowledge workers. The most valuable assets of the 20th century company was its production equipment [technology]. The most valuable asset of a 21st century institution (whether business or non-business) will be its knowledge workers [people] and their productivity [value]. (p. 79)

Drucker's statements continue to resonate because there must be a way to align people and technology within the workplace to add value and provide a competitive advantage for the organization. The five values of people and technology development provide alignment opportunities and ways for organizational leaders to create success through people and technology.

Employees seek high quality feedback for deeper understanding of their performance inefficiencies (Balcazar et al., 1985; Balzer et al., 1989; DeNisi & Murphy, 2017; Kluger & DeNisi, 1996; Hom et al., 2017). When managers cannot provide quality feedback that aligns directly with employees' performance, the employees may become demotivated about their work performance. Employees want to be regarded for the depth of their job performance and not just their surface understanding of work skills. They are not asking management to give up technological interests. Most employees know the cost of technology and like the way(s) technology can be leveraged to help them improve their performance (Bennett, 2022); however, they do not want their value to be marginalized by technology either (Baptiste, 2001; Brynjolfsson & McAfee, 2011; Cowen, 2011; Ford, 2009; Levy & Murnane, 2005; Pfau & Kay, 2002).

Data science has emerged to analyze and examine the value accuracy of technology (Yorks et al., 2022). Data scientists use technology to target information contained within big data. Targeting information requires some manipulation of the technology by highly qualified people. Technology allows people to leverage their technological abilities to the benefit of the organization when managed appropriately. The technological, globalized economy requires the contribution of ethical people to produce trustworthy desired output.

CREATION OF THE PEOPLE AS TECHNOLOGY (PT) THEORETICAL CONCEPT

The PT theory originated throughout my first few years of production experiences within the textile industry and was further enhanced during several additional years in the textile, healthcare and nutrition, bottling, and mining industries. The PT theoretical concept is also supported by research citations from leaders in the hotel and tourism, engineering, and retail industries. PT theory is still being examined and extended through the additional content in this book.

Finding the Competitive Advantage Through People, Equipment, Processes, Training, and Communication: A Case Study

The originating case for the PT concept occurred in the textile industry where adaptability to complexity was required to successfully process over 400 different styles of fabric in over 25,000 colors. Employees were consistently producing first quality products despite the complexity of their jobs and the fact that some employees were marking an X for their signature to receive their paychecks suggesting that they could not read or write.

This was confounding because the organization was very successful and meeting its goals. When the organization sought to achieve International Organization of Standards (ISO) certification, one of the key elements was training and development. In this specific case, many organization leaders perceived that their employees were the problem - implying that the lack of education of the workforce was the root cause of all problems – when nonconforming situations occurred during production. This was hard to believe and accept because the organization was successfully processing over 2.5 million yards of first quality product each week and investing millions of dollars in new equipment without additional funding for training and development of an underdeveloped workforce. In an effort to improve production capacity of employees, the decision was made by Banks (1995) to test and see if the reasons for off quality fabric were because of "people" problems. To succeed in "Finding the competitive advantage through people, equipment, processes, training, and communication" the simple, yet ingenious, theory was to consider people as a technology. The elements used to compare technology characteristics (on the left of the equal sign) to people characteristics (on the right side of the equal sign) were:

1. Location = Cohesiveness in assigned environment;
2. Use = Qualifications;
3. Maintenance = Continuous Training; and
4. Modification = Growth and Change.

The examination of these elements were made with the goal of the project being to help the employees to improve the processes needed to consistently produce first quality product and/or provide excellent service within the organization.

To assess whether production problems were indeed people problems, beam tickets (work order traceable tickets) were collected each time an operator reported a problem or defect within any lot of fabric during production. Beam tickets were collected from 1st and 3rd shift finishing operators on six finishing frames (dryers) for six months. The reported lots of fabric were examined after inspection to determine if information reported by finishing operators was confirmed by inspectors. Inspectors logged fabric defect information into a computer system for each inspected lot fabric. The researcher obtained this information from an electronic database and compared it against the information provided by the operators on the beam tickets. The inspectors were not informed about any reported beam tickets nor were they consulted during examination of their information inputted into the computer system. A limitation of the data is that the inspectors could have made errors, and no one was checking every lot of fabric that they examined. There were random checks of their work by senior inspectors, so their work was reliable.

Findings from the final project analysis of all data were:

1. Identified key problems and sources of the problems for each of the six finishing frame Recommendations for solving the problems were provided to operators and management. The specific key problems and sources of the problems are proprietary to the organization.

2. Confirmed the concept of "People as a Technology" because the people had responsibilities that they were held accountable for without proper financial and other resources. The disparity of investment in equipment/technology and the investment in people was so vast that people might need to be treated or viewed as a technology to inspire better treatment. The suggestion was made to further explore the following comparisons: Location = Cohesiveness in assigned environment; Use = Qualifications; Maintenance = Continuous Training; and Modification = Growth and Change.

3. Determined that many of the problems were equipment, process, training, and communication problems and not directly finishing operator problems or errors.

4. Recommended a shadow program and cross-training program for finishing operators to learn to recognize types of problems associated with job requirements that required finishing operators to move from frame to frame without understanding process changes for styles and finishes of fabric. Analyzing the differences in frame fabric without effective training caused employees to make errors such as missing fabric defects.

5. Acknowledged that producing a first quality product can be adversely affected by people, equipment, processes, training, and communication.
6. Discovered limited effectiveness of business strategies including ISO 9000, Total Quality Management (TQM), Just-in-Time (JIT), and teams employed in the organization because of the lack of effective management and leadership of people, equipment, processes, training, and communication resources.
7. Identified an under-educated and under-trained workforce.
8. Identified communication as a key to bring closure to problems.

The analogy of people to technology was made in this case because of the discrepancy in amount of money the organization was investing in new technology as opposed to people development. Construction engineers tore down walls to provide additional space to the facility for accommodating the new equipment while employees worked in cramped spaces within a plant that could reach well over 100 degrees during the summers. Thus, a consideration of the location value of equipment versus location value of people was warranted.

The new technologies were brought in with technical manuals and technical experts to install the equipment to make sure the technology was used appropriately. Thus, a consideration of the use value of people in the facility was merited. People were constantly perceived to be the problem when they made mistakes. When they made mistakes, they were required by human resource reprimand policies to remain on jobs that they may not have been best prepared to perform. There was no job rotation or changes allowed if employees received a certain number of reprimands. Ultimately, even if an employee had the potential to do a different job better, they were fired for not performing their current job.

Employees were trained on a particular finishing frame, but once trained for six weeks, they were often assigned to operate a different frame. There were seldom any employee development adjustments made for the different types of fabric being run on the frame to which they were assigned. For example, if they were trained on a polyester finishing frame, and then assigned to run a wool finishing frame, they had no frame of reference regarding how polyester fabric had different characteristics than wool fabric. They could operate the frame but could not adjust to any complexities or identify any defects within the fabric. Missing defects was one of the main reasons for which frame operators were reprimanded.

There was a high number of maintenance staff and a maintenance training program that the company developed and sold to other production companies. Maintenance employees were trained and developed to maintain all the technology and equipment in the plant. However, all production employees were not trained and developed or had their skills maintained in the same way. Consequently, the maintenance value of equipment or technology versus maintenance value of people was considered.

Some of the maintenance employees worked with the engineering department to modify equipment when needed. Hence, equipment modification value versus people modification value was considered since employees began to acquire GEDs and other skills outside the facility. At this point in the PT model development, time value was not a part of the model. The project results revealed that production employees were not the problem or cause of many of the problems that occurred within many production processes. The problems identified were more often equipment, processes, training, and communication.

An understanding of the PT concept requires one to alter traditional thought processes with regards to how people are treated and developed and how technologies, processes and procedures are managed. Using the PT concept contributed to organizational success because the blend of how to manage technology and develop people effectively could be directly attributed to efficiency increases. The PT concept has also been used to design training programs. Many organizations already know how to train people. The role of the PT concept is to help stakeholders recognize their best practices and leverage them through an ideal blend of people and technology in the workplace.

Time value was added to the model after managing a group of people that consisted of temporary, contract, and permanent employees. There was no knowledge of how long the temporary and contract employees would be needed during the transition from a research and development (R & D) production line to a traditional production line. Temporary employees are a highly unstable workforce, especially when assigned to third shift operations. The cost of technology is often depreciated over time on the balance sheet, but the time value for employees may not be documented. Besides, employment–at will allows employees and organizations to disengage from each other without cause, although there are exceptions (Koy et al., 1987; Malos, 1998; Muhl, 2001). Because there are exceptions, ethics implications should be considered when the employee-at-will doctrine is applied, and organizations should try to have an enforceable ethical environment when operating in an employment-at-will state (Hijal-Moghrabi et al., 2017)

A specific theoretical foundation to introduce the PT concept to academia or other areas of the business literature was not available at this point, because it was primarily applied in practice. The dilemma between theory and practice is continuously debated (Berger et al., 2004; Hughes & Gosney, 2016). The typical question was: How does one introduce theory into practice? This book provides one case where it is reversed; a simple concept that works in practice needed to be introduced into the theoretical and academic world of research. A discussion of the use of cognitive, behavioral, and cultural research sparked the beginning of the theoretical concept to introduce the PT concept to the scholarly community. After 28 years, the PT theoretical concept is still evolving.

The PT concept is using the word as, in the form of a simile not as a substitution. Therefore, it is asking stakeholders to consider humans as they do technology. Technology is readily recycled or discarded when it no longer serves our needs, but one cannot simply recycle or discard human beings. This is a huge ethical concern and aspects of this was addressed by laws that protect workers from age discrimination (Hughes, 2019).

Some concerns expressed regarding the five-point model's stability included: productivity gains, skill development, supply risks, and time to market. Productivity gains are addressed within the model through better understanding and application of the five values. Skill development is clearly covered in the maintenance and modification areas of the model and by adding talent management to the discussion of the values. Supply risks are often addressed through quality systems such as ISO certifications and through government laws and regulations. Supply risk will be included and discussed in the context of diversity intelligence™ (Hughes, 2016) and risking the supply of human capital for the organization because of a lack of diversity intelligent leaders. Supply risk (Zsidisin, 2003) in the context of technology management will be covered under maintenance value and modification value because if the technology supply is limited as is the case for many products due to the COVID-19 pandemic, it becomes a major concern. Time to market is address through lead time that is built into the production processes and procedures

Enhancing the PT Theoretical Concept

Humans have enriched their lives through the labor of other humans using positive and negative methods. Methods have included slavery, feudal systems, indentured servitude, apprenticeship, child labor, and prison labor and some of these methods continue today. Since the first industrial revolution, technology has received more recognition for productivity gains than human effort (Drucker, 1999). We are now in the fourth industrial revolution and the debate continues regarding organizations trying to define their competitive advantage in the marketplace. There is beginning to be talk about the fifth industrial revolution which seeks to leverage the blend of humans and technology.

Organizations continuously look for ways to win (Carrig & Wright, 2006; Drucker, 1992; Hamel & Prahalad, 1994; Hoskisson et al., 2008; Porter, 1980; Welch, 2005; Womack & Jones, 1996) as they compete for their market share. Some new ideas include the employee experience (Morgan, 2017) and workforce inter-personnel talent management systems (Hughes, 2018). Sometimes leaders become complacent in their views with regards to opportunities for employee growth and development. Organizations conduct in-depth audits of their financial and technical assets on a routine basis. However, the audit of people is often limited to the number of employees, hourly wages, or yearly performance evaluations and seldom goes beyond the surface to truly examine their value or worth to the organization. Executive employees including board members have placed significant value on themselves based upon their salary, stock options, and other perks (Edmans et al., 2017; O'Reilly III et al., 2014). How valid are their assessments and why do they not use this same process to value their employees? The makeup of hourly wages is not clear to all workers and the hesitation of organizations to raise the minimum wage for workers has been a source of contention in American Society (Neumark & Shirley, 2022). The COVID-19 pandemic exacerbated the need for a higher minimum wage (Baena-Díez et al., 2020; Perry et al., 2021, Van Barneveld et al., 2020) and workers began the Great Resignation (Cook, 2021; Jiskrova, 2022; Kaplan, 2021; Serenko, 2022).

The focus of this book is targeted at determining where workers' value, outside of the executive suite and corporate board room, resides? Is their value to the organization found in their location, use, maintenance, modification, time value or a combination thereof (Hughes, 2010)? As organizations persist in searching for ways to inspire their employees to perform at peak levels, they could begin to understand the five values of each employee. The COVID-19 pandemic has indeed forced organization to address the five values. Organizations are having to address the five values from an ethical perspective as it relates to preventing employees' illness and/or death while seeking to meet organizational goals (Jecker et al., 2020; Kursumovic et al. 2020; Lusk & Chandra, 2021; Robert et al., 2020; Turale et al., 2020; Waltenburg et al., 2020; White et al., 2021). Low and middle-skilled workers in farming, poultry, healthcare, grocery, food service, hospitality, manufacturing, and other essential jobs were most susceptible to unethical treatment and did become ill at work and died. Most of these workers, in the U. S., were minorities and immigrants.

The worldwide COVID-19 pandemic has opened room for more extensive discussion of the five values. As economies in nations around the world sit at the precipice of collapse, low and middle-skilled workers are beginning to rebel against low pay, unethical treatment, and what they perceive as unfair distribution of wealth along with jobs that jeopardize their health and ability to stay alive. In contrast, technology was not at risk (Brakman et al., 2021) per se, but the use of needed technology (e.g., ventilators) was a major ethical concern due to supply risk (Birkel et al., 2020; Chu et al., 2020; Laffey et al. 2020; White & Lo, 2020). Also, the intellectual property protections for some technologies were at risk (Bloom et al., 2021; Jecker & Atuire, 2021). Determining whom to save during the height of the onset of the COVID-19 pandemic was daunting. Technology in the workplace that is valued more than people is being further scrutinized as stakeholders struggle to determine how technology and people can best help them achieve organization goals. Dead and severely ill employees should not be a hard choice for leaders; yet, in some instances during the COVID-19 pandemic that seemed to be the case. It has been revealed through remote work requirements during the COVID-19 pandemic that people do not need to be in a physical workplace with all other employees to be productive (Brynjolfsson et al., 2020).

Technology has been displacing workers for generations (Acemoglu & Restrepo, 2019; Hughes 2010, 2012) without much fanfare. However, someone must operate the technology, so many essential roles exist for people in organizations. However, technology became a central focus during the COVID-19 pandemic as organizations began funding technology such as robots, drones, mobile internet, laptops, smart phones, virtual meeting tools, 3D printing, artificial intelligence (AI), machine learning (Acemoglu & Restrepo, 2020; Li, 2013; Chua, 2020) at astronomical speed to meet vaccine development, education, training, remote work, food delivery and distribution, and other immediate needs (Caselli et al., 2022; Chu et al., 2020; Yamey et al., 2020). Many of these technologies were distributed to people who had no idea how to use them (Hughes, 2021), and in other cases, employees who had been requesting advances in technology from their employers for years finally received it in record time. The position or location value of the person and the technology has shifted. With this shift, there is now a need for the employee to possess more knowledge through training (maintenance value) or education (modification value) (Hughes, 2010) and a need to place emphasis on the placement of valued critical and remote technologies (Brynjolfsson et al., 2020). Training and education are not one and the same (Antonacopoulou, 2001; Banks, 2002; Garavan, 1997).

Differences Between Education and Training

Training and/or education is often used to introduce new technological innovations to individuals within organizations (Banks, 2002; Bennett, 2022; Hughes 2010, 2012, 2020; Hughes et al., 2019; Kim & Park, 2020; Wang, 2011). Lewin (1993) stated that "It is also important to distinguish between training as a preparation for existing jobs, training intended to lead to job creation, and training designed to improve performance on the job" (p. 221). Training enhances human performance by bridging the gap that exists between job needs and the lack of knowledge or skill required to perform the job (Silberman, 1998). Training focuses on the "gap" in knowledge or the assessed immediate need of the individual to acquire some specific knowledge and/or skill. It is often short-term and limited to a particular environment or task. It also focuses on the process and/or procedures needed to perform one or more tasks by providing specific 'need to know' information to the individual. Training is closely linked to time value because the pace and need for training is usually closely aligned. For example, when the need is urgent, training is rapidly deployed and administered.

Education is much broader than training and is designed to prepare individuals for future aspirations more often than immediate needs. Education provides in-depth content and information to meet general, as opposed to specific, knowledge and/or skills, and is more long-term. Education focuses more on theory and background of applications as opposed to practical application although experiential activities are included depending on the educational content being taught. Training and education are similar regarding their primary purpose of transferring knowledge to individuals.

Training and education are administration processes that impact the quality of the results for trainees. Training professionals and practitioners identify training problems through needs analysis techniques. Once the problem is identified, methods to address the problem are determined using assessment techniques such as surveys, interviews, and/or observations. After the appropriate method has been selected to address the training problem, proper development and delivery of the training methods and instruction for the learner becomes crucial. There are various models available to assist with instructional design and methodologies (Andrews & Goodson, 1980; Conley et al., 2017; Hughes & Byrd, 2015; Wang, 2011).

In contrast to training, education follows a prescribed curriculum that is designed to address broad needs of the learners and are sanctioned by accreditation agencies or other governing bodies. Educators follow curriculum guidelines as opposed to learner specific guidelines. The education instructional materials usually include a textbook as opposed to instructional materials developed for training need. Ultimately, education is the transfer of knowledge and practice in a discipline or field of study; whereas training is learning and practicing activities and skills to complete a specific task or work practice (Hughes, 2012). Individuals often benefit most from a combination of both education and training because training builds on what trainees learned in school environments and education builds upon and broadens the trainees' knowledge in specific skill areas (Banks, 2002; Hughes, 2012; Schein 1988).

Education relates to modification value and training relates to maintenance value.

Maintenance value is to maintain the organization's status quo through training employees while employees often seek education to self-develop and expand development and promotional opportunities. Sometimes training is a long-term process within jobs and careers. Should the long-term process of training be considered long-term just as education is considered long-term from a time value perspective? Education (reading, writing,) makes employees capable of training, which is a good point, but historically many workers could not read or write. Yet they were still trained to perform their jobs in the workplace.

Organizations expect to receive consistent, peak performance from employees. Without knowledge and skills, employees cannot meet performance expectations. Employees must know and understand the expectations or intentions of employers. In addition to the earlier described case study from which the PT concept originated, the objectives of this chapter are to discuss:

1. The philosophical perspectives that influence organizational culture.
2. The expectations and intentions of management with regards to people and technology development within organizations.
3. Some of the ways that managers and leaders currently value people and technology in the workplace.
4. The role of ethics in managing people and technology in the workplace.

Solutions and Recommendations

There are many theories and definitions of motivation (Herzberg, 1966; Kanfer et al., 2017; Maslow, 1987; Steers, & Porter, 1979; Weiner, 1972). Psychologists have directed their motivation studies of drive and expectancy theory towards filling in the missing empirical content of hedonism (Harrell & Stahl, 1986; House et al.,1974; Ramlall, 2004). People are assumed to behave in ways that maximize rewards, satisfiers, positive reinforcements, etc. and minimize punishments, dissatisfiers, negative reinforcements, etc. (Steers et al., 2004).

Technology is only as effective as the persons who is developing, designing, managing, programming, writing the algorithms, and/or monitoring the technology. Individuals within workplaces may be more educated and/or diverse; however, their ability to apply their educational knowledge within the context of the organization and to leverage their inter-personal diversity to strengthen organizational performance is only as effective as the individual determines. The adaptable workforce was seen to be lacking at the onset of the COVID-19 pandemic and many organizations were scrambling to help employees adapt and are still struggling with maintaining the needed workforce. The adaptability of the workforce is essential within the continuously changing global economic environment in which organizations operate. The speed with which technology has improved has increased the opportunity for communication within and across organizations. North American firms indicated their concern with their ability to "pass knowledge along from older to younger workers (39 percent versus 28 percent worldwide) and their ability to bring new employees up to speed (39 percent versus 24 percent)" (Ringo & MacDonald, 2008, p. 59). This may have changed dramatically due to the Great Resignation. Many older employees have retired and may not have passed on their knowledge (Serenko, 2022). Also, the speed at which employees left organizations during the Great Resignation leaves doubt that new employees were brought up to speed.

Organizations use many initiatives to increase productivity. Some of these initiatives have been successful while others have been detrimental. Some organizations no longer exist because of technology reliance, and some no longer exist because of people reliance. There must be a blend of commonalities between people and technology that is beneficial to the organization.

FUTURE RESEARCH DIRECTIONS

Future research can examine case studies to test the PT concept. Research on the ways that location, use, maintenance, modification, and time value can provide insight to stakeholders on how employees improve efficiency and productivity in alignment with technology. Future research can also examine training methods that are used ensure that employees are most effective within their assigned jobs. How effective are the training methods? How adaptable are organizations to the changes and growth of employees?

CONCLUSION

The World Economic Forum (2020) in its "The future of jobs report 2020" stated that AI and automation is expected to create 97 million jobs by 2025. The pace of AI and automation requires that all employees adopt technology and increase their technology skills rapidly. This change is going to require HRD professionals, practitioners, and scholars to be at the forefront of using and teaching others how to use technology (Hughes, 2020) and to expand their collaboration with technology specialists including information systems technologists, computer scientists and engineers among others. Today's global marketplace demands that organizations compete with effective people and productive technology. Without a strategic focus, organizations will isolate people from technology and struggle to win competitive advantage.

COVID-19 IMPACT MINI CASE STUDY

Hybrid work is here to stay after the lockdowns that forced employees to work from home during the COVID-19 pandemic. Forcing employees to work from centralized workplaces is no longer an option as employees have chosen to resign rather than return to work (Melin & Egkolfopoulou, 2021). The workers are in control of the labor market and are choosing their personal well-being. Organizations are having to adjust policies to recruit and retain workers. The continuous changes are making it necessary for HRD professionals, practitioners, and scholars to be leaders of the strategies to ensure that training and development needs of workers in all locations are met and that they champion programs supporting employee well-being (Hamouche & Chabani, 2021).

1. How can the PT concept be used to help organizations understand the location value of employees when employees are involved in hybrid or remote work?
2. How can the PT concept be used to help stakeholders adjust to continuous employee changes?
3. How can the PT concept help organization leaders improve retention of workers?

REFERENCES

Acemoglu, D., & Restrepo, P. (2019). Automation and new tasks: How technology displaces and reinstates labor. *The Journal of Economic Perspectives*, *33*(2), 3–30. doi:10.1257/jep.33.2.3

Acemoglu, D., & Restrepo, P. (2020). Robots and jobs: Evidence from US labor markets. *Journal of Political Economy*, *128*(6), 2188–2244. doi:10.1086/705716

Adams, J. S. (1963). Toward an understanding of inequity. *Journal of Abnormal and Social Psychology*, *67*(5), 422–436. doi:10.1037/h0040968 PMID:14081885

Antonacopoulou, E. P. (2001). The paradoxical nature of the relationship between training and learning. *Journal of Management Studies*, *38*(3), 327–350. doi:10.1111/1467-6486.00239

Arrieta, A. B., Díaz-Rodríguez, N., Del Ser, J., Bennetot, A., Tabik, S., Barbado, A., Garcia, S., Gil-Lopez, S., Molina, D., Benjamins, R., Chatila, R., & Herrera, F. (2020). Explainable artificial intelligence (XAI): Concepts, taxonomies, opportunities and challenges toward responsible AI. *Information Fusion*, *58*, 82–115. doi:10.1016/j.inffus.2019.12.012

Baena-Díez, J. M., Barroso, M., Cordeiro-Coelho, S. I., Díaz, J. L., & Grau, M. (2020). Impact of COVID-19 outbreak by income: Hitting hardest the most deprived. *Journal of Public Health*, *42*(4), 698–703. doi:10.1093/pubmed/fdaa136 PMID:32776102

Balcazar, F., Hopkins, B. L., & Suarez, Y. (1985). A critical, objective review of performance feedback. *Journal of Organizational Behavior Management, 7*(3-4), 65–89. doi:10.1300/J075v07n03_05

Baldi, F., & Trigeorgis, L. (2020). Valuing human capital career development: A real options approach. *Journal of Intellectual Capital, 21*(5), 781–807. doi:10.1108/JIC-06-2019-0134

Balzer, W. K., Doherty, M. E., & O'Connor, R. Jr. (1989). Effects of cognitive feedback on performance. *Psychological Bulletin, 106*(3), 410–433. doi:10.1037/0033-2909.106.3.410

Banks, C. H. (1995). *Finding the competitive advantage through people, equipment, processes, training, and communication* [Unpublished master's degree project, North Carolina State University].

Banks, C. H. (2002). A descriptive analysis of the perceived effectiveness of Virginia Tech's faculty development institute. *Dissertation Abstracts International, 64*(8). (UMI No. 3102585)

Baptiste, I. (2001). Educating lone wolves: Pedagogical implications of human capital theory. *Adult Education Quarterly, 51*(3), 184–201. doi:10.1177/074171360105100302

Becker, G. S. (1964). *Human capital: A theoretical and empirical analysis, with special reference to education.* University of Chicago Press.

Becker, G. S. (1993). *Human capital: Atheoretical and empirical analysis, with special reference to education* (3rd ed.). University of Chicago Press. doi:10.7208/chicago/9780226041223.001.0001

Bennett, E. E. (2022). Leveraging technology to design and deliver human resource development. In P. Holland, T. Bartram, T. Garavan, and K. Grant (Eds.). The Emerald handbook of work, workplaces and disruptive issues in HRM (pp. 261-276), Emerald Publishing Limited. doi:10.1108/978-1-80071-779-420221026

Berger, N. O., Kehrhahn, M. T., & Summerville, M. (2004). Research to practice: Throwing a rope across the divide. *Human Resource Development International, 7*(3), 403–409. doi:10.1080/1367886042000246003

Betz, F. (1993). *Strategic technology management.* McGraw-Hill.

Birkel, H. S., & Hartmann, E. (2020). Internet of Things–the future of managing supply chain risks. *Supply Chain Management*, *25*(5), 535–548. doi:10.1108/SCM-09-2019-0356

Bloom, N., Davis, S. J., & Zhestkova, Y. (2021, May). Covid-19 shifted patent applications toward technologies that support working from home. *AEA Papers and Proceedings. American Economic Association*, *111*, 263–266. doi:10.1257/pandp.20211057

Brakman, S., Garretsen, H., & van Witteloostuijn, A. (2021). Robots do not get the coronavirus: The COVID-19 pandemic and the international division of labor. *Journal of International Business Studies*, *52*(6), 1215–1224. doi:10.105741267-021-00410-9 PMID:33758437

Brynjolfsson, E., Horton, J. J., Ozimek, A., Rock, D., Sharma, G., & Tu, H. Y. (2020). *COVID-19 and remote work: An early look at US data* (No. w27344). National Bureau of Economic Research.

Brynjolfsson, E., & McAfee, A. (2011). *Race against the machine: How the digital revolution is accelerating innovation, driving productivity, and irreversibly transforming employment and the economy*. Digital Frontier Press.

Carrig, K., & Wright, P. M. (2006). *Building profit through building people: Making your work-force the strongest link in the value-profit chain*. Society for Human Resource Management.

Caselli, M., & Fracasso, A. (2022). COVID-19 and technology. In K. F. Zimmermann (Ed.), *Handbook of labor, human resources and population economics*. Springer., doi:10.1007/978-3-319-57365-6_331-1

Champy, J., & Hammer, M. (1993). *Reengineering the corporation*. HarperBusiness.

Chu, Q., Correa, R., Henry, T. L., McGregor, K. A., Stoklosa, H., Robinson, L., Jha, S., Annamalai, A., Hsu, B. S., Gupta, R., Patton, D. U., Moreno-Walton, L. A., Butts, C., Chai, C., & Kuy, S. (2020). Reallocating ventilators during the coronavirus disease 2019 pandemic: Is it ethical? *Surgery*, *168*(3), 388–391. doi:10.1016/j.surg.2020.04.044 PMID:32616345

Chua, C. K. (2020). The global rise of 3D printing during the COVID-19 pandemic. *Nature Reviews. Materials*, *5*(9), 637–639. doi:10.103841578-020-00234-3 PMID:35194517

Conley, Q., Lutz, H. S., & Miller, C. L. (2017). The flipped training model: Six steps for getting employees to flip out over training. *Performance Improvement, 56*(5), 18–31. doi:10.1002/pfi.21692

Cook, I. (2021, September 15). Who is driving the Great Resignation? *Harvard Business Review*. https://hbr.org/2021/09/who-is-driving-the-great-resignation

Cowen, T. (2011). *The great stagnation: How America ate all the low-hanging fruit of modern history, got sick, and will(eventually) feel better*. Penguin Group Publishing.

De Clercq, D., Dayan, M., & Ng, P. Y. (2023). When performance demands enable change: How employees can overcome emotional dissonance and organizational underappreciation. *European Management Journal*, 1–11. doi:10.1016/j.emj.2023.02.004

DeNisi, A. S., & Murphy, K. R. (2017). Performance appraisal and performance management: 100 years of progress? *The Journal of Applied Psychology, 102*(3), 421–433. doi:10.1037/apl0000085 PMID:28125265

Drucker, P. F. (1992). *Managing for the future*. Butterworth Heinemann.

Drucker, P. F. (1999). Knowledge-worker productivity: The biggest challenge. *California Management Review, 41*(2), 79–94. doi:10.2307/41165987

Edmans, A., Gabaix, X., & Jenter, D. (2017). Executive compensation: A survey of theory and evidence. The Handbook of the Economics of Corporate Governance, 1, 383-539.

Ford, M. (2009). *The lights in the tunnel: Automation, accelerating technology and the economy of the future*. Acculant Publishing.

Formica, S., & Sfodera, F. (2022). The great resignation and quiet quitting paradigm shifts: An overview of current situation and future research directions. *Journal of Hospitality Marketing & Management, 31*(8), 899–907. doi:10.1080/19368623.2022.2136601

Formosa, P., & Ryan, M. (2021). Making moral machines: Why we need artificial moral agents. *AI & Society, 36*(3), 839–851. doi:10.100700146-020-01089-6

Freedman, S. M. (1978). Some determinants of compensation decisions. *Academy of Management Journal*, *21*(3), 397–409. doi:10.2307/255722 PMID:10246525

Friedman, M. (1994). *Money mischief: Episodes in monetary history*. Harcourt Brace.

Funding the development and manufacturing of COVID-19 vaccines. *The Center for Policy Impact in Global Health., Duke Global Working Paper Series*, (20), 1-26.

Garavan, T. N. (1997). Training, development, education and learning: Different or the same? *Journal of European Industrial Training*, *21*(2), 39–50. doi:10.1108/03090599710161711

Hamel, G., & Prahalad, C. K. (1994). *Competing for the future*. Harvard Business School Press.

Hamouche, S., & Chabani, Z. (2021). COVID-19 and the new forms of employment relationship: Implications and insights for human resource development. *Industrial and Commercial Training*, *53*(4), 366–379. doi:10.1108/ICT-11-2020-0112

Heinrich, T., & Witko, C. (2021). Technology-induced job loss and the prioritization of economic problems in the mass public. *The Review of Policy Research*, *38*(2), 164–179. doi:10.1111/ropr.12418

Herzberg, F. (1966). Work and the nature of man. *WORLD (Oakland, Calif.)*.

Hijal-Moghrabi, I., Sabharwal, M., & Berman, E. M. (2017). The importance of ethical environment to organizational performance in employment at will states. *Administration & Society*, *49*(9), 1346–1374. doi:10.1177/0095399715581043

Hom, P. W., Lee, T. W., Shaw, J. D., & Hausknecht, J. P. (2017). One hundred years of employee turnover theory and research. *The Journal of Applied Psychology*, *102*(3), 530–545. doi:10.1037/apl0000103 PMID:28125259

Hoskisson, R. E., Hitt, M. A., Ireland, R. D., & Harrison, J. S. (2008). *Competing for advantage* (2nd ed.). South-Western.

Hughes, C. (2010). "People as technology" conceptual model: Towards a new value creation paradigm for strategic human resource development. *Human Resource Development Review*, *9*(1), 48–71. doi:10.1177/1534484309353561

Hughes, C. (2012). *Valuing people and technology in the workplace: A competitive advantage framework*. IGI Global. doi:10.4018/978-1-4666-0240-3

Hughes, C. (2016). *Diversity intelligence: Integrating diversity intelligence alongside intellectual, emotional, and cultural intelligence for leadership and career development*. Palgrave MacMillan Publications. doi:10.1057/978-1-137-52683-0

Hughes, C. (2018). *Workforce inter-personnel diversity: The power to influence human productivity and career development*. Springer International Publishing.

Hughes, C. (2019). *Ethical and legal issues in human resource development: Evolving roles and emerging trends*. Springer International Publishing. doi:10.1007/978-3-319-99528-1

Hughes, C. (2021). The changing learning technological landscape for trainers in the wake of COVID-19. *Advances in Developing Human Resources*, *23*(1), 66–74. doi:10.1177/1523422320972108

Hughes, C., & Brown, L. (2018). Exploring leaders' discriminatory, passive-aggressive behavior toward protected class employees using diversity intelligence. *Advances in Developing Human Resources*, *20*(3), 263–284. doi:10.1177/1523422318778002

Hughes, C., & Byrd, M. (2015). *Managing human resource development programs: Current issues and evolving trends*. Palgrave Macmillan Publications. doi:10.1057/9781137492197

Hughes, C., & Gosney, M. (Eds.). (2016). *Bridging the scholar-practitioner gap in Human Resource Development*. IGI Global. doi:10.4018/978-1-4666-9998-4

Hughes, C., Robert, L., Frady, K., & Arroyos, A. (2019). *Managing technology and middle and low skilled employees: Advances for economic regeneration*. Emerald Publishing. doi:10.1108/9781789730777

Jacobs, R. (1989). Systems theory applied to hu-man resource development. In D. B. Gradous (Ed.), *Systems theory applied to human resource development* (pp. 27–60). American Society for Training and Development.

Jasson, C. C., & Govender, C. M. (2017). Measuring return on investment and risk in training–A business training evaluation model for managers and leaders. *Acta Commercii*, *17*(1), 1–9. doi:10.4102/ac.v17i1.401

Jecker, N. S., & Atuire, C. A. (2021). What's yours is ours: Waiving intellectual property protections for COVID-19 vaccines. *Journal of Medical Ethics*, *47*(9), 595–598. doi:10.1136/medethics-2021-107555 PMID:34233956

Jecker, N. S., Wightman, A. G., & Diekema, D. S. (2021). Vaccine ethics: An ethical framework for global distribution of COVID-19 vaccines. *Journal of Medical Ethics*, *47*(5), 308–317. doi:10.1136/medethics-2020-107036 PMID:33593876

Jiskrova, G. K. (2022). Impact of COVID-19 pandemic on the workforce: From psychological distress to the Great Resignation. *Journal of Epidemiology and Community Health*, *76*(6), 525–526. doi:10.1136/jech-2022-218826 PMID:35296522

Judge, T. A., Weiss, H. M., Kammeyer-Mueller, J. D., & Hulin, C. L. (2017). Job attitudes, job satisfaction, and job affect: A century of continuity and of change. *The Journal of Applied Psychology*, *102*(3), 356–374. doi:10.1037/apl0000181 PMID:28125260

Kanfer, R., Frese, M., & Johnson, R. E. (2017). Motivation related to work: A century of progress. *The Journal of Applied Psychology*, *102*(3), 338–355. doi:10.1037/apl0000133 PMID:28150980

Kaplan, J. (2021). The psychologist who coined the phrase 'Great Resignation' reveals how he saw it coming and where he sees it going. 'Who we are as an employee and as a worker is very central to who we are.' *Insider*. www.businessinsider.com/why-everyone-is-quitting-great-resig nationpsychologist-pandemic-rethink-life-2021-10

Kim, J., & Park, C. Y. (2020). Education, skill training, and lifelong learning in the era of technological revolution. *ADB Economics Working Paper Series*, (606), 1-15.

Klingenberg, C. O., Borges, M. A. V., & do Vale Antunes Jr, J. A. (2022). Industry 4.0: What makes it a revolution? A historical framework to understand the phenomenon. *Technology in Society*, *70*, 1–6. doi:10.1016/j.techsoc.2022.102009

Kluger, A. N., & DeNisi, A. (1996). The effects of feedback interventions on performance: A historical review, a meta-analysis, and a preliminary feedback intervention theory. *Psychological Bulletin*, *119*(2), 254–284. doi:10.1037/0033-2909.119.2.254

Kolbjørnsrud, V., Amico, R., & Thomas, R. J. (2016). How artificial intelligence will redefine management. *Harvard Business Review*, *2*(1), 3–10.

Koy, D. J., Briggs, S., & Grenig, J. (1987). State court disparity on employment-at-will. *Personnel Psychology*, *40*(3), 565–577. doi:10.1111/j.1744-6570.1987.tb00615.x

K. P. Kuchinke (Ed.). system levels. In K. P. Kuchinke (Ed.), *Proceedings of the 1999 AHRD Conference* (pp. 602-610). Academy of Human Resource Development.

Laffey, J. G., Chikhani, M., Bates, D. G., & Hardman, J. G. (2020). Supporting more than one patient with a single mechanical ventilator: Useful last resort or unjustifiable risk? *British Journal of Anaesthesia*, *125*(3), 247–250. doi:10.1016/j.bja.2020.05.029 PMID:32536443

Leventhal, G. S., & Whiteside, H. D. (1973). Equity and the use of reward to elicit high performance. *Journal of Personality and Social Psychology*, *25*(1), 75–83. doi:10.1037/h0034276

Levy, F., & Murnane, R. J. (2005). *The new division of labor: How computers are creating the next job market*. Princeton University Press.

Lewin, K. (1993). Investing in technical and vocational education: A review of the evidence. *The Vocational Aspect of Education*, *45*(3), 217–227. doi:10.1080/0305787930450303

Li, J. (2013). Web-based technology and the changing landscape of HRD. *Human Resource Development International*, *16*(3), 247–250. doi:10.1080/13678868.2013.799401

Loewenberg, A. (2015). Child care teachers: Underpaid and underappreciated. *New America*: https://www.newamerica.org/educationpolicy/edcentral/child-care-workers/

Lord, J. D. (2022). Quiet quitting is a new name for an old method of industrial action. *The Conversation*. https://usir.salford.ac.uk/id/eprint/65022/1/quiet-quitting-is-a-

Loyarte-López, E. & García-Olaizola, I. (2022). Machine learning based method for deciding internal value of talent. *Applied Artificial Intelligence*, *36*(1), 1-19, doi:10.1080/08839514.2022.2151160

Lusk, J. L., & Chandra, R. (2021). Farmer and farm worker illnesses and deaths from COVID-19 and impacts on agricultural output. *PLOS ONE, 16*(4), e0250621

Malos, S. (1998). Current legal issues in performance appraisal. In J. Smither (Ed.), Performance appraisal: State of the art in practice (pp. 49–94). Jossey-Bass Publisher.

Martelli, J. (1998). *Training for new technology: Midwest steel company.* ASTD.

Marx, K. (1906). *Capital* (Vol. 1). Kerr.

Maslow, A. (1987). *Motivation and personality* (3rd ed.). Harper & Row.

Melin, A. & Egkolfopoulou, M. (2021). Employees are quitting instead of giving up working from home. *Bloomberg Wealth.* www. bloomberg.com/news/articles/2021-06-01/return-to-officee mployees-are-quitting-instead-of-giving-up-work-from-home

Morgan, J. (2017). *The employee experience advantage: How to win the war for talent by giving employees the workspaces they want, the tools they need, and a culture they can celebrate.* John Wiley & Sons.

Morgan, J. (2019). Will we work in twenty-first century capitalism? A critique of the fourth industrial revolution literature. Economy and Society, 48(3), 371–398

Morgan, J. M., & Liker, J. K. (2020). *The Toyota product development system: integrating people, process, and technology.* Productivity press.

Muhl, C. J. (2001). The employment-at-will doctrine: Three major exceptions. Monthly Labor Review, 124, 3-11..

Murray, A., Rhymer, J. E. N., & Sirmon, D. G. (2021). Humans and technology: Forms of conjoined agency in organizations. *Academy of Management Review, 46*(3), 552-571. doi:10.5465/amr.2019.0186

Neumark, D., & Shirley, P. (2022). Myth or measurement: What does the new minimum wage research say about minimum wages and job loss in the United States? Industrial Relations, 61(4), 384–417.

O'Reilly III, C. A., Doerr, B., Caldwell, D. F., & Chatman, J. A. (2014). Narcissistic CEOs and executive compensation. The Leadership Quarterly, 25(2), 218–231.

Orr, J. E. (1996). *Talking about machines. An ethnography of a modern job.* ILR.

Pereira, V., Hadjielias, E., Christofi, M., & Vrontis, D. (2023). A systematic literature review on the impact of artificial intelligence on workplace outcomes: A multi-process perspective. *Human Resource Management Review, 33*(1), 1-22. doi:10.1016/j.hrmr.2021.100857

Perry, B. L., Aronson, B., & Pescosolido, B. A. (2021). Pandemic precarity: COVID-19 is exposing and exacerbating inequalities in the American heartland. *Proceedings of the National Academy of Sciences, 118*(8), e2020685118

Pfau, B. N., & Kay, I. T. (2002). *The human capital edge: 21 people management practices your company must implement (or avoid) to maximize shareholder value.* McGraw-Hill.

Pfeffer, J. (1994). *Competitive advantage through people: Unleashing the power of the workforce.* Harvard Business School Press.

Phillips, J. J. (2003). *Return on investment in training and performance improvement programs* (2nd ed.). Elsevier Science.

Pokrovskaia, N. N., Gildingersh, M. G., & Gornykh, E. V. (2018, July). Reengineering of corporate management in the innovative context and professional competencies of a reengineer. In *2018 Third International Conference on Human Factors in Complex Technical Systems and Environments (ERGO) s and Environments (ERGO)* (pp. 32-35). IEEE.

Porter, M. (1980). *Competitive strategy.* Free Press.

Prause, D., & Mujtaba, B. G. (2015). Conflict management practices for diverse workplaces. *Journal of Business Studies Quarterly, 6*(3), 13-22.

Rajecki, B. (2022). Go digital: How technology can mitigate the effects of the workforce shortage. *McKnight's Long-Term Care News, 43*(3), 14-15.

Ramlall, S. (2004). A review of employee motivation theories and their implications for employee retention within organizations. *Journal of American Academy of Business, Cambridge, 5*(1/2), 52–63.

Ramsey, M. (1986). *The super supervisor.* Positive Presentations, Inc.

Ransbotham, S., Kiron, D., Gerbert, P., & Reeves, M. (2017). Reshaping business with artificial intelligence: Closing the gap between ambition and action. MIT Sloan Management Review, 59(1), 1–17.

Rego, A., Souto, S., & Cunha, M. P. (2009). Does the need to belong moderate the relationship between perceptions of spirit of camaraderie and employees' happiness? *Journal of Occupational Health Psychology, 14*(2), 148–164. doi:10.1037/a0014767

Ringo, T., & McDonald, R. (2008). *Unlocking the DNA of the adaptable workforce: The global human capital study.* IBM Global Services.

RobertR.Kentish-BarnesN.BoyerA.LaurentA.AzoulayE.ReignierJ. (2020). Ethical dilemmas due to the Covid-19 pandemic. Annals of Intensive Care, 10(1), 1–9.

Sackett, P. R., Lievens, F., Van Iddekinge, C. H., & Kuncel, N. R. (2017). Individual differences and their measurement: A review of 100 years of research. *Journal of Applied Psychology, 102*(3), 254–273. doi:10.1037/apl0000151

Saulnier, C., & Frank, L. (2019). Unappreciated and underpaid: Early Childhood Educators in Nova Scotia. Canadian Centere for Policy Alternatives–Nova Scotia Office. https://www. policyalternatives. ca/publications/reports/early-childhood-educators-ns.

Schein, E. H. (1988). *Organizational socialization and the profession of management.* Sloan *Management Review*, 30(1), 53–65.

Serenko, A. (2022). The great resignation: The great knowledge exodus or the onset of the great knowledge revolution? Journal of Knowledge Management. Advance online publication. doi:10.1108/JKM-12-2021-0920

Shukla, P., Wilson, H.J., Alter, A. and Lavieri, D. (2017). Machine reengineering: Robots and people working smarter together. *Strategy & Leadership, 45*(6), 50-54. doi:10.1108/SL-09-2017-0089

Siegmann, K. A. (2020). From clapping for essential workers to revaluing them. Global Labour Column, (339), 1-2.

Silberman, M. (1998). *Active training* (2nd ed.). Jossey-Bass/Pfeiffer.

Sliter, M. T., & Boyd, E. M. (2014). Two (or three) is not equal to one: Multiple jobholding as a neglected topic in organizational research. Journal of Organizational Behavior, 35(7), 1042–1046.

Spring, M., Faulconbridge, J., & Sarwar, A. (2022). How information technology automates and augments processes: Insights from artificial-intelligence-based systems in professional service operations. *Journal of Operations Management, 68*(6-7), 592–618. doi:10.1002/joom.1215

Steers, R. M., Mowday, R. T., & Shapiro, D. L. (2004). The future of work motivation theory. Academy of Management Review, 29(3), 379–387.

Steers, R. M., & Porter, L. W. (1979). *Motivation and work behavior* (2nd ed.). McGraw-Hill.

Stewart, T. A. (1997). *Intellectual capital: The new wealth of organizations.* Doubleday.

Sull, D., Sull, C., & Zweig, B. (2022). Toxic culture is driving the great resignation. MIT Sloan Management Review, 63(2), 1–9.

Tarrant, K., & Nagasawa, M. (2020). New York Early care and education survey: Understanding the impact of COVID-19 on New York early childhood system. https://educate.bankstreet.edu/sc/2/

Torraco, R. J. (2000). The relationship of learning and performance improvement at different system levels. *Performance Improvement Quarterly, 13*(1), 60–83. doi:10.1111/j.1937-8327.2000.tb00157.

Turale, S., Meechamnan, C., & Kunaviktikul, W. (2020). Challenging times: Ethics, nursing and the COVID-19 pandemic. International Nursing Review, 67(2), 164–167.

Van Barneveld, K., Quinlan, M., Kriesler, P., Junor, A., Baum, F., Chowdhury, A., Junankar, P. N., Clibborn, S., Flanagan, F., Wright, C. F., Friel, S., Halevi, J., & Rainnie, A. (2020). The COVID-19 pandemic: Lessons on building more equal and sustainable societies. *The Economic and Labour Relations Review, 31*(2), 133-157.

Vergne, J. P. (2020). Decentralized vs. distributed organization: Blockchain, machine learning and the future of the digital platform. *Organization Theory, 1*(4), 1-26.

Wadors, P. (2016, August 10). Diversity efforts fall short unless employees feel that they belong. *Harvard Business Review*. Retrieved from https://hbr.org/2016/08/ diversity-efforts-fall-short-unless-employees-feel-that-they-belong

WaltenburgM. A.VictoroffT.RoseC. E.ButterfieldM.JervisR. H.FedakK. M.HoneinM. A. (2020). Update: COVID-19 among workers in meat and poultry processing facilities—United States, April–May 2020. Morbidity and Mortality Weekly Report, 69(27), 887.

Wang, M. (2011). Integrating organizational, social, and individual perspectives in Web 2.0-based workplace e-learning. Information Systems Frontiers, 13, 191–205.

Weiner, B. (1972). *Theories of motivation: From mechanism to cognition.* Markham.

Welch, J. (2005). *Winning.* HarperCollins.

Wen, L., Maani, S. A., & Dong, Z. (2023). Educational job mismatch, job satisfaction, on-the-job training, and employee quit behaviour: A dynamic analytical approach. *Applied Economics*, 1-22. doi:10.1080/00036846.2022.2161990

White, D. B., & Lo, B. (2020). A framework for rationing ventilators and critical care beds during the COVID-19 pandemic. Journal of the American Medical Association, 323(18).

White, E. M., Wetle, T. F., Reddy, A., & Baier, R. R. (2021). Front-line nursing home staff experiences during the COVID-19 pandemic. Journal of the American Medical Directors Association, 22(1), 199–203.

Wilson, C. (2012). Retaining good people through a focus on talent and purpose: Proper inductions make employees feel as though they truly belong. Human Resource Management International Digest, 20(2), 29–31.

Womack, J. P., & Jones, D. T. (1996). *Lean thinking.* Simon & Schuster.

World Economic Forum. (2020). *The future of jobs report 2020.* Geneva.

YameyG.SchäferhoffM.PateM.ChawlaM.RansonK.HatchettR.WilderR.

Yorks, L., Abel, A. L., & Rotatori, D. (2022). Using data and analytics for improved HRD performance in the age of digital technologies. In *Strategic human resource development in practice: Leveraging talent for sustained performance in the digital age of AI* (pp. 81-92). Springer International Publishing.

Zenger, J., & Folkman, J. (2022, August 31). Quiet quitting is about bad bosses, not bad employees. *Harvard Business Review.* https://hbr.org/2022/08/quiet-quittingis-about-bad-bosses-no t-bad-employees

Zsidisin, G. A. (2003). A grounded definition of supply risk. *Journal of Purchasing and Supply* Management, 9(5-6), 217–224.

Section 2
Applying the People as Technology Concept in HRD

Chapter 4

The People as Technology Model and the Five Values

ABSTRACT

Chapter four provides an overview of the people as technology (PT) model and the five common values between people and technology. Location value represents power of position, power to generate revenue, power to leverage resources, and power to serve as a catalyst for change. Use value is created when leaders motivate employees to use their knowledge, skills, and abilities to help organizations succeed. Use value relates to the quality factor in a worker's productivity. Employee maintenance value is expressed through a combination of training and development, motivation, and health and wellness. Modification value of people looks at how employees grow and change through activities that employees use for self-development including education. Time value is often directed but not measured accurately relative to cost for the organization or the individual. The COVID-19 pandemic made it abundantly apparent that employees are indeed the most important asset in organizations and understanding their values matters.

INTRODUCTION

The vastly different workforce that has emerged during the COVID-19 pandemic has made it imperative that organizations understand the value of each individual employee. The myriad of generations in the workforce from Gen Z to Baby Boomers has required that positions become more flexible

DOI: 10.4018/978-1-6684-5321-6.ch004

and suitable for each employee. When this was not occurring prior to the COVID-19 pandemic, many workers simply tolerated the situations. However, during the COVID-19 pandemic and the many forced adjustments, workers have begun to take control of their own careers. They are resigning as a part of the Great Resignation of 2022, they are quiet quitting by only doing the minimum required of them on their jobs, they are becoming entrepreneurs and contributing to society as a part of the GIG economy, or they are retiring as early as possible to enjoy their lives. Some workers are working remotely from home or anywhere that allows them the technological access to complete their work.

Adequate and accurate feedback through performance appraisal systems in the workplace influences employees' options for enrichment, vertical movement, lateral movement, realignment, relocation, and exploration of other potential location options. Stakeholders' ethical decision making should not include the use of unreliable systems on employees who expect their leaders to make trustworthy and dependable choices for their career success.

According to Pfeffer (1992),

organizations have career systems in place that tend to reward and encourage activities and skills more generously than others…Therefore, those who rise to positions of influence and who benefit from this career system have a particular set of skills and have engaged in a particular set of activities – those favored by the system" (p. 318).

Employees must be cognizant of the organizational culture and seek to build and develop relationships within the organization's career system. Are the culture and career systems ethical? Employees are essentially interdependent and rely on each other more in today's work environments where teamwork is required and expected. Are the processes of determining team members ethical processes. "It is critical that one be able to diagnose the relative power of various participants and comprehend the patterns of interdependence. One needs to know and understand not only the game, but also the players" (Pfeffer, 1992, p. 49). These concepts are being challenged by the COVID-19 pandemic regarding where the employee needs to be to develop or maintain interpersonal relationships. Software such Zoom, Microsoft Teams, and Webex have made virtual communication more accessible. Employees no longer need to be physically with each other in the workplace to communicate and develop interpersonal relationships.

Some organizations expect employees to work in teams and become a cohesive unit; however, the many personalities of team members require that motivation is sometimes needed to influence team unity. Definitions of motivation have three common denominators.

They are all principally concerned with factors or events that energize, channel, and sustain human behavior over time. In various ways, contemporary theories of work motivation derive from efforts to explicate with increasing precision how these three factors interrelate to determine behavior in organizations. (Steers et al., 2004, p. 379)

How do organization teams ethically energize, channel, and sustain team members' behavior? According to Steers & Porter (1979), a generalized model of motivation requires needs or expectations, behavior, goals, and some form of feedback. Banks' (2006) model incorporated all these elements and stressed that individuals address their personal goals and expectations.

Porter and Steers (1973) researched the potential role of "met expectations" on a person's withdrawal behavior, which is their tendency to be absent, avoid participation in optional organizational activities, or, in the extreme, quit. The Great Resignation is an example where millions of employees have reached the extreme limit because their expectations are not being met by their organizations. They defined met expectations as the "discrepancy between what a person encounters on this job in the way of positive and negative experiences and what he expected to encounter" (p.152). Using met expectations hypothesis, Porter and Steers predicted that when an individual's expectations are unmet, that person's propensity to withdraw will increase. Irving and Meyer (1995) tested the met expectations hypothesis using difference scores reflecting the discrepancy between post-entry experiences and pre-entry expectations and found problems. "Scores on the measure are assumed to reflect the "match" between these variables. If this is true, it should be possible to show that direct measures of met expectations reflect independently obtained measures of expectation and experiences approximately equally" (p. 1160). This concept can be used to measure employee perception of their location value. Are their perceptions of their location value in the organization what they expected (Hughes, 2012)?

Organizational Culture

Organizational culture considers the rules, written and unwritten, which influence how members of organizations should act to get along with each other (Chatman & Jehn, 1991; George et al., 1999; Ouchi, 1981; Pascale & Athos, 1981; Ritti & Funkhouser, 1982). Culture also influences employee behavior and performance outcomes, including economic efficiency (Camerer & Vepsalainen, 1988; Chatman & Cha, 2003; Deal & Kennedy, 1982). Comfort within the culture of the organization can enhance location value for employees. COVID-19 significantly impacted employee movement and some aspects of organizational culture were permanently altered.

Lawler (2003) discussed ways for employees to thrive through organizational nourishment. Career development and training and development are two ways that organizations can provide proper nourishment to employees. Organizations that become learning organizations can embed a culture of learning into the organization that supports knowledge sharing (Kucharska & Rebelo, 2022; Sari, 2022) Organization leaders and employees must communicate to understand each other's expectations, goals, and/or aspirations. The organization should seek to avoid establishing a career development or learning strategy of 'if we build it, they will come' - inferring that there is no need to encourage the employee to participate in the development of the strategy (Hughes, 2012). In this fast-paced economic environment, all employees need to be competent, flexible, and knowledgeable in all areas of their development and understand their role within career and learning management systems. Organizations should be fully prepared for adaptive learning (Konopka, 2018).

Employees must be aware of shifts in career planning and adapt accordingly especially if they are entering and reentering the workplace (Karsten & Igou, 2005; Hughes & Niu, 2021a, b). Many employees are entering and reentering different workplaces due to the COVID-19 pandemic. Many have switched careers as a part of the Great Resignation because their career aspirations no longer aligned with their organizations' values. Some employees value their life more than a career with an organization that appears to only value money or value money more than employees' health.

BACKGROUND

Organizations need assets to compete whether they are service organizations or product generating. The organization must be in a place that benefits its customers and so must its employees. However, the COVID-19 pandemic has caused organizations to become explicit regarding which employees are located. Essential employees needed to directly serve customers, technology was more targeted for customer interactions, and some office space became obsolete. Engineering expertise is tied directly to technological functionality. If the technology is not designed and integrated in the correct location within organizational systems and processes, organizations experience substantive revenue loss.

PT MODEL AND FIVE VALUES

The People as Technology (PT) model's central focus is on the development of technology and the development of people. The five common values between people and technology provides the opportunity for this model to be useful. Providing an overview of the five common values from the employee perspective more so than the technology perspective is done only to highlight the differences.

Organizations sometimes need to make infrastructure changes to accommodate the addition of new technology or expansion of current technologies. New or re-design of structures may be needed to house new technology. Rapid expansion often occurs to meet consumer needs; however, this was not the case for many rural communities. However, the COVID-19 pandemic has forced rapid expansion of technology availability for rural communities. The PT Model considers the risks and uncertainties that can occur with both people and technology development. Infrastructure changes are one example where risk and uncertainty happen. For example, transport trucks are the prime infrastructure of transportation companies such as FedEx, UPS, and JB Hunt. Knowing the location of the trucks is essential to meeting customer needs; therefore, the location value is the reason for the continuous investment in the technology to maintain location awareness. Global positioning systems (GPS) are used to track trucks and are a huge investment. Because these employees are on location with the organization's valuable infrastructure, the organization must understand where they are and why and how their placement benefits or hinders growth for the organization.

LOCATION VALUE

It is understood from the real estate market that location adds value to a commodity or entity (Figueroa, 1999; Gallimore et al., 1996; Thériault et al., 2003). Leaders spend inordinate amounts of time and resources locating the perfect placement for technology within and outside the organization. Maidique and Hayes (1984) noted that "the most successful high-technology firms lead one to conclude that they are highly focused. …the great bulk of their sales either from a single product line or from a closely related set of product lines" (p. 19). Successful organizations do not diversify away from their strengths. Yet, some leaders do not know the location value of their employees and may routinely ask employees to diversify away from their strength, leading to the employees' reduced effectiveness (Hughes, 2012). Many organizations learned during the COVID-19 pandemic that their employees' location value strength was not in there required business offices but in remote locations including employees as homes (Alipour et al., 2021). They also, in some instances, learned that the true value of the employee was in the employee and not the location itself.

Location value represents power. It can represent power of position, power to generate revenue, power to leverage resources, and power to serve as a catalyst for change. All these power dynamics were supported during the COVID-19 pandemic. As with any source of power, location value could provide an asset to or be a liability for the organization. Maidique and Hayes (1984) also noted that "organizational agility seems to be associated with organizational flexibility – frequent realignments of people and responsibilities as the firm attempts to maintain its balance on shifting competitive sands" (p.21). Realignments of people requires leaders to know the employees' location value to the organization. Organizations were forced to be agile at the onset and during the COVID-19 pandemic.

Power and structure inside organizations are tied to the central position of employees (Burkhardt & Brass, 1990; Brass & Burkhardt, 1993), and the impact of employees' actual and perceived power is determined by their strategic placement or location within the organization (Brass & Burkhardt, 1993; Pfeffer, 1994). Organization gain location value from employees occurs through employees' placement within the career development structure (Banks,

2006; Banks & Nafukho, 2008, Holland, 1973; Hughes & Niu, 2021a; Kaye, 1997, Schein, 1975, Super, 2002; Vardi, 1980; Vroom & MacCrimmon, 1968). Both internal and external location value of the employee to the organization (Vroom & MacCrimmon, 1968) matter. Vroom & MacCrimmon (1968) suggested that "organizations develop rules or policies that impose some control over personnel movements, such as retirement at 65, promotion from within, giving new college graduates a variety of training assignments before assigning them to positions of responsibility and so on" (p.28). Many control mechanisms are a part of organizations' talent management strategies (Yildiz & Esmer, 2023). Talent management emerged as a term that is used to replace personnel movement (Bolander et al., 2017; Jimoh & Kee, 2022).

Technology and employees both have location value within organizations (Nakajima, 1988; Rosenberg, 1972; Tushman & Anderson, 1986). Organizations use planning techniques to prepare themselves for integration of new technology. The British termed this process as "Terotechnology" in 1970 (Nakajima, 1988). Broadband infrastructure and server farms are examples of computer technology support that organizations invest in during the fourth industrial revolution.

In direct contrast, less preparation occurs within organizations for employees' cohesiveness in assigned environments including smaller financial investment in the areas of preparation, planning, or consideration (Hughes, 2012). Hughes (2010) proposed that if there were more investment by organizational leaders in employees' cohesiveness to their environment and adaptability to organizational culture, the location value of employees to the organization would increase (Nakajima, 1988; Tushman & Anderson, 1986). The extent to which the organization's core values are executed throughout the organization influences employee performance, retention, and location value to the organization (Wenstop & Myrmel, 2006; Hughes, 2012). Decisions for location of employees should align with employee performance and organizational needs. The employee's power to be effective is directly tied to the employee's location and whether the employee can perform the work. This may help explain the pushback from employees who do not want to return to the office due to COVID-19. They have shown that they are more productive in remote settings (Alipour, 2021); yet their organizations want them to return to the office. Some organizations are allowing employees to continue to work remotely (Brynjolfsson et al., 2020).

USE VALUE

Marx (1906) stated that the "utility of a thing makes it a use- value" (p.13). The economic implications of what Marx (1906) meant when he termed use-value has been debated by several scholars (Böhm-Bawerk et al., 1984; Clay, 2006; Fromm, 1989; Park, 2006; Wilson, 2004). People and technology each enhances the value of the other. "Information technology now enables knowledge and expertise to become drivers of value creation and organizational effectiveness" (Venkatraman & Henderson, 1998, p. 34). Ample time is allotted to determine how the use value of technology fits within the process systems of the organization (Nakajima, 1988). More time is needed to determine how an employee may integrate within the organizational structure and cultural environment (Baird & Meshoulam, 1988; Delery, 1998; Schneider et al., 2017; Wright & McMahan, 1992).

Without the right people in the right positions and locations at the right time and with the right technology, organizations may struggle to compete (Brache, 2002; Espedal, 2005; Hughes, 2012; Martelli, 1998; Pfeffer, 1994; Stewart, 1999). The COVID-19 pandemic proved this. Some organizations were prepared for rapid adjustments while others were not. Planning and process integration used for technology development is much more sophisticated than that used for employee development (Aguinis & Kraiger, 2009; Baird & Meshoulam, 1988; Becker et al., 2009; Delery, 1998; Morgeson & Campion, 1997; Wright & McMahan, 1992; Vroom, 1973).

The resume and interview process provide limited information on the usefulness of the person to the organization (Bossidy, 2001; Ployhart et al., 2017) because employees are very complex (Huselid, 1995; Huselid et al., 1997; Ployhart et al., 2017; Ramsey 1986). The complexity of employees' KSAs are not easily measurable during the selection process (Hughes, 2012). The use of technology is only as valuable as the extent of the employee knowledge regarding the technology. This was made abundantly clear during the COVID-19 pandemic as many employees were ill prepared to use available technology (Hughes, 2021).

Use value has had negative connotations when employees felt they were being used by the organization because their pay was perceived as not equating to their KSAs or performance. Sometimes the positions, individual tasks, and/ or responsibilities that employees are assigned might no longer represent the best use of their KSAs. This, though received negatively in some instances, was what was being communicated with the use of the terms essential and nonessential employees during the COVID-19 pandemic. Employees and organizations had to critically exam their KSAs and usefulness of their KSAs to the COVID-19 pandemic forced work environment.

Technology Use Value, Process Control, and Strategic Planning

Technology use value is often predicated by customer needs and demands. Competitive organizations can predict or anticipate and understand customer needs ahead of time (Maidique & Hayes, 1984). Technology use value begins within the engineering strategy (Cyert & March, 1963; Olmosk, 1972). Engineers sometimes give the impression that technical skills are more important than interpersonal skills (Badawy, 1995) and technical employees need help to enhance their interpersonal skills for better execution of technical strategies (Robles, 2012; Stewart et al., 2016). Data science examines information flow (Larson & Chang, 2016; Yorks et al., 2022) and is used by organizations to better develop technical strategies.

The control process consists of three separate and distinct steps: (1) measuring actual performance, (2) comparing actual performance against a standard; and (3) taking managerial action to correct deviations or inadequate standards (Robbins & Coulter, 2007). The control process examines existing standards of performance. The validity of the standards is tested against what employees do during job performance. For example, how does the control process work for diversity, equity, and inclusion (DEI) activities? Are leaders and employees adhering to DEI standards of performance? Does the organization have DEI standards of performance? Many different techniques are used to monitor the control of projects and activities within organizations. Deming (1982) introduced TQM processes, including control charts for managers to track and post employee productivity.

Organizations use strategic planning to try and anticipate customer needs and purchase the technology needed to beat their competition to market. Sometimes circumstances do not allow for strategic planning to take place. The public was able to witness some of these processes during the rush for companies to create a viable vaccine against the COVID-19 virus and its variants. The willingness of companies to openly collaborate was ethically and morally beneficial to worldwide societies. Strategic planning methods including, cost-leadership, balanced scored, meta-SWOT, and appreciative inquiry that have been proven effective (Agarwal et al., 2012) for organizations.

People Use Value

Knowing the dominant philosophical perspective (cognitive, behavioral, or cultural) within which the organization is operating becomes essential when determining people use value. Organization leaders should be open-minded to the possibilities that can occur if they allow their employees to show their creativity and capabilities in the workplace. Sutton (2001) suggested that organizations consider hiring employees that are not perfect fits to meet the creative and innovative needs of the organization. He noted

If I were running a company that depended on innovation, I would go even further to import fresh knowledge: I would hire some people who had never tried to solve problems like the ones I was addressing. In the creative process, ignorance is bliss, especially in the early stages. People who don't know how things are "supposed to be" aren't blinded by preconceptions. (p. 99)

Encouraging organizations to devote more time, people, and money to exploring new ideas is difficult when some organization leaders are content with exploiting the old ways of doing things (Sutton, 2001). The COVID-19 pandemic and Great Resignation has forced organization to look at new ways of hiring and retaining employees. Many employees had to be creative without any ideas about what the COVID-19 virus would do. Some, alongside their employers were surprised by their ingenuity during a crisis. Chalutz Ben-Gal (2022) suggested that a new model of person job fit called person-skill fit is needed.

MAINTENANCE VALUE

To be effective employees must be active participants (Silberman, 1998) in their own learning. Employees must learn how to learn the required knowledge, skills, and abilities needed to improve in their positions (Argyris & Schön, 1978). Individuals bring their own expectations into every situation (Banks, 2002) and should be able to channel those expectations into alignment with position requirements and organization strategy. Maintenance value requires that the organization and the employee understand the formal knowledge needed by the employee to perform his work.

Maintenance value of technology is revealed in preventive maintenance systems and processes and investment in tools needed to maintain technology

(Nakajima, 1988). Stakeholder value creation for organizations is expressed through growth, market share, profitability, and liquidity; whereas employee value creation is expressed through job satisfaction, motivation, salary, and job security (Hax & Majluf, 1996; Hughes, 2012; Huselid, 1995, Huselid et al., 1997).

Some organizations have limited training and development plans for employees while others are extensively learning organizations (Argyris & Schön, 1978; Garvin et al., 2008; Newbold & Pharoah, 2009; Odor, 2018; Sari, 2022). The variation in employee development strategies and educational backgrounds of workers create differentiation in employees' KSAs and capabilities. Becker et al. (2009) suggested that a differentiated workforce may be the key to transforming talent within the workplace; however, not all employees' differences are valued by organizations.

Organizations are spending billions of dollars to maintain and support technology (Aguinis & Kraiger, 2009), but not as much is spent of employees. Health and wellness of the employee are impacts maintenance value to the organization (Hughes, 2012) and became a central focus during the COVID-19 pandemic. However, many workplaces do not offer healthcare for employees nor do all US states offer viable healthcare options for their citizens. All states did not opt into opportunities from the Affordable Care Act better known as Obamacare. The COVID-19 pandemic is forcing organizations to consider this question: How favorably do organizations value the maintenance value of their employees from a health perspective?

Maintenance is associated with technology and equipment (Liyanage & Kumar, 2003); however, people require maintenance as well (Maslow, 1987). A worker spends more time at work than any place else during their lifetime, especially the low wage, manual worker. Preventive maintenance systems and processes are scheduled for maintaining capability and functioning of technology to meet productivity goals and customer demands (Sim & Endrenyi, 1988; Thompson, 1968). Yet workers are continuously negotiating with organizations for preventive healthcare options and mental healthcare services.

To ensure that technology is maintained, organizations invest in the tools needed to support technology upkeep. Not losing productivity or having to replace technology too soon is a value add for the organization (Liyanage & Kumar, 2003; Womack & Jones, 1996). Maintenance value of the employees is focused on training and development, motivation, and health and wellness. Many of the health and wellness benefits and offerings were designed to motivate the employee to continue working for the employer (Hughes, 2012) and the COVID-19 pandemic has made these benefits central to organizational strategies to retain employees. The ethics surrounding health and wellness of employees directly affects organization success.

Training and Development

Training and development are one of the three pillars of human resource development (HRD) (Swanson, 2001) and were not originally developed as a method to benefit employees but as a necessary benefit for the organization to consistently, mass produce product during the industrial revolution (Bell et al., 2017). Training and education are different because training is to meet immediate needs of the organization, while education is for long term benefit of the individual. Organizations such as the Society for Human Resource Management (SHRM) and the Association for Talent Development (ATD) have certification programs through which they offer external professional development seminars. These programs and seminars supplement what most organizations consider important to job performance. The necessity of these certifications is questionable. How do these certifications translate to on-the- job performance that benefits the organization as opposed to supplying revenue to SHRM or ATD? This question is especially relevant as it pertains to ethics and diversity efforts within organizations. How is it that many of these certified professionals have not contributed to the success of ethics and diversity efforts within their organizations? Romani et al., (2018) suggested that some HR professionals are blind to the harm of diversity initiatives.

Training must also be aligned to the job for appropriate transfer to occur (Andoh et al., 2022; Montesino, 2002). Training transfer is a huge issue of debate within the training field (Abiddin et al., 2021; Awais Bhatti et al., 2014; Baldwin & Ford, 1988; Bell et al., 2017; Blume et al., 2010; Blume et al., 2019; Burke & Hutchins, 2007, 2008; Chiaburu & Lindsay, 2008; Garavaglia, 1993; Grossman & Salas, 2011; Martin, 2010). How and when does training transfer occur? Are employees applying information received off-the-job when they are on-the-job? What is the credibility and validity of trainers who have never spent any time performing the work for which they are readily providing technical training? (Hughes, 2012). Do these trainers understand their content? Technical training problems were evident during the COVID-19 pandemic when it was revealed that many trainers were technologically illiterate (Hughes, 2021). Workers do not participate in training because they do not see the benefit to them. This does not apply to most soft skills training such as ethics training, although it would be helpful if trainers modeled behavior they are training about. Many trainers in organizations have no or limited frames of reference for what they attempt to train and are often perceived to be experts only because of their education and/certifications.

It has become acceptable in many organizations for trainers to have no practical training in the work for which they are designing or providing training (Hughes, 2012). The ability to train for job performance requires experience; therefore, trainers without experience should partner, with someone who does have the experience, to provide the training. Historically, workplace trainers were experienced supervisors, but because of complexity of the jobs, professional trainers were hired (Bell et al., 2017). This is fine if trainers recognize that it would be best for experienced workers to deliver the training. Professional trainers can assist with material development and coordination of training activities (Lundgren & Poell, 2022; Tripathi & Dhir, 2022). Employees need to be trained in job functions by experienced employees who know and have performed the work or similar work.

Organization leaders must understand the difference between education and training and ensure they are using either education or training appropriately to remain competitive. should understand job functions and how the job responsibilities align with organizational goals. Trainers should be able to speak workplace vernacular and gain credibility. Another alternative would be for organizations to understand the use value of all their employees and choose employees to be trainers who have the KSAs and experience to be effective. Train-the-trainer should become a primary function of professional trainers. Value creation through training (Andoh et al., 2022; Qureshi et al., 2006) must occur for organizational success. Collins's (2001) suggestion of determining first who, then what, applies with training in the workplace. Organizations must determine who should be trainers of their employees, and then establish the type of information the employees need to receive through training activities (Lundgren & Poell, 2022; Potnuru & Sahoo, 2016; Tripathi & Dhir, 2022). The mismatch is evident with those leading diversity efforts. Organization must do a better job of determining who can provide specific types of training. Not everyone, with a training title can be efficient and effective at providing specific types of training. Diversity and ethics training are two areas where the selection of the right trainer is vital.

Work Motivation and Maintenance Value

Employee work motivation is a component of the maintenance value of the employee to the organization. Organizations can use motivational techniques that enhance the employee's self-perception. Motivating employees only to meet organization needs can be demotivating for the employees. The working poor are employees who come to work every day and struggle to survive financially in a capitalistic society (Hughes, 2012). It is difficult to motivate a worker who is living paycheck-to-paycheck to peak performance when they can discern no appreciable solution to their daily dilemma.

The organization may not be directly responsible for the worker when they are not at work, but the organization is directly affected if the worker does not meet productivity goals. It can be difficult to persuade a worker that they are valued by their organization and should be motivated to give their full effort when they see their organization's continuous investment in technology and do not perceive that they are receiving a reasonable or comparable wage and/or treatment. Some leaders view procedural justice from person-to-person comparisons made by employees, they should begin to look at it from a person to technology comparison and make needed adjustments.

MODIFICATION VALUE

Modification value of technology has been studied for centuries (Babbage, 1835) and in operational and engineering literature (Liyanage & Kumar, 2003; Maidique & Hayes, 1984; Nakajima, 1988; Thompson, 1968; Womack & Jones, 1996). Employees routinely modify themselves for personal reasons and these modifications may contribute to their work performance. Individuals are continuously learning both on and off the job. Continuous learning can include obtaining higher education, attending training and professional development seminars, or engaging in individualized study. Learning from peers and co-workers is another possibility. Sometimes, forced change, which occurs rapidly, can be stressful for employees. The market collapse in September 2008 was a prime example as was the onset of the COVID-19 pandemic.

Drucker (1999) stated that "making knowledge workers more productive requires changes in attitude not only on the part of the individual knowledge worker, but [also] on the part of the whole organization" (p. 92). Modification of people examines how the person grows and changes through activities that people use for self-development that may or may not align with their current jobs. Organizations can benefit by understanding how employees want to grow and change. Upgrades and minor/major modification of the technology (Rosenberg, 1972; Tushman & Anderson, 1986) shows its modification value (Hughes, 2010, 2012). Modification value of employees is their growth, change, and the job enrichment actions of organizational leaders (Hughes, 2010; 2012). Organizations should have HRD systems (Swanson & Holton, 2001) in place to adjust to employee growth and change like organization adjustments to technological changes (Betz, 1993; Vroom, 1973). Employees bring "hardware": the employee's physical well-being, fitness, health, and well-ness; and "software": their skills, expertise, stock of knowledge, and its currency; which require maintenance and planned modifications or upgrades (Disselkamp, 2009).

When employees are not rewarded for their growth and change through incentive methods such as job enrichment, they are more likely to leave (Drucker, 1999). Many employees felt or feel that their growth and change was not rewarded during the COVID-19 pandemic, so they left and were part of the Great Resignation and quiet quitting phenomenon. Enhancing employee growth is just as important as modifying technology (equipment) to adjust to changes (Burkhardt & Brass, 1990). Modification value includes the personal expectations that employees and organizational leaders bring to the organization (Cyert et al., 1958; Vroom, 1964). Integration of the concepts of the PT model (Hughes, 2010) into management practice can help managers gain a competitive advantage (Espedal, 2005; Pfeffer, 1994).

Dalziel and Schoonover (1988) defined change as the planned or unplanned responses of an organization to the pressures brought about by individuals, teams, coalitions, and special-interest groups inside and outside the organization. Extensive research has been focused on helping employees accept change in the workplace (Choi, 2011; Judge et al., 2017); however, very little research has been focused on the value of employees to the organization when they do change. The concern becomes whether the change is superficial which could mean that the employees are delivering a performance for their economic survival (Goffman, 1959; Horniman, 2004; Mangham & Overington, 1983) or whether it is a true change, and the employee has transformed their beliefs and abilities? Sometimes employees change to the extent that they become incompatible with the organization. They become unable to perform because their performance would be in stark contrast to their personal goals and beliefs.

Horniman (2004) described leadership as a performing art. The employees' job performance can be a performing art if they grow and change, and the job does not grow and change along with them. Their work responsibilities can become incongruent to their personal goals. Their ability to accept job constraints that would have them ignore their changes is reduced. In some instances, organizations encourage employees to change (i. e., tuition reimbursement for degree attainment) but are incapable of incorporating the new skills into their corporate strategy (Benson et al., 2004; Makarius & Srinivasan, 2017).

Technological Forced Change

Because computers can do routine, repetitive tasks better than humans, many entry-level jobs will either be eliminated or upgraded. For society, worker obsolescence means that a certain percentage of employable individuals will always be out of work because their jobs were eliminated or upgraded by technology (Hunter et al., 2001). Changes in technology have reduced the stability of most employees' KSAs. New technologies driven by computers, reengineering, TQM, and flexible manufacturing systems are changing the demands of jobs and the skills needed to perform. Individuals who want the best jobs in the future must cultivate skills in computer literacy, interpersonal communication, creative problem-solving, and the self-discipline to work autonomously. This information was validated during the COVID-19 pandemic.

The Job Characteristic Model (JCM) (Fried & Ferris, 1987; Hackman & Oldham, 1974; Hackman & Oldham, 1975) described dimensions that must be present for workers to find their jobs important, meaningful, valuable, and worthwhile. Work that provides task significance and affects the lives or work of others can create a sense of pride in workers. Furthermore, jobs that possess autonomy enable workers to feel personally responsible for outcomes.

Hughes's (2012) assessment of the JCM model was that:

First, the JCM assumes that workers want to be challenged, want to perform multiple tasks, and have a variety of skills and talents. It ignores the employees who want to get paid as much as possible for doing as little as possible. Second, the model assumes that workers want their efforts to be identified, that they want to take responsibility for the final product. It ignores workers who would rather blame others for their failures than accept that they are personally responsible for anything. Third, the model assumes that workers care whether their work is useful to anyone else. It ignores those workers who only care about getting paid or getting by. Fourth, the model assumes that workers will accept honest feedback that will allow them to realistically assess their current on-the-job performance and to improve in the future. It ignores workers who cannot or will not accept constructive criticism and those who do not want to improve. (p. 127)

Not all employees want to grow and change educationally. There is still place for these workers because they are expected to maintain productivity levels and they can receive training that is required to enhance their job performance.

Job enrichment asks employees to do more work for the same amount of pay, and there may be incentives associated with the enrichment that motivates the employee to perform. Organizations also use techniques such as job rotation (cross-training) and job enlargement to enrich the job. Job rotation can reduce employee boredom and benefit the organization by allowing managers more flexibility in scheduling work, adapting to changes, and filling vacancies. Downsides to job rotation include increased training costs, potential for productivity to be reduced, adjustments of work groups to accommodate new employees, and demotivation of trainees who prefer to specialize as opposed to cross-train.

Some organizations have entrepreneurial cultures that accommodate the growth of employees. Employees are allowed to take leaves of absences to further their education or fulfill a personal passion. Robbins and Judge (2011) describe six elements of organization structure: work specialization, departmentalization, chain of command, span of control, centralization/decentralization, and formalization. All these elements of the organization structure may be areas where people modification value can be incorporated into organization design strategies.

People modification incorporates aspects of organizational development and organizational design. How do organization development initiatives affect the changes in people? Is the organization willing to make needed organizational design changes if warranted? These questions are important to consider as organizations recognize growth and change of employees, especially within the new global economy, and with the availability of many methods for employees to develop themselves. Another significant concern with organization development efforts is the ethics of the organization. All organization development strategies should contain ethical guidelines including codes of ethics that all employees adhere to (Coughlan, 2005;

Somers, 2001). Those codes of ethics should also be in alignment with the DEI goals of the organization.

TIME VALUE

Within organizations time essentially equals money; or does it? Should it be that employee output is equal to money as opposed to their time on the job (Hughes, 2012)? How is employee time valued in work? can employees say no to preserve their time with the organization? Time is an important resource that is often directed but not measured accurately. Time in many organizations is measured based upon absence from work (Nicholson & Johns, 1985) as opposed to productivity.

Organizations also face issues related to the length of time employees choose to remain with the organization. Employee time is bought by the employer (Taylor, 1974), and there are issues related to absence and when an employee can legitimately miss work. Nicholson and Johns (1985) stated

On the one hand are the shared expectations that employees' time has been "purchased" and that the employer has the right to set and enforce work schedules. On the other are shared expectations that some absence from work is necessary, legitimate, and mutually beneficial for employer and employee. (p.400)

Organizations must reconcile with employees how they both benefit from employee time. Time becomes a part of the organization's culture and employees endure leaders', and sometimes peer pressure, to be at work a certain amount of time regardless of how they feel or if there is actual work to perform.

Time is measured in a continuum despite efforts to segregate its value in the workplace (Taylor, 1911). Knowledge workers introduced the thought concept of knowledge value. How do you value knowledge? Knowledge value relates to time value because organizations still pay many knowledge workers in derivatives based upon hourly rates. Knowledge workers charge billable hours along and other fees to provide a measure for their knowledge value.

Leaders' effort and time are seen as predictors of outcome results (Heck, Larsen, & Marcoulides, 1990; Owens, 1987). Rogers (2003) studied the relevance of time with regards to how technology or innovation is introduced and disseminated throughout an organization. He studied: "(1)

the innovation-diffusion process, (2) innovativeness and (3) an innovation's rate of adoption" (p.37). The rate of adoption of a new activity or concept can be measured. Sometimes, time can be a stressor when individuals attempt to meet established deadlines (Driskell et al., 2001; Yu & Wang, 2022). As organizations implement new technology and introduce change initiatives, the effect of time constraints on employee performance should be examined (Vroom, 2003).

Different individuals perform the same tasks at different rates of time. Many organizations tend to frustrate employees who produce more work in less time by demanding their presence at work despite the employee completing the assigned tasks (Hughes, 2012). Younger employees become frustrated when forced to spend time in a physical location to be "seen" by their bosses to be perceived as working or being effective (Erickson, 2008; Latkovikja & Popovskab, 2020). Different kinds of work require different amounts of time and requiring all employees to be at work for the same amount of time because it is an organizational cultural norm is problematic for employees and organizations (Hughes, 2012). It has been revealed as a major problem during the COVID-19 pandemic and a contributor to the Great Resignation and quiet quitting. Organizations can still plan for employee length of time in position and develop ethically and morally sound downsizing/rightsizing strategies that are economically beneficial (Drucker, 2002; Eby & Buch, 1998; Vroom & MacCrimmon, 1968). Employees and organizations have the legal right through employment-at-will laws to choose whether an employee stays with or leaves the organization (Koy et al., 1987; Malos, 1998).

Time value of technology and people is critical to organizations. When technology does not keep up with marketplace changes, it becomes obsolete (Arthur, 1994; Damanpour, 1991; Hogan, 1987; Tushman & Anderson, 1986). Employees also become obsolete if their value is not measured, enhanced, and rewarded (Arthur, 1994; Staw, 1980). The management of the core technology (Bossert et al., 1982; MacKenzie, 1986; March & Simon, 1959) has been studied and accepted practices regarding the time value of technology abound. The same has not been done with regards to people.

People time value is the value of employee performance of work that adds value to the organization. Being present does not necessarily equate to adding value to the organization. The assumption is that visible presence equates to productivity, insinuating that an employee will work just because he is present (Nicholson & Johns, 1985). The concept of quiet quitting shows that to be untrue. Researchers have identified two themes related to employee absence: 1) the relationship between job satisfaction and absence implying that an employee will not come to work if they are not satisfied with their job and 2) the association between personal characteristics and absence (Muchinsky, 1977; Nicholson & Johns, 1985; Porter & Steers, 1973; Steers & Rhodes, 1978). There are many existing variables and parameters that conflict with or contradict these two premises. For example, some employee will remain on a job just to collect their salary. Nicholson and Johns (1985) stated

… persons in high discretion roles (such as professions) operate under high trust psychological contracts that reinforce the work ethic and internalized commitment to the organization. Those in low discretion roles are parties to a lower trust psychological contract that fosters a more detached view of organizational participation. (p. 399)

Their summary of Fox's (1974) concept of the "trust dynamic" suggested that the position level of the employee influences the work ethic or time on the job. Workers were to do as much work as possible in the least amount of time (Taylor, 1911).

Employees struggle with managing internal control of their time and external control of their time within the workplace (Kohn, 1981). The level of the employee's position within the organization also controls this factor. If an employee is a hourly employee, their time is most likely externally controlled within workplace. If they are salaried employees, their time is more internally controlled, and they have more autonomy to operate at their own time discretion. There are exceptions where some hourly employees have internal control, and some salaried employees have external constraints on their time (Hughes, 2012).

Researchers have found that American workers spend more time on the job than most other developed countries and are less productive (Hall & Jones, 1999; Schor, 1991). Although workers may be physically present at work, their lack of productivity may be attributed to them not being fully present mentally or emotionally (Kahn, 1990; May et al., 2004). Workers under excess stress are less productive (Crampton et al., 1995; Fraser, 2001). Employee monitoring is expanding and not being reduced by employers as they seek to get the most work that they can from their employees (Blumenfeld et al., 2020; Hartman, 2001; Hartman & Bucci, 2004; Jandl et al., 2023; Loch et al., 1998; Martin & Freeman, 2003). The ethics of employee monitoring is being examined by researchers as employees become more frustrated by the invasion of and perceive invasion of their privacy by employers (Jandl et al., 2023). The push for organization to provide support for employee mental health and self-care has become more pronounced during the COVID-19 pandemic. When employees began working from home during the COVID-19 pandemic, employee privacy became a major concern as employers tried to monitor their activities and work in their homes.

Length of time in position is another measure of people time value to the organization. Having long-term, mature employees within organizations or employees with seniority has not always been favored; else, why would we have age protection laws for employees over 40 years old? There are times when the most senior person may not be the most adequate person for the job. There are also many instances where minority employees are always the last hired and the first fired because of seniority policies. From an ethical standpoint these policies need to be reviewed and considered before termination of minority employees.

Downsizing and/or rightsizing usually benefits the organization and not most employees (Birati & Tziner, 2000; Buch, 1992; Cameron, 1994; Drucker, 1999; Kozlowski et al., 1993; Sheaffer et al., 2009). Downsizing and/or rightsizing can result in burnout of the employees and lower customer satisfaction as employee productivity and performance is diminished (Fraser, 2001). This is being challenged as workers have chosen to rebel against organization policies and are choosing to resign as a part of the Great Resignation during the COVID-19 pandemic.

INTERSECTION OF PEOPLE, TECHNOLOGY, AND TIME

Technology affects employee time when employee must be present to monitor a machine's functions and record any synchronization and/or deviations from operational specifications (Brynjolfsson & Mcafee, 2011; Drucker, 1999; Nicholson & Johns, 1985; Taylor, 1911). Technology also tracks employee time, movement, and monitors employee performance. Sometimes employees manipulate the system by not completing their work during normal work hours to be able to work overtime hours (Gowler, 1969; Steers & Rhodes, 1978). This is unethical behavior. Tracking systems (Disselkamp, 2007, 2009; Scott & Markham, 1982) have revealed that technology is neither as sophisticated as the human mind nor capable of completing all physical tasks in the workplace. Employees determine whether they want to come to work (Porter & Steers, 1973).

ISSUES, CONTROVERSIES, PROBLEMS

Location value may provide employees with a sense of belonging to an organization and this in turn may increase their productivity (Hughes, 2012). Length of service on a job often leads to higher productivity as employees usually become more proficient performing their job over time. When employees are inadequately placed within organizations work time is wasted. Employees doing the wrong job in the wrong location are limited in their ability to maximize their potential to benefit organization (Swamy, 2004; Qureshi et al., 2006). Employees who feel ostracized (Zhang et al., 2023) at work may feel that they have no location value and leave.

Hughes (2010) also proposed that: 1) employee performance increases as their comfort with the environment increases and their location value is known and valued by the organization; 2) as organizational investment, not necessarily monetary, in employee cohesiveness to environment and adaptability to organizational culture increases, employee performance and retention increase; and 3) organizations' career development strategies' success or failure may depend upon the proper placement of employees internally and externally to the organization. Item three is relevant to the Great Resignation. Employees or making career changes due to employer improper placement during the COVID-19 pandemic.

Organizations and commissions have been trying to determine the use value of employees within the organization. The SCANS commission (1991) issued five directives based on its discussions and meetings with business owners, public employers, unions, and workers and supervisors in shops, plants, and stores. The first directive pertains to use value within the workplace and provided five competencies in accordance with the ability to efficiently use (a) resources, (b) interpersonal skills, information, (d) systems, and (e) technology. Organizations can incorporate these competencies to determine the way(s) use value of employees is essential to organizational productivity and/or competitive advantage.

Acceptance of employee stagnation is detrimental to their use value to the organization. Some of the employee stagnation can be attributed to unethical treatment of employees in the workplace. Ethical treatment of diverse, protected class employees cannot be overlooked when expecting high performance from employees. Mistreated employees may give the organization the bare minimum of contribution towards productivity goals.

Lack of Career Paths

Career paths represent the linear order of career progression in organizations (Isaacson & Brown, 1997; Leibowitz et al., 1986), are used to assist with development of career plans for employees, and are determined based on organizational promotional practices (Isaacson & Brown, 1997). Many organizations do not have documented, clear career paths for employees to follow for career advancement. There are many opportunities for employees to obtain career development information both inside and outside of the organization. Without clear career paths, both employees and the organization can become confused about employees' career progression, and employees may distrust and become frustrated regarding advancement and promotion opportunities within their organizations.

Because of historical, discriminatory practices in position placement in the US, there are several protected class laws that organizations must adhere to (i.e., sexual harassment, racial and ethnic, age, disability) so that organization leaders cannot make stereotypical and adversely judgmental decisions. These laws are warranted, but there still needs to be ways organizations can determine how to manage the location value of employees from positions that are not mandated, preventatively influenced to avoid punishment, and because of fear of legal action. Leaders should make the right position placement because it is the right thing to do (Alder & Gilbert, 2006; Muir et al., 2022). They must also not use AI to make discriminatory decisions (Kiron, 2022; Roche, 2022; Stahl et al., 2023; Wilson et al., 2022).

Baptiste (2001) argued that human capital theorists had an idealistic view of education as an answer for all society's troubles.

For instance, regarding the mediating effects of technology, human capital theorists assume that more educated workers are always more technologically savvy than their less educated counterparts and that their superior technological savvy renders them always more productive than their less educated peers. In short, human capital theorists do not envisage situations in which less educated workers might enjoy a productive advantage over their more educated peers. (p.190)

Some human capital theorists supported the mechanized, scientific management philosophy that believed that workers had no cognitive abilities and needed to rely on the behavioral abilities supported by their employers. It was impossible for some human capital theorists to believe that lower skilled workers had KSAs and learning capabilities that were superior to their more educated coworkers. These human capital theorists found it difficult to ask someone who they believed had limited knowledge of organizational processes to strategically align training to organizational goals. Some training leaders just do not know the answer and should seek as much input as possible from less educated workers. This was the case with essential workers during the COVID-19 pandemic. The work that these employees do was finally seen by trainers and customers.

Organizations leaders do not always understand employee growth and changes or the modification value of its employees. They can also define the relationship between decision making with regards to people and technology in the workplace. Organizations have more patience for technology downtime than they do with employee downtime (Gale, 1980). Hughes (2012) suggested the following 11 questions for leaders to consider when evaluating employee time value to the organization:

1.   What pressures are placed upon employees from a time perspective within the workplace? [Are these pressures ethical?]
2.   How do they handle these pressures and remain productive?
3.   What is the time value of employees within the organization?
4.   In what way(s) is time value of employees essential to productivity and/ or competitive advantage of an organization?
5.   How much of a predictor is time value to achieving organizational outcomes?
6.   What is the role of time in the development of organizational climate (Denison, 1996; Hellriegel & Slocum, 1974; Jones & James, 1979; Litwin & Stringer, 1968; Schneider, 1975; Schneider & Reichers, 1983; Tagiuri & Litwin, 1968) and ultimately culture?
7.   Do leaders enhance or sabotage employee productivity by demanding time presence?
8.   How much money do organizations lose just because they pay for time presence?
9.   How much time is spent in meetings when no productive action occurs?
10. Do leaders just have meetings to use up required work time?
11. To what extent are employees allowed to say no? (p. 139)

Work Life Balance Issues

Money has been found to not be the number one motivator for employees (Kohn, 1993; Pfeffer, 1998; Wiley, 1997). Many workers are seeking work life balance to be productive both at home and at work (Hall,1990; Hall & Richter, 1988). The COVID-19 pandemic is forcing organization leaders to respond to these concerns. The Family Medical Leave Act (FMLA) does allow employees unpaid time away from work to deal with family medical issues (Waldfogel, 1999). However, employees have other family related experiences that they value such as time with their children and some just need a retreat from burnout (Fraser, 2001; Rumbles & Ree, 2013).

Solutions and Recommendations

Employees and organizations should understand the location value that employees provide to for organizations. In contrast to technology, where organizations recognize technology's value by insuring the technology against failure. The value of the technology is also immediately seen when it stops working. Whitman (2010) succinctly described an example of the value of technology when EBay encountered a system outage and EBay had to compensate its customers millions of dollars because of their loss during the outage. There are ways to ensure that the employees are placed in the positions that bring the most value to organizations. Sometimes employees are moved from one location to another or placed in positions that were unsuitable for their KSAs to the detriment of the employee and the organization.

Organization leaders know that there are differences in technical and non-technical staffs' use value to the organization. There are dual career ladders for technical personnel to attain similar status, compensation, and recognitions that are provided for other high-level managers. High-technology managers efficiently manage technology by understanding:

1. How the technology works;
2. Its limits, as well as its potential (together with the limits and the potential of competitors' technologies);
3. What these various technologies require in terms of technical and economic resources;
4. The direction and speed of change; and

5. The available technological options, their cost, probability of failure, and potential benefits if they prove successful. (Maidique & Hayes, 1984)

Leaders of employees should know:

1. How the employee does his job.
2. What the limitations are as well as the potential for the employee to do his job better and more efficiently than competitors' employees.
3. What resources, technical and economic, employees need to perform or be trained to perform his job better.
4. What changes are needed and how quickly the change needs to be understood by the employee.
5. What available options the employees have to ensure success and how much will needed options cost?
6. How will the employees' successes affect the organization?

The competition between education and training must end if organizations are to value all the dimensions that workers bring to the workplace. How can organizations distinguish training from education? This author suggests that training is a maintenance value and education is a modification value. Strategic training interventions can be developed through communication among training professionals, organizational leaders, and all employees. When employees are left out, key information that will enhance the strategy is often missed and implementation of the strategy becomes complicated. Employees should not be left out of their own development strategies (Hughes, 2012). Employee growth and change, when possible, should be integrated into organization strategy. Some of the barriers to change may be the leaders themselves, especially the unethical leaders (Luan et al., 2022).

Moran and Brightman (2000) provided five detailed observations of organizations that have launched successful change initiatives:

(1) *Change is nonlinear; there is often no clearly defined beginning or end.*
(2) *Effective change interweaves multiple improvement efforts.*
(3) *Change is top-down and bottom-up.*
(4) *Organizational change has an important personal dimension.*
(5) *Measurement is key to successful and sustainable change.* (pp. 66-67)

Modification value addresses all of Moran and Brightman's (2000) five observations. However, items three, four, and five are most relevant.

Strengthening employee involvement requires that employees not be marginalized by their leaders and feel valued by their organization (Hughes, 2012; Hughes, 2016; Hughes & Brown, 2018). Organization leaders who recognize the bottom-up approach should value employees who choose to self-develop and change. Organization leaders should allow employees to grow and change according to some of the employees' own values and beliefs and provide clear and measurable goals. Leaders should also understand "the three most powerful drivers of work behavior: purpose, identity, and mastery" (Moran & Brightman, 2000, p.66) in individuals. Leaders of change efforts can try to inspire individuals to align their purpose – what people desire and value; identity – a person's sense of who they are; and mastery – one's ability to manage oneself and the environment effectively to the necessary organizational change effort (Moran & Brightman, 2000). Without this alignment, employees and organizations will struggle to accomplish organizational goals.

"[T]he demand from the market place for speed, quality, customization, timeliness, and a variety of products and services has changed the landscape for doing business. The use of technology, the relentless speed of change, and the skills that working people need have changed the nature of work itself" (Kunneman et al., 2000, p. 51). To keep up with continuous change, organization learning activities should be equal to or greater than the pace of change (Browell, 2000). Many organizations found that they were not providing learning equal to or greater than the pace of change and were incapable of doing so during the COVID-19 pandemic (Hughes, 2021).

Kiesler et al., (1969) noted that there is no single definition of attitude acceptable to all attitude researchers. Heneson et al., (1978) indicated that "unlike the heart rate, attitude infers through words and actions. They further described attitude as… a tool that serves the human need to see order and consistency in what people say, think and do, so that given certain behaviors, predictions can be made about future behaviors" (p. 11). Individuals' attitudes influence their ability to change or accept change Schleicher et al., 2011). Several researchers have asserted that some of the factors that contribute to acceptance or resistance to change include age, gender, and education (Choi, 2011; Dohmann, 1970; Halloran, 1967; Judge et al., 2017; Kirton & Mulligan, 1973; Rogers, 1995; Strebel, 1996; Trumbo, 1958; Trumbo, 1961). Organization leaders must be acceptable to change for modification value to be respected and welcomed in workplaces. Leaders may require socialization interventions (Wiener, 1988) to execute the values necessary to integrate modification value into the workplace. Marcoulides and Heck (1993) found that the largest effect on organizational performance was worker attitude and organization activities. If workers are not allowed to grow and change to maintain a positive attitude, organization performance may be reduced.

Time value has the potential to strengthen relationships and help to establish cultural norms. However, sometimes "U. S. workers often form stronger allegiances to their occupations than they do their work organizations-- an outcome that may be neither desirable nor inevitable" (Beyer & Trice, 1987, p.13). Organizations and workers both benefitted when the workers formed allegiances to both the organization and the occupation (O'Reilly III et al., 1991). When workers can take their occupational skills to other organizations, worker power increases even if their time value with a particular organization may have decreased.

Solutions to time value concerns may require cultural adjustments (Munck, 2001). Some organizational climate researchers (Guion, 1973; James & Jones, 1974) placed "greater emphasis on organizational members' perceptions of 'observable' practices and procedures that are closer to the 'surface' of organizational life" (Denison, 1996, p. 622). Climate includes how an individual reacts to organizational conditions (Litwin & Stringer, 1968; Denison, 1996). How an employee reacts to time-related policies within organizations help determine how employees value the role of time within organizational climate. Some leaders and peers seek to manipulate employees' time in organizations. when employees feel that they cannot say no, it becomes a major problem. Some countries have passed laws that allow workers to say no to their employers when it comes to using technology to manipulate workers, especially through smart phones and e-mail. Time is limited to the length of life (Bloom, 1974) and that is all everyone has.

FUTURE TRENDS

Location value is essential to the employees' ability to establish unity within their assigned environment; to adapt to the organizational culture; and 3) develop a sustainable career (Hughes, 2012). Organizations may want to understand the extent to which the cultural environment affects the location value of employees in the workplace. An unethical cultural environment may ensure that the employee chooses to leave the organization, especially if that unethical environment supports mistreatment of protected class employees. Organizations may also want to understand the way(s) location value is essential to productivity and competitive advantage (Hughes, 2010).

Flexible and hybrid work policies and their effect on employees is a future trend that HRD professionals, practitioners, and scholars should continue to examine. These policies are shifting the career realities of employees in many organizations (Hughes & Niu, 2021a, b, c). Without an understanding of location value of employees, organizations will not be able to train and develop, manage careers, or institute OD initiatives that can help them retain employees.

Some organizations are reversing the trend from employees with only specialized skills back to employees with "all around" skills that were dominant prior to the industrial revolution (Bowden, 1947). The rapidly changing workplace is requiring workers that can do many things on the job. Organizations are asking employees to be entrepreneurial in their performance. Organizations are asking their employees to be innovative within cultures that are stifling creativity. To multitask and be innovative, traditional practices of being present just to be seen at work must end (Munck, 2001). Munck (2001) recognized that the culture of the organization was repressing the use value of employees at Marriott and decided to make a change by listening to employees. Many organizations were forced to do this without the luxury of a pilot program during the COVID-19 pandemic and are still reeling from the rapid changes. The impossible, with regards to job flexibility and remote work, was proven to be possible in rapid time.

Organizations must begin to institute targeted training efforts. Just-in-time training must continue, but training should also be more anticipatory. To be anticipatory, trainers with experience must be able to anticipate the next solution for potential problems. Training after the fact forces the organization to be reactionary as opposed to proactive in solving problems. The training must be relevant, accurate, and effective to meet the specific needs of organizations (Hughes, 2012). Silberman (1998) noted that training should provide need to know information.

FUTURE RESEARCH DIRECTIONS

Future research should evaluate how and why training and development is perceived to be more valued outside the organization through certification programs than it is inside the organization from the people who are doing the job every day. Researchers could seek to determine exactly what employees are doing on their jobs and then determine what needs to be added or eliminated.

Researchers could also examine time value and the ethical implications of employee location value.

Organizations are continuing to offer flex time to employees in some service industries; however, in many manufacturing industries this is not a feasible option unless employee output becomes the measure and not their 40 hour per week presence (Christensen & Staines, 1990; Ezra & Deckman, 1996; Hughes, 2012; Rainey, Jr. & Wolf, 1981). It is often inferred that if a person is present, they will devote time and effort to their task within the organization. Understanding the influence of time from the employee's perspective is needed. More research is needed to empirically examine the relationship between individual perceptions of time within the context of motivational theories such as expectancy theory (Vroom, 1964, 1995) and performance (Campbell, 1990; Gilley & Maycunich, 2000; Gordon & DiTomaso, 1992; Hanna, 1988; Kotter & Heskett, 1992; Marcoulides & Heck, 1993; Wilkins & Ouchi, 1983). One example is the United Kingdom is pilot testing a four-day work week.

CONCLUSION

The concepts in this chapter provide a direct contrast to the ways technology's value is respected when people value is not respected. Location value of people and technology are both important. Hamrick and MacMillan (1984) stated that "No sane management deliberately makes a capital investment to bring about low ROI." (p.68). The same can be said regarding people investment.

Organizational leaders must understand both people and technology to enhance and improve organizational performance. Location value must be cultivated and supported so that employees can reach their potential within the organization. The location value of people and technology in the workplace can serve as asset or liability depending upon placement. Making the necessary realignments of people requires knowledge of their location value within the organization. The physical location value of employees is a final component for organizational success. The COVID-19 pandemic made this abundantly apparent when employees were no longer able to work in their typical locations and workplace environments.

Organizations seek alternative uses for technological assets (Hambrick & MacMillan, 1984) and employees' use value is just as important. Organizations must consider the multidimensionality of the person prior to hiring and plan to adjust as needed. The multidimensionality of each employee must be considered along with their imperfections (Whitman, 2010). Sometimes organizational leaders choose not to move employees to other work areas where they may be more effective because of political ties and power struggles (Pfeffer, 1992). Political ties and power struggles (Pfeffer, 1992) must be ethically examined so that they do not impede leaders' decision making when determining the best use of employees' KSAs.

The required work performance of the individual should not stifle individual creativity and innovation for value to be produced for the organization. Organization leaders must be adaptable to change and willing to recognize that their beliefs, knowledge, or practices can be irrelevant in the face of continuously changing situations in the marketplace (Bowden, 1947). "Economic value for a company is nothing more than the gap between price and cost, and it is reliably measured only by sustained profitability" (Porter, 2001, p. 65). Technology enhances employee productivity, and the employee enhances technology productivity.

The Internet has been the most prominent technological innovation thus far and is still being integrated into organizations, worldwide. Often, employees are asked to compete against each when their time could be better spent focusing on how to defeat external competitors through the collective use of their vast capabilities. Division of labor was introduced during the industrial revolution to be able to mass produce product (Bowden, 1947) and there is still a need for mass production, but there is more of a need for employees to communicate with each other on the job (Prusak & Cohen, 2001). Technology does not fight against itself unless designed to do so by a person.

Bowden (1947) stated that:

The executives of these companies assumed that new employees could be added to the payroll roughly in the same manner that a new machine is added to the shop. Apparently, they thought that relatively little formal attention to selection and training of employees was necessary, and that the old timers in the shop would take care of whatever was needed informally. This lack of a systematic program increased the errors of placement and thereby contributed to high rates of labor turnover. The lack of carefully worked out job descriptions made expansion unnecessarily difficult. Without these it was hard to develop training programs. And without job descriptions companies were overdependent on individuals. When a long- service employee was absent, the details of job knowledge which he carried around in his mind were absent with him, and vital routines of communication were disrupted. (p.536)

Bowden's work is still relevant today in many organizations. There is a lack of respect for the complexity of employees. Organizations leaders tend to believe that the replacement of one employee by another is an equivalent exchange because they are doing the same job. The basic requirements of the job may get done, but the extra effort will not be exerted as is evident with quiet quitting during the COVID-19 pandemic.

Changing people to meet organizational needs to be adjusted to accommodate employee growth and change like how organization leaders modify technology to meet consumer demands. Some organizational constraints are the unwillingness of some organization leaders to allow flexible work hours and remote work to continue as the COVID-19 pandemic is lessening. Employees have proven that they can perform productively while having flexible work hours and locations. Researchers can develop measures for how modification value is affected by the attitude of leaders and their willingness to consider people modification value. Employee attitudes in the workplace are strongly predicted by organizational values and directly effects the level of organizational performance (Marcoulides & Heck, 1993).

Ultimately, the nature of time (Schein, 1990) must be defined by the organization leaders, communicated to employees, and managed throughout the organization. This is abundantly clear with the required changes during the COVID-19 pandemic. Many organizations cannot and should not want to go back to their pre-COVID-19 pandemic ways. The ability to keep people who are productive and meeting organizational standards should provide an advantage over competitors. Some organizations have cultures that are not time sensitive regarding micromanagement of employees.

COVID-19 ETHICAL IMPACT MINI CASE STUDY

The impact of COVID-19 brought visibility to the tasks that all employees performed on their jobs. The perceived non-essential job functions were found to be essential for some organizations' survival. Employees who were most close to other people were exposed to a deadly virus at work.

Rapid analysis and decision making became important as time became a vital element of life-or-death results. Battling a virus that had no cure, forced work life to be sped up for workers in healthcare, food, transportation, and cleaning supplies industries. Rapid technological changes occurred out of necessity. Questions to consider are:

1. In what way(s) has time value of people and technology become an ethical focal point during the COVID-19 pandemic?
2. How does location value relate to employee visibility and belonging?
3. How can location value become an unethical decision?

REFERENCES

Abiddin, N. Z., Ismail, A., & Nasreen, A. (2021). The role of organizational and individual factors in predicting training transfer: A conceptual model. *Review of International Geographical Education Online*, *11*(8), 24–35.

Agarwal, R., Grassl, W., & Pahl, J. (2012). Meta-SWOT: Introducing a new strategic planning tool. *The Journal of Business Strategy*, *33*(2), 12–21. doi:10.1108/02756661211206708

Aguinis, H., & Kraiger, K. (2009). Benefits of training and development for individuals and teams, organizations, and society. *Annual Review of Psychology, 60*, 451–474. doi:. psych.60.110707.163505 doi:10.1146/annurev

Alder, G. S., & Gilbert, J. (2006). Achieving ethics and fairness in hiring: Going beyond the law. *Journal of Business Ethics*, *68*(4), 449–464. doi:10.100710551-006-9039-z

Alipour, J. V., Fadinger, H., & Schymik, J. (2021). My home is my castle–The benefits of working from home during a pandemic crisis. *Journal of Public Economics*, *196*(104373), 1–11. doi:10.1016/j.jpubeco.2021.104373

Andoh, R. P. K., Owusu, E. A., Annan-Prah, E. C., & Boampong, G. N. (2022). Training value, employee internal states and training transfer: Examining the web of relationships. *The Learning Organization*, *29*(6), 674–691. doi:10.1108/TLO-09-2022-0100

Argyris, C., & Schön, D. (1978). *Organizational learning*. Addison-Wesley.

Arthur, J. B. (1994). Effects of human resource systems on manufacturing performance and turnover. *Academy of Management Journal*, *37*(3), 670–687. doi:10.2307/256705

Awais Bhatti, M., Ali, S., Mohd Isa, M. F., & Mohamed Battour, M. (2014). Training transfer and transfer motivation: The influence of individual, environmental, situational, training design, and affective reaction factors. *Performance Improvement Quarterly, 27*(1), 51–82. doi:10.1002/piq.21165

Babbage, C. (1835). *On the economy of machinery and manufacturers.* Frank Cass & Co.

Badawy, M. K. (1995). *Developing managerial skills in engineers and scientists: Succeeding as a technical manager* (2nd ed.). Van Nostrand Reinhold.

Baird, L., & Meshoulam, I. (1988). Managing two fits of strategic human resource management. *Academy of Management Review, 13*(1), 116–128. doi:10.2307/258359

Baldwin, T. T., & Ford, J. K. (1988). Transfer of training: A review and directions for future research. *Personnel Psychology, 41*(1), 63–105. doi:10.1111/j.1744-6570.1988.tb00632.x

Banks, C. H. (2002). A descriptive analysis of the perceived effectiveness of Virginia Tech's faculty development institute. *Dissertation Abstracts International, 64*(08). (UMI No. 3102585)

Banks, C. H. (2006). Career planning: Toward an inclusive model. In M. Karsten (Ed.), *Gender, race and ethnicity in the workplace* (Vol. 3, pp. 99–116). Greenwood Publishing Group, Inc.

Banks, C. H., & Nafukho, F. M. (2008). Career transitions across and within organizations: implications for human resource development. In T.M. Chermack & J. Storberg-Walker (Eds.), *2008 Academy of Human Resource Development Annual Research Conference Proceedings,* (pp. 1096- 1102). Bowling Green, OH: Academy of Human Resource Development.

Baptiste, I. (2001). Educating lone wolves: Pedagogical implications of human capital theory. *Adult Education Quarterly, 51*(3), 184–201. doi:10.1177/074171360105100302

Becker, B. E., Huselid, M. A., & Beatty, R. W. (2009). *The differentiated workforce: Transforming talent into strategic impact.* Harvard Business Press.

Bell, B. S., Tannenbaum, S. I., Ford, J. K., Noe, R. A., & Kraiger, K. (2017). 100 years of training and development research: What we know and where we should go. *The Journal of Applied Psychology*, *102*(3), 305–323. https://psycnet.apa.org/doi/10.1037/apl0000142. doi:10.1037/apl0000142 PMID:28125262

Benson, G. S., Feingold, D., & Mohrman, S. A. (2004). You paid for the skills, now keep them: Tuition reimbursement and voluntary turnover. *Academy of Management Journal*, *47*(3), 315–331. doi:10.2307/20159584

Betz, F. (1993). *Strategic technology management*. McGraw-Hill.

Beyer, J. M., & Trice, H. M. (1987). How an organization's rites reveal its culture. *Organizational Dynamics*, *8*(3), 5–24. doi:10.1016/0090-2616(87)90041-6

Birati, A., & Tziner, A. (2000). Cost-benefit analysis of organizational interventions: The case of downsizing. *Journal of Business and Psychology*, *15*(2), 277–286. doi:10.1023/A:1007894018069

Bloom, B. (1974). Time and learning. *The American Psychologist*, *29*(9), 682–688. doi:10.1037/h0037632

Blume, B. D., Ford, J. K., Baldwin, T. T., & Huang, J. L. (2010). Transfer of training: A meta-analytic review. *Journal of Management*, *36*(4), 1065–1105. doi:10.1177/0149206309352880

Blume, B. D., Ford, J. K., Surface, E. A., & Olenick, J. (2019). A dynamic model of training transfer. *Human Resource Management Review*, *29*(2), 270–283. doi:10.1016/j.hrmr.2017.11.004

Blumenfeld, S., Anderson, G., & Hooper, V. (2020). Covid-19 and employee surveillance. *New Zealand Journal of Employment Relations*, *45*(2), 42–56. doi:10.24135/nzjer.v45i2.28

Böhm-Bawerk, E. V., Hilferding, R., & Sweezy, P. M. (1984). *Karl Marx and the close of his system*. Orion Editions.

Bolander, P., Werr, A., & Asplund, K. (2017). The practice of talent management: A framework and typology. *Personnel Review*, *46*(8), 1523–1551. doi:10.1108/PR-02-2016-0037

Bossert, S., Dwyer, D., Rowan, B., & Lee, G. (1982). The instructional management role of the principal. *Educational Administration Quarterly*, *18*(3), 34–64. doi:10.1177/0013161X82018003004

Bossidy, L. (2001). The job no CEO should delegate. *Harvard Business Review*, *79*(3), 46–49. PMID:11246923

Bowden, G. T. (1947). The adaptive capacity of workers. *Harvard Business Review*, *25*, 527–542.

Brache, A. P. (2002). *How organizations work: Taking a holistic approach to enterprise health*. John Wiley & Sons, Inc.

Brass, D. J., & Burkhardt, M. E. (1993). Potential power and power use: An investigation of structure and behavior. *Academy of Management Journal*, *36*(3), 441–470. doi:10.2307/256588

Browell, S. (2000). Staff development and professional education: A cooperative model. *Journal of Workplace Learning: Employee Counseling Today*, *12*(2), 57–65. doi:10.1108/13665620010316208

Brynjolfsson, E., Horton, J. J., Ozimek, A., Rock, D., Sharma, G., & TuYe, H. Y. (2020). *COVID-19 and remote work: An early look at US data* (No. w27344). National Bureau of Economic Research.

Brynjolfsson, E., & McAfee, A. (2011). *Race against the machine: How the digital revolution is accelerating innovation, driving productivity, and irreversibly transforming employment and the economy*. Digital Frontier Press.

Buch, K. (1992). How does downsizing affect employee involvement? *Journal for Quality and Participation*, *15*, 74–77.

Burke, L. A., & Hutchins, H. M. (2007). Training transfer: An integrative literature review. *Human Resource Development Review*, *6*(3), 263–296. doi:10.1177/1534484307303035

Burke, L. A., & Hutchins, H. M. (2008). A study of best practices in training transfer and proposed model of transfer. *Human Resource Development Quarterly*, *19*(2), 107–128. doi:10.1002/hrdq.1230

Burkhardt, M. E., & Brass, D. J. (1990). Changing patterns or patterns of change: The effects of a change in technology on social network structure and power. *Administrative Science Quarterly*, *35*(1), 104–127. doi:10.2307/2393552

Camerer, C., & Vepsalainen, A. (1988). The economic efficiency of corporate culture. *Strategic Management Journal*, *9*(Special Issue), 115–126. doi:10.1002mj.4250090712

Cameron, K. S. (1994). Strategies for successful organizational downsizing. *Human Resource Management*, *33*(2), 189–211. doi:10.1002/hrm.3930330204

Campbell, J. P. (1990). Modeling the performance prediction problem in industrial and organizational psychology. In M. D. Dunnette & L. M. Hough (EDs.), Handbook of industrial and organizational psychology (2nd ed., Vol. 1, pp. 687–732). Consulting Psychologists Press.

Chalutz Ben-Gal, H. (2022). Person–skill fit: Why a new form of employee fit is required. *Academy of Management Perspectives*. doi:10.5465/amp.2022-0024

Chatman, J. A., & Cha, S. E. (2003). Leading by leveraging culture. *California Management Review*, *45*(4), 20–34. doi:10.2307/41166186

Chatman, J. A., & Jehn, K. A. (1991). Assessing the relationship between industry characteristics and organizational culture: How different can you be? *Academy of Management Journal*, *37*(3), 522–553. doi:10.2307/256699

Chiaburu, D. S., & Lindsay, D. R. (2008). Can do or will do? The importance of self-efficacy and instrumentality for training transfer. *Human Resource Development International*, *11*(2), 199–206. doi:10.1080/13678860801933004

Choi, M. (2011). Employees' attitudes toward organizational change: A literature review. *Human Resource Management*, *50*(4), 479–500. doi:10.1002/hrm.20434

Christensen, K. E., & Staines, G. L. (1990). Flextime: A viable solution to work/family conflict? *Journal of Family Issues*, *11*(4), 455–476. doi:10.1177/019251390011004007

Clay, J. (2006). The deep difference between labor and use-value. *Science and Society*, *70*(3), 375–378. doi:10.1521iso.70.3.375

Collins, J. (2001). *Good to great*. HarperCollins.

Coughlan, R. (2005). Codes, values and justifications in the ethical decision-making process. *Journal of Business Ethics*, *59*(1–2), 45–53. doi:10.100710551-005-3409-9

Crampton, S. M., Hodge, J. W., Mishra, J. M., & Price, S. (1995). Stress and stress management. *S.A.M. Advanced Management Journal*, *60*(3), 10–29.

Cyert, R. M., Dill, W. R., & March, J. G. (1958). The role of expectations in business decision making. *Administrative Science Quarterly, 3*(3), 307–340. doi:10.2307/2390716

Cyert, R. M., & March, J. G. (1963). *A behavioral theory of the firm.* Prentice Hall.

Dalziel, M. M., & Schoonover, S. C. (1988). *Changing ways: A practical tool for implementing change within organizations.* AMACOM.

Damanpour, F. (1991). Organizational innovation: A meta-analysis of effects of determinants and moderators. *Academy of Management Journal, 34*(3), 555–590. doi:10.2307/256406

Deal, T., & Kennedy, A. (1984). *Corporate cultures.* Addison-Wesley.

Delery, J. E. (1998). Issues of fit in strategic human resource management: Implications for research. *Human Resource Management Review, 8*(3), 289–309. doi:10.1016/S1053-4822(98)90006-7

Deming, W. E. (1982). *Out of the crisis.* MIT Center for Advanced Engineering Study.

Denison, D. R. (1996). What is the difference between organizational culture and organizational climate? A native's point of view on a decade of paradigm wars. *Academy of Management Review, 21*(3), 619–654. doi:10.2307/258997

Disselkamp, L. (2007). *Working the clock: How to win the race for productivity and profits with workforce management technology.* The Oaklea Press.

Disselkamp, L. (2009). *No boundaries: How to use time and labor management technology to win the race for profits and productivity.* John Wiley & Sons, Inc.

Dohmann, C. W. (1970). Teachers' perception toward innovations and change. *UMI Dissertation Services, 70*(25), 019. (University Microfilms No, 70-25, 019)

Driskell, J. E., Johnston, J. H., & Salas, E. (2001). Does stress training generalize to novel settings? *Human Factors, 43*(1), 99–110. doi:10.1518/001872001775992471 PMID:11474766

Drucker, P. F. (1999). Knowledge-worker productivity: The biggest challenge. *California Management Review, 41*(2), 79–94. doi:10.2307/41165987

Drucker, P. F. (2002). *Managing in the next society.* Saint Martin's Press.

Eby, L. T., & Buch, K. (1998). The impact of adopting an ethical approach to employee dismissal during corporate restructuring. *Journal of Business Ethics, 17*(12), 1253–1264. doi:10.1023/A:1005758628414

Erickson, T. (2008). Plugged. In *The generation Y guide to thriving at work*. Harvard Business School Press.

Espedal, B. (2005). Management development: Using internal or external resources in developing core competence. *Human Resource Development Review, 4*(2), 136–158. doi:10.1177/1534484305276217

Ezra, M., & Deckman, M. (1996). Balancing work and family responsibilities: Flextime and childcare in the federal government. *Public Administration Review, 56*(2), 174–179. doi:10.2307/977205

Figueroa, R. A. (1999). Modelling the value of location in Regina using GIS and spatial auto correlation statistics. *Assessment Journal, 6*(6), 29–37.

Fox, A. (1974). *Beyond contract: Work, power, and trust relations*. Faber.

Fraser, J. A. (2001). *White-collar sweatshop*. W. W. Norton & Co.

Fried, Y., & Ferris, G. R. (1987). The validity of the job characteristics model: A review and meta-analysis. *Personnel Psychology, 40*(2), 287–322. doi:10.1111/j.1744-6570.1987.tb00605.x

Fromm, E. (1989). *Marx's concept of man*. The Continuum Publishing Company.

Gale, B. T. (1980). Can more capital buy higher productivity? *Harvard Business Review, 58*(4), 78–86.

Gallimore, P., Fletcher, M., & Carter, M. (1996). Modelling the influence of location on value. *Journal of Property Valuation Investment, 14*(1), 6–19. doi:10.1108/14635789610107444

Garavaglia, P. L. (1993). How to ensure transfer of training. *Training & Development, 47*(10), 63–69.

Garvin, D. A., Edmondson, A. C., & Gino, F. (2008). Is yours a learning organization? *Harvard Business Review, 86*(3), 109–134. PMID:18411968

George, G., Sleeth, R., & Siders, M. (1999). Organizing culture: Leader roles, behaviors, and reinforcement mechanisms. *Journal of Business and Psychology, 13*(4), 545–560. doi:10.1023/A:1022923005165

Gilley, J. W., & Maycunich, A. (2000). *Organizational learning, performance, and change: An introduction to strategic human resource development.* Perseus Publishing.

Goffman, E. (1959). *The presentation of self in everyday life.* Doubleday.

Gordon, G., & DiTomaso, N. (1992). Predicting corporate performance from organizational culture. *Journal of Management Studies, 29*(6), 783–798. doi:10.1111/j.1467-6486.1992.tb00689.x

Gowler, D. (1969). Determinants of the supply of labour to the firm. *Journal of Management Studies, 6*(1), 73–95. doi:10.1111/j.1467-6486.1969.tb00582.x

Grossman, R., & Salas, E. (2011). The transfer of training: What really matters. *International Journal of Training and Development, 15*(2), 103–120. doi:10.1111/j.1468-2419.2011.00373.x

Guion, R. (1973). A note on organizational climate. *Organizational Behavior and Human Performance, 9*(1), 120–125. doi:10.1016/0030-5073(73)90041-X

Hackman, J. R., & Oldham, G. R. (1974). The job diagnostic survey: An instrument for the diagnosis of jobs and the evaluation of job redesign projects. *Catalog of Selected Documents in Psychology, 4,* 148.

Hackman, J. R., & Oldham, G. R. (1975). Development of the job diagnostic survey. *The Journal of Applied Psychology, 60*(2), 159–170. doi:10.1037/h0076546

Hall, D. T. (1990). Telecommuting and the management of work-home boundaries. In *Paradigms revised: The annual review of communications in society-1989* (pp. 177–208). Institute for Information Studies.

Hall, D. T., & Richter, J. (1988). Balancing work life and home life: What can organizations do to help? *The Academy of Management Executive, 3*(3), 213–223. doi:10.5465/ame.1988.4277258

Hall, R. E., & Jones, C. I. (1999). Why do some countries produce so much more output per worker than others? *The Quarterly Journal of Economics, 114*(1), 83–116. doi:10.1162/003355399555954

Halloran, J. D. (1967). *Attitude formation and change.* Leicester University Press.

Hamrick, D. C., & MacMillan, I. C. (1984). SMR forum: Asset parsimony-Managing assets to manage profits. *Sloan Management Review, 25*(2), 67–74.

Hanna, D. P. (1988). *Designing organizations for high performance*. Addison-Wesley.

Hartman, L. P. (2001). Technology and ethics: Privacy in the workplace. *Business and Society Review*, *106*(1), 1–27. doi:10.1111/0045-3609.00099

Hartman, L. P., & Bucci, G. (2004). The economic and ethical implications of new technology on privacy in the workplace. *Business and Society Review*, *102*(1), 1–24. doi:10.1111/0045-3609.00021

Hax, A. C., & Majluf, N. S. (1996). *The strategy concept and process: A pragmatic approach* (2nd ed.). Prentice Hall.

Heck, R. H., Larsen, T. J., & Marcoulides, G. A. (1990). Instructional leadership and school achievement: Validation of a causal model. *Educational Administration Quarterly*, *26*(2), 94–125. doi:10.1177/00131 61X90026002002

Hellriegel, D., & Slocum, J. W. Jr. (1974). Organizational climate: Measures, research, and contingencies. *Academy of Management Journal*, *17*(2), 255–280. doi:10.2307/254979

Heneson, M. E., Morris, L. L., & Fitz-Gibbon, C. T. (1978). How to measure attitudes. *Sage (Atlanta, Ga.)*.

Hogan, W. T. (1987). *Minimills and integrated mills: A comparison of steelmaking in the United States*. Heath.

Holland, J. L. (1973). *Making vocational choices: A theory of careers*. Prentice-Hall.

Horniman, A. B. (2004). Leading: A performing learning art. In M. Goldsmith, H. J. Morgan, & A. J. Ogg (Eds.), *Leading organizational learning: Harnessing the power of knowledge*. Jossey-Bass.

Hughes, C. (2010). "People as technology" conceptual model: Towards a new value creation paradigm for strategic human resource development. *Human Resource Development Review*, *9*(1), 48–71. doi:10.1177/1534484309353561

Hughes, C. (2012). *Valuing people and technology in the workplace: A competitive advantage framework*. IGI Global. doi:10.4018/978-1-4666-0240-3

Hughes, C. (2016). *Diversity intelligence: Integrating diversity intelligence alongside intellectual, emotional, and cultural intelligence for leadership and career development*. Palgrave MacMillan Publications. doi:10.1057/978-1-137-52683-0

Hughes, C. (2021). The changing learning technological landscape for trainers in the wake of COVID-19. *Advances in Developing Human Resources*, *23*(1), 66–74. doi:10.1177/1523422320972108

Hughes, C., & Brown, L. (2018). Exploring leaders' discriminatory, passive-aggressive behavior toward protected class employees using diversity intelligence. *Advances in Developing Human Resources*, *20*(3), 263–284. doi:10.1177/1523422318778002

Hughes, C., & Niu, Y. (Eds.). (. (2021a). How COVID-19 is shifting career reality: Ways to navigate career journeys. *Advances in Developing Human Resources*, *23*(3). doi:10.1177/15234223211017847

Hughes, C., & Niu, Y. (2021b). Preface: Shifting career realities and navigating career journeys. *Advances in Developing Human Resources*, *23*(3), 195–202. doi:10.1177/15234223211017847

Hughes, C., & Niu, Y. (2021c). Responding to career development uncertainties and successfully navigating career journeys. *Advances in Developing Human Resources*, *23*(3), 267–272. doi:10.1177/15234223211017852

Hunter, L., Bernhardt, A., Hughes, K., & Skuratowicz, E. (2001). It's not just the ATMs: Technology, firm strategies, jobs, and earnings in retail banking. *Industrial & Labor Relations Review*, *54*(2A), 402–424. doi:10.1177/001979390105400222

Huselid, M. A. (1995). The impact of human resource management practices on turnover, productivity, and corporate financial performance. *Academy of Management Journal*, *38*(3), 635–872. doi:10.2307/256741

Huselid, M. A., Jackson, S. E., & Schuler, R. S. (1997). Technical and strategic human resource management effectiveness as determinants of firm performance. *Academy of Management Journal*, *40*(1), 171–188. doi:10.2307/257025

Irving, P. G., & Meyer, J. P. (1995). On using direct measures of met expectations: A methodological note. *Journal of Management*, *21*(6), 1159–1176. doi:10.1177/014920639502100608

Isaacson, L. E., & Brown, D. (1997). *Career information, career counseling, and career development* (6th ed.). Allyn & Bacon.

James, L., & Jones, A. (1974). Organizational climate: A review of theory and research. *Psychological Bulletin, 18*(12), 1096–1112. doi:10.1037/h0037511

Jandl, C., Zafari, S., Taurer, F., Hartner-Tiefenthaler, M., & Schlund, S. (2023). Location-based monitoring in production environments: Does transparency help to increase the acceptance of monitoring? *Production & Manufacturing Research, 11*(1), 1–20. doi:10.1080/21693277.2022.2160387

Jimoh, L. A., & Kee, D. M. H. (2022). Talent management: The way out of poor task performance. *Industrial and Commercial Training, 54*(4), 623–636. doi:10.1108/ICT-03-2022-0016

Jones, A. P., & James, L. R. (1979). Psychological climate: Dimensions and relationships of individual and aggregated work environment perceptions. *Organizational Behavior and Human Performance, 23*(2), 201–250. doi:10.1016/0030-5073(79)90056-4

Judge, T. A., Weiss, H. M., Kammeyer-Mueller, J. D., & Hulin, C. L. (2017). Job attitudes, job satisfaction, and job affect: A century of continuity and of change. *The Journal of Applied Psychology, 102*(3), 356–374. doi:10.1037/apl0000181 PMID:28125260

Kahn, W. A. (1990). Psychological conditions of personal engagement and disengagement at work. *Academy of Management Journal, 33*(4), 692–724. doi:10.2307/256287

Karsten, M. F., & Igou, F. (2005). Career planning: A model for a diverse workforce. *Refereed Proceedings of the North American Management Society track at the 2005 Midwest Business Administration Association Conference.* MBAA.

Kaye, B. (1997). *Up is not the only way.* Davies-Black.

Kiesler, C. A., Collins, B. E., & Miller, N. (1969). *Attitude change.* John Wiley & Sons, Inc.

Kiron, D. (2022). AI can change how you measure-and how you manage. *MIT Sloan Management Review, 63*(3), 24–28.

Kirton, M. J., & Mulligan, G. (1973). Correlates of managers' attitudes toward change. *The Journal of Applied Psychology, 58*(1), 101–107. doi:10.1037/h0035425

Kohn, A. (1993). Why incentive plans cannot work. *Harvard Business Review, 71*(5), 54–63.

Kohn, M. L. (1981). Personality, occupation, and social stratification: A frame of reference. In D. J. Treiman & R. V. Robinson (Eds.), *Research in social stratification and mobility* (Vol. 1, pp. 267–297). JAI Press.

Konopka, Z. J. (2018). Prepare your organization for adaptive learning. *TD Magazine, 72*(5), 20–22.

Kotter, J., & Heskett, J. (1992). *Corporate culture and performance.* Free Press.

Koy, D. J., Briggs, S., & Grenig, J. (1987). State court disparity on employment-at-will. *Personnel Psychology, 40*(3), 565–577. doi:10.1111/j.1744-6570.1987.tb00615.x

Kozlowski, S. W. J., Chao, G. T., Smith, E. M., & Hedlund, J. (1993). Organizational downsizing: Strategies, interventions, and research implications. *International Review of Industrial and Organizational Psychology, 6*, 263–332.

Kucharska, W., & Rebelo, T. (2022). Knowledge sharing and knowledge hiding in light of the mistakes acceptance component of learning culture- knowledge culture and human capital implications. *The Learning Organization, 29*(6), 635–655. doi:10.1108/TLO-03-2022-0032

Kunneman, D. E., Key, J. P., & Sleezer, C. M. (2000). Management training activities and training needs within selected business and industry organizations in Oklahoma. *Journal of Career and Technical Education, 16*(2), 51–56. doi:10.21061/jcte.v16i2.551

Larson, D., & Chang, V. (2016). A review and future direction of agile, business intelligence, analytics and data science. *International Journal of Information Management, 36*(5), 700–710. doi:10.1016/j.ijinfomgt.2016.04.013

Latkovikja, M. T., & Popovskab, M. B. (2020, June). How millennials, Gen z, and technology are changing the workplace design. In *Proceedings of the 6th International Workshop on Socio-Technical Perspective in IS Development (STPIS 2020).* CEUR.

Lawler, E. E. III. (2003). *Treat people right! How organizations and individuals can propel each other into a virtuous spiral of success.* Jossey-Bass.

Leibowitz, Z. B., Farren, C., & Kaye, B. L. (1986). *Designing career development systems.* Jossey-Bass.

Litwin, G. H., & Stringer, R. A. (1968). *Motivation and organizational climate.* Harvard Business School, Division of Research.

Liyanage, J. P., & Kumar, U. (2003). Towards a value-based view on operations and maintenance performance management. *Journal of Quality in Maintenance Engineering, 9*(4), 333–350. doi:10.1108/13552510310503213

Loch, K. D., Conger, S., & Oz, E. (1998). Ownership, privacy and monitoring in the workplace: A debate on technology and ethics. *Journal of Business Ethics, 17*(6), 653–663.

Luan, Y., Zhao, K., Wang, Z., & Hu, F. (2022). Exploring the antecedents of unethical pro-organizational behavior (UPB): A meta-analysis. *Journal of Business Ethics.* doi:10.100710551-022-05269-w

Lundgren, H., & Poell, R. F. (2022). How do HRD professionals and business managers interact in organizing HRD activities? *Human Resource Development Quarterly,* 1–23. doi:10.1002/hrdq.21485

Mackenzie, K. D. (1986). *Organizational design: The organizational audit and analysis technology.* Ablex Publishing Corporation.

Maidique, M. A., & Hayes, R. H. (1984). The art of high-technology management. *Sloan Management Review, 25*(2), 17–31.

Makarius, E. E., & Srinivasan, M. (2017). Addressing skills mismatch: Utilizing talent supply chain management to enhance collaboration between companies and talent suppliers. *Business Horizons, 60*(4), 495–505. doi:10.1016/j.bushor.2017.03.007

Malos, S. (1998). Current legal issues in performance appraisal. In J. Smither (Ed.), *Performance appraisal: State of the art in practice* (pp. 49–94). Jossey-Bass Publisher.

Mangham, I. L., & Overington, M. A. (1983). Dramatism and the theatrical metaphor: Really playing at critical distances. In G. Morgan (Ed.), *Beyond method: Social research strategies* (pp. 219–233). Sage.

March, J., & Simon, H. (1959). *Organizations.* Wiley and Sons.

Marcoulides, G. A., & Heck, R. H. (1993). Organizational culture and performance: Proposing and testing a model. *Organization Science*, *4*(2), 209–225. doi:10.1287/orsc.4.2.209

Martelli, J. (1998). Training for new technology: Midwest steel company. In Rothwell, W. (Ed.), Linking HRD programs with organizational strategy (pp. 85–96). ASTD.

Martin, H. J. (2010). Workplace climate and peer support as determinants of training transfer. *Human Resource Development Quarterly*, *19*(1), 87–104. doi:10.1002/hrdq.20038

Martin, K., & Freeman, R. E. (2003). Some problems with employee monitoring. *Journal of Business Ethics*, *43*(4), 353–361. doi:10.1023/A:1023014112461

Marx, K. (1906). *Capital* (Vol. 1). Kerr.

Maslow, A. (1987). *Motivation and personality* (3rd ed.). Harper & Row.

May, D. R., Gilson, R. L., & Harter, L. (2004). The psychological conditions of meaningfulness, safety, and availability and the engagement of the human spirit at work. *Journal of Occupational and Organizational Psychology*, *77*(1), 11–37. doi:10.1348/096317904322915892

Montesino, M. U. (2002). Strategic alignment of training, transfer-enhancing behaviors, and training usage: A post training study. *Human Resource Development Quarterly*, *13*(1), 89–108. doi:10.1002/hrdq.1015

Moran, J. W., & Brightman, B. K. (2000). Leading organizational change. *Journal of Workplace Learning: Employee Counseling Today*, *12*(2), 66–74. doi:10.1108/13665620010316226

Morgeson, F. P., & Campion, M. A. (1997). Social and cognitive sources of potential inaccuracy in job analysis. *The Journal of Applied Psychology*, *82*(5), 627–655. doi:10.1037/0021-9010.82.5.627

Muir, C. P., Sherf, E. N., & Liu, J. T. (2022). It's not only what you do, but why you do it: How managerial motives influence employees' fairness judgments. *The Journal of Applied Psychology*, *107*(4), 581–603. doi:10.1037/apl0000898 PMID:34197139

Munck, B. (2001). Changing a culture of face time. *Harvard Business Review*, *79*(10), 125–131.

Nakajima, S. (1988). *Introduction to total productive maintenance*. Productivity Press.

Newbold, C., & Pharoah, N. (2009). What it means to be a learning organization. *Strategic HR Review*, *8*(3), 12–16. doi:10.1108/14754390910946521

Nicholson, N., & Johns, G. (1985). The absence culture and the psychological contract—Who's in control of absence? *Academy of Management Review*, *10*, 397–407.

O'Reilly, C. A. III, Chatman, J., & Caldwell, D. F. (1991). People and organizational culture: A profile comparison approach to assessing person-organization fit. *Academy of Management Journal*, *34*(3), 487–516. doi:10.2307/256404

Odor, H. O. (2018). A literature review on organizational learning and learning organizations. *International Journal of Economics & Management Sciences*, *07*(01). doi:10.4172/2162-6359.1000494

Olmosk, K. E. (1972). Seven pure strategies of change. In J. W. Pfeiffer & J. E. Jones (Eds.), *The 1972 annual handbook for group facilitators*. Pfeiffer & Company.

Ouchi, W. (1981). *Theory Z*. Addison-Wesley.

Owens, R. (1987). *Organizational behavior in education*. Prentice-Hall.

Park, C. S. (2006). Reply. *Science and Society*, *70*(3), 379–380. doi:10.1521iso.70.3.379

Pascale, R., & Athos, A. (1981). *The art of Japanese management*. Simon &Schuster. doi:10.1016/0007-6813(81)90032-X

Pfeffer, J. (1992). *Managing with power*. Harvard Business School Press.

Pfeffer, J. (1994). *Competitive advantage through people: Unleashing the power of the workforce*. Harvard Business School Press. doi:10.2307/41165742

Pfeffer, J. (1998). *The human equation: Building profits by putting people first*. Harvard Business School Press.

Ployhart, R. E., Schmitt, N., & Tippins, N. T. (2017). Solving the Supreme Problem: 100 years of selection and recruitment at the Journal of Applied Psychology. *The Journal of Applied Psychology*, *102*(3), 291–304. doi:10.1037/apl0000081 PMID:28125261

Porter, L. W., & Steers, R. M. (1973). Organizational, work, and personal factors in employee turnover and absenteeism. *Psychological Bulletin*, *80*(2), 151–176. doi:10.1037/h0034829

Porter, M. (2001). Strategy and the Internet. *Harvard Business Review*, *79*(3), 62–78. PMID:11246925

Potnuru, R. K. G., & Sahoo, C. K. (2016). HRD interventions, employee competencies and organizational effectiveness: An empirical study. *European Journal of Training and Development*, *40*(5), 345–365. doi:10.1108/EJTD-02-2016-0008

Prusak, L., & Cohen, D. (2001). How to invest in social capital. *Harvard Business Review*, *79*(6), 86–93. PMID:11408980

Qureshi, S., Briggs, R. O., & Hlupic, V. (2006). Value creation from intellectual capital: Convergence of knowledge management and collaboration in the intellectual bandwidth model. *Group Decision and Negotiation*, *15*(3), 197–220. doi:10.100710726-006-9018-x

Rainey, G. W. Jr, & Wolf, L. (1981). Flex-time: Short-term benefits; long-term...? *Public Administration Review*, *41*(1), 52–63. doi:10.2307/975724

Ramsey, M. (1986). *The super supervisor*. Positive Presentations, Inc.

Ritti, R., & Funkhouser, G. (1982). *The ropes to skip and the ropes to know*. Grid.

Robbins, S., & Coulter, M. (2007). *Management* (9th ed.). Prentice Hall.

Robbins, S., & Judge, T. (2011). *Organizational behavior* (14th ed.). Prentice Hall.

Robles, M. M. (2012). Executive perceptions of the top 10 soft skills needed in today's workplace. *Business Communication Quarterly*, *75*(4), 453–465. doi:10.1177/1080569912460400

Roche, C., Wall, P.J. & Lewis, D. (2022). Ethics and diversity in artificial intelligence policies, strategies and initiatives. *AI Ethics,* 1-21. doi:10.1007/s43681-022-00218-9

Rogers, E. M. (1995). *Diffusion of innovations* (4th ed.). The Free Press.

Rogers, E. M. (2003). *Diffusion of innovations* (5th ed.). The Free Press.

Romani, L., Holck, L., & Risberg, A. (2018). Benevolent discrimination: Explaining how human resources professionals can be blind to the harm of diversity initiatives. *Organization*, *26*(3), 371–390. doi:10.1177/1350508418812585

Rosenberg, N. (1972). *Technology and American economic growth*. M. E. Sharp.

Rumbles, S., & Rees, G. (2013). Continuous changes, organizational burnout and the implications for HRD. *Industrial and Commercial Training*, *45*(4), 236–242. doi:10.1108/00197851311323538

Sari, D. Y. (2022). The study of learning organization models: A literature review. *Journal Research of Social, Science, Economics, and Management*, *2*(02), 188–202. doi:10.36418/jrssem.v2i2.251

SCANS. (1991). What work requires of schools. *A SCANS report for America 2000*. Washington, DC: U.S. Department of Labor, The Secretary's Commission on Achieving Necessary Skills (SCANS).

Schein, E. (1990). Organizational culture. *The American Psychologist*, *45*(2), 109–119. doi:10.1037/0003-066X.45.2.109

Schein, E. H. (1975). How career anchors hold executives to their career paths. *Personnel*, *52*, 11–24.

Schleicher, D. J., Hansen, S. D., & Fox, K. E. (2011). Job attitudes and work values. In S. Zedeck (Ed.), APA handbook of industrial and organizational psychology, Vol. 3. Maintaining, expanding, and contracting the organization (pp. 137–189). American Psychological Association. doi:10.1037/12171-004

Schneider, B. (1975). Organizational climate: An essay. *Personnel Psychology*, *28*(4), 447–479. doi:10.1111/j.1744-6570.1975.tb01386.x

Schneider, B., González-Romá, V., Ostroff, C., & West, M. A. (2017). Organizational climate and culture: Reflections on the history of the constructs in the Journal of Applied Psychology. *The Journal of Applied Psychology*, *102*(3), 468–482. doi:10.1037/apl0000090 PMID:28125256

Schneider, B., & Reiehers, A. E. (1983). On the etiology of climates. *Personnel Psychology*, *36*(1), 19–40. doi:10.1111/j.1744-6570.1983.tb00500.x

Schor, J. (1991). *The overworked American: The unexpected decline of leisure*. Basic Books.

Scott, D., & Markham, S. (1982). Absenteeism control methods: A survey of practices and results. *The Personnel Administrator, 27*(6), 73–84.

Sheaffer, Z., Carmeli, A., Steiner-Revivo, M., & Zionit, S. (2009). Downsizing strategies and organizational performance: A longitudinal study. *Management Decision, 47*(6), 950–974. doi:10.1108/00251740910966677

Silberman, M. (1998). *Active training* (2nd ed.). Jossey-Bass/Pfeiffer.

Sim, S. H., & Endrenyi, J. (1988). Optimal preventive maintenance with repair. *IEEE Transactions on Reliability, 37*(1), 92–96. doi:10.1109/24.3721

Somers, M. J. (2001). Ethical codes of conduct and organizational context: A study of the relationship between codes of conduct, employee behavior and organizational values. *Journal of Business Ethics, 30*(2), 185–195. doi:10.1023/A:1006457810654

Stahl, B. C., Schroeder, D., & Rodrigues, R. (2023). Unfair and illegal discrimination. In *Springerbriefs in research and innovation governance* (pp. 9–23). Springer Briefs in Research and Innovation Governance. doi:10.1007/978-3-031-17040-9_2

Staw, B. M. (1980). The consequences of turnover. *Journal of Occupational Behaviour, 1*, 253–273.

Steers, R. M., Mowday, R. T., & Shapiro, D. L. (2004). The future of work motivation theory. *Academy of Management Review, 29*(3), 379–387. doi:10.2307/20159049

Steers, R. M., & Porter, L. W. (1979). *Motivation and work behavior* (2nd ed.). McGraw-Hill Book Company.

Steers, R. M., & Rhodes, S. R. (1978). Major influences on employee attendance: A process model. *The Journal of Applied Psychology, 63*(4), 391–407. doi:10.1037/0021-9010.63.4.391

Stewart, C., Wall, A., & Marciniec, S. (2016, July). Mixed signals: Do college graduates have the soft skills that employers want? In Competition forum (Vol. 14, p. 276). American Society for Competitiveness.

Stewart, T. A. (1999). *Intellectual capital: The new wealth of organizations.* Doubleday.

Strebel, P. (1996). Why do employees resist change? *Harvard Business Review, 74*(3), 86–92.

Super, D. (2002). A life-span, life-space approach to career development. In D. Brown & L. Brooks (Eds.), *Career choice and development* (2nd ed.). Jossey-Bass. doi:10.1016/0001-8791(80)90056-1

Sutton, R. I. (2001). The weird rules of creativity. *Harvard Business Review*, *79*(8), 94–103. PMID:11550634

Swamy, M. R. K. (2004). Does non-inclusion of intangible asset values lead to distortion of financial statements and mislead judicious financial decision making? Focus on environmental accounting and estimation of knowledge capital values. *Journal of Financial Management and Analysis*, *17*(1), 77–91.

Swanson, R. A. (2001). The discipline of human resource development. In R. A. Swanson & E. F. Holton (Eds.), *Foundations of human re- source development* (pp. 88–100). Berrett-Koehler Publishers.

Swanson, R. A., & Holton, E. F. (2001). *Foundation of human resource development*. Berrett-Koehler Publishers.

Tagiuri, R., & Litwin, G. H. (Eds.). (1968). *Organizational climate: Exploration of a concept*. Harvard Business School, Division of Research.

Taylor, F. W. (1911). *The principles of scientific management*. Harper & Row.

Taylor, P. J. (1974). Sickness absence: Factors and misconceptions. *Journal of the Royal College of Physicians*, *8*, 315–334. PMID:4841341

Thériault, M., Des Rosiers, F., Villeneuve, P., & Kestens, Y. (2003). Modelling interactions of location with specific value of housing at- tributes. *Property Management*, *21*(1), 25–62. doi:10.1108/02637470310464472

Thompson, G. L. (1968). Optimal maintenance policy and sale date of a machine. *Management Science*, *14*(9), 543–550. doi:10.1287/mnsc.14.9.543

Tripathi, A., & Dhir, S. (2022). HRD interventions, learning agility and organizational innovation: A PLS-SEM modelling approach. *The International Journal of Organizational Analysis*. doi:10.1108/IJOA-12-2021-3064

Trumbo, D. A. (1958). *An analysis of attitudes toward change among the employees of an insurance company*. [Unpublished Doctoral dissertation, Michigan State University].

Trumbo, D. A. (1961). Individual and group correlates of attitudes toward work-related change. *The Journal of Applied Psychology*, *45*(5), 338–344. doi:10.1037/h0040464

Tushman, M. L., & Anderson, P. (1986). Technological discontinuities and organizational environments. *Administrative Science Quarterly, 31*(3), 439–465. doi:10.2307/2392832

Vardi, Y. (1980). Organizational career mobility: An integrative model. *Academy of Management Review, 5*(3), 341–355. doi:10.2307/257109

Venkatraman, N., & Henderson, J. C. (1998). Real strategies for virtual organizing. *Sloan Management Review, 34*(2), 73–87.

Vroom, V. H. (1964). *Work and motivation.* John Wiley & Sons, Inc.

Vroom, V. H. (1973). A new look at managerial decision making. *Organizational Dynamics, 1*(4), 66–80. doi:10.1016/S0090-2616(73)80024-5

Vroom, V. H. (1995). *Work and motivation.* Jossey-Bass.

Vroom, V. H. (2003). Educating managers for decision making and leadership. *Management Decision, 41*(10), 968–978. doi:10.1108/00251740310509490

Vroom, V. H., & MacCrimmon, K. R. (1968). Toward a stochastic model of managerial careers. *Administrative Science Quarterly, 13*(1), 26–46. doi:10.2307/2391260

Waldfogel, J. (1999). The impact of the family and medical leave act. *Journal of Policy Analysis and Management, 18*(2), 281–302. doi:10.1002/(SICI)1520-6688(199921)18:2<281::AID-PAM5>3.0.CO;2-J

Wenstop, F., & Myrmel, A. (2006). Structuring organizational value statements. *Management Research News, 29*(11), 673–683. doi:10.1108/01409170610715990

Whitman, M. (2010). *The power of many: Values for success in business and in life.* Three Rivers Press.

Wiener, Y. (1988). Forms of value systems: A focus on organizational effectiveness and cultural change and maintenance. *Academy of Management Review, 13*, 534–545.

Wiley, C. (1997). What motivates employees ac- cording to over 40 years of motivation surveys. *International Journal of Manpower, 18*(3), 263–280. doi:10.1108/01437729710169373

Wilkins, A. L., & Ouchi, W. G. (1983). Efficient cultures: Exploring the relationship between culture and organizational performance. *Administrative Science Quarterly*, *28*(3), 468–481. doi:10.2307/2392253

Wilson, H. T. (2004). Use value and substantive rationality in the work of Marx and Weber. *Journal of Classical Sociology*, *4*(1), 4–30. doi:10.1177/1468795X04040650

Wilson, M., Robertson, P., Cruickshank, P., & Gkatzia, D. (2022). Opportunities and risks in the use of AI in career development practice. *Journal of the National Institute for Career Education and Counselling*, *48*(1), 48–57. doi:10.20856/jnicec.4807

Womack, J. P., & Jones, D. T. (1996). *Lean thinking*. Simon & Schuster.

Wright, P. M., & McMahan, G. C. (1992). Theoretical perspectives for strategic human resource management. *Journal of Management*, *18*(2), 295–320. doi:10.1177/014920639201800205

Yildiz, R. O., & Esmer, S. (2023). Talent management strategies and functions: A systematic review. *Industrial and Commercial Training*, *55*(1), 93–111. doi:10.1108/ICT-01-2022-0007

Yorks, L., Abel, A. L., & Rotatori, D. (2022). Using data and analytics for improved HRD performance in the age of digital technologies. In *Strategic human resource development in practice: Leveraging talent for sustained performance in the digital age of AI* (pp. 81–92). Springer International Publishing. doi:10.1007/978-3-030-95775-9_5

Yu, W., & Wang, Z. (2022). Dual influencing paths of time pressure on employee creativity. *International Journal of Stress Management*, 1–12. doi:10.1037tr0000267

Zhang, R., Kang, H., Jiang, Z., & Niu, X. (2023). How does workplace ostracism hurt employee creativity? Thriving at work as a mediator and organization-based self-esteem as a moderator. *Applied Psychology*, *72*(1), 211–230. doi:10.1111/apps.12374

Chapter 5

People as Technology and Systems Thinking in the Context of Human Resource Development

ABSTRACT

Chapter five describes the people as technology (PT) concept and the complex relationships of technology development and people development within organizations. Systems theory is a foundational theory of human resource development. This chapter describes how the PT concept relates to systems theory in the context of HRD. Implications for how ethical and unethical behavior influences organizational systems are provided. Comparison of the five values of people and technology development to six themes of high technology development, the six major factors to determine knowledge-worker productivity, and the COVID-19 pandemic are also included.

INTRODUCTION

Organizations say people are their greatest asset, yet they sometimes refer to them as employees, human resources, human capital, associates, union members, subordinates, indirect labor, direct labor, knowledge worker, among other names. Gale's (1980) concept of value added can be used to measure "the physical output of each worker and the value of that output (p.79). The

DOI: 10.4018/978-1-6684-5321-6.ch005

value-added concept does not measure employees' effort to create output. The five values of people and technology development may assist stakeholders as they continue to strive to measure and understand people and technology's value to the organization.

AI and automation have added a new dimension to the workplace as it relates to the understanding of people and technology in the workplace. AI and automation not only have a productivity impact, but also an ethical impact as organization managers and leaders seek to strike the right balance when displacing employees with technology, use technology to monitor employee performance and behavior, and use AI in employee selection (Acemoglu & Restrepo, 2019; Donahoe & Metzger, 2019; Gordon, 2020; Kalimeri & Tjostheim, 2020; Müller, 2020). Despite exorbitant profits daily, some organizations continuously work toward maintaining and enhancing their competitiveness. They try to have the right blend of people and technology to achieve the highest possible return on investment (ROI) (Gale, 1980; Jasson & Govender, 2017; Phillips, 2003; Wang et al., 2002).

Southwest Airlines was one of the first organizations that had a University for People (Hollis, 2003). As valuable assets, people should be acknowledged as such. Understanding the character and mind of the people that work for the organization is what matters (Hughes, 2012). The mind of the employee has been undervalued by organizations. Jack Welch (2005) wrote that "A middle-aged appliance worker who was at one Work-Out spoke for thousands of people when he told me, 'For twenty-five years, you paid for my hands when you could have had my brain as well - for nothing'" (p. 56). Ramsey (1986) noted that employees are three dimensional: body [behavioral], spirit [cultural], and mind [cognitive]. It would seem that organizations would want to work with all aspects of an employee's body, mind, and spirit through behavioral, cultural, and cognitive initiatives in the workplace. Ramsey also suggested that management only cares about the body and not the spirit and mind of the employee which can reduce the employees' will and zeal to perform productively for the organization. This chapter discusses and explains how the PT concept relates to systems theory in the context of HRD. This content has become much more relevant during the fourth industrial revolution and the COVID-19 pandemic.

BACKGROUND

The emergence of the fourth industrial revolution has made the ethical treatment of people in the workplace a central interest. AI technology and digital media including robotics and avatars alongside drones and machine learning requires that people, through the study of human interactions with computers, be examined not only by HRD experts but in collaboration with computer information system, computer science, and computer engineering experts. Programmers who are writing and creating the computer algorithms must view people through an ethical lens and not just focus on the capabilities of the technology. Many algorithms and unexplainable AI errors have been made that have proven to be detrimental to people in the workplace (Cheng et al., 2021; Henriksen & Bechmann, 2020; Kim, 2018; Lang et al., 2021).

These and other important interactions between technology and people at work require immediate action; hence, the development of the PT concept (Hughes, 2010). The purpose of the PT concept is to assist stakeholders with the process of thinking of people as they would think of technology in the workplace. Location, use, maintenance, modification, and time value considerations provide a context for making appropriate decisions. Appropriate technology must be used by fully trained employees.

Reich (1992) suggested ways a country could prepare all its citizens to share in the new global economy. He stated that "neither the profitability of a nation's corporations nor the successes of its investors necessarily improve the standard of living of most of the nation's citizens (p.8). The incentive that guided their operational focus was economic gain regardless of where the organizations were located in the world. The COVID-19 pandemic has exposed the offshoring of necessary supply manufacturing and has forced many of these corporations to begin producing needed supplies in America, again (Kajjumba et al., 2020; Simonite, 2020; van Hoek & Dobrzykowski, 2021). Several examples include swabs, car parts, face masks, and surgical gloves. Even baby formula had to be imported from offshore manufacturing plants during a shortage.

The fourth industrial revolution and the COVID-19 pandemic together have exacerbated the divide between the rich (1%) and the other 99% of workers in America. The lack of investment in the nation's schools was especially exposed during the COVID-19 pandemic when kids had to go home during lockdowns and be taught online. Many teachers nor students were prepared for online learning. The lack of computer and internet access that had been being discussed in the digital divide for decades became front and center news. Some kids without technology were left behind academically.

Organization leaders and employees adapt to the changes in society. They need research, development, and technological skills to identify and help solve societal problems. External and internal conditions are always changing with new competitors, opportunities, processes, and employees. Powell (1995) stated that "When the environment changes, you have to change with it and try to get ahead of it" (pp. 319-320). Attaining needed KSAs will be an employee's only opportunity to survive as America becomes more economically divided, so organizations cannot falter in producing the most knowledgeable workers possible. The COVID-19 pandemic has proven that organizations without technology skilled employees took much longer to adapt to society's needs during lockdown periods (Agrawal et al., 2020; Howe et al., 2021; Hughes, 2021).

PEOPLE AS TECHNOLOGY AND LEARNING ORGANIZATIONS

As technology advances, individuals, together with organizations, must be ready to adapt to new trends and incorporate new ideas into the workplace. They must be willing to learn new processes, develop new methods, and acquire and use the knowledge that is available and attainable. Learning technologies play a significant role in the learning process (Githens et al., 2008; McWhorter, 2014; Oh et al., 2018; Upadhyay & Khandelwal, 2019; Wang, 2011) and workplace learning effects the competitive advantage strategy of organizations (Lee & Lan, 2007; Fenwick, 2008, Kuchinke, 1995). Organization leaders should meet the demands for workplace learning by supplying the technological tools necessary to meet workforce needs regardless of levels, and specific individual needs (Hughes, 2012; 2021). The attainment of solutions for the above-mentioned issues is crucial to the success of organizations, yet many organizations did not have the capability to adjust during the COVID-19 pandemic (Amankwah-Amoah et al., 2021; Hughes, 2021). Many were not learning organizations (Garvin, 1993; Garvin et al., 2008, Griego et al., 2000; Luhn, 2016; Marsick & Watkins, 1994; Newbold & Pharoah, 2009; Senge, 1990) even though they provided organizational learning opportunities to employees (Huysman, 2000; Kontoghiorghes et al., 2005; Liu, 2014; Mutamba, 2017; Odor, 2018; Örtenblad, 2018; Sun, 2003).

New technologies and processes are developed or enhanced daily such as the Internet, intelligent tutoring systems, learning objects, AI, voice recognition, virtual reality, machine learning, and ChatGPT (Bassi et al., 1998; Floridi & Chiriatti, 2020; Lund & Wang, 2023; Short, 2013; Wang, 2011). Providers of learning opportunities for employees must be knowledgeable of the changes and able to integrate those changes and technologies into the workplace as needed. The enormous changes during the COVID-19 pandemic proved this statement to be true. The COVID-19 pandemic did not allow room for fear or time to motivate. Hence, the need for continuous development so that employees are always prepared for all kinds of potential disruptions.

Technology Development

Betz (1993) defined technology as "the knowledge of the productive capabilities of the firm's businesses" (p. xv) and listed five basic technology principles. The principles are:

1. Technology should be conceived of as a competitive factor within a business system.
2. New technological potential should be forecast.
3. Technology forecasts should be implemented through planned technology strategies.
4. New products using the new technology must be marketed with special attention to the problems of new markets.
5. Technology strategy and business strategy must be closely integrated. (p.9)

Betz's principles apply to AI and is relevant to 21st century technologies. London and Diamante (2002) described technology-focused expansive individuals as early adopters of technology who continuously sought technological advancements, could acquire new technological knowledge and skills, and were fascinated by technological developments.

These individuals often find the problems in the algorithms and flaws that the innovators missed during development. They help innovators make needed adjustments because they are the first to repeatedly use new technology.

US organizations' ability to organize, manage, and succeed with technological developments has been and continues to be admired by other countries (Arora & Gambardella, 2005; Servan-Schreiber, 1967) especially since America created the internet, but many countries are surpassing the US

(Thoben et al., 2017) because of educational deficiencies in science, technology, engineering, and math (STEM). Organizations such as Amazon, Microsoft, Apple, Alphabet, Meta, General Electric (GE), Ford Motor Company, Boeing, and International Business Machines (IBM) all have international reputations for technological success. Maidique and Hayes's (1984) six themes for high technology development success within organizations are "(1) business focus; (2) adaptability; (3) organizational cohesion; (4) entrepreneurial culture; (5) sense of integrity; and (6) "hands-on" top management" (p.18). In some organizations only the sixth theme has been visible leading to a separation of people and technology from the perspective that the only people who have played a role in the initial integration of technology into the workplace have been upper management and engineering leaders (Hughes, 2012). Because of this detachment, employees who are supposed to ensure technology's function within organizational processes have only been engaged when told exactly what to do without any room for deviation from established processes and procedures. This approach can be successful, but it has also led to abject failure.

Betz (1993) noted that the overhead support to a firm included activities of technology development, human resource management, and firm infrastructure and three kinds of technology which are used by any economic value-adding firm. The three kinds of technology are:

1. Product technologies in the design of the firm's products,
2. Production technologies in the production of the firm's products, and
3. Service technologies in overhead functions that serve the direct productive activities of the firm and provide external services to customers. (p. 223)

Companies such as Coca-Cola and AT&T embraced the concept of economic value added (EVA™) (Abdeen & Haight, 2002; Chen & Dodd, 1997; Sabol & Sverer, 2017; Sharma & Kumar, 2010). Specific examples of the three kinds of technology are (1) the AutoCAD machine, (2) Ford's assembly line (Hounshell, 1984), and (3) the computer and AI. Technology designers and developers of technologies should interact with organizations' production and service teams to ensure customer satisfaction. Xerox and Apple were initially able to leverage their technology into production or sales. Yet, today, both companies have made the required adjustments and are dominant technology market leaders.

Technologies are dependent upon human performance. Maidique and Hayes (1984) suggested the following questions that should be answered to understand technology development:

1. How technology works? (Its limits, as well as its potential (together with the limits and potential of competitor's technologies).
2. What these various technologies require in terms of technical and economic resources?
3. The direction and speed of change.
4. The available technological options, their costs, probability of failure and potential benefits if they prove successful. (p. 26)

Similar questions should be asked when trying to understand people development.

1. How do people work? (What are employees' limits, as well as their potential (together with the limits and potential of competitor's people)?
2. What do these multidimensional people require in terms of technical and economic resources?
3. What is the direction and speed of employee change?
4. What are the available people options, their costs, probability of failure, and potential benefits if they prove successful? (Hughes, 2012, p. 34)

Answering these questions keeps organizations aware of the needs of their employees and could help organizations adjust during disruptions caused by pandemics and other unforeseen changes.

Technology is used by organization because it provides multiple uses and flexibility within its current strategy. New technologies are extensively evaluated to determine if they integrate with or can replace current technologies in ways that are advantageous for the organization (Hughes, 2012). The amount of disruption expected from the introduction of new technology is also considered. Sometimes technologies are selected not because they are the most advanced, but because they are the most reliable, produces consistent results, and generates revenue.

Organizations would like to hire new employees with similar characteristics; however, these expectations may not be communicated to employees when they enter the organization, or the expectations may be beyond the capabilities of the employees who have been hired. Often the multidimensionality of the technology is known upfront, but the multidimensionality of the employee is not. Using the five values during the hiring process can help organizations make not only better hiring decisions but also more effective change strategies.

People Development

During the Great Recession, reemployment was limited because of workers' lack of knowledge for the jobs that were available and many manual workers from construction and traditional manufacturing industries made up a majority of the unemployed (Hughes, 2012). Most businesses "manual workers as a cost. To be productive, knowledge workers must be considered a *capital asset*. Costs need to be controlled and reduced. Assets need to be made to grow" (Drucker, 1999, p. 87). The COVID-19 pandemic has led to a labor-controlled market. Seismic worker shifts are occurring with the workers in control. For example, Amazon and Apple employees have formed unions for the first time. The Great Resignation is forcing organizations to consider workers' needs. This has led to a paradigm shift in how organizations develop its employees.

Kincheloe (1999) discussed the disrespect of workers and how modernism had shaped US society's view of work and education by delineating the characteristics of positivism, the power of corporations and their influence on politics, and the lack of democracy in the workplace. Some employers were concerned more with the attitude (or behavior) of workers rather than their mental capacity or social concerns, but the COVID-19 pandemic has forced the consideration of the employees' mental capacity and social concerns (Hughes & Niu, 2021; Park et al., 2021). The ethics of responding to workers' deaths forced changes in worker treatment and healthcare benefits (Cimarolli et al., 2022).

Technology has displaced millions of workers. Very few reasons for not meeting expectations are accepted as excuses from workers by organization leadership when goals are not met, but leadership failures are seldom addressed. Thus, the focus of people development has been meeting stated goals similar to how teaching to the test has become the mantra in some public schools. Both concerns are being reassessed during the COVID-19 pandemic. Many standardized tests are being eliminated, and goals are being reconsidered. The ethics of testing and goal establishment are being examined.

Workers want to see concrete, consistent examples of caring from management that will allow them to trust them (Ramsey, 1986). The COVID-19 pandemic revealed this to be true with regards to life and death situations with the virus. Hospital and medical workers without proper personal protective equipment (PPE) is but one example. The location value of workers including teachers are being reexamined because work that was thought to be incapable of being accomplished remotely has been proven to be possible to accomplish at extremely high success rates. Forced change is sometimes the best and only change.

Drucker (1999) listed six major factors to determine knowledge-worker productivity. They are:

1. Knowledge-worker productivity demands that we ask the question: *"What is the task?"*
2. It demands that we impose the responsibility for their productivity on the individual knowledge workers themselves.
3. Knowledge workers have to manage themselves. They have to have autonomy.
4. Continuing innovation has to be part of the work, the task and the responsibility of knowledge workers.
5. Knowledge work requires continuous learning on the part of the knowledge worker, but equally continuous teaching on the part of the knowledge worker. Productivity of the knowledge worker is not – at least not primarily – a matter of the quantity of output. Quality is at least as important.
6. Finally, knowledge-worker productivity requires that the knowledge worker is both seen and treated as an "asset" rather than a "cost." It requires that knowledge workers want to work for the organization in preference to all other opportunities. (pp. 83-84)

Many knowledge workers were part of the Great Resignation because these six factors were not met during the COVID-19 pandemic. Optimum quality is usually an essential functional goal of the knowledge-worker and Drucker (1999) suggested the need to define that quality. Learning to value the five values of the employees will help organization leaders to define their employees' functional qualities.

Swanson (2007) defined Human Resource Development (HRD) as "a process of developing and unleashing human expertise through training and development and organization development for the purpose of improving performance" (p.331). He proposed that HRD is a process, "not profession or organizational function; the notion of human expertise, not just knowledge; the notion of systems/organization, not just individuals; and the notion of performance as a purpose that is of value to both the organization and the individual" (p. 331). Individuals perceive that because they are paying for something, they will receive value; this may or may not be true (Hughes, 2012). The assumption that you get what you pay for is not always true when dealing with unethical humans who have knowledge but lack expertise; unethical systems or organizations that are designed to deceive; and performance that is lackluster as opposed to optimal when the capability for optimal performance exists. This is why the ethics rug is a part of Swanson's (2001) theory of HRD; to undergird all HRD functions so that HRD scholars, professionals, and practitioners will consider the ethics of all of their actions. Once an employee has been trained and is knowledgeable, that knowledge must be managed effectively. However, Ernst and Young's Center for Business Intelligence identified the following four difficulties that create challenges to leaders who are seeking to effectively managing knowledge within corporations: Changing people's behavior; measuring the value and performance of knowledge assets; determining what knowledge should be managed; and justifying the use of scarce resources for knowledge initiatives (Bassi et al.,1998). These challenges are common because people control and change their own behavior. Employees must be active participants in the change process for change to be successful, and employees should be provided appropriate feedback, rewards, and/or incentives to continuously progress. One key question becomes: Where does training end and the employee's application of knowledge and accountability for his actions and behavior begin?

As organizations continue to grow, all employees must be trained and developed for an organization's survival. Some learning technologies directly generate revenue and organizations are still learning how to integrate and effectively manage these technologies (Argote & Hora, 2017; Lee & Lan, 2007; Morkunas et al., 2019). Determining which technologies are useful to an individual and/or organization must be done with care. Consideration of organization strategy and providing the knowledge and skills to meet employee demands has to be done without sacrificing quality of the learning or knowledge required. The challenge and opportunities for achieving these objectives are as near as the Internet or as far away as an organization that is unwilling to invest in the necessary tools and resources for achieving its goal (Hughes, 2012). These organizations were revealed during the COVID-19 pandemic and many of them were K-12 school districts and colleges and universities in the US. Many restaurants that could not adjust to delivery options were also adversely affected. Companies such as Lyft, Uber, DoorDash, Amazon, Wal-Mart, Zoom, etc. thrived or saw very little or no disruptions. Many were able to rapidly adapt to required changes.

Although, there is a myriad of useful information available to organizations for people development, it is critical that the information be relevant for each specific organization. How value is defined determines whether it is received. Carrig and Wright (2006) suggested that every organization "needs to prioritize its own outcomes" (p. 20) and suggested in their Value-Profit Chain (VPC) model that a firm should have core capabilities consisting of people, technology, and processes. They defined "core capability as a group of people using a particular technology (or technologies) in a set of business processes to create a set of valued customer outcomes" (p. 21). They opined that organization

success cannot be achieved by just bringing in really good people but not equipping them with technology or processes" [and that] "even more it is even truer that technology and processes without people are without value. It is people who design and execute processes. It is people who design, work with, and leverage technology. (p. 21)

Pfeffer (1994) also noted that "If competitive success is achieved through people, then the skills of those people are critical" (p.16). In today's knowledge economy, employees are asked to learn to use continuously changing technology(ies). The time, money, and effort spent on research and development of new technology is forever increasing and a proportionally, equivalent amount of that time, money, and effort should be invested for developing employees.

Systems Theory in the Context of HRD

The four steps of the basic systems model are input, process, output, and organizational context (Jacobs, 2003; Swanson & Holton, 2009). In the context of HRD, Jacobs (2003) suggested that in the system model, inputs are the people involved, training location, the information be learned, and the technology used to deliver the information. He described the process as the training process which included preparing the training, delivering the information, and ensuring that the trainee had learned. He described the output as what happened after combining the inputs and the process. The organizational context is the environment within which the input, process, and output occurred. The system of training interacts with other organizational systems.

Table 1 provides examples of how the people as technology and systems theory interact within the context of the organization.

Table 1. Five Values and The Basic Systems Model

Five Values/ Desirable/ Undesirable Inputs	Processes/Ethical Behavior	Desirable Intended/ Expected Outputs	Undesirable, Unintended, or Unexpected Outputs
Location Value	Ethical environment that places employees on teams where they do not have to question whether they belong. Unethical environment	Increased team productivity and effectiveness	Low employee morale; Degradation of organizational systems can occur because of unethical actions.
Use Value	Is the job title genuine? Is the position power genuine? What value does the position provide to the organization? Does the individual in the powerful position have the actual power to add value to the organization or are they a figure head in a symbolic position?	Increased morale; effective, powerful leadership capability	
Maintenance Value	DQ	Leaders who are capable of leading all employees	
Modification Value	Employers have had to accept employee modifications during the COVID-19 pandemic. Conformity to the culture can be negative and make leaders valueless	Higher employee retention	Avoidance of quiet quitting because employers do not always know when an employee has stopped going beyond performance standards
Time Value	1. Listening to learn the needs of people for the effective employee development. 2. Vacation time 3. Time on the job 4. Productivity diminishes after a certain amount of time on the job (hours); 8 hours versus 12 hours; 3–4-day work weeks	Reduce errors; Improve performance; Identify problems; Communicate needs; Execute strategy; Reduce loss time; Learn from the employees to help them; Test for understanding	

Issues, Controversies, Problems

What does this mean when the knowledge of the individual knowledge worker becomes an asset – and, in more and more cases, the main asset – of an institution? What does this mean for personnel policy? What is needed to attract and to hold the highest producing knowledge workers? What is needed to increase their productivity and to convert their increased productivity into performance capacity for the organization? (Drucker, 1999, p. 88)

Drucker's questions are even more important to answer for workplaces in the fourth industrial revolution and the PT concept can help. The PT concept was created using practical efforts to help organizations implement employee development and productivity projects through the optimal use of available resources and services. The PT concept has been used to help develop people, improve processes, better utilize equipment/technology, expand communication, and enhance career development.

Organizations seek and many thrive on their abilities to be innovating and at the cutting edge of research to meet consumer demands. They seek ways to motivate their employees to be innovative within their work. Davis and North (1970) developed an institutional theory model where the motivation for innovation was rooted in financial concepts and identified three exogenous change agents that potentially put institutional innovation at risk. They were:

1. Potential income from arrangemental innovation might increase because some exogenous change could lead to the emergence of an externality where none existed before, to a restructuring of risks, to a shift in transaction costs, or to the application of a new technology subject to increasing returns.
2. The costs of organizing and/or operating a new institution might change because of the invention of a new arrangemental technology, of institutional change in the non-economic sector, or because the price of the factors used in the new or in competing existing institutions may change.
3. Some legal or political change might alter the economic environment and make it possible for some group to effect a redistribution or take advantage of an existing external profit opportunity. (p. 139)

As cost and organizational leverage factors change or become at risk due to innovation, HRD can become a risk-mitigating factor because HRD manages human capital risk (Bhattacharya & Wright, 2005). HRD in an organization may be tasked with change management and assisting with the acceptance of change strategies. It may assist the organization in learning new technologies or ways of behaving with technologies. HRD may also aid in mitigating external risks from political or legal pressure by helping the organization comply with legal or political mandates (Hughes, 2016, 2019).

Solutions and Recommendations

Organizations should communicate, throughout the organization, that there are strong alliances between people and technology. Consider the strong alliance between the two during the COVID-19 pandemic. Table 2 shows how technology development as identified by Maidique and Hayes (1984) and people development as defined by Drucker (1999) overlap with the five values of people and technology development. They each have elements of location, use, maintenance, modification, and time value.

FUTURE RESEARCH DIRECTIONS

Research analysis of the items in Table 2 will help organizations strengthen their focus on people and technology development and value the elements of both. Without both during the COVID-19 pandemic, some organizations and their employees were left behind. The PT concept continues to provide positive implications for organizational growth and development. Research can be conducted on leaders who recognize similarities and differences between people and technology development and are willing to leverage these similarities and differences. An examination of organizations' ethical communication strategies could also be conducted to learn how organizations succeed through its people with technology.

CONCLUSION

Organizations must continue to evolve during and after the COVID-19 pandemic to meet customer needs within the global economy. They need knowledge workers and superior technology to outperform competitors. Organizations with superior technology have and will continue to outpace other organizations especially if they continue to innovate new, applicable, and relevant technologies. Organizations are seeking the best technology and the best people wherever in the world that they can find either. All facets of the individual's knowledge base must be used to succeed. Today, the

Table 2. Comparing the five values of people and technology development to six themes of high technology development, the six major factors to determine knowledge-worker productivity, and the COVID-19 pandemic

Hughes (2011) Five Values of People and Technology Development	*Maidique & Hayes (1984) Six Themes of High Technology Development*	*Drucker (1999, pp. 83-84)) Six Major Factors to Determine Knowledge-worker Productivity*	*COVID-19 Pandemic*
Location and Use	Business Focus	Knowledge-worker productivity demands that we ask the question: *"What is the task?"*	Essentials tasks were identified during lockdowns. Work that had to be done and could be done from home became the identified tasks.
Modification	Adaptability	It demands that we impose the responsibility for their productivity on the individual knowledge workers themselves. Knowledge workers must manage themselves. They must have autonomy.	Workers who worked from home were responsible for their own productivity. They were at times monitored electronically, but they had to have the autonomy to do their work and manage themselves.
Location	Organizational cohesion	Continuing innovation must be part of the work, the task, and the responsibility of knowledge workers.	These workers were innovative in their transition from the office to home. Many workers quit to become entrepreneurs because of what they learned during forced pandemic disruptions.
Use, Modification, Maintenance	Entrepreneurial culture	Knowledge work requires continuous learning on the part of the knowledge worker, but equally continuous teaching on the part of the knowledge worker.	These workers learned new technologies and ways of doing things to adapt to changes required during the pandemic. They taught themselves and their peers continuously.
Use and Time	Sense of Integrity	Productivity of the knowledge worker is not – at least not primarily – a matter of the quantity of output. Quality is at least as important.	The quality of work increased along with the output of work produced. Working from home within all the various constraints of being at home required innovative ways to produce the required outputs.
Location	"Hands-on" Top Management	Finally, knowledge-worker productivity requires that the knowledge worker is both seen and treated as an "asset" rather than a "cost." It requires that knowledge workers want to work for the organization in preference to all other opportunities.	The pandemic forced organization leaders to see their knowledge workers as assets. In fact, some costs were reduced because these workers could work from home and the organization no longer needed as much office space. The Great Resignation and Quiet Quitting revealed which knowledge workers wanted to work for their organizations in preference to all other opportunities.

projected top job is Information Security Analyst. This job is critical because of cybersecurity concerns. As America seeks to create jobs, traditional fields of study and ways of studying are becoming obsolete. Online education and training were the wave of the future and self-directed learning (Caffarella, 1993; Garrison, 1997; Karakas & Manisaligil, 2012; Rana et al., 2016) was becoming the norm. Being static and resistant to change will cause organizations and employees to be left behind. Those who chose not to adapt to online learning and training were left behind and are still scrambling to adjust during the worldwide, COVID-19 pandemic.

COVID-19 ETHICAL IMPACT MINI CASE STUDY

Some of the ethical impacts of COVID-19 are provided in Table 2., but COVID-19 also impacted many of the world's children who were left behind due to the lack of access to online education during the COVID-19 pandemic. They did not have the broadband infrastructure nor the technology tools and systems to access their education. Many working women were being left behind because of work life unbalance. They could not take care of their children's education and work from home. Many employees were left behind because their work was deemed nonessential (Hughes, 2021) and training professionals and practitioners were unskilled in the ability to use training technologies, as were the trainees. Some questions for further discussion are:

1. In what way(s) is it ethical to leave children uneducated because they lack technological resources and broadband access?
2. In what way(s) is it unethical to leave women out of workplace advancement opportunities because of limitations that they faced as an impact of COVID-19?

REFERENCES

Abdeen, A. M., & Haight, G. T. (2002). A fresh look at economic value added: Empirical study of the fortune five-hundred companies. [JABR]. *Journal of Applied Business Research*, *18*(2), 27–36.

Acemoglu, D., & Restrepo, P. (2019). Automation and new tasks: How technology displaces and reinstates labor. *The Journal of Economic Perspectives*, *33*(2), 3–30. doi:10.1257/jep.33.2.3

Agrawal, S., De Smet, A., Lacroix, S., & Reich, A. (2020). *To emerge stronger from the COVID-19 crisis, companies should start reskilling their workforces now. McKinsey Insights*. Issue May.

Amankwah-Amoah, J., Khan, Z., & Wood, G. (2021). COVID-19 and business failures: The paradoxes of experience, scale, and scope for theory and practice. *European Management Journal*, *39*(2), 179–184. doi:10.1016/j.emj.2020.09.002

Argote, L., & Hora, M. (2017). Organizational learning and management of technology. *Production and Operations Management*, *26*(4), 579–590. doi:10.1111/poms.12667

Arora, A., & Gambardella, A. (2005). The globalization of the software industry: Perspectives and opportunities for developed and developing countries. *Innovation Policy and the Economy*, *5*, 1–32. doi:10.1086/ipe.5.25056169

Bassi, L., Cheney, S., & Lewis, E. (1998). Trends in workplace learning: Supply and demand in interesting times. *Training & Development*, *52*(11), 51–75.

Betz, F. (1993). *Strategic technology management*. McGraw-Hill.

Bhattacharya, M., & Wright, P. M. (2005). Managing human assets in an uncertain world: Applying real world options theory to HRM. *International Journal of Human Resource Management*, *16*(6), 929–948. doi:10.1080/09585190500120574

Caffarella, R. S. (1993). Self-directed learning. *New Directions for Adult and Continuing Education*, *1993*(57), 25–35. doi:10.1002/ace.36719935705

Carrig, K., & Wright, P. M. (2006). *Building profit through building people: Making your work force the strongest link in the value-profit chain*. Society for Human Resource Management.

Chen, S., & Dodd, J. L. (1997). Economic value added (EVA™): An empirical examination of a new corporate performance measure. *Journal of Managerial Issues*, *9*(3), 318–333.

Cheng, L., Varshney, K. R., & Liu, H. (2021). Socially responsible ai algorithms: Issues, purposes, and challenges. *Journal of Artificial Intelligence Research*, *71*, 1137–1181. doi:10.1613/jair.1.12814

Cimarolli, V. R., Bryant, N. S., Falzarano, F., & Stone, R. (2022). Job resignation in nursing homes during the COVID-19 pandemic: The role of quality of employer communication. *Journal of Applied Gerontology*, *41*(1), 12–21. doi:10.1177/07334648211040509 PMID:34428936

Davis, L., & North, D. (1970). Institutional change and American economic growth: A first step to-wards a theory of institutional innovation. *The Journal of Economic History*, *30*(1), 131–149. doi:10.1017/S0022050700078633

Donahoe, E., & Metzger, M. M. (2019). Artificial intelligence and human rights. *Journal of Democracy*, *30*(2), 115–126. doi:10.1353/jod.2019.0029

Drucker, P. F. (1999). Knowledge-worker productivity: The biggest challenge. *California Management Review*, *41*(2), 79–94. doi:10.2307/41165987

Fenwick, T. (2008). Workplace learning: Emerging trends and new perspectives. *New Directions for Adult and Continuing Education*, *2008*(119), 17–26. doi:10.1002/ace.302

Floridi, L., & Chiriatti, M. (2020). GPT-3: Its nature, scope, limits, and consequences. *Minds and Machines*, *30*(4), 681–694. doi:10.100711023-020-09548-1

Gale, B. T. (1980). Can more capital buy higher productivity? *Harvard Business Review*, *58*(4), 78–86.

Garrison, D. R. (1997). Self-directed learning: Toward a comprehensive model. *Adult Education Quarterly*, *48*(1), 18–33. doi:10.1177/074171369704800103

Garvin, D. (1993). Building a learning organization. *Harvard Business Review*, *71*(4), 78–91. PMID:10127041

Garvin, D. A., Edmondson, A. C., & Gino, F. (2008). Is yours a learning organization? *Harvard Business Review*, *86*(3), 109–134. PMID:18411968

Githens, R. P., Dirani, K., Gitonga, J., & Teng, Y. T. (2008). Technology-related research in HRD publications: An analysis of content and metaperspectives from 2000 to 2006. *Human Resource Development Quarterly*, *19*(3), 191–215. doi:10.1002/hrdq.1236

Gordon, J. S. (2020). Building moral robots: Ethical pitfalls and challenges. *Science and Engineering Ethics*, *26*(1), 141–157. doi:10.100711948-019-00084-5 PMID:30701408

Griego, O. V., Geroy, G. D., & Wright, P. C. (2000). Predictors of learning organizations: A human resource development practitioner's perspective. *The Learning Organization*, *7*(1), 5–12. doi:10.1108/09696470010313632

Henriksen, A., & Bechmann, A. (2020). Building truths in AI: Making predictive algorithms doable in healthcare. *Information Communication and Society*, *23*(6), 802–816. doi:10.1080/1369118X.2020.1751866

Hollis, E. (2003). Southwest Airlines: Employee education takes flight. *Chief Learning Officer Magazine, 3*.

Hounshell, D. A. (1984). *From the American system to mass production, 1800-1932: The development of manufacturing technology in the United States*. Johns Hopkins University Press. doi:10.56021/9780801829758

Howe, D. C., Chauhan, R. S., Soderberg, A. T., & Buckley, M. R. (2021). Paradigm shifts caused by the COVID-19 pandemic. *Organizational Dynamics*, *50*(4), 100804. doi:10.1016/j.orgdyn.2020.100804 PMID:33191959

Hughes, C. (2010). "People as technology" conceptual model: Towards a new value creation paradigm for strategic human resource development. *Human Resource Development Review*, *9*(1), 48–71. doi:10.1177/1534484309353561

Hughes, C. (2012). *Valuing people and technology in the workplace: A competitive advantage framework*. IGI Global. doi:10.4018/978-1-4666-0240-3

Hughes, C. (2016). *Diversity intelligence: Integrating diversity intelligence alongside intellectual, emotional, and cultural intelligence for leadership and career development*. Palgrave MacMillan Publications. doi:10.1057/978-1-137-52683-0

Hughes, C. (2019). *Ethical and legal issues in human resource development: Evolving roles and emerging trends*. Springer International Publishing. doi:10.1007/978-3-319-99528-1

Hughes, C. (2021). The changing learning technological landscape for trainers in the wake of COVID-19. *Advances in Developing Human Resources*, *23*(1), 66–74. doi:10.1177/1523422320972108

Hughes, C., & Niu, Y. (Eds.). (. (2021). How COVID-19 is shifting career reality: Ways to navigate career journeys. *Advances in Developing Human Resources*, *23*(3). doi:10.1177/15234223211017847

Huysman, M. (2000). An organizational learning approach to the learning organization. *European Journal of Work and Organizational Psychology*, *9*(2), 133–145. doi:10.1080/135943200397905

Jacobs, R. L. (2003). *Structured on-the-job training: Unleashing employee expertise in the Workplace* (2nd ed.). Berrett-Koehler.

Jasson, C. C., & Govender, C. M. (2017). Measuring return on investment and risk in training– A business training evaluation model for managers and leaders. *Acta Commercii*, *17*(1), 1–9. doi:10.4102/ac.v17i1.401

Kajjumba, G. W., Nagitta, O. P., Osra, F. A., & Mkansi, M. (2020). Offshoring-outsourcing and onshoring tradeoffs: The impact of coronavirus on global supply chain. In *Outsourcing and offshoring*. IntechOpen. doi:10.5772/intechopen.95281

Kalimeri, K., & Tjostheim, I. (2020, July). Artificial intelligence and concerns about the future: A case study in Norway. In *International Conference on Human-Computer Interaction* (pp. 273-284). Springer. 10.1007/978-3-030-50344-4_20

Karakas, F., & Manisaligil, A. (2012). Reorienting self-directed learning for the creative digital era. *European Journal of Training and Development*, *36*(7), 712–731. doi:10.1108/03090591211255557

Kim, P. T. (2018). Big Data and artificial intelligence: New challenges for workplace equality. *University of Louisville Law Review*, *57*, 313–328.

Kincheloe, J. (1999). *How do we tell the workers? The socioeconomic foundations of work and vocational education*. Westview Press.

Kontoghiorghes, C., Awbre, S. M., & Feurig, P. L. (2005). Examining the relationship between learning organization characteristics and change adaptation, innovation, and organizational performance. *Human Resource Development Quarterly*, *16*(2), 185–212. doi:10.1002/hrdq.1133

Kuchinke, K. P. (1995). Managing learning for performance. *Human Resource Development Quarterly*, *6*(3), 307–316. doi:10.1002/hrdq.3920060309

Lang, M., Bernier, A., & Knoppers, B. M. (2021). AI in cardiovascular imaging: "Unexplainable" legal and ethical challenges? *The Canadian Journal of Cardiology, 38*(2), 225–233. doi:10.1016/j.cjca.2021.10.009 PMID:34737036

Lee, M. R., & Lan, Y. (2007). From Web 2.0 to conversational knowledge management: Towards collaborative intelligence. *Journal of Entrepreneurship Research, 2*(2), 47–62.

Liu, Z. R. (2014). Perspectives on organizational learning and learning organization. *Applied Mechanics and Materials, 644*(650), 5917–5920. doi:10.4028/www.scientific.net/AMM.644-650.5917

London, M., & Diamante, T. (2002). Technology-focused expansive professionals: Developing continuous learning in the high-technology sector. *Human Resource Development Review, 1*(4), 500–524. doi:10.1177/1534484302238438

Luhn, A. (2016). The learning organization. *Creative and Knowledge Society, 6*(1), 1–13. doi:10.1515/cks-2016-0005

Lund, B. D., & Wang, T. (2023). Chatting about ChatGPT: How may AI and GPT impact academia and libraries? *Library Hi Tech News, 1-4.* doi:10.1108/LHTN-01-2023-0009

Maidique, M. A., & Hayes, R. H. (1984). The art of high-technology management. *Sloan Management Review, 25*(2), 17–31.

Marsick, V. J., & Watkins, K. E. (1994). The learning organization: An integrative vision for HRD. *Human Resource Development Quarterly, 5*(4), 353–360. doi:10.1002/hrdq.3920050406

McWhorter, R. R. (2014). A synthesis of new perspectives on Virtual HRD. *Advances in Developing Human Resources, 16*(3), 391–401. doi:10.1177/1523422314532126

Morkunas, V. J., Paschen, J., & Boon, E. (2019). How blockchain technologies impact your business model. *Business Horizons, 62*(3), 295–306. doi:10.1016/j.bushor.2019.01.009

Müller, V. C. (2020). Ethics of artificial intelligence and robotics. In E. N. Zalta (Ed.), *The Stanford encyclopedia of philosophy.*

Mutamba, C. (2017). The inter-relationship of organizational learning, learning organizations, virtual technology, and virtual communities of practice. *New Horizons in Adult Education and Human Resource Development*, *29*(3), 4–14. doi:10.1002/nha3.20186

Newbold, C., & Pharoah, N. (2009). What it means to be a learning organization. *Strategic HR Review*, *8*(3), 12–16. doi:10.1108/14754390910946521

Odor, H. O. (2018). A literature review on organizational learning and learning organizations. *International Journal of Economics & Management Sciences*, *7*(1), 1–6. doi:10.4172/2162-6359.1000494

Oh, E. G., & Huang, W. D. (2018). A review of technology research in HRD from design-based research perspective. *Human Resource Development Review*, *17*(3), 258–276. doi:10.1177/1534484318784798

Örtenblad, A. (2018). What does "learning organization" mean? *The Learning Organization*, *25*(3), 150–158. doi:10.1108/TLO-02-2018-0016

Park, S., Jeong, S., & Chai, D. S. (2021). Remote e-workers' psychological well-being and career development in the era of COVID-19: Challenges, success factors, and the roles of HRD professionals. *Advances in Developing Human Resources*, *23*(3), 222–236. doi:10.1177/15234223211017849

Pfeffer, J. (1994). *Competitive advantage through people: Unleashing the power of the workforce.* Harvard Business School Press. doi:10.2307/41165742

Phillips, J. J. (2003). *Return on investment in training and performance improvement programs* (2nd ed.). Elsevier Science.

Ramsey, M. (1986). *The super supervisor*. Positive Presentations, Inc.

Rana, S., Ardichvili, A., & Polesello, D. (2016). Promoting self-directed learning in a learning organization: Tools and practices. *European Journal of Training and Development*, *40*(7), 470–489. doi:10.1108/EJTD-10-2015-0076

Reich, R. B. (1992). The work of nations: Preparing ourselves for 21st century capitalism (Rev. ed.). Vintage Books.

Sabol, A., & Sverer, F. (2017). A review of the economic value-added literature and application. *UTMS Journal of Economics (Skopje)*, *8*(1), 19–27.

Senge, P. M. (1990). *The fifth discipline: the art and practice of the learning organizations*. Doubleday.

Servan-Schreiber. J.-J. (1967). The American challenge. Atheneum Publishers.

Sharma, A. K., & Kumar, S. (2010). Economic value added (EVA)-literature review and relevant issues. *International Journal of Economics and Finance*, *2*(2), 200–220. doi:10.5539/ijef.v2n2p200

Short, D. C. (2013). Designing a 3D virtual HRD environment from a scholar-practitioner perspective. *Advances in Developing Human Resources*, *15*(3), 270–283. doi:10.1177/1523422313487838

Simonite, T. (2020). How decades of offshoring led to a mask shortage in a pandemic. *Wired*. https://www.wired.com/story/decades-offshoring-led-mask-shortage-pandemic/

Sun, H. C. (2003). Conceptual clarifications for 'organizational learning', 'learning organization' and 'a learning organization'. *Human Resource Development International*, *6*(2), 153–166. doi:10.1080/13678860110086465

Swanson, R. A. (2001). Human resource development and its underlying theory. *Human Resource Development International*, *4*(3), 299–312. doi:10.1080/13678860110059311

Swanson, R. A. (2007). Theory framework for applied disciplines: Boundaries, contributing, core, useful, novel, and irrelevant components. *Human Resource Development Review*, *6*(3), 321–339. doi:10.1177/1534484307303770

Swanson, R. A., & Holton, E. F. III. (2009). *Foundations of human resource development* (2nd ed.). Berrett-Koehler Publishers, Inc.

Thoben, K. D., Wiesner, S., & Wuest, T. (2017). "Industrie 4.0" and smart manufacturing-a review of research issues and application examples. *International Journal of Automotive Technology*, *11*(1), 4–16. doi:10.20965/ijat.2017.p0004

Upadhyay, A. K., & Khandelwal, K. (2019). Artificial intelligence-based training learning from application. *Development and Learning in Organizations*, *33*(2), 20–23. doi:10.1108/DLO-05-2018-0058

van Hoek, R., & Dobrzykowski, D. (2021). Towards more balanced sourcing strategies–are supply chain risks caused by the COVID-19 pandemic driving reshoring considerations? *Supply Chain Management*, *26*(6), 689–701. doi:10.1108/SCM-09-2020-0498

Wang, G. G., Dou, Z., & Li, N. (2002). A systems approach to measuring return on investment for HRD interventions. *Human Resource Development Quarterly*, *13*(2), 203–224. doi:10.1002/hrdq.1024

Wang, M. (2011). Integrating organizational, social, and individual perspectives in Web 2.0-based workplace e-learning. *Information Systems Frontiers*, *13*(2), 191–205. doi:10.100710796-009-9191-y

Welch, J. (2005). *Winning*. Collins.

Chapter 6
Diversity Intelligence® and Workforce Inter-Personnel Diversity

ABSTRACT

Chapter six discusses workers' characteristics that influence their location, use, maintenance, modification, and time value. Organization leaders should be able to recognize and leverage each employee's strengths using diversity intelligence® (DQ). Once leaders are diversity intelligent, they will then be capable of understanding the organizations' workforce inter-personnel diversity which looks at the differences of each individual employee. They will also be able to use workforce inter-personnel diversity as a talent management strategy tool.

INTRODUCTION

Historically, all individuals in the workplace have not been perceived to be as valuable as others. Organizational leaders are encouraged to acknowledge and understand all employees and use that knowledge to enhance and improve organizational performance (Hughes & Stephens, 2012). However, this does not occur as often as one would like. Some leaders made choices that tended to exclude some employees which led to the creation of Affirmative Action (AA) policies, protected class laws, and the creation of the Equal Employment Opportunity Commission (EEOC).

DOI: 10.4018/978-1-6684-5321-6.ch006

No worker is the same and the differences necessitates finding a "fit" between organizational and employee goals ((Becker et al., 2009; Baird & Meshoulam, 1988; Delery, 1998; Wright & McMahan, 1992; Vroom, 1973). Boudreaux (2001) suggested that career development focuses "on the alignment of individual subjective career aspects and the more objective career aspects of the organizations in order to achieve the best fit between individual and organizational needs as well as personal characteristics and career roles" (p. 806). His statement suggests that leaders should find ways to understand the personal characteristics of workers. Hughes's (2010) five values is one way that leaders can begin to better understand the personal characteristics of the employees. Both the employees and organization leaders can benefit from understanding the five values. The employees include diverse employees who have not been previously considered mainstream (Avery, 2011).

The objectives of this chapter are to help organization leaders: 1) determine ways that employees' diversity influences career development; 2) explore the intersection of Hughes's (2010) five values and workplace inter-personnel diversity; and 3) suggest ways that leaders can understand diversity intelligence™ (DQ) to become diversity intelligent.

BACKGROUND

The power and structure inside organizations influences the organization's diversity and diversity efforts (Burkhardt & Brass, 1990; Brass & Burkhardt, 1993; Pfeffer, 1994). The valuation an organization places on diversity is connected to the organization's development of the career development plans for its employees (Pitts, 2006). Organization policies that encourage diversity and career development make the organization desirable for all workers, especially women and minorities, to remain in the organization (Pitts, 2006).

Avery (2011) suggested that "prioritizing diversity throughout organizational human-resource management practices" (p. 251) unlocks diversity's potential inside the organization. He also noted that

Through their human-resource management policies and procedures, organizations have a considerable impact on the diversity climates they facilitate and the employees they attract and retain. If they wish to encourage employee diversity activism, it is imperative that they take steps to ensure that the climates, supervisors, and coworkers employees routinely encounter convey that diversity is valued and supported. (p. 252)

These suggestions could extend to all leaders within organizations as it relates to providing career development, training and development, and other developmental opportunities for employees. Organizations should provide a supportive climate, supervisors, and coworkers for diverse employees to feel comfortable interacting with mentors (Bingham et al., 2005; Thomas, 2008). As employees compete for jobs, they are competing against low wage, high skilled workers throughout the world (Friedman & Mandelbaum, 2011) and should not feel restricted by lack of development from their organization simply because they are different.

DIVERSITY INTELLIGENCE® (DQ)

Without the leaders' ability to understand diversity intelligence® (DQ), they cannot effectively recognize the five values of their employees. As I began to think about the different ways to measure each individual employee, I realized that something was missing. I kept asking myself, how can leaders value each individual person in the workplace if they do not see each individual person in the workplace? Or how can leaders value each individual employee if they are marginalizing some of their employees? These questions gave me pause as I attempted to expand on the constructs of the people as technology (PT) model and the use the *Hughes HRD Value Creation Model for Competitive Advantage.* I realized that there was no way that leaders could really and truly value every employee in the workplace if they did not see all of them. At that point, I began to think of a way to help leaders see all their employees. At the same time there was constant, unrelenting conversations about diversity in the workplace all around me. As I began to read some of the work on diversity and think about the impact of diversity in the workplace and all the failures of diversity in the workplace as noted by Department of Labor settlements, class action lawsuits, and EEOC filings and settlements. I began to ask; how can this be when there is so much diversity training going on inside organizations.? The failings could only be attributed to leadership failures. This is true because leadership knows that there have been federal laws and mandates since 1964 in American workplaces that requires protection of protected class employees and categories. Therefore, if those laws are being followed, why are there so many complaints? I made the presumption that the leaders could not truly know who their protected class employees were or the laws, mandates, and categories that they are required to know to lead and treat their employees fairly. It was either that or leaders are willfully neglecting and violating the laws and mandates.

At that point I conducted a research study to see if leaders knew the protected class laws and mandates. The results revealed that leaders did not know the laws and mandates and these leaders were at all different levels in the workplace. So, how do we resolve this problem? My solution was the development of the diversity intelligence™ theory and scale. Once I thought of the idea of DQ, the problem became proving it as a theoretical construct or concept. So, I spent the last eight years developing and proving this construct of DQ. The definition of DQ is "the capability of individuals to recognize the value of workplace diversity and to use this information to guide thinking and behavior" (Hughes & Brown, 2018, p. 264). When I wrote this definition in 2018, I did not realize that I had basically, defined DQ in 2012. Elements of the definition DQ is found throughout book (Hughes, 2012).

Many people see DQ as just compliance and DQ does involve compliance, but it involves compliance that organization leaders should have already been doing since 1964. DQ goes beyond compliance and includes the knowledge and education of leaders and the behaviors of leaders. Since there has been so much pushback against DQ and a lack of understanding of how to measure leaders' behavior towards protected class groups in the workplace, I created a DQ assessment to measure their behavior. The content of the tool came from the research study results. The fact that there is a DQ assessment, and the DQ assessment has been validated using confirmatory and exploratory factor analysis from responses of to over 1,300 leaders is a major accomplishment. With DQ, leaders can now see each individual employee and began to measure the five values. They can no longer ignore any employee in the workplace. Now that it has been proven and validated with the DQ assessment that leaders can see each individual person in the workplace, leaders no longer have an excuse for not recognizing the value of each individual employee that they lead in the workplace. The *Hughes HRD Value Creation Model* with the Workforce Inter-personnel Diversity Talent Management system can be used to bridge the gap between people and technology in the workplace and help organizations accomplish talent management goals. Leaders that are diversity intelligent or become diversity intelligent can:

1. Implement and practice workforce inter-personnel diversity as a talent management system.
2. Lead and protect each individual employee within the right location on the job.

3. Assist employees with utilizing all of their use value that is applicable to the job performance of the employee.
4. Help employees maintain their levels of knowledge and training needed to accomplish tasks on the job
5. Recognize and accept that employees will modify themselves and will grow and change; they will enhance who they are personally.
6. Recognize that the time value of an employee, especially protected class employees, are vital to their survival in society. When you have a workplace system that is built on promotion and advancement from the perspective that time equals money or the lack of money because leaders choose not to recognize the employees, it becomes vital for leaders to be diversity intelligent. Diversity unintelligent leaders do not pay their employees and because they do not pay them, they cannot survive in society.

Diversity unintelligent leaders do a disservice to employees, their organization, and society because they do not recognize, value, and reward their employees. They, instead, choose to discriminate because they lack DQ and do not seek to improve it.

Organizations who truly want the best from their employees and to improve the employee experiences at work must insist that their leaders become diversity intelligent. Organizations who do not compel their leaders to be diversity intelligent can look forward to issues competing worldwide. They brand their organizations as diversity inclusive; but this mantra will ring hollow to people who are diversity intelligent and know the difference. Many people do not know the difference; they just see the diversity platitudes, slogans, and symbols but the workers inside the organizations do not feel that they are being treated fairly. A lot of them have become a part of the Great Resignation and are taking their power back from their organization and giving it to unions. I am not saying that all workers are mistreated. I am saying that you can use turnover numbers to be sure that none of your workers are mistreated by becoming a diversity intelligent organization. It is simple to fix issues related to diversity. It is just that the organization must have the will to do what is necessary to accomplish this. The number one thing they can do is stop allowing leaders who choose not to be diversity intelligent to lead employees in the workplace. They do it all the time after lawsuits and settlements. They fire that leader, or they make a change in leadership. Why wait, when you know that there are issues inside your organization?

Diversifying Employees' Career Development Opportunities

The Global Recession of 2007 shed light on the limitations of the career development plans and strategies of organizations. Widespread, uncontrollable layoffs revealed that many organizations and employees had no career strategy or career plan for successful transitioning or adaptation to the rapid changes (Friedman & Mandelbaum, 2011). Some organizations still did not have plans when the COVID-19 pandemic began.

Organizations are learning that they should expand beyond typical career development models and understand how the diversity of employees can influence their career strategies throughout their careers (Banks, 2006). Unplanned disruptions on the careers of diverse employees are much more strident than white males. The impact of the COVID-19 pandemic on womens' careers was exponentially different than those of men and the impact on white women was exponentially different than that of Black women. Employees usually move from job to job seeking a career because they usually have no career plan (Banks, 2006; Hayes, 2000; Hughes, 2012; Karsten & Igou, 2005). The impact of the COVID-19 pandemic revealed the lack of career plans for many employees. Employees during the COVID-19 pandemic were entering, re-entering, and transitioning within the workplace because of the shifting nature of career planning (Hayes, 2000; Hughes & Niu, 2021; Karsten & Igou, 2005). They were adapting to the rapidly changing nature of the impacts of the COVID-19 pandemic. The organization's culture must be accepting of diversity and career development (Avery, 2011; Deal & Kennedy, 1984). Organizations must do their part to educate their leaders to recognize and value the diversity of their workforce.

Five Values and Differences of Employees

There are differences amongst employee characteristics that can be clearly seen using the five values. Using the five values allows leaders to see all employee differences without discrimination and/or stereotyping. Employees want to be seen and valued for who they are and what they can do.

Location Value

The location value (Hughes, 2010, 2012) is partially explained through employee placement within organizations (Banks, 2006; Banks & Nafukho, 2008, Holland, 1973; Kaye, 1997, Schein, 1975, Super, 2002; Vardi, 1980; Vroom & MacCrimmon, 1968). Employees provide both internal and external location value and "organizations develop rules or policies that impose some control over personnel movements, such as retirement at 65, promotion from within, giving new college graduates a variety of training assignments before assigning them to positions of responsibility and so on" (Vroom & MacCrimmon, 1968, p. 28). Employees' location value (Hughes, 2010) provides the organization leaders access to the diversity of talent. Recognition of the strengths and weaknesses of employees' location value enables organization leaders the opportunity to use the KSAs of all employees (Hughes & Stephens, 2012). Location value not only relies on an employee's capability but also on the organization's capability to appreciate employees' contributions. Organizational capability depends on the contributions of all workers else why are they employed. Whether essential or non-essential, they are all workers who are contributing something to and receiving compensation from the organization. Not using all the KSAs of all employees is detrimental to organizations achieving all of its capacity (Danquah et al, 2023).

Use Value

Employees' actions should translate into measurable performance (Kerno & Kuznia, 2007). detailed performance criteria should be equal to employees' use value (Hughes, 2010) when all employees are contributing their KSAs they are providing use value. Diverse employees contribute to productivity, competitive advantage, and long-term performance strategy of organizations.

When workers change jobs, organization leaders and employees realize employees' true use value. The explosion of entrepreneurial activity during the COVID-19 pandemic supports this assertion. Employees used the time to assess their work values against their family and our health values. Making life versus potential death decisions inspired many employees to make job and career changes. Employees' use value contributes directly to the transformative power of workplace diversity.

Maintenance Value

Employee maintenance value includes training and development, motivation, and health and wellness. Leaders who recognize the diversity of employees performing the same job also understand that all employees do not need the same on-the-job training at the same time. These leaders have the option to use Just- In-Time (JIT) training to meet the varied needs of individual employees and measure and document employees' success. To increase or maintain the motivation levels of employees, employers must begin to recognize and reward differences.

Modification Value

Viable organizations should always have employees who are growing and changing and adding to the diversity of the organization's strengths. Without growth and change employees and organizations can become stagnant. If an organization becomes stagnant, it will most likely end its business operations. If an employee becomes stagnant, he will be replaced or may self-select from the workplace. Stagnation can also be a sign of quiet quitting by employees,

Time Value

Some employees perform tasks quicker and much better than other employees on the same job; yet some organization leaders expect employees to perform equal amount of work in the same number of hours for the same pay. This provides no motivation for the faster worker to perform more work which leads to quiet quitting. Time value includes the time an employee works, the length of time an employee remains with the organization, and how the employees' time contributes to the organization's success.

The five values provide criteria of assessment. Hughes (2012) suggested some questions leaders should consider when using the five values are:

1. Is the employee located on a job that best suits his use value to the organization?
2. Does the training and development provided to the employee align with the maintenance value of the employee?

3. As the modification value of the employee increases through the employee's own self-development, is the organization able to leverage the strengths of the employee to organizational goals?
4. As the time value of the employee increases, does the organization provide opportunities where they show the employee that his time is needed, valued, and treasured?

LEADERS' USE OF HUGHES'S FIVE VALUES TO MEET WORKFORCE DIVERSITY GOALS

Hughes's (2010) five values, when understood, allows for workforce diversity to enhance organizational performance. Leaders who use the five values will have the ability to objectively explain measurable differences between employees without discriminating against employees. If leaders do not discriminate in placement of employees on the right job, employees' location value will be accurate. If leaders do not discriminate against employees, they are most likely to have employees who will display their use value without inhibitions. If leaders do not discriminate against employees, employees are most likely to be included in all activities that support their maintenance and modification values. If leaders do not discriminate against employees, employees are more likely to come to work and provide time value that enhances the employees' job performance and contributes to organization success.

ISSUES, CONTROVERSIES, PROBLEMS

Unfair treatment of employees is seen through the Equal Employment Opportunities Commission (EEOC) and Department of Labor (DOL) settlements, the numerous lawsuits, and workplace disputes. Employees differ in their perception of whether they are treated fairly regardless of organizational systems and policies regarding procedural justice (Folger & Greenberg, 1985; Küçük, 2022). Some employees see disparity and unfairness when they observe organizations investing in new equipment/technology and not investing in employee development initiatives.

Organizations leaders need training in legal aspects of discrimination, but they should also be able to discern and document clear differences between employees from a positive perspective. Illegal discrimination addresses the negative perspective that organization leaders have and display towards some employees. Leaders do not empower employees by discriminating against them.

SOLUTIONS AND RECOMMENDATIONS

Using the five values will highlight for the employees that they are indeed different, not from a negative perspective but because of their positive contributions to the organization (Hughes, 2012). Negative treatment from leaders lessens motivation and contributes to low morale of employees (Gotsis & Grimani, 2016; Hughes & Brown, 2018). Leaders impact employee performance in so many positive and negative ways. Yet, little focus is placed on the negative implications of leaders and their unethical behavior towards employees. There is ample evidence about leaders who behave unethically and their effect on the well being of the business but not on their subordinates. Leaders' unethical, discriminatory behavior has been detrimental to many employees' careers; yet laws like Sarbanes Oxley have not been passed. Yes, the EEOC exists to help deter leaders from discriminating but many of the incidents never make it to the EEOC. The discriminatory incidents that do still have not deterred some leaders from continuing to discriminate against some protected class employees.

Evaluator Ability and Motivation to Provide Accurate Ratings

Some leaders have used the performance evaluation systems in organizations to discriminate against diverse employees (Gelfand et al., 2005; Shen et al., 2009; Triana et al., 2021). They do not provide accurate performance evaluations for many employees, but it occurs more often with diverse employees even though there is no reason for them not to provide accurate performance ratings for all employees. Campbell's (1990) theory of job performance three determinants for any component of job performance are declarative knowledge, procedural knowledge, and motivation. The first two determinants relate to employee ability and the third is motivation. Despite knowing these three determinants, evaluators do not do a very good job of providing accurate performance evaluations (Cleveland & Murphy, 1992; Murphy, 2008; Welch, 2005).

Banks and Murphy (1985) suggested that evaluators are unwilling to evaluate accurately. Murphy and Cleveland (1991) also stated that "Raters do not fail to give accurate ratings because they are incapable of accuracy but rather because they are unwilling to rate accurately" (p. 209). Evaluators' unwillingness to provide accurate performance appraisals centers upon their personal motivations (Harris, 1994) and the lack of being held accountable for their inaccurate evaluations. If there is nothing or no one holding them accountable for their actions, why should any of these evaluators change their behavior? Some evaluators would attribute their employees' low ratings to their own effectiveness as leaders (Harris, 1994: Murphy & Cleveland, 1991). The ethics of evaluators who fail to evaluate employees fairly have long-term implications for employee career success, pay, and longevity with the organization. Welch (2005) suggested the use of formative evaluations aimed at improving performance on a daily, weekly, or monthly. Conducting yearly evaluations provide little opportunity for employees to improve their performance (Banks, 2006). Regardless of the time frame for administering evaluations, evaluators must be ethical in their actions when conducting evaluations of their employees.

Researchers have evaluated and determined factors that affect the accuracy of performance evaluations (Arvey & Murphy, 1998; Bernardin & Buckley, 1981; Bernardin et al., 2000; Bernardin & Villanova, 1986; Mero & Motowidlo, 1995); however, the extent to which those factors improve evaluator accuracy is unknown. Two of the factors identified to influence evaluator accuracy were ability and motivation (Bernardin et al., 2000). "Performance appraisals are inaccurate because raters lack the motivation, lack the ability, or lack both, for doing accurate appraisals" (Personal communication, November 2005).

For motivation to exist there must be both positive outcomes and connection between behavior and the outcomes (Banks, 2002). Viswesvaran (2001) stated that "although a person's job performance depends on some combination of ability, motivation and situational constraints, it can be measured only in terms of some outcomes" (p. 114). Four factors that may influence evaluator ability are communication of policy, understanding of policy, frame of reference training, and time.

Communicating and Understanding Rating Policy

Cleveland and Murphy (1991) found that "organizations rarely reward good raters or punish bad ones" (p. 159) and stated that organizations "create conditions that motivate raters to provide accurate ratings when they can establish and implement a clear policy linking the quality of the rating data to rewards" (1992, p.172). The rating policy should be communicated to the evaluator. Cleveland and Murphy (1992) also suggested that rewards that are valued by the evaluator should be tied to rating behavior; negatively valued outcomes of accuracy must be reduced; and evaluators must see clear links between their rating behavior and valued outcomes. Organizations must also ensure that procedures that are likely to produce accurate ratings are articulated to and understood by the raters (Tziner et al., 2001; Murphy & Cleveland, 1992). Organizations should not ask evaluators to execute performance appraisals using unclear policies and procedures (Murphy and Cleveland, 1992).

Frame of Reference (FOR) Training

Bernardin and Buckley (1981) suggested that a common frame of reference for observing and rating be created to enhance rating accuracy. Day and Sulsky (1995) suggested the need for FOR training. Woehr and Huffcutt's (1994) found that FOR training led to the largest overall increase in rating accuracy and that FOR training is effective when raters are trained on a specific theory of performance. Bernardin et.al (2000) also believed that the "major transferring element of FOR training was experience with clearly defined and precise performance criteria and the use of these criteria as a context for the observation and subsequent rating of performance" (p. 268). Obtaining consistency and accuracy through training can only be effective if the evaluator has the ethical mindset, attitude, and desire to be accurate.

Time

Research has shown that "[p]erformance appraisal often occupies only a minimum of the busy supervisor's time" (Cleveland and Murphy, 1992, p.159). Viswesvaran (2001) also noted that "conscientious individuals are likely to spend more time on the task and less time daydreaming. This investment of time will result in greater acquisition of job knowledge, which in turn will result in greater productivity and which in turn will result in positive ratings" (p. 122). Supervisors believed that lack of time was a major reason for inaccurate performance appraisals (Bernardin & Villanova, 1986; Murphy, 2008; Tziner et al., 2001).

Rater Motivation

Drive and expectancy theories focus on the concept that people have behavior response "expectations" or "anticipations" about future events. Porter and Lawler (1968) stated that:

The differences between the theories are that expectancy argues that the anticipation of the positively valent outcome functions selectively on actions which are expected to lead to it. Drive theory views the magnitude of goal as a source of general excitement – a nonselective influence on performance. (p. 11)

Expectancy theory (Vroom, 1964,1995) places more emphasis on anticipation of the future than upon past learning (Porter & Lawler, 1968). So, when there is no future consequence for an evaluator to complete an accurate performance evaluation, he is less likely to do so. Vroom's models included a job satisfaction, work motivation, and job performance (Vroom, 1995) and were developed to address the following three phenomena within the interrelationship of work and motivation:

1. The choices made by persons among work roles.
2. The extent of their satisfaction with their chosen work roles.
3. The level of their performance or effectiveness in their chosen work roles (Vroom, 1995, p.7).

According to Ormond (1999) motivation increases an individual's energy and activity level, directs the individual toward certain goals, promotes initiation and persistence in certain activities, and affects the learning strategies and cognitive processes employed by individuals. Cleveland and Murphy (1992) found that "one factor that influences motivation is rewards (pp. 144-145). They also suggested that "valued rewards are clearly linked to accuracy in performance appraisal" (Cleveland & Murphy, 1992, p.172).

Harris' (1994) model of rater motivation described situational and personal variables that affected motivational factors which in turn impacted performance evaluation behaviors of observations, storage, retrieval, integration, rating, and feedback. Harris also suggests that the "effect of rater motivation on accuracy may be an indirect rather than direct effect" (1994, p. 750).

As an indirect effect, it suggests that it may be difficult to motivate evaluators to change their behavior.

Rewards

Murphy and Cleveland (1992) suggested that "the best way to convince raters that they will be rewarded for accurate ratings is to give rewards, in as public a way as possible, to raters who comply" (p.172). In contrast, Harris (1994) suggested that an evaluator is "uninterested in being accurate, which is most likely caused by a lack of any rewards" (p. 751). Why should evaluators need to be rewarded for doing their job accurately?

The Porter-Lawler (1968) model of expectancy theory measured supervisor effort, peer effort, and self-effort and focused on the value of the reward, the perceived effort required relative to attaining the expected reward, the actual effort, abilities and traits, role perceptions, performance (accomplishment), rewards (fulfillment), perceived equitable rewards and satisfaction. The major ethical concern is that organizations know that they have evaluators who are not providing accurate performance evaluations for their subordinates, and they continue to allow them to lead employees. The subordinates are being held accountable to evaluators who do not care enough, morally, or ethically to provide them with accurate job performance feedback through the organization's performance evaluation system.

Accountability

Mero & Motowidlo (1995) showed that evaluators were more accurate when held accountable by having to justify their evaluations. However, Harris (1994) found that "increased accountability to subordinates will typically decrease rater motivation to make accurate ratings" (p. 744). Holding evaluators accountable requires effort by the organization to provide clear, objective tools and resources (Murphy, 2008). With regards to increasing workforce diversity, accurate performance evaluations may be one way for diverse individuals to feel valued and respected within organizations. It may also reduce the number of EEOC complaints, labor disputes, and lawsuits associated with diversity and unfairness in the workplace (D'Netto & Sohal, 1999; Fulkerson & Schuler, 1992; Jayne & Dipboye, 2004; Loden & Rosener, 1991; Morrison, 1992; Powell & Butterfield, 1994; Schreiber et al., 1993; Schuler et al.,1992).

Legal and Ethical Consideration of Diversity Management

Sometimes diversity is mistaken for Equal Employment Opportunity (EEO) and Affirmative Action (AA); however, diversity goes beyond legal requirements (Kelly & Dobbin, 1998). Actually, "for many organizations, the definition of diversity has evolved from a focus on legally protected attributes such as race, gender, and age to a much broader definition that includes the entire spectrum of human differences" (Jayne & Dipboye, 2004, p. 410). This definition supports the ways that Hughes's (2010) five values can be used to promote workforce inter-personnel diversity because Hughes's five values examines all employees' differences.

There are human, psychological, organization and institutional resistance to the implementation of diversity (Konrad, 2006; Avery, 2011). For these reasons, "building support for a diversity initiative requires a clearly defined strategy for communicating the business case and clear roles and responsibilities for the senior leadership team, managers, and employees" (Jayne & Dipboye, 2004, p.418). Some researchers support building the business case for diversity so that diversity could be tied to the organizations' profits. However, that has not stopped discrimination from occurring regardless of the organizations' earnings. Hughes's (2010) five values can help build the business case for diversity, but it still may not be enough for some leaders to stop discriminating against some protected class employees. Marques (2007) explains "if conscientiously applied and facilitated at all levels, diversity can elevate an organization's long-term performance to levels that are beyond all expectations" (p. 24). Diversity is an ethical behavioral choice for the leaders who chose to conscientiously apply it.

FUTURE RESEARCH DIRECTIONS

Ethics should also be a part of a rater's willingness to provide accurate evaluations. Performance evaluations are used to determine employees' pay, their promotion, and their advancement opportunities. It is totally unethical for an evaluator not to consider these things when performing their evaluation responsibility to their employees. Future research should examine the extent that evaluator ethical beliefs align with the extent to which they provide accurate employee evaluations.

The future success of organizations depends on a workforce with KSAs to perform technological work (Friedman & Mandelbaum, 2011; Reich, 2010). How do organizations ensure that they are providing all workers with the opportunity to use their KSAs without encountering discrimination? Answers to this question may help researchers better explain how workers experience discrimination at work.

There is no longer room in many organizations for leaders of employees to feign ignorance of diversity needs within organizations. Without diversity intelligence™ leaders are incapable of properly leading all employees in the workplace (Hughes, 2016). Younger employees within protected class groups and categories are less tolerant with leaders who ignore the microaggressions against them or are the ones mistreating them. They are becoming quiet quitters are part of the Great Resignation. Researchers can interview quiet quitters and other employees who were a part of the Great Resignation to find out exactly how diversity intelligence affects employees.

CONCLUSION

Global workplace expansion requires leaders to understand different cultures and the needs of employees who are of different nationalities (Friedman & Mandelbaum, 2011). Leaders must also learn how to quickly recognize and adapt to people differences, despite their willingness to perform the same tasks (Hughes, 2010). This chapter is suggesting that organizational leaders acknowledge and understand all employees and use that knowledge to enhance and improve organizational performance. Diversity intelligent leaders can do this, so all leaders should work towards becoming diversity intelligent.

COVID-19 ETHICAL IMPACT MINI CASE STUDY

Diverse employees were most likely to die from contracting the COVID-19 virus and its different strains at work when completing low paid, essential work. Many low paid employees worked in meat processing plants, nursing homes, and other lower paying jobs and were required to go to work during the COVID-19 pandemic. Many of these workers did not have health insurance or ways to protect their families from contracting the virus from them when they went home from work.

1. In what way(s) was it unethical for organization leaders to require diverse employees with known underlying conditions susceptible to the COVID-19 virus to continue coming to work?
2. Should employers have an ethical duty to protect their workers and their workers family from sickness?

REFERENCES

Aliaga, O. A. (2001). Academy of HRD 2001 Conference Proceedings (pp. 805-812). Academy of Human Resource Development.

Arvey, R. D., & Murphy, K. R. (1998). Performance evaluation in work settings. *Annual Review of Psychology, 49*, 141–168. doi:. psych.49.1.141 doi:10.1146/annurev

Avery, D. R. (2011). Support for diversity in organizations: A theoretical exploration of its origins and offshoots. *Organizational Psychology Review, 1*(3), 239–256. doi:10.1177/2041386611402115

Baird, L., & Meshoulam, I. (1988). Managing two fits of strategic human resource management. *Academy of Management Review, 13*(1), 116–128. doi:10.2307/258359

Banks, C. G., & Murphy, K. R. (1985). Toward narrowing the research-practice gap in performance appraisal. *Personnel Psychology, 38*(2), 335–345. doi:10.1111/j.1744-6570.1985.tb00551.x

Banks, C. H. (2002). A descriptive analysis of the perceived effectiveness of Virginia Tech's faculty development institute. *Dissertation Abstracts International, 64*(08). (UMI No. 3102585)

Banks, C. H. (2006). Career planning: Toward an inclusive model. In M. Karsten (Ed.), *Gender, race and ethnicity in the workplace* (Vol. 3, pp. 99–116). Greenwood. Publishing Group, Inc.

Banks, C. H., & Nafukho, F. M. (2008). Career transitions across and within organizations: Implications for human resource development. In T.M. Chermack & J. Storberg-Walker (Eds.), *2008 Academy of Human Resource Development Annual Research Conference Proceedings,* (pp. 1096- 1102). Academy of Human Resource Development.

Becker, B. E., Huselid, M. A., & Beatty, R. W. (2009). *The differentiated workforce: Transforming talent into strategic impact.* Harvard Business Press.

Bernardin, H. J., & Buckley, M. R. (1981). Strategies in rater training. *Academy of Management Review, 6*(2), 205–212.

Bernardin, H. J., Buckley, M. R., Tyler, C. L., & Weise, D. S. (2000). A reconsideration of strategies in rater training. *Research in Personnel and Human Resources Management, 18,* 221–274.

Bernardin, H. J., & Villanova, P. (1986). Performance appraisal. In E. A. Locke (Ed.), *Generalizing from laboratory to field settings* (pp. 43–62). Lexington Books.

Bingham, K., Gewin, A., Hu, C., Thomas, K., & Yanchus, N. (2005). The roles of protégé race, gender, and proactive socialization attempts on peer monitoring. *Advances in Developing Human Resources, 7*(4), 540–555. doi:10.1177/1523422305279681

Boudreaux, M. A. (2001). *Career development: What is its role in human resource development?*

Brass, D. J., & Burkhardt, M. E. (1993). Potential power and power use: An investigation of structure and behavior. *Academy of Management Journal, 36*(3), 441–470. doi:10.2307/256588

Burkhardt, M. E., & Brass, D. J. (1990). Changing patterns or patterns of change: The effects of a change in technology on social network structure and power. *Administrative Science Quarterly, 35*(1), 104–127. doi:10.2307/2393552

Campbell, J. P. (1990). Modeling the performance prediction problem in industrial and organizational psychology. In M. D. Dunnette & L. M. Hough (Eds.), *Handbook of industrial and organizational psychology* (2nd ed., Vol. 1, pp. 687–732). Consulting Psychologists Press.

Cleveland, J. N., & Murphy, K. R. (1992). Analyzing performance appraisal as goal-directed behavior. *Research in Personnel and Human Resources Management, 10,* 121–185.

D'Netto, B., & Sohal, A. (1999). Human resource practices and workforce diversity: An empirical assessment. *International Journal of Manpower, 20*(8), 530–547. doi:10.1108/01437729910302723

Danquah, J. K., Crocco, O. S., Mahmud, Q. M., Rehan, M., & Rizvi, L. J. (2023). Connecting concepts: Bridging the gap between capacity development and human resource development. *Human Resource Development International*, 1–18. doi:10.1080/13678868.2022.2108992

Day, D. V., & Sulsky, L. M. (1995). Effects of frame-of-reference training and information configuration on memory organization and rating accuracy. *The Journal of Applied Psychology*, *80*(1), 158–167. doi:10.1037/0021-9010.80.1.158

Deal, T., & Kennedy, A. (1984). *Corporate cultures*. Addison-Wesley.

Delery, J. E. (1998). Issues of fit in strategic human resource management: Implications for research. *Human Resource Management Review*, *8*(3), 289–309. doi:10.1016/S1053-4822(98)90006-7

Folger, R., & Greenberg, J. (1985). Procedural justice: An interpretive analysis of personnel systems. *Research in Personnel and Human Resources Management*, *3*, 141–183.

Friedman, T. L., & Mandelbaum, M. (2011). *That used to be us: How America fell behind in the world it invented and how we can come back*. Farrar, Strauss, and Giroux.

Fulkerson, J. R., & Schuler, R. S. (1992). Managing worldwide diversity at Pepsi-Cola International. In S. E. Jackson (Ed.), *Diversity in the workplace: Human resources initiatives, society for industrial and organisational psychology (The Professional Practice Series)*. Guildford Press.

Gelfand, M. J., Nishii, L. H., Raver, J. L., & Schneider, B. (2005). Discrimination in organizations: An organizational-level systems perspective. In R. L. Dipboye & A. Colella (Eds.), *Discrimination at work: The psychological and organizational bases* (pp. 117–144). Psychology Press.

Gotsis, G., & Grimani, K. (2016). Diversity as an aspect of effective leadership: Integrating and moving forward. *Leadership and Organization Development Journal*, *37*(2), 241–264. doi:10.1108/LODJ-06-2014-0107

Harris, M. M. (1994). Rater motivation in the performance appraisal context: A theoretical framework. *Journal of Management*, *20*(4), 737–756. doi:10.1016/0149-2063(94)90028-0

Hayes, K. H. (2000). *Managing career transitions: Your career as a work in progress* (2nd ed.). Prentice Hall.

Holland, J. L. (1973). *Making vocational choices: A theory of careers.* Prentice-Hall.

Hughes, C. (2010). "People as technology" conceptual model: Towards a new value creation paradigm for strategic human resource development. *Human Resource Development Review, 9*(1), 48–71. doi:10.1177/1534484309353561

Hughes, C. (2012). *Valuing people and technology in the workplace: A competitive advantage framework.* IGI Global. doi:10.4018/978-1-4666-0240-3

Hughes, C., & Brown, L. (2018). Exploring leaders' discriminatory, passive-aggressive behavior toward protected class employees using diversity intelligence. *Advances in Developing Human Resources, 20*(3), 263–284. doi:10.1177/1523422318778002

Hughes, C., & Stephens, D. M. (2012). Leveraging workforce diversity through a career development paradigm shift. In C. L. Scott and M. Y. Byrd (Eds.) Handbook of research on workforce diversity in a global society: Technologies and concepts, (pp. 262-272). IGI Global. doi:10.4018/978-1-4666-1812-1.ch015

Jayne, M., & Dipboye, R. (2004). Leveraging diversity to improve business performance: Research findings and recommendations for organizations. *Human Resource Management, 43*(4), 409–424. doi:10.1002/hrm.20033

Karsten, M. F., & Igou, F. (2005). Career planning: A model for a diverse workforce. *Refereed Proceedings of the North American Management Society track at the 2005 Midwest Business Administration Association Conference.* MBAA.

Kaye, B. (1997). *Up is not the only way.* Davies-Black.

Kelly, E., & Dobbin, F. (1998). How affirmative action became diversity management: Employer response to antidiscrimination laws, 1961 to 1996. *The American Behavioral Scientist, 41*(7), 960–984. doi:10.1177/0002764298041007008

Kerno, S., & Kuznia, K. (2007). Modern career navigation: Preparing for success despite uncertainties. *Industrial Engineering (American Institute of Industrial Engineers), 39*(10), 31–33.

Konrad, A. (2006). Leveraging workplace diversity in organizations. *Organizational Management Journal, 3*(3), 194–189. doi:10.1057/omj.2006.18

Küçük, B. A. (2022). Understanding the employee job satisfaction depending on manager's fair treatment: The role of cynicism towards the organization and co-worker support. *European Review of Applied Psychology, 72*(6), 1–21. doi:10.1016/j.erap.2022.100795

Lawler, E. E. III. (2003). *Treat people right! How organizations and individuals can propel each other into a virtuous spiral of success.* Jossey-Bass.

Loden, M., & Rosener, J. B. (1991). *Workforce America! Managing employee diversity as a VITAL resource.* Business One Irwin.

Marques, J. (2007). Diversity as a win-win strategy. *Management Services, 51*(1), 22–24.

Mero, N. P., & Motowidlo, S. J. (1995). Effects of rater accountability on the accuracy and the favorability of performance ratings. *The Journal of Applied Psychology, 80*(4), 517–524. doi:10.1037/0021-9010.80.4.517

Morrison, A. M. (1992). *The new leaders: Guide-lines on leadership diversity in America.* Jossey-Bass Publishers.

Murphy, K. R. (2008). Explaining the weak relationship between job performance and ratings of job performance. *Industrial and Organizational Psychology: Perspectives on Science and Practice, 1*(2), 148–160. doi:10.1111/j.1754-9434.2008.00030.x

Murphy, K. R., & Cleveland, J. N. (1991). *Performance appraisal: An organizational perspective.* Allyn & Bacon.

Ormond, J. E. (1999). *Human learning* (3rd ed.). Prentice-Hall Inc.

Pfeffer, J. (1994). *Competitive advantage through people: Unleashing the power of the workforce.* Harvard Business School Press. doi:10.2307/41165742

Pitts, D. (2006). Modeling the impact of diversity management. *Review of Public Personnel Administration, 26*(3), 245–268. doi:10.1177/0734371X05278491

Porter, L. W., & Lawler, E. E. (1968). *Managerial attitudes and performance.* Richard D. Irwin, Inc.

Powell, G. N., & Butterfield, D. A. (1994). Race, gender and the glass ceiling: An empirical study of actual promotions to top management. Paper presented at the *annual meeting of the Academy of Management*. Emerald Insight.

Reich, R. B. (2010). *Aftershock: The next economy and America's future.* Alfred A. Knopf.

Schein, E. H. (1975). How career anchors hold executives to their career paths. *Personnel, 52,* 11–24.

Schreiber, C. T., Price, K. F., & Morrison, A. (1993). Workplace diversity and the glass ceiling: Practices, barriers, possibilities. *Human Resource Planning, 16*(2), 51–69.

Schuler, R. S., Dowling, P. J., Smart, J. P., & Huber, V. L. (1992). *Human resource management in Australia* (2nd ed.). Harper Educational Publishers.

Shen, J., Chanda, A., D'netto, B., & Monga, M. (2009). Managing diversity through human resource management: An international perspective and conceptual framework. *International Journal of Human Resource Management, 20*(2), 235–251. doi:10.1080/09585190802670516

Super, D. (2002). A life-span, life-space approach to career development. In D. Brown & L. Brooks (Eds.), *Career choice and development* (2nd ed.). Jossey-Bass., doi:10.1016/0001-8791(80)90056-1

Thomas, K. M. (2008). *Diversity resistance in organizations.* Lawrence Erlbaum.

Triana, M. D. C., Gu, P., Chapa, O., Richard, O., & Colella, A. (2021). Sixty years of discrimination and diversity research in human resource management: A review with suggestions for future research directions. *Human Resource Management, 60*(1), 145–204. doi:10.1002/hrm.22052

Tziner, A., Murphy, K. R., Cleveland, J. N., & Roberts-Thompson, G. P. (2001). Relationships between attitudes toward organizations and performance appraisal systems and rating behavior. *International Journal of Selection and Assessment, 9*(3), 226–239. doi:10.1111/1468-2389.00176

Vardi, Y. (1980). Organizational career mobility: An integrative model. *Academy of Management Review, 5*(3), 341–355. doi:10.2307/257109

Viswesvaran, C. (2001). Assessment of individual job performance: A review of the past century and a look ahead. In N. Anderson, D. S. Ones, H. K. Sinangil, & C. Viswesvaran (Eds.), *Handbook of industrial, work and organizational psychology* (Vol. 1, pp. 110–126). Sage. doi:10.4135/9781848608320.n7

Vroom, V. H. (1964). *Work and motivation.* John Wiley & Sons, Inc.

Vroom, V. H. (1973). A new look at managerial decision making. *Organizational Dynamics, 1*(4), 66–80. doi:10.1016/S0090-2616(73)80024-5

Vroom, V. H. (1995). *Work and motivation.* Jossey-Bass.

Vroom, V. H., & MacCrimmon, K. R. (1968). Toward a stochastic model of managerial careers. *Administrative Science Quarterly, 13*(1), 26–46. doi:10.2307/2391260

Welch, J. (2005). *Winning.* HarperCollins.

Woehr, D. J., & Huffcutt, A. I. (1994). Rater training for performance appraisal: A quantitative review. *Journal of Occupational and Organizational Psychology, 67*(3), 189–205. doi:10.1111/j.2044-8325.1994.tb00562.x

Wright, P. M., & McMahan, G. C. (1992). Theoretical perspectives for strategic human resource management. *Journal of Management, 18*(2), 295–320. doi:10.1177/014920639201800205

Chapter 7
Understanding the Need for Strategic Human Resource Development (SHRD)

ABSTRACT

Chapter seven provides information to help HRD scholars, professionals, and practitioners better understand the need for strategic human resource development (SHRD). The struggle of comparing people to technology and respectfully integrating people and technology in the workplace continues to be debated to the detriment of individual and organizational success. The COVID-19 pandemic revealed how far behind HRD scholars, professionals, and practitioners are when needed to integrate and enhance the relationship between people and technology in the workplace.

INTRODUCTION

Strategic human resource development (SHRD) has been researched and defined by several authors (Alagaraja, 2013; Becker et al., 2001; Beer & Spector, 1989; Ericson, 2006; Garavan, 1991, 2007; Garavan et al., 1995, 2016; Gilley & Eggland, 1989; Gilley & Maycunich, 2000; Grieves, 2003; Harrison, 1993, 1997; Lee, 2003; Nadler & Wiggs, 1986; Rothwell & Kazanas, 1991; Tseng & McLean, 2008). Garavan (1991) suggested nine SHRD key characteristics suggested by Garavan (1991) are: (1) integration with organizational missions and goals; (2) top management support; (3)

DOI: 10.4018/978-1-6684-5321-6.ch007

environmental scanning; (4) HRD plans and policies; (5) line manager commitment and involvement; (6) existence of complementary HRM activities; (7) expanded trainer role; (8) recognition of culture; and (9) emphasis on evaluation. Garavan et al. (2016) further expanded on the topic of SHRD by examining the Dynamic capabilities of SHRD by suggesting Dynamic SHRD capabilities (DSHRDC) and a DSHRDC framework consisting of enabling factors, specific components, underlying processes, and unique SHRD dynamic capabilities. The COVID-19 pandemic has spotlighted the need for strategic human resource development (SHRD) and the DSHRDC framework. The area of technology became an indispensable necessity for human survival during the onset of the COVID-19 pandemic when human-human interaction was a life-threatening endeavor. Human-machine and machine-machine interactions became the norm and remain an integral part of organization functionality. Technology needs to be a focus of SHRD.

"Man and machine are as essential to organizational prosperity as air and water is to living" (Hughes & Gosney, 2012, p.759). HRD researchers have published very few empirical articles on people and technology in organizations (Githens et al., 2008). HRD publications only mention computer technology used to administer training, facilitate communication, and/or to track training results (Bennett, 2022; Githens et al., 2008; Werner & DeSimone, 2012). Githens, et al. (2008) noted that the technology areas addressed in the five primary HRD publications between the years 2000-2006 were "educational technology (86), ... virtual teams (18), and workers, knowledge management, and other, had less than ten articles each" (p. 203). HRD is the leading educational field of study for training and development, and they are behind on researching and understanding how AI, robots (Pham et al., 2018), machine learning, ChatGPT, and other technologies are affecting employees in the workplace (Righetti et al., 2019; Ruiner et al., 2023; Vrontis et al., 2022). Kim (2022) has conducted some research to provide HRD scholars, practitioners, and professionals with insights on human-machine interactions when dealing with robots.

The main three areas of focus within the field of HRD has been training and development, career development, and organization development (OD) (Mankin, 2001; Swanson & Holton, 2001). The field is expanding into to areas including critical HRD, diversity, equity, and inclusion (DEI), strategic HRD, evaluation, and cross-cultural HRD. Technology is still not included as a main area of focus. The global recession with its high number of unemployed workers shined a light on the need for HRD (Hughes & Gosney, 2012) and the COVID-19 pandemic has exacerbated the need for HRD and SHRD in particular. Yet many HRD scholars professionals and practitioners were not prepared to make the necessary technological adjustments for themselves or for their organizations (Hughes, 2021).

Aguinis and Kraiger (2009) suggested that there is "[a]n important challenge for the practice of training... to integrate the training function with employee selection, performance, management, rewards, and other human resource practices (Aguinis, 2009; Aguinis & Pierce, 2008; Cascio & Aguinis, 2005)" (p. 467). Strategic HRD (SHRD) is an opportunity HRD to better integrate people and technology development. SHRD is defined as "the process of facilitating organizational learning, performance, and change through organized interventions and initiatives and management actions for the purpose of enhancing an organization's performance capacity, capability, competitive readiness, and renewal" (Gilley & Maycunich, 2000, p. 6) and is designed to integrate HRD initiatives with business strategy (Gilley & Maycunich, 2000; Kandula, 2001; Werner & DeSimone, 2012) through OD.

HRD researchers have described OD as involving the principles, processes, and performance within organizations (McLagan, 1989; McLean & McLean, 2001; Egan, 2001; Egan, 2002; Cummings & Worley, 2005; McLean, 2006). McLean (2006) broadly describes OD as:

... any process or activity, based on the behavioral sciences, that, either initially or over a long term, has the potential to develop in an organization set-ting enhanced knowledge, expertise, productivity, satisfaction, income, interpersonal relationships, and other desired outcomes, whether for interpersonal or group/team gain or for the benefit of an organization, community, region, or, ultimately, the whole of humanity. (p. 9)

Gilley and Maycunich, (2000) suggested that employees participated in interventions and initiatives that could expand their knowledge and skills and improve their performance, and "Organizations create work environments, systems, and processes that increase employee productivity and managers provide feedback and reinforcement useful in encouraging continuous employee growth and development" (p. 5). One main area for this is the ample use of new technologies throughout organizations (Wilson & Daugherty, 2019). Instead of technologies helping employees better perform their work, many of the new technologies such as AI are being developed to replace employees and the ethics of these decisions should be examined by HRD researchers (Attard-Frost et al., 2022; Eitel-Porter, 2021; Stahl et al., 2023) because there are some researchers such as Munn (2022) who believe that AI ethics is useless.

There are many questions that come to mind when thinking about HRD's lack of focus on technology and people interactions in the workplace. Questions include:

1. Could HRD professionals' lack of the ability through OD to integrate people and technology in the workplace help to explain why many HRD professionals do not have a seat at the table in organizations (Beyer & Trice, 1987)?
2. "Are HRD professionals and researchers denying that there is a relationship between people and technology in organizations?
3. Are HRD professionals and researchers limited by their beliefs concerning the comparison of people to technology" (Hughes & Gosney, 2012, p.759)?

Until HRD scholars, professionals, and practitioners be transparent about why they are avoiding conversations about the relationships between people and technology in the workplace, employees will continue to be seen as less valued than technology in organizations. These employees are sometimes referred to as precarious (Anderson, 2022), vulnerable, (Bazzoli & Probst, 2023), and middle-skill level employees (Hughes et al., 2019)

BACKGROUND

Zakaria (2010) noted that "technology and globalization are shattering the middle class" in America (p. 31). American workers were being displaced by technology and high skilled, low wage workers in a globalized economy (Friedman & Mandelbaum, 2011). Until HRD helps to resolve these issues, middle class workers will remain at a disadvantage within the global economy (Hughes & Gosney, 2012; Hughes et al., 2019). HRD professionals and practitioners should design developmental initiatives that allow workers to integrate their KSAs with technology (Weintraub & Martineau, 2002; Wilson & Daugherty, 2019).

The lessons learned during Just-in-Time (JIT) training can be directly incorporated by the worker into an evolving understanding of the task, more easily recalled, and used effectively when needed (Collins et al., 1997).

HRD professionals and practitioners know that JIT training or learning was not invented by "workplace educators and performance specialists within the human resource development field, but rather it is conceptualized as an evolutionary response to the demands of a knowledge-driven and speed-oriented marketplace" (Brandenburg & Ellinger, 2003, p. 311). They also know that

"Just-in-Time" learning systems deliver training to workers when and where they need it. Rather than sitting through hours of traditional classroom training, users can tap into Web-based tutorials, interactive CD-ROMs, and other tools to zero in on just the information they need to solve problems, perform specific tasks, or quickly update their skills. (Sambataro, 2000, p. 50)

Although Brandenburg and Ellinger (2003) espoused the relationship of the JIT learning to the core values of HRD. They noted that

JIT learning relates to the core values of HRD as exemplified by the [three] common ground statements .... [1] Leveraging available technology, without losing the human touch and social component of learning. ... [2] Intellectual capital as the life blood of the organization. ... [3] Effective management of knowledge and learning. (pp. 316-317)

Brandenburg and Ellinger's (2003) suggested that HRD professionals and practitioners enhance their role of integrating HRD with JIT learning. This book expands Brandenburg and Ellinger's (2003) idea of "Leveraging available technology, without losing the human touch and social component of learning" (p. 316). It also provides an opportunity for HRD professionals and practitioners to go beyond their understanding of computer technology for knowledge management and learning purposes to a greater understanding of how employees use the equipment/technology required to do their job to enhance productivity for organizations. The right information is just as important as the learning methodologies.

PEOPLE, TECHNOLOGY, AND SHRD

Most of the research regarding technology and HRD involves computer technology and its relationship to educating employees in the workplace. Learning Management Systems (LMS's) that manage employee training and development are important tools; however, HRD professionals, practitioners, and researchers should aid employees as they seek to operate technological equipment within the workplace. The technological equipment and systems are displacing some middle-class workers (Zakaria, 2010; Hughes et al., 2019) because the workers are not equipped or educated to operate high technology and cannot be trained quickly enough to meet the rapidly changing global organizations' needs (Hughes & Gosney, 2010). Githens et al. (2008) found that only 10% of 1675 articles in the top five HRD publications were technology related. This lack of interest in technology by HRD researchers, practitioners, and professionals was discouraging because HRD should understand technology's role in workplace success (Hughes, 2012, 2021). Hughes' (2010) PT conceptual model described ways to integrate people and technology into organizations' value creation strategies. Organizations struggle when they do not have the best people in the right jobs at the right time with the best technology (Brache, 2002; Espedal, 2005; Hughes, 2012; London & Diamante, 2002; Martelli, 1998; Pfeffer, 1994; Snell & Dean, 1992; Stewart, 1999).

Robots, AI, machine learning, and other simulation systems have been introduced into workplaces and are replacing employees (Brynjolfsson & McAfee, 2011; Cowen, 2011; Ford, 2009; Levy & Murnane, 2005). This is not a new phenomenon but visible during the Great Recession. It is even more recognized during the COVID-19 pandemic as employers are using drones, robots, and chat bots to replace employees' work tasks. HRD professionals, practitioners, researchers, and organizations must adjust to these changes and develop people and technology together.

SHRD allows more productivity in alignment with business strategies (Werner & DeSimone, 2012; Garavan et al., 2016). Understanding the business means that HRD professionals and practitioners are learning the operational processes and are actively involved in understanding process flow so that their training and development and organization development activities sufficiently meets the needs of the organization and employees (Hughes, 2012). Despite, billions of dollars being spent on training and development in the US each year, yet the perception persists that employees are not properly trained. Employees are receiving training that does not meet their job specific needs; training that is not linked to employee productivity. Most training goes to leaders to help them better manage employees (Hughes 2012; Hughes et al., 2019), but if employees do not receive skill enhancement training, all the leadership in the world will not help them perform any better. The failure of leadership needs to be studied extensively by HRD scholars.

Most employees receive entry level training, but many do not advance beyond entry level to troubleshoot equipment or make higher level decisions without management intervention. This issue is being resolved with technology enhancements at the job. Not having the higher level, critical thinking and problem-solving ability is one of the most, if not the most, challenging problem for employees. Machines can be programmed to identify defects in products and modified to fix them. Employees are humans and miss defects, and their modification takes time and training. Time and training incur costs for organizations that they do not want. Organizations want to maximize efficiency within specific timeframes, and want employees trained at the lowest cost.

ISSUES, CONTROVERSIES, PROBLEMS

Technology has helped revolutionize and expand productivity in organizations, but human input has always been present (Pfau & Kay, 2002). Humans developed technology to displace employees and after witnessing the Great Recession were beginning to rethink past technological philosophy and offer ways to reassess economic models of supply and demand (Brynjolfsson & McAfee, 2011; Cowen, 2011; Ford, 2009; Hughes, 2012; Levy & Murnane, 2005). Hughes (2012) noted three controversies of concern within HRD related to people and technology development:

1. HRD practitioners' and professionals' lack the ability through OD to integrate people and technology in the workplace (Beyer & Trice, 1987).
2. HRD professional, practitioners, and researchers tend not to want to discuss the relationship between people and technology in organizations. The idea of replacing people with technology has been a source of contention (Baptiste, 2001). However, if HRD professionals want to expand their role within the workplace, they must openly acknowledge that employees are being replaced by technology and explore ways to enhance human performance with technology (Pfau & Kay, 2002).
3. HRD professionals, practitioners, and researchers must constrain their beliefs concerning the comparison of people to technology and conduct empirical research to support and/or challenge their beliefs (Buchholz, 1977; Githens et al.; Hughes & Gosney, 2012). Without the research evidence to support their beliefs, HRD will continue to espouse

unsubstantiated opinions regarding the ability of people and technology to both enhance productivity in organizations. (p. 151)

The COVID-19 pandemic support that these issues are still relevant. These controversies are not insurmountable.

Solutions and recommendations

Davis and North's (1970) idea regarding how the costs associated with organizing and/or operating a new institution may change because of the invention of a new arrangemental technology relates most closely to the PT model and may be addressed using *Hughes's HRD Value Creation Model*. As cost and organizational leverage factors change or come at risk due to innovation, HRD can become a risk-mitigating factor (Hughes & Gosney, 2011). HRD manages human capital risk (Bhattacharya & Wright, 2005) and by successfully managing this risk, HRD helps organizations maximize profit. Organization leaders may task HRD practitioners and professionals with managing OD and change initiatives.

FUTURE RESEARCH DIRECTIONS

SHRD may also assist organizations in learning new technology (Hughes & Gosney, 2011). SHRD can aid in mitigating political, ethical, and/or legal external risks and pressures by assisting the organization in complying with legal or political mandates through training and development and OD activities. Scott (1987) described institutionalization as

the social process by which individuals come to accept a shared definition of reality – a conception whose validity is seen as independent of the actor's own views or actions but is taken for granted as defining the 'way things are' and/or the 'way things are to be done.' (p. 496)

HRD, using institutional theory, could become the entity through which the "shared definition of reality" is transmitted or diffused throughout the organization (Hughes & Gosney, 2011; Rogers, 1995). Kuchinke (2000) proposed that institutional theory become a theoretical framework used by HRD scholars to conduct empirical research to assist organizations seeking transformational change.

Githens, et al. (2008) revealed that HRD technology-related research "focused on educational technology in higher education settings, while non-profit organizations and government/military settings were underrepresented. Overall, non-training topics were [also] underrepresented" (p. 1). Their findings are still relevant today. The opportunity for research in technology related research within HRD is needed. The US workforce also needs training and re-training in high-tech skills, and this is also an area where HRD researchers, practitioners, and professionals' skills are most needed.

HRD professionals, practitioners, and researchers must also be willing to continuously change and evolve to help organizations achieve their goals. Hughes and Gosney (2011) suggested the following key strategies that are applicable here and are areas where HRD scholars can focus their research agendas:

1. HRD professionals, [practitioners], and researchers must find a way to bridge the gap between research and practice (Argyris, 1985; Beer, 2001; Berger et al., 2004; Burack, 1999; Hamlin, 2002; Hughes et al., 2010; Mohrman et al., 2001; Muchinsky, 2004; Rynes et al., 2001; Short, 2006; Short et al., 2004; Van de Ven & Johnson, 2006; Yorks, 2005).

2. HRD professionals, [practitioners], and researchers must understand the relationship between people and technology and not focus on one or the other in isolation. They must develop methods of valuing both people and technology within the workplace (Hughes, 2010, 2012).

3. Technological innovations in the workplace are on an explosive upward trend. HRD researchers and professionals must understand these innovations to ensure that as people are developed their roles are not diminished or further eliminated but enhanced by technology.

4. HRD professionals, [practitioners], and researchers must work to meet the business needs of workers in all organizations and provide technological based solutions along with their people-based solutions. The same way that engineers cannot accomplish their design goals without people implementing their designs, HRD professionals and researchers cannot plan people strategies without understanding technological implications (Betz, 1993).

5. Ultimately, HRD must consider public policy as a potential future area of research. Understanding the broader labor relations and economic implications of their decisions within the public policy arena can only strengthen HRD practice. (p. 765)

Item number five is evident with the economic impact of COVID-19. There are many ways that HRD can use learning content management systems (LCMS) (Abazi-Bexheti, 2008; Alassaf et al., 2014; Cohen & Nycz, 2006; Ismail, 2001; Jovanovic et al., 2007; Qwaider, 2017; Wright et al., 2010) to help with employee career development needs, but LCMS is seldom mention in the HRD empirical research literature.

CONCLUSION

There is very little research in HRD publications that supports their effort to understand the relationship between people and technology within organizations. HRD professionals, practitioners, and researchers can be supportive of the relationship between people and technology so that organizations do not value one over the other (Carrig & Wright, 2006). Welch (2005), states "To manage people well, companies should [e]levate HR to a position of power and primacy in the organization, and make sure HR people have the special qualities to help managers build leaders and careers" (p. 98). The future of HRD is bright (Vince, 2003), but HRD scholars, professionals, and practitioners must be open to change and be adaptable to the opportunities that technology brings. The future of SHRD and DSHRDC are brighter because there are numerous ways that SHRD can be developed to meet organizations' needs for global competitive advantage. Without competent, capable, well-trained employees, organizations will not be able to compete to win (Hughes, 2012; Welch, 2005).

COVID-19 ETHICAL IMPACT MINI CASE STUDY

The COVID-19 pandemic, while extremely disruptive, has technological impacts that can be viewed positively and negatively. HRD scholars, professionals, and practitioners should be able to deal with both the positive and negative implications of technology. They should be able to use the technologies to help employees and organizations which have been negatively impacted.

They must also consider the ethical implications of how they best use technology to both stem the negative effects on employees and strengthen employees using some of the same technologies. Questions to consider include:

1. To what extent should HRD scholars, professionals, and practitioners use technology in their services despite the same technology diminishing the need for employees?
2. In what way(s) is it ethical or unethical for HRD professionals and practitioners not to use known technologies to improve organizational performance to protect employees form downsizing?

REFERENCES

Abazi-Bexheti, L. (2008). Development of a learning content management system. *WSEAS Transactions on Information Science and Applications*, *5*(6), 1001–1010.

Aguinis, H. (2009). *Performance management* (2nd ed.). Pearson Prentice Hall.

Aguinis, H., & Kraiger, K. (2009). Benefits of training and development for individuals and teams, organizations, and society. *Annual Review of Psychology, 60*, 451–474. doi:.psych.60.110707.163505 doi:10.1146/annurev

Aguinis, H., & Pierce, C. A. (2008). Enhancing the relevance of organizational behavior by embracing performance management research. *Journal of Organizational Behavior*, *29*(1), 139–145. doi:10.1002/job.493

Alagaraja, M. (2013). Mobilizing organizational alignment through strategic human resource development. *Human Resource Development International*, *16*(1), 74–93. doi:10.1080/13678868.2012.740794

Alassaf, N., Harfoushi, O., Obiedat, R., & Hammouri, T. (2014). Learning management systems and content management system: Definitions and characteristics. *Life Science Journal*, *11*(12), 39–41.

Ambrosini, V., & Bowman, C. (2009). What are dynamic capabilities and are they a useful construct in strategic management? *International Journal of Management Reviews*, *11*(1), 29–49. doi:10.1111/j.1468-2370.2008.00251.x

Anderson, V. (2022). Human resource development, professions and precarious workers. In P. Holland, T. Bartram, T. Garavan, & K. Grant (Eds.), *The Emerald handbook of work, workplaces and disruptive issues in HRM* (pp. 277–301). Emerald Publishing Limited. doi:10.1108/978-1-80071-779-420221028

Argyris, C. (1985). Making knowledge more relevant to practice: Maps for action. In E. E. Lawler (Ed.), *Doing research that is useful for theory and practice* (pp. 29–125). Jossey-Bass.

Attard-Frost, B., De los Ríos, A. & Walters, D.R. (2022). The ethics of AI business practices: A review of 47 AI ethics guidelines. *AI Ethics*, 1-18. doi:10.1007/s43681-022-00156-6

Baptiste, I. (2001). Educating lone wolves: Pedagogical implications of human capital theory. *Adult Education Quarterly*, *51*(3), 184–201. doi:10.1177/074171360105100302

Bazzoli, A., & Probst, T. M. (2023). Vulnerable workers in insecure jobs: A critical meta-synthesis of qualitative findings. *Applied Psychology*, *72*(1), 85–105. doi:10.1111/apps.12415

Becker, B. E. (Ed.), *The HR scorecard: Linking people, strategy, and practice* (pp. 1–26). Harvard Business School.

Becker, B. E., Huselid, M., & Ulrich, D. (2001). *HR as a strategic partner: The measurement challenge.*

Beer, M. (2001). Why management research findings are unimplementable: An action science perspective. *Reflections: The SoL Journal*, 2(3), 58–65. doi:10.1162/152417301570383

Beer, M., & Spector, B. (1989). Corporate wide transformations in human resource management. In R. E. Walton & P. R. Lawrence (Eds.), *Human resource management: Trends and Challenges*. Harvard University School Press.

Bennett, E. E. (2022). Leveraging technology to design and deliver human resource development. In P. Holland, T. Bartram, T. Garavan, K. and Grant. (Eds.) The Emerald handbook of work, workplaces and disruptive issues in HRM (pp. 261-276). Emerald Publishing Limited. doi:10.1108/978-1-80071-779-420221026

Berger, N. O., Kehrhahn, M. T., & Summerville, M. (2004). Research to practice: Throwing a rope across the divide. *Human Resource Development International*, *7*(3), 403–409. doi:10.1080/1367886042000246003

Betz, F. (1993). *Strategic technology management*. McGraw-Hill.

Beyer, J. M., & Trice, H. M. (1987). How an organization's rites reveal its culture. *Organizational Dynamics*, *8*(3), 5–24. doi:10.1016/0090-2616(87)90041-6

Brache, A. P. (2002). *How organizations work: Taking a holistic approach to enterprise health*. John Wiley & Sons.

Brandenburg, D. C., & Ellinger, A. D. (2003). The future: Just-in-time learning expectations and potential implications for human resource development. *Advances in Developing Human Resources*, *5*(3), 308–320. doi:10.1177/1523422303254629

Brynjolfsson, E., & McAfee, A. (2011). *Race against the machine: How the digital revolution is accelerating innovation, driving productivity, and irreversibly transforming employment and the economy*. Digital Frontier Press.

Buchholz, R. A. (1977). The belief structure of managers relative to work concepts measured by a factor analytic model. *Personnel Psychology*, *30*(4), 567–587. doi:10.1111/j.1744-6570.1977.tb02328.x

Burack, E. H. (1999). Bridging research to corporate application. In L. Larwood & U. E. Gattiker (Eds.), *Impact analysis: How reach can enter application and make a difference* (pp. 17–46). Erlbaum.

Carrig, K., & Wright, P. M. (2006). *Building profit through building people: Making your workforce the strongest link in the value-profit chain*. Society for Human Resource Management.

Cascio, W. F., & Aguinis, H. (2005). *Applied psychology in human resource management* (6th ed.). Pearson Prentice Hall.

Cohen, E., & Nycz, M. (2006). Learning objects and e-learning: An informing science perspective. *Interdisciplinary Journal of E-Learning and Learning Objects*, *2*(1), 23–34. doi:10.28945/399

Collins, J. A., Greer, J. E., Kumar, V. S., McCalla, G. I., Meagher, P., & Tkatch, R. (1997). Inspectable user models for just-in-time workplace training. In A. Jameson, C. Paris, & C. Tasso (Eds.), *User Modeling: Proceedings of the Sixth International Conference UM97* (pp. 327-337). Springer Wien. 10.1007/978-3-7091-2670-7_33

Cowen, T. (2011). *The great stagnation: How America ate all the low-hanging fruit of modern history, got sick, and will(eventually) feel better*. Peguin Group Publishing.

Cummings, T. G., & Worley, C. G. (2005). Organizational development and change (8th ed.). South-Western/Thomson.

Davis, L., & North, D. (1970). Institutional change and American economic growth: A first step towards a theory of institutional innovation. *The Journal of Economic History*, *30*(1), 131–149. doi:10.1017/S0022050700078633

Egan, T. M. (2001). *Organization development: An examination of definitions and dependent variables*. Human Resource Development Research Center, University of Minnesota.

Egan, T. M. (2002). Organization development: An examination of definitions and dependent variables. *Organization Development Journal*, *20*(2), 59–70.

Eitel-Porter, R. (2021). Beyond the promise: Implementing ethical AI. *AI and Ethics*, *1*(1), 73–80. doi:10.100743681-020-00011-6

Ericson, M. (2006). Strategic HRD and the relational self. *Human Resource Development Quarterly*, *17*(2), 223–229. doi:10.1002/hrdq.1170

Espedal, B. (2005). Management development: Using internal or external resources in developing core competence. *Human Resource Development Review*, *4*(2), 136–158. doi:10.1177/1534484305276217

Ford, M. (2009). *The lights in the tunnel: Automation, accelerating technology and the economy of the future*. Acculant Publishing.

Friedman, T. L., & Mandelbaum, M. (2011). *That used to be us: How America fell behind in the world it invented and how we can come back*. Farrar, Strauss, and Giroux.

Garavan, T. N. (1991). Strategic human resource development. *Journal of European Industrial Training*, *15*(1), 17–30. doi:10.1108/EUM0000000000219

Garavan, T. N. (2007). A strategic perspective on human resource development. *Advances in Developing Human Resources*, *9*(1), 11–30. doi:10.1177/1523422306294492

Garavan, T. N., Costine, P., & Heraty, N. (1995). The emergence of strategic human resource development. *Journal of European Industrial Training*, *19*(10), 4–10. doi:10.1108/03090599510095816

Garavan, T. N., Shanahan, V., Carbery, R., & Watson, S. (2016). Strategic human resource development: Towards a conceptual framework to understand its contribution to dynamic capabilities. *Human Resource Development International*, *19*(4), 289–306. doi:10.1080/13678868.2016.1169765

Gilley, J., & Eggland, S. A. (1989). *Principle of human resource development*. Perseus.

Gilley, J. W., & Maycunich, A. (2000). *Organizational learning, performance, and change: An introduction to strategic human resource development*. Perseus Publishing.

Githens, R. P., Dirani, K., Gitonga, J. W., & Teng, Y. T. (2008). Technology-related research in HRD publications: An analysis of content and meta perspectives from 2000 to 2006. *Human Resource Development Quarterly*, *19*(3), 191–215. doi:10.1002/hrdq.1236

Grieves, J. (2003). Strategic Human Resource Development. *Sage (Atlanta, Ga.)*.

Hamlin, R. G. (2002). In support of evidence- based management and research-informed HRD through HRD professional partnerships: An empirical and comparative study. *Human Resource Development International*, *5*(4), 467–491. doi:10.1080/13678860210122643

Harrison, R. (1993). Developing people – for whose bottom line? In R. Harrison (Ed.), *Human resource management. Issues and strategies* (pp. 299–329). Addison-Wesley.

Harrison, R. (1997). *Employee development*. Institute of Personal and Development.

Hughes, C. (2010). People as technology conceptual model: Towards a new value creation paradigm for strategic human resource development. *Human Resource Development Review*, *9*(1), 48–71. doi:10.1177/1534484309353561

Hughes, C. (2012). *Valuing people and technology in the workplace: A competitive advantage framework*. IGI Global. doi:10.4018/978-1-4666-0240-3

Hughes, C. (2021). The changing learning technological landscape for trainers in the wake of COVID-19. *Advances in Developing Human Resources*, *23*(1), 66–74. doi:10.1177/1523422320972108

Hughes, C., & Gosney, M. W. (2012). People, technology and human resource development (HRD) philosophy. In V. C. X. Wang (Ed.), *Encyclopedia of e-leadership, counseling and training* (pp. 759–771). IGI Global. doi:10.4018/978-1-61350-068-2.ch055

Hughes, C., Robert, L., Frady, K., & Arroyos, A. (2019). *Managing technology and middle and low skilled employees: Advances for economic regeneration.* Emerald Publishing. doi:10.1108/9781789730777

Hughes, C., Wang, J., Zheng, W., & McLean, L. (2010). Implementation concerns scholar-practitioners: A pilot study of the link between research and practice. *International Journal of Asian Business and Information Management, 1*(2), 32–46. doi:10.4018/jabim.2010040104

Ismail, J. (2001). The design of an e-learning system: Beyond the hype. *The Internet and Higher Education, 4*(3-4), 329–336. doi:10.1016/S1096-7516(01)00069-0

Jovanovic, J., Gasevic, D., Brooks, C., Devedzic, V., Hatala, M., Eap, T., & Richards, G. (2007). Using semantic web technologies to analyze learning content. *IEEE Internet Computing, 11*(5), 45–53. doi:10.1109/MIC.2007.116

Kandula, S. R. (2001). *Strategic human resource development.* Prentice-Hall of India Private Limited.

Kim, S. (2022). Working with robots: Human resource development considerations in human–robot interaction. *Human Resource Development Review, 21*(1), 48–74. doi:10.1177/15344843211068810

Kuchinke, K. P. (2000). Debates over the nature of HRD: An institutional theory perspective. *Human Resource Development International, 3*(3), 279–283. doi:10.1080/13678860050128474

Lee, M. (2003). *HRD in a complex world.* Routledge.

Levy, F., & Murnane, R. J. (2005). *The new division of labor: How computers are creating the next job market.* Princeton University Press.

London, M., & Diamante, T. (2002). Technology-focused expansive professionals: Developing continuous learning in the high-technology sector. *Human Resource Development Review, 1*(4), 500–524. doi:10.1177/1534484302238438

Mankin, D. A. (2001). A model for human resource development. *Human Resource Development International*, *4*(1), 65–85. doi:10.1080/13678860121714

Martelli, J. (1998). Training for new technology: Midwest steel company. In Rothwell, W. (Ed.), Linking HRD programs with organizational strategy (pp. 85–96). ASTD.

McLagan, P. (1989). *Models for HRD practice*. American Society for Training and Development.

McLean, G. N. (2006). *Organization development*. Berrett-Koehler.

McLean, G. N., & McLean, L. D. (2001). If we can't define HRD in one country, how can we define it in as international context? *Human Resource Development International*, *4*(3), 313–326. doi:10.1080/13678860110059339

Mohrman, S., Gibson, C., & Mohrman, A. (2001). Doing research that is useful to practice: A model and empirical exploration. *Academy of Management Journal*, *44*(2), 357–375. doi:10.2307/3069461

Muchinsky, P. M. (2004). When the psychometrics of test development meets organizational realities: A conceptual framework for organizational change, examples and recommendations. *Personnel Psychology*, *57*(1), 179–205. doi:10.1111/j.1744-6570.2004.tb02488.x

Munn, L. (2022). The uselessness of AI ethics. *AI and Ethics,* 1-9. doi:022-00209-w doi:10.1007/s43681

Nadler, L., & Wiggs, G. (1986). *Managing human resource development: A Practical guide*. Jossey-Bass.

Pfau, B. N., & Kay, I. T. (2002). *The human capital edge: 21 people management practices your company must implement (or avoid) to maximize shareholder value*. McGraw-Hill.

Pfeffer, J. (1994). *Competitive advantage through people: Unleashing the power of the workforce*. Harvard Business School Press.

Pham, Q., Madhavan, R., Righetti, L., Smart, W., & Chatila, R. (2018). The impact of robotics and automation on working conditions and employment [ethical, legal, and societal issues]. *IEEE Robotics & Automation Magazine*, *25*(2). https://doi.org/10.1109/mra.2018.2822058

Qwaider, W. Q. (2017). Information security and learning content management system (LCMS). *International Journal of Advanced Computer Science & Applications, 8*(11). https://doi.org/10.14569/IJACSA.2017.081174

Righetti, L., Madhavan, R., & Chatila, R. (2019). Unintended consequences of biased robotic and artificial intelligence systems [ethical, legal, and societal issues]. *IEEE Robotics & Automation Magazine, 26*(3), 11–13. https://doi.org/10.1109/MRA.2019.2926996

Rothwell, W., & Kazanas, H. (1991). *Strategic human resource planning and management*. Prentice-Hall.

Ruiner, C., Debbing, C. E., Hagemann, V., Schaper, M., Klumpp, M., & Hesenius, M. (2023). Job demands and resources when using technologies at work-development of a digital work typology. *Employee Relations: The International Journal, 45*(1), 190–208. doi:10.1108/er-11-2021-0468

Rynes, S. L., Bartunek, J. M., & Daft, R. L. (2001). Across the great divide: Knowledge creation and transfer between practitioners and academics. *Academy of Management Journal, 44*, 340–355. doi:10.2307/3069460

Sambataro, M. (2000, April). Just-in-time learning. *Computerworld.* http://www.computerworld.com/news/2002/ story/0,11280.44312, 00.html

Scott, W. R. (1987). The adolescence of institutional theory. *Administrative Science Quarterly, 32*, 493–511. doi:10.2307/2392880

Short, D. (2006). Closing the gap between research and practice in HRD. *Human Resource Development Quarterly, 17*(3), 343–350. doi:10.1002/hrdq.1178

Short, D. C., Sherlock, J. J., & Sugrue, B. (2004). Time to recognize those who link research and practice. *Human Resource Development Quarterly, 15*(3), 259–262. doi:10.1002/hrdq.1102

Snell, S. A., & Dean, J. W. (1992). Integrated manufacturing and human resource management: A human capital perspective. *Academy of Management Journal, 35*(3), 467–504. doi:10.2307/256484

Stahl, B. C., Schroeder, D., & Rodrigues, R. (2023). The ethics of artificial intelligence: A conclusion. In Springerbriefs in research and innovation governance (pp. 107–111). SpringerBriefs in Research and Innovation Governance. https://doi.org/10.1007/978-3-031-17040-9_9.

Stewart, T. A. (1999). Intellectual capital: The new wealth of organizations. Doubleday. Swanson, R. A. (1982). Industrial training. In W. H. Mitzel (Ed.), 5th encyclopedia of educational research (pp. 864-870). Macmillan.

Swanson, R. A. (1999). The foundations of performance improvement and implications for practice. In R. Torraco (Ed.), *Performance improvement theory and practice: Advances in developing human resources* (pp. 1–25). Sage. doi:10.1177/152342239900100102

Swanson, R. A., & Holton, E. F. (2001). *Foundation of human resource development*. Berrett-Koehler Publishers.

Swanson, R. A., & Torraco, R. J. (1994). Technical training's challenges and goals. *Technical & Skills Training*, *5*(7), 18–22.

Tseng, C. C., & McLean, G. N. (2008). Strategic HRD practices as key factors in organizational learning. *Journal of European Industrial Training*, *32*(6), 418–432. https://doi.org/10.1108/03090590810886544

Van de Ven, A. H., & Johnson, P. E. (2006). Knowledge for theory and practice. *Academy of Management Review*, *31*(4), 802–821. doi:10.5465/AMR.2006.22527385

Vince, R. (2003). The future practice of HRD. *Human Resource Development International*, *6*(4), 559–563. doi:10.1080/13678860310001630656

Vrontis, D., Christofi, M., Pereira, V., Tarba, S., Makrides, A., & Trichina, E. (2022). Artificial intelligence, robotics, advanced technologies and human resource management: A systematic review. *International Journal of Human Resource Management*, *33*(6), 1237–1266.

Way, S. A., & Johnson, D. E. (2005). Theorizing about the impact of strategic human resource management. *Human Resource Management Review*, *15*(1), 1–19. doi:10.1016/j.hrmr.2005.01.004

Weintraub, R. S., & Martineau, J. W. (2002, June). The just-in-time imperative. *Training and Development Journal*, 51–57.

Welch, J. (2005). *Winning*. Harper Collins.

Werner, J. M., & DeSimone, R. L. (2012). *Human resource development* (6th ed.). South-Western.

Wilson, J., & Daugherty, P. (2019). Creating the symbiotic AI workforce of the future. *MIT Sloan Management Review*, *61*(1), 1–4. https://www.proquest.com/scholarly-journals/creating-symbiotic-ai-workforce-future/docview/2315489026/se-2

Wright, V. A., Vaughan, B. W., Laurent, T., Lopez, R., Brooksbank, C., & Schneider, M. V. (2010). Bioinformatics training: Selecting an appropriate learning content management system—an example from the European Bioinformatics Institute. *Briefings in Bioinformatics*, *11*(6), 552–562. https://doi.org/10.1093/bib/bbq023

Yorks, L. (2005). Nothing so practical as a good theory. *Human Resource Development Review*, *4*(2), 111–113. doi:10.1177/1534484305276176

Zakaria, F. (2010, November). Restoring the American dream. *Time*, *176*(18), 30–35.

Chapter 8

Aligning Organization Development Initiatives With Organizational Philosophical Perspectives

ABSTRACT

Organization development (OD) initiatives should align with the philosophical perspectives of the organization. Cognitive philosophical perspective organizations should use cognitive OD initiatives within its organizational culture to develop people and technology. Some cognitive OD initiatives include teaching, training, learning, procedures and processes, and motivation. Organizations that operate within the behavioral philosophical perspective focus more on the technology impact rather than employee role. The ethical and legal implications of behavioral OD initiatives are important. Organizations that operate form the cultural philosophical perspectives should consider how cultural OD initiatives are influenced by both internal and external cultures. Ethical employees, ethical workplace environments, and ethical use of technology are also discussed.

INTRODUCTION

Employees' value to organizations is a source of debate. The Great Resignation is a current example. Whomever introduced the terms essential and nonessential

DOI: 10.4018/978-1-6684-5321-6.ch008

worker created millions of workers' discontent. All people or essential. The work they do may or may not be essential. Intertwining and combining the employee and the work as one thing created the animosity from and among some workers. It also spurred entrepreneurship from many workers who were offended by their mistreatment by leaders within their organizations.

The voice of the employee (Morrison, 2023) is critical within organizations that depend on the cognitive ability of the employees to be effective. Morrison (2023) defined employee "voice as informal and discretionary communication of ideas, suggestions, concerns, problems, or opinions about work-related issues, with the intent to bring about improvement or change" (p. 80). Underestimating the cognitive value that employees place on being able to express and display their knowledge can cause problems for organization leaders (Peng & Wei, 2020). Employees leave or seek change within organizations that do not respect their cognitive value. They form new or join existing unions; change positions, leave the workplace, display quiet quitting tendencies, etc.

Myers (1925) questioned the development of new workers who were learning bad habits from employees with longer duration with the organizations. He asked: "Who can doubt the importance of determining such undeniably wasteful methods of movement and of preventing the novice from falling into such bad habits of work? Yet how little provision is made of training the worker scientifically, i.e., systematically" (p. 100)! He advised organizations to use professional trainers and used some sport analogies to support his suggestion.

In the case of sport, e.g., … in riding, skating or golfing, few of us would dispense with the instruction of a professional expert. But in the case of industrial work, the novice has in by far the majority of cases to pick up his methods as best he can, perhaps learning from a worker of experience who may, nevertheless, have acquired bad habits of movement, or from one who, if he has acquired good ones, may be quite useless as an instructor. (Meyers, 1925, p. 100)

One should acknowledge that organizations still have similar training problems today (Bell et al., 2017; Carolan et al., 2014; Clark, 2004; Martin, 2010). Some organizations still do not place enough emphasis on training or may have someone who has the knowledge but does not know how to deliver or transfer that knowledge to trainers or other workers.

Pettigrew (1979) was the first researcher to describe organizational culture. Employees and technology influences organizational culture and vice versa. Organizational cultural initiatives are influenced by both internal and external culture. Many researchers (Chatman & Cha, 2003; Hatch, 1993; Schein, 1983, 1988) have studied organizational culture since Pettigrew and some HRD scholars have tried to integrate HRD with culture (Bennett, 2014; Bunch, 2007; Plakhotnik & Rocco, 2011; Plakhotnik, 2014).

Drucker (1994) discussed the effect of social changes on society and organizations. The need for knowledge workers has forced cultural change inside organizations. Organizations seeking to meet labor needs cannot afford to overlook any worker with appropriate KSAs (Hughes, 2016, 2018, 2019). Since the 2008 Great Recession many organizations do not have jobs for the millions of uneducated and unskilled displaced older workers (Hughes, 2012; Hughes et al., 2019). The COVID-19 pandemic has only exacerbated the problem. Even more technological skills are needed. Apprenticeships are reemerging in the US as more manufacturing and technical jobs are returning. This becomes society's problem because without jobs providing income, people can become a burden on societal systems.

Drucker (1994) predicted that the economic challenge of this society would be the productivity of knowledge workers, and the social challenge would be the productivity of the non-knowledge or service workers. The challenge would be to determine how to give non- knowledge workers decent incomes with dignity and status. This has not happened and has contributed to the Great Resignation during the COVID-19 pandemic.

BACKGROUND

According to Wittrock (1978) the cognitive movement "encouraged research on comprehension, understanding and transfer" which are fundamental to education (p.15). Individuals need to first comprehend a construct, understand the construct, and then transfer that comprehension and understanding to others. This does not occur often enough, and social media has magnified the problem exponentially. Individuals without comprehension and understanding are fully transferring inaccurate, misinformation to billions of people. Wittrock also stated that

A cognitive approach indicates that "learning from instruction is scientifically more productively studied as an internally, cognitively mediated process

than as a direct product of the environment, people, or factors external to the learner. The approach involves understanding relations or interactions between the learners' cognitive processes and aptitudes, such as attribution, motivation, encoding, memory, cognitive styles, and cognitive structures, and the characteristics of instructional treatments. (p.15)

Essentially the person learns metacognitively and is unbothered by the influences and opinions of others. Wittrock would possibly be disillusioned by some of what occurs on some social media websites. In cognitive organizations, employees are actively and constructively involved in their own learning, take responsibility for, and are held accountable for what they know and learn. The accountability is essential. The scientific and technological revolutions have eroded the accountability and cognitive confidence of some learners. They depend on technology more than their own mind. They blame technology for their lack of personal accountability. Social media has elevated group think. They no longer think for themselves. The ethics of group think needs to be examined. Organizations that operate within the cognitive philosophical perspective use cognitive initiatives to develop people and technology.

Behavior is directly associated with what people do and what people do can be directly observed and judged. Behavioral researchers focus on what and not why people do what they do when performing work. Wittrock (1978) described his perception of Skinner's (1957) ability to introduce reinforcement into instruction. He noted that Skinner

emphasized the use for instruction of the notion that the environment, not the learner, determines the products of learning, the behaviors. This important concept led to the death of the mind, to accountability for teachers, who are part of the learners' environment, and to behavioral objectives, which are necessary if one teaches by associating behavior, rather than thoughts, to stimuli by frequently, immediately, and repeatedly reinforcing successive approximations of the desired behavior. (p. 17)

Wittrock suggested that Skinner's view did not value the person; that Skinner gave the environment and behavioral objective more credit for the person's learning than the mind and action of the person themselves (Hughes, 2012). Using Skinner's view, learners were not expected to think but to only do what they were told to do by their leaders.

Organizations operating from the behavioral philosophical perspective failed to appreciate the intrinsic worth of the individual (Lepper et al., 1973).

Behaviorists are "interested only in what can be observed directly" (Martinez, 2010, p. 6). Subsequently, employee behavior is controlled and not understood. Some methods managers and leaders have used to control employee behavior in the workplace are selection, new employee orientation, mentoring, goals, job design, formal regulations, direct supervision, training, performance appraisal, and organizational rewards. The people control methods have yielded mixed results for organizations.

Taylor (1911) introduced scientific management into the workplace and behaviorist adopted and indoctrinated the application of behaviorism (Watson, 1913) in the workplace. With the development of attribution theory, Weiner (1985) provided explanations of how we judge people differently depending on what meaning we attribute to a given behavior. Attribution theory suggested that by observing human behavior, observers can determine whether the manifestation of the behavior is due to internal or external factors and that the root of the behavior depends on three factors: 1) distinctiveness, (2) consensus, and (3) consistency.

For profit organizations existed to make money (Friedman, 1970), and they measured inputs and outputs. One of the inputs is the people who work for the organization. If people produced the desired outputs, the organization viewed them positively and objectively. However, if outputs fell below expectations, subjectivity occurred and allowed stakeholders to replace workers with machines and other technology that produced desired output with minimal disruption (Hughes, 2012). The ethics of these decisions were seldom questioned. Yet, Gale (1980) found that although

investment in equipment to automate production does allow each worker to add greater amounts of value, mechanization is not an all-purpose panacea for problems in labor output. For most businesses, unfortunately, we have also found that increased investment intensity reduces profitability. (p.79)

Gale suggested that rather than "evaluating investment in new equipment as a simple choice between increased capital costs and reduced labor costs, management needed to consider the long-term consequences of mechanization" (p. 79). Many of these decisions were made without ethical considerations of what could happen to workers and US Society as a whole.

Now that most of the manual labor jobs have been outsourced to other countries, there is a void in the US workplace in which the jobs that require highly skilled workers are not currently capable of being filled. Americans saw the fallacy in these decisions during the COVID-19 pandemic and are now backshoring (Stentoft et al., 2016; Xu et al., 2020) manufacturing jobs. Organizations are using government visa programs to bring workers to the US and are investing in training programs with community colleges and R & D departments of major universities to develop the talent needed to compete. These methods are also being used to try and recover from the COVID-19 pandemic and the loss of 2.5 million immigrants from the American workforce due to the immigration policies of the 45th president of the US and his administration (Cohen & Shampine, 2022; Pineo, 2020; Saenz & Sparks, 2020).

Organizational behavior (OB) is the systematic study of the actions and attitudes that people reveal within organizations (Robbins & Judge, 2011). The study of behaviors and attitudes occurs in the three areas of productivity, absenteeism, and turnover which are simple to measure and correct. Goals of OB include explanation, prediction, and control. Control can become an ethical issue because it can be perceived to violate employees' personal freedom. Some OB practitioners offers technologies that facilitate the control of people; whether or not those technologies should be used in organizations becomes an ethical question. One example is the company Axon where "Most of Axon's Ethics Board Resigns to Protest Drone Plans" in June of 2022 (News Staff, 2022. The ethics board protest led to a reconsideration and statement from the company's CEO.

Organizational citizenship was added as a determiner of organizational effectiveness (Tolman, 1938). Behaviorists deny employees a choice in what they do despite their unlimited potential to do other things. Sometimes this leads to employees being rewarded for doing less than they are capable (Thorndike, 1911). Pfeffer (1998) offered three basic principles (people work harder, people work smarter, and high commitment management practices), proven effective, to assist managers who were looking for ways to stop viewing employees as a cost item. He stated that:

People work harder, because of the increased involvement and commitment that comes from having more control over and say in their work. People work smarter; high performance management practices encourage the building of skills and competence and, as importantly, facilitate the efforts of people in actually applying their wisdom and energy to enhancing organizational performance. High commitment management practices, by placing more responsibility in the hands of people farther down in the organization, save on administrative overhead as well as other costs associated with having an alienated workforce in an adversarial relationship with management. (p. 33)

Pfeffer also provided seven components of high-performance management practices: employment security, selective hiring, self-managed teams, high compensation contingent on organizational performance, training, reduction of status differences, and sharing information. These seven factors should align with the business strategy of the organization. These factors still allow managers to have some control over employee behavior in a less stringent way. HRD professionals should be actively involved with managers to ensure effective training occurs ethically and continuously.

OD INITIATIVES

Organization development (OD) is one of the three pillars of human research development. HRD scholars, professionals, and practitioners have sought to define OD and found that OD involves the principles, processes, and performance within organizations (McLagan, 1989; McLean & McLean, 2001; Egan, 2002; Cummings & Worley, 2005; McLean, 2006). McLean (2006) described OD as:

… any process or activity, based on the behavioral sciences, that, either initially or over a long term, has the potential to develop in an organization setting enhanced knowledge, expertise, productivity, satisfaction, income, interpersonal relationships, and other desired outcomes, whether for interpersonal or group/team gain or for the benefit of an organization, community, region, or, ultimately, the whole of humanity. (p. 9)

Thus, there are many OD initiatives throughout organizations of which HRD professionals and practitioners have a central role. This chapter will discuss how OD initiatives should be aligned as closely as possible to the philosophical perspective(s) of organizations whether they be cognitive, behavioral, or cultural initiatives. Understanding the worker from the cognitive philosophical perspective and instituting OD initiatives that value the cognitive ability of the worker is what is needed in cognitive focused organizations.

COGNITIVE OD INITIATIVES

Cognitive initiatives that are popular in organizations include teaching, learning, procedures and processes, and motivation. These initiatives are used to help employees and leaders effectively execute organizational goals. Industrial and organizational psychologists and their research related to employee training contributed to cognitive initiatives. Viteles (1932) advocated for training in the workplace to increase efficiency and improve individual adjustment and noted that "A well-organized training program, based on a sound analysis of the job and applying well-established learning principles, enables the worker to employ the most effective methods in the performance of his task" (p. 393). Tiffin (1942) defined training as "the process by which, through some form of instruction, the necessary responses for correctly performing a job are developed" (p. 185). Ghiselli and Brown (1948) defined training as "a means of adjusting the worker in the working environment in such a way as to bring about the greatest returns to both the worker and the organization" (p. 308). Without a distinct purpose for and definition of training, organizations struggle to successfully develop people to implement work functions, with or without the use of technology.

Teaching

Teaching in organizations is usually accomplished through training and development (T & D). Methods for delivery of T &D include on-site and offsite consisting of learning universities, corporate universities, training departments, executive education, workshops led by consultant(s), mobile learning, certificate programs, professional development, coaching, technology-delivered instruction (TDI), career and technical education programs, and formal degree programs (Bell et al., 2017). On-site training was provided by the supervisor/expert to employees (Bell et al, 2017). As jobs became more complex training experts were introduced into the workplace to teach workers and supervisors how to perform work duties and adhere to government regulations including labor laws (Kraiger & Ford, 2007) and ethics training and education (Hughes, 2019; Luebker, 2021).

Kincheloe (1999) noted that training that was provided to the American worker was through vocational programs or schools. Many workers are still developed through these types of programs and schools and the name has been changed to career and technical education (CTE) (Hughes, 2012). Some problems within industry today occur because some academics are not communicating their theoretical ideas to individuals who can practically apply the ideas. They do not share their ideas because they did not think industry personnel can comprehend the information (Bartunek & Rynes, 2014; Hughes

& Gosney, 2016; Kieser & Leiner, 2012; Patton, 2012). Kraiger and Ford's (2007) described four eras through which training or people development has evolved relevant to managing work within organizations. These eras were:

(a) the scientific management era (circa 1900- 1930); (b) the human relations era (circa 1930- 1960); (c) the participative management era (circa 1960- 1990); and (d) the strategic learning era (circa 1990 to present). [They] contend[ed] that these time periods represent[ed] not only fundamentally different perspectives of organization work but also different perspectives on what is meant by learning and development. (p. 281)

Kraiger and Ford showed that management did not begin to value the workers' humanistic persona until the 1930s; began to value workers' knowledge in the 1990s; and the transformation of understanding the knowledge worker continues to evolve. Even though it was understood through Münsterberg (1913) that learning was needed for the worker to perform their jobs, he stated that "Every form of economic labor in the workshop and in the factory, in the field and in the mine, in the store and in the office, must first be learned" (p. 145). He also questioned how the most economic method of learning practical activities could be determined. Professionals, practitioners, and researchers are still trying to answer Münsterberg's question even though Goldstein (1974) noted that "there is a wide gulf separating learning theories and principles from what is actually needed to improve performance" (p. 92). Knowing exactly what is needed to be learned will help determine the most economical way of providing the training. Pass (2019) has suggested a return to the humanistic roots of OD.

Teaching is used to pass knowledge from one individual to another. The traditional view of teaching is that "the learner is treated as 'an empty vessel' to be (inertly) filled with knowledge" (Fox, 2001, p. 25). Organizations have made a paradigm shift away from the focus on the teacher to a focus on the learner to adapt to change more rapidly. This shift to the focus on the learner requires stakeholders to determine ways to enhance the learners' ability to learn using all available materials and resources, technologically and in-person (Bennett, 2022; Conley et al., 2017; Hughes, 2021; Wang, 2011). This paradigm shift was evident in some ways using simulations and computer-based instruction and the emergence of cloud computing contributed to the shift along with AI and machine learning becoming the norm (Yorks et al., 2022). Theoretical knowledge is becoming less valued and practical and immediately applicable knowledge is becoming more valued (Hughes, 2012).

Evidence that supports this change away from theoretical knowledge is the shifting of federal research funding in the U.S. away from traditional four-year colleges and universities towards community and technical colleges to improve and increase the development of students who can be more quickly trained to enter the workplace.

In many workplaces, the term training is used simultaneously with teaching. Training is more of a behavior-based term because of the perception that it deals with skill attainment as opposed to long term knowledge acquisition. However, some skill attainment is also long term. The type of workplace and the level of knowledge attainment that is needed for mastery of content (Bloom, 1968) determines what teaching or training workers require. Teaching or training occurs in all organizations, formally or informally, and understanding the organization's philosophical perspective is imperative. For example, employees employed by organizations that operate within the cognitive philosophical perspective, such as educational institutions, consulting firms, legal firms, hospitals, and investment firms, employees spend inordinate amounts of time mastering their knowledge content to effectively perform their job. The complexity that arises in cognitive philosophical perspective workplaces occurs when workers feel that their knowledge is being exploited or undervalued by the organization (Drucker, 1969). Thus, determining the value of employee knowledge contribution becomes a point of contention as has been seen during the COVID-19 pandemic.

Learning

According to Silberman (1998), there are three specific learning problem goals organizations typically trying to solve:

1. Cognitive goals are the priority when there is a lack of knowledge. This is often referred to as a "don't know" situation.
2. Behavioral goals are the priority when there is a lack of skill. This is often referred to as a "can't do" situation.
3. Affective goals are the priority when there is a lack of desire or fear about using new knowledge or skills. This is often referred to as a "won't do" situation. (p.40)

Developers of cognitive OD initiatives can target one or all three goals (Hughes, 2012). Learning organizations seek to learn, adapt, and/or change (Gephart et al., 1996; Levitt & March, 1988; Senge, 1990) and employees must be willing to share their knowledge, management must encourage flexibility and experimentation on the job, and the culture must sustain the culture of learning once developed (Drucker, 1999; Tannenbaum, 1997). Learning only occurs when there is a transfer of knowledge (Argote & Hora, 2017; Argote & Miron-Spektor, 2011; Baumgartel & Jeanpeiere, 1972; Frisque & Kolb, 2008; Garavaglia, 1993; Goldstein, 1974; Leifer & Newstrom, 1980; Martin, 2010), and the individual and organization controls the extent to which transfer occurs. Transfer of knowledge occurs tacitly within organizations and capturing the extent of knowledge transfer becomes irrelevant when organizations are achieving their financial goals (Hughes, 2012). There are no easy ways to include tacit knowledge on the balance sheet (Hall & Andriani, 2000; Thoene & Buszko, 2014; Welch, 2005) despite the extent that training transfer is occurring relative to the bottom-line financial performance of the organization. Many executives agree that they do not know exactly when knowledge transfer occurred, but they know success when they see it in their organization and will reward successful training results (Hughes, 2012).

Kraiger and Ford (2007) suggested that workplace learning struggles to find an acceptable place in organizations. There needs to be a shift away from proving the necessity of training to acknowledging the value of people and technology through a multidimensional understanding of the person and the technology used in organizations (Hughes, 2012). The value of people and how they learn in organizations has been viewed from a behavioral philosophical perspective and analysis of their actions. Cognitive learning is supported by the constructivist view. Some of the ways constructivist theorists viewed cognitive learning are expressed in Table 1.

Procedures and Processes and Ethical Decision-making

Organizations operate within three primary systems: social, political, and input-output and the social system consists of subsystems with several distinctive characteristics and goals, "but their activities must be coordinated or the parent system cannot function" (Beckhard & Harris, 1987, p. 24). Political systems are centered on power and influence (Pfeffer, 1992). Organizations are input-output systems because they use and learn to perfect some process to convert inputs (human and material resources) into outputs (services or products) desired by their customers (Hughes, 2012). All areas of the systems use procedures and processes, but the input-output systems requires that procedures and processes be followed for the best employee performance.

Table 1. Cognitive learning supported by constructivist view

Constructivist Belief	Authors
Learning in the cognitive orientation is viewed as an active, generative process where meaning and understanding must be constructed from experiences.	Neisser, 1967; Smith, 1975; Wittrock, 1978, 1989; Osborne & Wittrock, 1985
It is recognized that meaning and comprehension (i.e., learning) is a function of the interaction between the organization of what is to be presented and the characteristics of individual students' own memory units.	Ausubel, 1963, 1978; Di Vesta,1974; Johnson, 1975; Voss, 1978
Learning occurs as a result of self-regulated behavior including assimilation and accommodation.	Bandura, 1986; Hardy III et al., 2019; Piaget, 1970; Sitzmann & Ely, 2011; Zimmerman, 2002
Learning is a case of self-organization and internal restructuring.	Koopmans, 2014; Kostromina, 2013; Piaget, 1959
Learning is a constructive building process of meaning-making that results in reflective abstractions, producing symbols within a medium. These symbols then become part of the individual's repertoire of assimilatory schemes, which in turn are used when perceiving and further conceiving.	Vygotsky, 1987; Liu & Matthews, 2005
Learning is not a result of development; learning is development.	Dewey, 1938; Gredler, 2012; Kolb, 1984; Lewin, 1946; Piaget, 1970; Vygotsky, 1978
Learning proceeds toward the development of structures. As learners struggle to make meaning, progressive structural shifts in perspective are constructed –in a sense, "big ideas"	Schifter & Fosnot, 1993; Fosnot & Perry, 1996

Procedures and processes are used to reduce uncertainty and the impact of change while also reducing overlapping and wasteful activities (Hughes, 2012). The use of procedures establishes standards that, when followed, facilitate control within work processes (Hughes, 2012).

Procedures and processes can become institutionalized and normalized within organizations and, as procedures and processes have become more complex, cognitive understanding is expected from employees to make necessary adjustments to meet quality standards and customer specifications (Hughes, 2012). It became necessary for organizations to depend on employees to solve problems that occur within jobs. They were expected to use ethical reasoning when solving problems without specific ethics training. Doing the right thing simply because it was the right thing to do was the expectation. In some organizations ethics training is provided and becoming normalized (Luebker, 2021).

Motivation for Employee Retention and Ethics

Motivation is associated with retention in the workplace (Chaumont, 2014; Kanfer et al., 2017; Ramlall, 2004; Thompson & Gregory, 2012) and some of these theories include Maslow's (1987) hierarchy of needs theory, McGregor's (2006) Theory X and Theory Y, Herzberg's (1966) two-factor theory, or the motivation-hygiene theory; McClelland's theory of needs; goal setting theory; equity theory; Skinner's (1957) reinforcement theory; and Vroom's (1995) expectancy theory. The theories that are more cognitively based have been better received by employees. As the workplace has changed to adjust to the knowledge worker, more emphasis has been placed on cognitive theories to inspire cognitive action from employees.

Maslow's Hierarchy of Needs Theory

The best-known approach to motivation is Maslow's (1987) hierarchy of needs theory where he suggested that human beings have an internal hierarchy of five needs: 1) Physiological needs— hunger, thirst, shelter, sex, and other bodily needs; 2) Safety needs—security and protection from physical and emotional harm; 3) Social needs— affection, a sense of belonging, acceptance, and friendship; 4) Esteem need—internal factors such as self-respect, autonomy, and achievement and external factors such as status, recognition, and attention; and 5) Self-actualization needs—the drive to become what one is capable of becoming; includes growth, achieving one's potential, and self-fulfillment. Physiological and safety needs were identified as lower order needs and are predominately satisfied through external resources. These physiological and safety needs became paramount and higher order for workers during the COVID-19 pandemic. Organizations that did not make them higher order needs experienced the most worker losses during the Great Resignation. Social, esteem, and self-actualization needs were categorized as higher-order needs and are satisfied internally. Within the workplace and society contexts, it can be inferred that in prosperous economic times, almost all permanently employed workers will have their lower order needs met. However, as the COVID-19 workplace environment and 2008-2009 recession proved, these needs are becoming more precarious for middle class US workers to meet. Many lost jobs and homes with no foreseeable solutions. How do we motivate workers to continue looking for jobs to meet their lower order needs during recessionary times? The COVID-19 pandemic presented similar problems for lower- and middle-skilled workers. When lower order needs are not being met despite full employment, one begins to question the ethics of organization and societal leaders who support a pay structure that does not support a livable wage for employees.

McGregor's Theory X and Theory Y

McGregor (2006) proposed two distinct views of human beings: basically negative, labeled Theory X and basically positive, labeled Theory Y. Theory X consist of four assumptions that promote negative connotations toward employees. Theory X implies that employees 1) inherently dislike work and, whenever possible, will attempt to avoid it; 2) must be coerced, controlled, or threatened with punishment to achieve desired goals since they dislike work; 3) will avoid responsibilities and seek formal direction whenever possible; and 4) place security above all other factors associated with work and will display little ambition. Theory Y has four positive assumptions regarding employees; that employee: 1) view work as being as natural as rest or play; 2) who are committed to the objectives will exercise self- direction and self-control; 3) can learn to accept, and even seek responsibility; and 4) can make innovative decisions is widely dispersed throughout the population and is not necessarily the sole province of those in management positions. Using McGregor's analysis, one would assume that employees who embody Theory X would have lower order needs and those who align with Theory Y would have higher order needs. From an ethical perspective Theory X employees would most likely behave unethically as related to job performance. Theory X employees would not perform to the job standards in alignment with the pay they receive. Is it unethical to underperform on the job when being paid to perform?

Herzberg Two-Factor Theory

Herzberg (1966) introduced the two-factor theory, or the motivation-hygiene theory investigating what people want from their jobs. His findings revealed a significant difference between how people replied when they felt good versus bad about their jobs. Internal factors included advancement, recognition, responsibility, and achievement which related to job satisfaction. Extrinsic factors included supervision, pay, company policies, and working conditions which related to job dissatisfaction. To motivate employees, Herzberg recommended emphasizing factors associated with the work itself or to outcomes directly derived from work including promotional opportunities and personal growth opportunities for employees. Ethically, leaders cannot focus on the work itself to the detriment of employees' mental and psychological well-being. They should also be concerned with extrinsic factors that affect the job itself or that the job effects, such as the environment. Ethically sound regulations are needed to not only protect employees but also the community, society, and the environment.

McClelland's Theory of Needs

McClelland's (1961) Theory of Needs describes the following three needs of the individual: 1) The need for achievement(nAch) which is the drive to excel or striving to succeed by achieving in relation to a set of standards; 2) The need for power (nPow) which is the need to make others behave in a way they would not have behaved otherwise; and 3) The need for affiliation (nAff) which is the desire for friendly, close interpersonal relationships. If employees can meet these needs within the workplace, they may feel more comfortable there; however, a question remains regarding the extent to which each of these needs are to be met. What is the right amount of drive, power, and/or affiliation for the person to feel that their needs have been met? From an ethical perspective, how are these needs being met for protected class employees?

Locke's Goal Setting Theory

Locke's (1969) Goal-Setting Theory is based on the idea that human action is purposeful and directed by conscious goals. Goal-setting theory is a contributing factor to motivation. Goals can be short-term or long-term depending on the task to be accomplished (Latham & Locke, 1991). Aligning individual goals to organizational goals is a constant endeavor (Boswell, 2006; Kheirandish, 2014; Paarlberg & Perry, 2007; Rumbles & Rees, 2013) as organizations strive to remain competitive. The alignment of people and technological goals within organizations must be complementary for organizations. Ethics should be embedded in the goals. Some organizations have developed motivational strategies to operationalize the goal setting theory. One such strategy is Management by Objectives (MBO) (Deming, 1982; Drucker, 1954; Kyriakopoulos, 2012; Levinson, 1970; Odiorne, 1965;

Roth, 2009). MBO emphasizes participatively established goals that are tangible, verifiable, and measurable. The four elements common to MBO programs are goal specificity, participative decision making, an explicit time period, and performance feedback. Goal-setting theory demonstrates that hard goals result in a higher level of individual performance and feedback on one's performance leads to higher performance. MBO and goal-setting theory differ in terms of participation; MBO strongly advocates participation, while goal-setting theory demonstrates that assigning goals to subordinates works just as well.

Skinner's Reinforcement Theory

Reinforcement Theory was Skinner's (1953) approach to motivation. It was not designed to consider the cognitive ability of the individual and was a counterpoint to goal-setting theory. Goal setting theory is a cognitive approach which proposes that an individual's purposes direct his actions, and reinforcement theory uses a behavioristic approach, which argues that reinforcement conditions behavior. The ethics of how much reinforcement theory should be used to control employees' behavior should be examined. The power of leaders to control employees' behavior by conditioning employees to exceed normal physical capabilities.

Adams's Equity Theory

Equity theory (Adams, 1963) offered the assumption that employees weigh what they put into a job situation (input) against what they get from it (outcome) and then compare their input-outcome ratio with the input-outcome ratio of relevant others. Employee perception is central to equity theory. If employees perceive equity of treatment, they feel that their situation is fair. If employees perceive that their treatment is unequal, inequity exists, and employees view themselves as under or over rewarded and they injustice is present. Depending on the social context when inequities occurred, employees would attempt to correct them (Adams, 1965). The referent variable that employees compare themselves against is important in equity theory. The three referent categories in the workplace are classified as "other," "system," and "self." The other category includes other individuals with similar jobs in the same organization. The system category considers organizational pay policies and procedures as well as how this system is administered. The self-category refers to input-outcome ratios that are unique to the individual. This category is influenced by criteria such as past jobs or family commitments. The ethical environment of the organization will determine how employees perceive others, the system, and themselves while at work.

Vroom's Expectancy Theory

Expectancy theory (Vroom, 1964, 1995) argued that the strength of a tendency to act in a certain way depends on the strength of an expectation that the act will be followed by a given outcome and on the attractiveness of that outcome to the individual. The three variables make up expectancy theory are 1) Attractiveness—the importance the individual places on the potential outcome or reward that can be achieved on the job; 2) Performance/reward linkage—the degree to which the individual believes that performing at a particular level will lead to the attainment of a desired outcome; and 3) Effort/performance linkage—the probability perceived by the individual that exerting a given amount of effort will lead to performance. The strength of a person's motivation to perform (effort) depends on how strongly he believes he can achieve what he attempts. The attractiveness, performance of, and effort exerted towards ethical behavior by leaders and employees depends on how they will be rewarded and if they can truly be ethical towards others.

Vroom (1964, 1995) developed expectancy theory to explain work behavior. Researchers have designed, developed, and modified models to explain expectations, values, and instrumentations (Mitchell, 1974). Porter and Steers (1973) focused on the role of met expectations and withdrawal behavior of an individual and defined met expectations as the difference between the positive and negative experiences a person faces on the job and what he expected to encounter. Porter and Steers found that when an individual's expectations were not substantially met, his inclination to withdraw increased. Irving and Meyer (1995) utilized difference scores to test met expectations hypothesis to examine the discrepancy between post-entry experiences and pre-entry expectations and learned that the difference scores produced artificial relations with outcome variables. Using direct measures required participants to indicate whether their pre-entry expectations concerning their jobs were confirmed (Irving & Meyer, 1995). A weakness of direct measures of met expectations was that it required participants to recall (Bem, 1972) their prior expectations after having been on the job for some time. It was a weakness because participant recollections of pre-entry expectations were filtered by more recent experiences and behaviors (Irving & Meyer, 1995). Therefore, individuals' personal ethics could be questioned and tested if they were not honest about their recollections.

Employees' and organizational leaders' expectations can have a positive or negative effect on employee performance and organizational success (Lovallo & Kahneman 2003). As leaders implement the PT concept throughout organizations, there are three questions they should consider:

1. How do the ethical expectations of the organization affect leaders' ethical decision-making?
2. How do leaders' ethical expectations of employees impact their employees' ethical decisions on the job?
3. How do employees' ethical decisions on the job impact the success of the organization?

The ethical use of the PT model could be incorporated into management practice to help gain competitive advantage (Espedal, 2005; Hughes, 2010, 2012; Pfeffer, 1994). For many employees, personal motivation, desire, and the will to be ethical are more important to their success than the influence of other employees and leaders (Beu et al., 2003; Lin et al., 2022).

Ormond (1999) revealed four general effects of motivation: 1) increase an individual's energy and activity level; 2) direct an individual toward certain goals; 3) promote initiation of certain activities and persistence in those activities; and 4) affect the learning strategies and cognitive processes an individual employs. Cascio (1998) found four factors that motivated trainees to do well in training: (1) a favorable work environment; (2) a belief in the soundness of the judgment by others that the trainee has strengths or weaknesses that training can improve on; (3) a personal belief in one's ability to master the content of the training (high self-efficacy); and (4) a belief on the part of the trainee that successful completion of the program will lead to outcomes that he or she personally values (personal development, promotion, an increase in pay). The combination of their findings suggest that the individual must be actively involved in motivation efforts expended by leaders. The individual is important because Banks (2002) found that regardless of how much leaders communicate with individuals, they still come to training programs with personal expectations and goals.

BEHAVIORAL OD INITIATIVES

The behavioral environments in many organizations have transitioned from Taylorism (1911) to operations research during the 1940s, to Deming's statistical process control in the 1950s, to Motorola's introduction of six sigma in 1986, to International Business Machines (IBM) modeling workers in 2005, and currently AI (Yorks et al., 2022), machine learning, robotics, and automation. Many organizations have also used business strategies for managing technological processes with people being a secondary focus such as Just-in-Time (JIT), lean manufacturing, International Organization of Standards (ISO), Total Quality Management (TQM), and Six Sigma.

Technology's Organizational Environmental Impact and Ethics

Technology is one major way organizations converted inputs into outputs while substituting machinery for human labor since the First Industrial Revolution (Hughes, 2012). Employees' behaviors are influenced advances in technologies. Technology advancements helped organizations increase output with less labor, capital, and materials. It has expanded to AI and other forms of digital technology in the 21st century that has been termed the fourth industrial revolution and has helped bolster the GIG economy. The GIG economy gives the worker more entrepreneurial power and autonomy with their work.

Technology requires continuous maintenance and modification to remain flexible and useful. Employees also need flexibility to do their jobs. How do we value an employees' identities and sustain their flexibility within the workplace? Horniman (2004) described leadership as a performing art and noted that leaders must be able to adjust to workplace situations regarding people and technology when they arise. Communication through social media has created both pros and cons as some workers have not been successful separating their home identity from their work identity and have lost jobs due to their home identity negatively affecting their work identity and that of their organization (Drouin et al., 2015). Society had been able to malign organizations who employ individuals with home identities that contrast with what they deem to be immoral and/or unethical behavior some examples include racism, ableism, among others (Martinez, 2019).

Three specific issues influenced by technology are: 1) continuous improvement processes, 2) process reengineering, and 3) mass customization. Continuous improvement processes (Deming, 1982) help develop and introduce new technology into the workplace. Deming provided 14 points for transforming organizations. These transforming points remain relevant and align with the *Hughes HRD Value Creation Model* as described in Table 2.

Organization leaders should determine if any of the 14 points are applicable to attaining their transformation goals. Deming's (1982) points were aimed at assisting behavioral focused organizations to change its philosophical perspective to a more cognitively focused operation which would include a cultural change within the organization.

Organization leaders must determine if the change they are implementing is in response to a break in the status quo, such as the Great Recession, and the change is needed only in occasional situations; or if the change is a natural state and managing change is a continual process (Lewin, 1946). Deming's (1982) framework may be useful in change situations and may also be effective for disruptive change such as the COVID-19 pandemic.

Process reengineering (Champy & Hammer, 1993) has three main elements which are: 1) identifying an organization's distinctive competencies—the unique skills and resources that determine an organization's competitive weapons; assessing core processes--these are the processes that customers value; and 3) reorganizing horizontally by process--flattening the structure and relying more on teams. Process reengineering changes also incorporates lean thinking (Bittencourt et al., 2019; Womack & Jones, 1996) with the purpose of inspiring rethinking and comprehensive redesign of essential business processes.

Behavior within Organizational Culture

Business environments experience change due to by seven forces: the changing nature of the workplace, technology, economic shocks, domestic and global competition, new social trends, world politics, and any unforeseen circumstances such as the COVID-19 worldwide pandemic. These changes have an impact on the organizational culture and employees must learn new ways to complete their work to change their behavior. Gredler (2009) identified three basic assumptions held by behaviorist theorists about learning:

1. Observable behavior rather than internal mental events or verbal reconstruction of events should be the focus of study.

Table 2. Deming's 14 Points and the Hughes HRD Value Creation Model

Deming's 14 Points for Transforming an Organization (**Deming, 1982, pp. 23-24**)	*Hughes HRD Value Creation Model Components*
1. Create constancy of purpose toward improvement of product and service, with the aim to become competitive and to stay in business, and to provide jobs.	Time Value
2. Adopt the new philosophy. We are in a new economic age. Western management must awaken to the challenge, must learn their responsibilities, and take on leadership for change.	Philosophical Perspectives
3. Cease dependence on inspection to achieve quality. Eliminate the need for inspection on a mass basis by building quality into the product in the first place.	OD Initiatives
4. End the practice of awarding business on the basis of price tag. Instead, minimize total cost. Move toward a single supplier for any one item, on a long-term relationship of loyalty and trust.	OD Initiatives and Competitive Advantage
5. Improve constantly and forever the system of production and service, to improve quality and productivity, and thus constantly decrease costs.	OD Initiatives and Competitive Advantage
6. Institute training on the job.	Maintenance Value
7. Institute leadership. The aim of supervision should be to help people and machines and gadgets to do a better job. Supervision of management is in need of overhaul, as well as supervision of production workers.	Diversity Intelligence and OD Initiatives
8. Drive out fear, so that everyone may work effectively for the company.	Diversity Intelligence and Workforce inter-personnel Diversity Talent Management System
9. Break down barriers between departments. People in research design, sales, and production must work as a team, to foresee problems of production and in use that may be encountered with the product or service.	Use Value, Location Value and Workforce inter-personnel Diversity Talent Management System
10. Eliminate slogans, exhortations, and targets for the workforce asking for zero defects and new levels of productivity. Such exhortations only create adversarial relationships, as the bulk of the causes of low quality and low productivity belong to the system and thus lie beyond the power of the workforce.	Workforce inter-personnel Diversity Talent Management System & OD Initiatives; Cultural Philosophical Perspective
11a. Eliminate work standards (quotas) on the factory floor. Substitute leadership.	Cognitive versus Behavioral Philosophical Perspective; OD Initiatives Cognitive versus Behavioral Philosophical Perspective
11.b Eliminate management by objective. Eliminate management by numbers, numerical goals. Substitute leadership.	Cognitive versus Behavioral Philosophical Perspective; OD Initiatives
12a. Remove barriers that rob the hourly worker of his right to pride of workmanship. The responsibility of supervisors must be changed from sheer numbers to quality.	Cognitive versus Behavioral Philosophical Perspective; Use Value; and OD Initiatives
12b. Remove barriers that rob people in management and in engineering of their right to pride or workmanship. This means inter alia, abolishment of the annual or merit rating and of management by objective.	Cognitive versus Behavioral Philosophical Perspective; OD Initiatives
13. Institute a vigorous program of education and self-improvement.	Maintenance and Modification Values
14. Put everybody in the company to work to accomplish the transformation. The transformation is everybody's job.	Cultural Philosophical Perspective; Workforce Inter-personnel Diversity Talent Management System

2.   Behavior should be studied in terms of its simplest elements, i.e., specific stimuli and specific responses.

3.   The process of learning is behavioral change. That is a particular response becomes associated with the occurrence of a particular stimulus. (p. 37)

Despite Gredler's findings management still needed to know if learning occurred. To ensure that learning had occurred and there were changes in employee behavior, management began using assessments. There are debates in HRD about how to define learning (Garavan, 1997; Masadeh, 2012; Slotte et al., 2004), so this is an area where specificity of what is being assessed to measure learning is important. Bass and Vaughn (1966) noted that

the primary objective of training is to bring about certain desired changes in [employee] behavior as efficiently as possible, and since the essence of learning is change in behavior, the importance of an understanding of the principles of learning to any training endeavor becomes obvious [and essential to the organization]. (p. 4)

Likert (1961) developed attitude surveys to identify participative management. He explained four types of management: exploitative and authoritarian, benevolent autocracy, consultative, and participative and suggested participative as the best options for managing employee behavior. Likert's tools measured the attitudes of the employees, predicted their behavior, and predicted their likely job performance. Likert appeared to want to inspire ethical interactions between employees and management. He wanted to stop the blind obedience and corporate coercion of employees and provided a way for employees to provide feedback to their employers. If employees' needs are not being met, they will never fully align themselves to the organizational culture. This was seen in many organizations during the COVID-19 pandemic in as some employees became tired of and frustrated with employee satisfaction surveys.

Unlimited amounts of information are available to organizations in real time through social media and other new age technological methods. With so much information, organization leaders are sometimes unable to troubleshoot problems because of information overload (Carr, 2003). Big data analysis has emerged as a tool that is being used by data scientists and HRD professionals and practitioners to help resolve some of these issues (Yorks et al., 2022).

Align People Initiatives with Technological Goals

Aligning people initiatives with technological goals require innovative ideas. Innovative organizations have structural, cultural, and human resource innovations facilitated by flexibility, adaptation, and synthesis of ideas. Innovative organizations actively train and develop their employees to use current or new technologies and do not marginalize its workers (Deng et al., 2016; Hughes, 2020; Isaac & Elrick, 2021). Innovation can occur through people as well as through technology and the *Hughes HRD Value Creation Model* can assist organizations with identifying ways to innovate with people. Some employees are inimitable and can help their organizations sustain a competitive advantage (Hatch & Dyer, 2004; Hoskisson et al., 2008).

Remote Work

Some people initiatives include flextime, job sharing, and using telecommuting to increase organizational flexibility. Remote work emerged as an imperative due to the COVID-19 pandemic, and many employees no longer want to be in centralized workplaces. Flextime allows employees some discretion in choosing their work hours. Job sharing gives the organization access to two or more employees for the price of one. Telecommuting reduces the costs of maintaining permanent work areas for employees and increases employee flexibility by eliminating commuting time and allowing workers to better balance work and family responsibilities. More research is now available on the benefits of remote work and work life balance (Como et al., 2021; Park et al., 2021; Yarberry & Sims, 2021; Zamarro & Prados, 2021).

Organizations and employees should be willing to change. Moran and Brightman (2000) Identified the three most powerful drivers of work behavior: purpose (what they desire and value); identity (which is their sense of who they are); and mastery (their ability to manage themselves and the environment). They suggested that change leaders must inspire employees to align their purpose, identity, and mastery with the necessary organizational change efforts. Even AI has proven to be unsuccessful without people. Explainable AI has been required to improve the problem (Arrieta et al., 2020; Robbins, 2019). Bandura (1977) noted that "Expectations alone will not produce desired performance if the component capabilities are lacking. Moreover, there are many things that people can do with certainty of success that they do not perform because they have no incentives to do so" (p. 194). Lawler (2000) suggested that employees who provided excellent performance needed to be rewarded to feel valued by organizations.

CULTURAL OD INITIATIVES

Schein (1983) defined organizational culture as:

the pattern of basic assumptions that a given group has invented, discovered, or developed in learning to cope with its problems of external adaptation and internal integration – a pattern of assumptions that has worked well enough to be considered valid and, therefore, to be taught to new members as the correct way to perceive, think, and feel in relation to those problems. (p, 14)

Robbins and Judge (2011) provided seven primary characteristics of organizational culture: innovation and risk taking, attention to detail, outcome orientation, people orientation, team orientation, aggressiveness, and stability. The strength of the culture is only as important as having all employees know what the culture is and adapting to the culture (Hughes, 2012). Assimilating toward the bad aspects of an organization's culture can destroy the careers of new employees before they ever can share their expertise (Anand et al., 2002; Becker & Bish, 2021; Caldwell & Peters, 2018; Liu et al., 2022; Trevino, 1986; Trevino & Brown, 2004). A strong organizational culture is characterized by the organization's core values being both intensely held and widely shared whether positive or negative. This can be negative for organizations that do not have strong ethical core values. Culture can be a liability for the organization when the shared values do not agree with values that increase the organization's effectiveness.

An organization's current customs, traditions, and general way of doing things are usually maintained when what they are doing is consistently successful, but the ultimate source of an organization's culture is its founders (Schein, 1983). Three forces are most important to sustaining a culture: selection practices, the actions of top management, and socialization methods (Schein, 1988). The wrong employees, bad leadership, and their socialization methods can also sustain an unethical culture.

Organizations share their cultures with its employees through stories, rituals, and messaging. Rituals are repetitive sequences of activities that express and reinforce the key values of the organization, the most important goals and people, and which goals and people are expendable (Caplow,

1954). To be ethically sound, organizations must tell ethical stories, develop ethical rituals, and provide ethical messaging. Sometimes a dramatic crisis forces cultural change to their messaging, stories, and rituals to take place. Regarding anti-racism, it took the death of George Floyd and worldwide protests for organizations to begin making ethical changes against racism when it has been required by law since 1964. Sports teams have cultures that are associated with the organization, communities, cities, and states within which they exist. Currently, the name, image, and likeness (NIL) opportunities for college athletes are beginning to change the culture of recruiting in college athletics (Kadlec, 2020). The transfer portal has also contributed to cultural change in the NCAA (O'Brien, 2021).

Ethics has become a major emphasis within the culture of organizations. Ethical standards were assumed within organizations; however, as the economy became more globalized, it has had to be taught to employees. The Sarbanes-Oxley law (Sarbanes, 2022) also forced ethics training into organizations. The different cultural norms across countries where organizations do businesses forced organizations to understand what is acceptable in each country. Saying no to traditional bribes and other influences is required to meet some legal standards. Not all unethical behavior is illegal, but some unethical behavior may violate organizational policies.

Organizations must be able to socialize and integrate new employees to accept the organization's core cultural values; however, these employees should not be asked to do things that are detrimental to their core personal values and beliefs. Sometimes an employee can be loyal to the organization without denying who they are as an individual. Management must openly acknowledge and demonstrate support for the differences that employees bring to the workplace especially if the employee is a member of a protected class group.

Pareek (1989) observed that organizational climate is created by the interaction of an organization's "structure, systems, culture, leader behavior, and psychological needs of employees" (p. 161). Through a review of studies by Likert (1967), Litwin and Stringer (1968), and others, Pareek (1989) identifies the following 12 dimensions of organizational climate:

These 12 dimensions offer a starting point for organizations to enhance their culture to benefit all stakeholders. Organizations can embed ethics into all 12 dimensions as noted in Table 3.

Table 3. Pareek's (1989) 12 Dimensions of Organizational Climate and Ethical Implications

Pareek's (1989) 12 Dimensions of Organizational Climate (pp. 162-163)	Ethical Implications
1. Orientation: members' principal concern (control, excellence, and so on).	All members of the organization should be aligning ethics with their principal concerns. Achieve excellence with ethical behavior.
2. Interpersonal relations: such as cliques or dependency.	Interpersonal relations should be ethical such that all employees feel that they belong. Unethical treatment by creating cliques or teams that are intentionally exclusive of protected group employees can be unethical.
3. Supervision: supervisors' influence on employee motivation.	Leaders' behavior should be ethical and not coercive when seeking to influence employee motivation. Honesty and integrity should be the norm.
4. Problem management: how the organization views and solves problems.	Problem solving procedures should be aligned with ethical standards of operation. Deviations from rules to solve problems can be unethical and harmful if safety regulations are not adhered to.
5. Management of mistakes: leaders' attitudes toward subordinates' errors	Leaders' unethical treatment of subordinates because of mistakes such as retaliation and creating a hostile work environment are unacceptable.
6. Conflict management: processes used to resolve conflict.	Processes used in conflict management should follow procedural just protocols and be fair and just for all employees. Favoritism is unethical.
7. Communication: prevalent styles and characteristics of communications.	Ethical, moral, and honest communication that does not embarrass employees are needed.
8. Decision making: how decisions are made and by whom; how the decision making process affects relationships;	Decision making should be as transparent as legally allowed. All stakeholders affected by the decision should be a part of the decision-making process as much as possible and all ethical concerns addressed.
9. Trust: who trusts whom for what.	Building trust requires leaders and followers to exhibit ethical trustworthy behavior in all interactions.
10. Management of rewards: what behaviors are reinforced.	Rewards for ethical behaviors should be included in the rewards and incentives system of the organization.
11. Risk taking: the organization's way of handling risky situations.	Before taking a risk, organization leaders should consider moral and ethical implications and whom and what they are risking.
12. Innovation and change: who is responsible for instigating change, by what methods, and to what effect?	Leaders should consider the ethical implications of who will be directly and indirectly affected by innovation and change. What are the collateral damages that could occur?

Embedding Ethics into The Organizational Environment

Schein (1983) stated that "The basic process of embedding a cultural element – a given belief or assumption – is a "teaching" process, but not necessarily an explicit one" (p. 21). He provided a list of mechanism used to embed and transmit culture within organizations. These mechanisms are:

1. Formal statements of organizational philosophy, charters, creeds, materials used for recruitment and selection, and socialization.
2. Design of physical spaces, facades, buildings.
3. Deliberate role modeling, teaching, and coaching by leaders.
4. Explicit reward and status system, promotion criteria.
5. Stories, legends, myths, and parables about key people and events.
6. What leaders pay attention to, measure and control.
7. Leader reactions to critical incidents and organizational crises (times when organizational survival is threatened, norms are unclear or are challenged, insubordination occurs, threatening or meaningless events occur, and so forth).
8. How the organization is designed and structured. (The design of work, who reports to whom, degree of decentralization, functional or other criteria for differentiation, and mechanisms used for integration carry implicit messages of what leaders assume and value.)
9. Organizational systems and procedures. (The types of information, control, and decision support systems in terms of categories of information, time cycles, who gets what information, and when and how performance appraisal and other review processes are conducted carry implicit messages of what leaders assume and value.)
10. Criteria used for recruitment, selection, promotion, leveling off, retirement, and "excommunication" of people (the implicit and possibly unconscious criteria that leaders use to determine who "fits" and who doesn't "fit" membership roles and key slots in the organization). (p.22)

The most effective way to get employees to accept an organization's culture has been through leadership behavior (Hughes, 2012). If leaders exemplify the cultural behavior of the organization, employees will follow their lead. Leaders' behavior has been an asset and a detriment to the success of cultural initiatives within organizations. Leaders should not delegate their responsibility to provide cultural adaptation and teaching for their followers. In today's boundaryless career (Robbins & Judge, 2011) environment, employees are adopting cultural norms from multiple organizations. There must be a consistency of ethical behavior at all levels of the organization (Luebker, 2021).

Leadership by Inspiration

Inspirational leadership is a form of transformational leadership. Bass (1999) described transformational leadership as referring "to the leader moving the follower beyond immediate self- interests through idealized influence (charisma), inspiration, intellectual stimulation, or individualized consideration" (p. 11). Leadership by Inspiration occurs when charismatic leaders embody the culture of the organization and employees follow because of their inspiring presence (Friedland, 1964; House, 1977; Kelman, 1961; Trice & Beyer, 1986a,1986b; Weber, 1947). These leaders produce achievements through people because they are capable of inspiring, intellectually stimulating, and being considerate to them (Bass, 1999). Inspirational leaders' influences can be positive or negative (Graham, 1991), and transformational leadership is beneficial when dealing with complexity (Crane & Hartwell, 2018). Dr. Martin Luther King, Jr. was an inspirational leader during the civil rights movement as was Mohandas Gandhi in India. Steve Jobs of Apple was an inspirational leader because of his resiliency and creativity (Isaacson, 2011). Mary Kay was an inspirational leader because of her ability to encourage women to become self-sufficient (Ash, 1981). Inspiring leaders and their followers share common beliefs about what is wrong, and the leader will articulate these beliefs publicly.

[Inspirational leaders] have the ability to influence subordinates to exert themselves beyond their own expectations and self-interest. The overlapping components of inspirational leadership behavior can be perceived to include: 1. managing meaning, 2. managing impressions, 3. molding follower expectations, 4. envisioning, and 5. intellectually stimulating followers. (Bass, 1988, p. 21)

Leadership by inspiration is a cultural phenomenon because it has characteristics of cultural change, encourages adoption of cultural norms that is represented by the leader, and becomes an embedded part of the organizational culture (Hughes, 2012).

EVIDENCE-BASED MANAGEMENT

Sackett (1997) defined evidence-based medicine as the "conscientious, explicit and judicious use of current best practice in making decisions about the care of individual patients" (p. 3). Pfeffer and Sutton (2006) suggested that evidence-based practice was much more needed in management. The pace of business forces them not to make decisions based upon the evidence and adjust along the way (Whitman, 2010). The pace of business can also lead to unethical decision-making that may be incapable of being rectified. Rousseau (2006) questioned whether evidence-based management was being applied in the workplace and provided the features that characterize evidence-based practice:

- Learning about *cause-effect* connections in professional practices;
- Isolating the variations that measurably affect desired outcomes;
- Creating a culture of evidence-based decision making and research participation;
- Using information-sharing communities to reduce overuse, underuse, and misuse of specific practices;
- Building decision supports to promote practices the evidence validates, along with techniques and artifacts that make the decision easier to execute or perform (e.g., checklists, protocols, or standing orders); and
- Having individual, organizational, and institutional factors promote access to knowledge and its use. (pp. 259- 260)

Managers can use these features to gauge whether evidence-based practice is being used in their organizations. Data science and its evaluation of big data can assist organizations with evidence-based management goals.

ISSUES, CONTROVERSIES, PROBLEMS

Learning organizations, although popular throughout the 1990s are not as prevalent today (DiBella, 1995; Ege et al., 2017; Fisher & White, 2000; Garvin, 1993; Garvin et al., 2008; Griego et al., 2000; Huysman, 2000; Kontoghiorghes et al., 2005; Luhn, 2016; Marsick & Watkins,1994; Mutamba, 2017; Newbold & Pharoah, 2009; Odor, 2018; Örtenblad, 2001, 2018; Rana et al., 2016Sun, 2003; Watkins & Marsick, 1993). The learning organization process was designed for leaders could try to extract knowledge that is applicable to the function of the organization from employees (Stewart, 1997). Senge (1990) introduced the five disciplines, systems thinking, personal mastery, mental models, shared vision, and team learning of the learning organization. Organization leaders should know the philosophical perspective(s) within which their organization operates before designating the organization as a learning organization. If the organization operates within the cognitive philosophical perspective, organization leaders should focus on the cognitive OD initiatives that will help the organization achieve its goals.

The biggest challenge for organizations dominated by the behavioral philosophical perspective is managing knowledge workers. Knowledge workers will not accept displacement by technological innovations. This has been proven during the Great Recession and the COVID-19 pandemic as workers are leaving their employers in the Great Resignation. The GIG economy also shows this to be true as workers continue to create jobs for themselves through independent or collaborative entrepreneurial efforts. The human mind has always been compared to the computer (Martinez, 2010). Although there are similarities, the differences, specifically, the computer's lack of consciousness must not be overlooked (Dwivedi et al., 2021; Mittelstadt, 2019). Yet, it has been overlooked to the detriment of some organizations.

Organizations continuously seek to improve quality and productivity using quality management, reengineering, and other techniques. They are seeking to:

1. Improve people skills.
2. Manage workforce diversity—a key challenge since organizations are becoming more heterogeneous in terms of race, and ethnicity.
3. Respond to globalization.
4. Responsible for managing.
5. Stimulate innovation and change.
6. Cope with temporariness as the workforce becomes more part time and contingency based.
7. Deal with declining employee loyalty.
8. Improve ethical behavior. (Hughes, 2012, p. 68)

Hughes's HRD Value Creation Model can affect these issues by providing a better understanding of how both people and technology are integral to organizational success. Cultural initiatives are extremely difficult to measure quantitatively and can be unexplainable. Some AI is unexplainable. The new AI 2.0 will be even more complex and unexplainable as it seeks to enhance the intelligence of technology. There has to be an interface between human beings and technology.

Solutions and Recommendations

This chapter provided teaching, learning, processes and procedures, and motivation related initiatives that are cognitively based that can be further developed to help organizations that operate predominantly from the cognitive philosophical perspective. Lee and Allen (1982) provided three general ways for technical staff in research and development to remain current about and introduce new technology into the workplace. They are:

1. Through readership of the scientific and engineering literature and other forms of documentation.
2. Through contact directly or indirectly with knowledgeable individuals outside the organization.
3. Through hiring and assimilation of new technically trained personnel. (p. 1405)

These suggestions fit within the cognitive philosophical perspective.

Organizations can also use evaluations to measure the compatibility of its initiatives to its philosophical perspective. Formative evaluations are useful because they are applied during the development stage of the process (Patton, 2012). Some formative evaluation techniques include one-to-one interviews, focus groups, pilot tests, observations, and surveys. The summative evaluation process is an overall review of the program. Conducting a summative evaluation after completion of a program provides a view of the overall program.

The cognitive philosophical perspective can be measured through use, maintenance and modification value. Legal, investment, and educational firms which depend upon the cognitive ability of employees could be studied using the cognitive aspects of the PT model (Hughes, 2010). The behavioral philosophical perspective can be measured through location and time value. IBM is used a process called modeling workers that is "building mathematical models of its own employees ... to improve productivity and automate management" (Baker, 2008a, p. 33). Baker(2008b) explained how employee behavior is being studied to add value to organizational performance.

Organizations that operate successfully within the cultural philosophical perspective include Alphabet, SAS Institute, and Gore-Tex and have very low employee turnover. Evaluation of the influence of historical, social, and political structures within the cultural philosophical perspective on location, use, modification, maintenance, and time value of employees may provide: 1) an understanding of the culture that is embedded in the workplace environment; 2) how employees adopt cultural norms of the organization; 3) how leadership by inspiration is effective (Mintzberg, 1998); and 4) how evidence-based management practices are implemented (Pfeffer & Sutton, 2006). Pfeffer and Sutton (2006) suggested that the best way to encourage employee performance was to build a high-performance culture using evidence-based management.

FUTURE RESEARCH DIRECTIONS

The debate between theory and practice continues and as employees and managers learn to be scholar-practitioners, the divide, while not completely bridged, is lessening (Argyris, 1985; Beer, 2001; Burack, 1999; Fang, 2023; Hamlin, 2002; Hughes & Gosney, 2016; Hughes et al., 2010; Mohrman et al., 2001; Muchinsky, 2004; Rynes et al., 2001; Van de Ven & Johnson, 2006). However, research is needed to help eliminate the gap that remains. Theory and practice must collaborate to keep up with rapid technological changes and people development.

Many OD initiatives that are used to develop people and technology require the use of cognitive ability. To derive and implement strategies that are successful requires an understanding of employees' cognitive perception of their location, use, maintenance, modification, and time value within the organization. This understanding could lead HRD professionals, practitioners, and researchers to develop of better teaching, learning, procedures and processes, motivational adjustments to enhance the five values. Schmidt et al., (1986) developed a causal model that showed cognitive ability as the single most important cause of job performance, and that the relationship between cognitive ability and job performance remains invariant or grows stronger over time. Murphy (1989) noted some instability in skilled performance associated with cognitive ability but did not take into consideration the job environment along with the job itself. More research can be conducted on the job environment's impact on the five values.

"What the learners believe or think influences their behavior" (Wittrock, 1978, p.18). Cognitive thoughts and capabilities influence behavior. Table 4 provides three ways that learning occurs, behaviorally.

Table 4. Learning behaviorally

Behaviorist View	Authors
Learning is more or less a permanent change in behavior that can be detected by observing an organism over a period of time.	Skinner, 1953
There are many schedules of reinforcement such as shaping, chaining etc.... that are useful for maintaining the change in behavior necessary for learning to have occurred.	Skinner, 1957
Learning is a system of behavioral responses to physical stimuli.	Pavlov, 1927

Organizations and their employees resist change overtly, implicitly, immediately, and/or by deferring. Tactics that have been effective in overcoming resistance to change include communication, participation, providing support, rewarding acceptance of change, and creating a learning organization. Leaders have introduced learning organizations into organizations using knowledge management (KM) (Alavi & Leidner, 2001; Penrose, 1959). KM is a process of organizing and distributing an organization's collective wisdom (Allen, 2022; Allen et al., 2019) so the right information gets to the right people at the right time. Researchers can examine how behavioral learning help the integration of people and technology.

Sitzmann et al. (2008) found that trainees are more influenced by their training environment than their own characteristics or organizational support. Thus, the training environment should reflect the work that employees are asked to perform (Belasco & Stayer, 1993; Kupritz, 2002). The location value of employee training is an area for future research. Virtual training during the COVID-19 pandemic has provided a rich environment to study virtual location value. Gagné (1962) noted that "performance comes first, and learning is often considered to result from practice of this performance" (p. 85). The location value of training will be revealed in this way.

Sustainability and spirituality in the workplace are two examples that have impacted cultural changes in organizations (Byrd, 2016; Halsell, 2014). Corporate social responsibility (CSR) is also affecting how organizations interact with employees and society (Jang & Ardichvili, 2020). More research is needed on how employees' location value and use value intersect with sustainability, spirituality, and CSR.

CONCLUSION

Wittrock (1978) noted that

From a cognitive point of view, accountability pertains to every person involved with the instruction. The teacher is responsible for teaching; the learner is responsible for learning; which is an internal process involving attention and the mental elaboration of information. A cognitive approach also raises serious questions about the effects upon learners of the belief that someone else controls and is accountable for their learning. The belief may foster dependency, retard student effort, and retard the development of a positive self-concept and of a feeling of ability to influence one's own learning. (p. 19)

Wittrock's statements may help to explain employees' inaction when do not feel that they control what and how they learn. Knowledge workers expect to feel motivated and empowered to influence some of their own learning. Attributing failure to lack of effort in cognitively based organizations is an accurate assessment when there is not a lack of ability. Organizations currently thrive on the minds of some of its people through individual effort and group performance and must begin to appreciate and value the minds of all its employees to enhance its competitiveness. Diversity, equity, and inclusion (DEI) efforts depend on engaging with all employees (Hughes, 2016). It is no longer acceptable to selectively dismiss and ignore the minds of diverse employees.

COVID-19 ETHICAL IMPACT MINI CASE STUDY

Computers are incapable of logical, cognitive reasoning which is essential to problem solving and troubleshooting in the workplace (Brynjolfsson & McAfee, 2011; Vergano, 2011). This became abundantly evident during the pandemic. Essential employees were needed at work. Some may have thought that essential workers were only knowledge workers, but that was not the case. Workers who were considered to be less knowledgeable and working in behaviorally based organizations were essential workers. Technology has impacted the workplace environment in both positive and negative ways. Warehouse workers for companies such as Amazon were felt over worked despite the robust technological systems that Amazon uses to take customer orders. To fulfill those orders, manual labor of workers became excessive. Adaptability became the norm during the COVID-19 pandemic. Some questions to consider:

1. Is it ethical for organizations to overwork manual workers because their technology is capable of receiving high volumes of orders?
2. Should organizations make promises to customers that they do not have the employees to fulfill?
3. Is it ethical for organizations to place excessive stress on workers when they know that their goals are not accomplishable?
4. How can organizations ethically align their people initiatives with their technological initiatives and goals?

REFERENCES

Adams, J. S. (1963). Toward an understanding of inequity. *Journal of Abnormal and Social Psychology*, *67*(5), 422–436. doi:10.1037/h0040968 PMID:14081885

Adams, J. S. (1965). Inequity in social exchange. *Advances in Experimental Social Psychology*, *2*, 267–299. doi:10.1016/S0065-2601(08)60108-2

Alavi, M., & Leidner, D. E. (2001). Review: Knowledge management and knowledge management systems: Conceptual foundations and research issues. *Management Information Systems Quarterly*, *25*(1), 107–136. doi:10.2307/3250961

Allen, J. M. (2022). *Fostering wisdom at work*. Routledge. doi:10.4324/9781003018759

Allen, J., Bracey, P., Aguilar, M., & Zimmerman, T. (2019). Supporting workforce wisdom in a global economy. In C. Hughes (Ed.), *Handbook of research on attracting, maintaining, and balancing a mature workforce*. IGI Global.

Anand, V., Glick, W. H., & Manz, C. C. (2002). Thriving on the knowledge of outsiders: Tapping organizational social capital. *The Academy of Management Executive*, *19*(1), 87–101. doi:10.5465/ame.2002.6640198

Argote, L., & Hora, M. (2017). Organizational learning and management of technology. *Production and Operations Management*, *26*(4), 579–590. doi:10.1111/poms.12667

Argote, L., & Miron-Spektor, E. (2011). Organizational learning: From experience to knowledge. *Organization Science, 22*(5), 1123–1137. https://www.jstor.org/stable/41303106. doi:10.1287/orsc.1100.0621

Argyris, C. (1985). Making knowledge more relevant to practice: Maps for action. In Lawler, E. E. III, Mohrman, A. M., Mohrman, S. A., Led- ford, G. E. Jr, & Cummings, T. G. (Eds.), Doing research that is useful for theory and practice (pp. 29–125). Jossey-Bass.

Arrieta, A. B., Díaz-Rodríguez, N., Del Ser, J., Bennetot, A., Tabik, S., Barbado, A., Garcia, S., Gil-Lopez, S., Molina, D., Benjamins, R., Chatila, R., & Herrera, F. (2020). Explainable artificial intelligence (XAI): Concepts, taxonomies, opportunities and challenges toward responsible AI. *Information Fusion, 58*, 82–115. doi:10.1016/j.inffus.2019.12.012

Ash, M. K. (1981). *Mary Kay*. Harper and Row.

Ausubel, D. (1963). *The psychology of meaningful verbal learning*. Holt, Rinehart & Winston.

Ausubel, D. P. (1978). In defense of advance organizers: A reply to the critics. *Review of Educational Research, 48*(2), 251–257. doi:10.3102/00346543048002251

Baker, S. (2008a, September 8). Management by the numbers. *Business Week*, pp. 32-36.

Baker, S. (2008b). *The numerati*. Houghton Mifflin.

Bandura, A. (1977). Self-efficacy: Toward a unifying theory of behavioral change. *Psychological Review, 84*(2), 191–215. doi:10.1037/0033-295X.84.2.191 PMID:847061

Bandura, A. (1986). *Social foundations of thought and action: A social cognitive theory*. Prentice Hall.

Banks, C. H. (2002). A descriptive analysis of the perceived effectiveness of Virginia Tech's faculty development institute. *Dissertation Abstracts International, 64*(08). (UMI No. 3102585)

Bartunek, J. M., & Rynes, S. L. (2014). Academics and practitioners are alike and unlike: The paradoxes of academic-practitioner relationships. *Journal of Management, 40*(5), 1181–1201. doi:10.1177/0149206314529160

Bass, B. M. (1988). The inspirational process of leadership. *Journal of Management Development*, *7*(5), 21–31. doi:10.1108/eb051688

Bass, B. M. (1999). Two decades of research and development in transformational leadership. *European Journal of Work and Organizational Psychology*, *8*(1), 9–32. doi:10.1080/135943299398410

Bass, B. M., & Vaughn, J. A. (1966). *Training in industry: The management of learning*. Brooks/Cole.

Baumgartel, H., & Jeanpeiere, F. (1972). Applying new knowledge in the back home setting: A study of Indian managers' adoptive efforts. *The Journal of Applied Behavioral Science*, *8*(6), 674–694. doi:10.1177/002188637200800603

Becker, K., & Bish, A. (2021). A framework for understanding the role of unlearning in onboarding. *Human Resource Management Review*, *31*(1), 1–13. doi:10.1016/j.hrmr.2019.100730

Beckhard, R., & Harris, R. T. (1987). *Organizational transitions: Managing complex change* (2nd ed.). Addison-Wesley Publishing Company.

Beer, M. (2001). Why management research findings are unimplementable: An action science perspective. *Reflections: The SoL Journal*, *2*(3), 58–65. doi:10.1162/152417301570383

Belasco, J. A., & Stayer, R. C. (1993). *Flight of the buffalo: Soaring to excellence, learning to let employees lead*. Warner Books, Inc.

Bell, B. S., Tannenbaum, S. I., Ford, J. K., Noe, R. A., & Kraiger, K. (2017). 100 years of training and development research: What we know and where we should go. *The Journal of Applied Psychology*, *102*(3), 305–323. doi:10.1037/apl0000142 PMID:28125262

Bem, D. J. (1972). Self-perception theory. In L. Berkowitz (Ed.), Vol. 6, pp. 1–62). Advances in experimental and social psychology. Academic Press.

Bennett, E. E. (2014). How an intranet provides opportunities for learning organizational culture: Implications for virtual HRD. *Advances in Developing Human Resources*, *16*(3), 296–319. doi:10.1177/1523422314532093

Bennett, E. E. (2022). Leveraging technology to design and deliver human resource development. In P. Holland, T. Bartram, T. Garavan, and K. Grant (Eds.). The Emerald handbook of work, workplaces and disruptive issues in HRM (pp. 261-276), Emerald Publishing Limited. doi:10.1108/978-1-80071-779-420221026

Beu, D. S., Buckley, M. R., & Harvey, M. G. (2003). Ethical decision–making: A multidimensional construct. *Business Ethics (Oxford, England)*, *12*(1), 88–107. doi:10.1111/1467-8608.00308

Bittencourt, V. L., Alves, A. C., & Leão, C. P. (2019). Lean thinking contributions for industry 4.0: A systematic literature review. *IFAC-PapersOnLine*, *52*(13), 904–909. doi:10.1016/j.ifacol.2019.11.310

Bloom, B. (1968). Learning for mastery. *Evaluation Comment*, *1*(2), 1–12.

Boswell, W. (2006). Aligning employees with the organization's strategic objectives: Out of 'line of sight', out of mind. *International Journal of Human Resource Management*, *17*(9), 1489–1511. doi:10.1080/09585190600878071

Brynjolfsson, E., & McAfee, A. (2011). *Race against the machine: How the digital revolution is accelerating innovation, driving productivity, and irreversibly transforming employment and the economy*. Digital Frontier Press.

Bunch, K. J. (2007). Training failure as a consequence of organizational culture. *Human Resource Development Review*, *6*(2), 142–163. doi:10.1177/1534484307299273

Burack, E. H. (1999). Bridging research to corpo- rate application. In L. Larwood & U. E. Gattiker (Eds.), *Impact analysis: How reach can enter application and make a difference* (pp. 17–46). Erlbaum.

Byrd, M. Y. (2016). The enlightened revelation: Toward a spirit-centered, socially just workplace. *New Directions for Adult and Continuing Education*, *152*(152), 85–94. doi:10.1002/ace.20215

Caldwell, C., & Peters, R. (2018). New employee onboarding – psychological contracts and ethical perspectives. *Journal of Management Development*, *37*(1), 27–39. doi:10.1108/JMD-10-2016-0202

Caplow, T. (1954). *The sociology of work*. McGraw-Hill Book Company.

Carolan, T. F., Hutchins, S. D., Wickens, C. D., & Cumming, J. M. (2014). Costs and benefits of more learner freedom: Meta-analyses of exploratory and learner control training methods. *Human Factors*, *56*(5), 999–1014. doi:10.1177/0018720813517710 PMID:25141602

Carr, N. G. (2003). IT doesn't matter. *Harvard Business Review*, *81*(5), 41–49. PMID:12747161

Cascio, W. F. (1998). *Applied psychology in human resource management* (5th ed.). Prentice Hall.

Champy, J., & Hammer, M. (1993). *Reengineering the corporation.* HarperBusiness.

Chatman, J. A., & Cha, S. E. (2003). Leading by leveraging culture. *California Management Review*, *45*(4), 20–34. doi:10.2307/41166186

Chaumont, F. (2014). *Does corporate culture have a positive impact on motivation?* [Doctoral dissertation, Dublin Business School].

Clark, N. (2004). HRD and the challenges of assessing learning in the workplace. *International Journal of Training and Development*, *8*(2), 140–156. doi:10.1111/j.1468-2419.2004.00203.x

Cohen, E., & Shampine, S. (2022, May 11). Immigration shortfall may be a headwind for labor supply. *Economic Bulletin*, 1–4.

Como, R., Hambley, L., & Domene, J. (2021). An exploration of work-life wellness and remote work during and beyond COVID-19. *Canadian Journal of Career Development*, *20*(1), 46–56.

Conley, Q., Lutz, H. S., & Miller, C. L. (2017). The flipped training model: Six steps for getting employees to flip out over training. *Performance Improvement*, *56*(5), 18–31. doi:10.1002/pfi.21692

Crane, B., & Hartwell, C. J. (2018). Developing employees' mental complexity: Transformational leadership as a catalyst in employee development. *Human Resource Development Review*, *17*(3), 234–257. doi:10.1177/1534484318781439

Deming, W. E. (1982). *Out of the crisis.* MIT Center for Advanced Engineering Study.

Deng, X., Joshi, K. D., & Galliers, R. D. (2016). The duality of empowerment and marginalization in microtask crowdsourcing. *Management Information Systems Quarterly, 40*(2), 279–302. doi:10.25300/MISQ/2016/40.2.01

Di Vesta, F. J. (1974). Cognitive structures and symbolic processes. *Teachers College Record, 75*(3), 357–370. doi:10.1177/016146817407500302

DiBella, A. J. (1995). Developing learning organizations: A matter of perspective. *Academy of Management Journal, 38*, 287–290.

Drouin, M., O'Connor, K. W., Schmidt, G. B., & Miller, D. A. (2015). Facebook fired: Legal perspectives and young adults' opinions on the use of social media in hiring and firing decisions. *Computers in Human Behavior, 46*, 123–128. doi:10.1016/j.chb.2015.01.011

Drucker, P. F. (1954). *The practice of management.* Harper.

Drucker, P. F. (1969). *The age of discontinuity.* Butterworth-Heinemann.

Drucker, P. F. (1994). The age of social transformation. *Atlantic Monthly, 274*(5), 53–80.

Drucker, P. F. (1999). Knowledge-worker productivity: The biggest challenge. *California Management Review, 41*(2), 79–94. doi:10.2307/41165987

Dwivedi, Y. K., Hughes, L., Ismagilova, E., Aarts, G., Coombs, C., Crick, T., & Williams, M. D. (2021). Artificial Intelligence (AI): Multidisciplinary perspectives on emerging challenges, opportunities, and agenda for research, practice and policy. *International Journal of Information Management, 57*, 101994

Ege, T., Esen, A., & Aşik Dizdar, Ö. (2017). Organizational learning and learning organizations: An integrative framework. *International Journal of Management Economics & Business / Uluslararasi Yönetim Iktisat ve Isletme Dergisi, 13*(2), 439–460. doi:10.17130/ijmeb.2017228693

Espedal, B. (2005). Management development: Using internal or external resources in developing core competence. *Human Resource Development Review, 4*(2), 136–158. doi:10.1177/1534484305276217

Fang, B. (2023). Bridging the gap between research and practice of engagement: Toward a collaborative human resource development. *Advances in Developing Human Resources, 0*(0), 1–21. doi:10.1177/15234223231156627

Fisher, S. R., & White, M. A. (2000). Downsizing in a learning organization: Are there hidden costs? *Academy of Management Review, 25*(1), 244–251. doi:10.2307/259273

Fosnot, C. T., & Perry, R. S. (1996). Constructivism: A psychological theory of learning. *Constructivism: Theory, Perspectives, and Practice, 2*(1), 8–33.

Fox, R. (2001). Constructivism examined. *Oxford Review of Education, 27*(1), 23–35. doi:10.1080/03054980125310

Friedland, W. H. (1964). For a sociological concept of charisma. *Social Forces, 43*(1), 18–26. doi:10.2307/2575961

Friedman, M. (1970, September 13). The social responsibility of business is to increase its profits. *The New York Times Magazine.*

Frisque, D. A., & Kolb, J. A. (2008). The effects of an ethics training program on attitude, knowledge, and transfer of training of office professionals: A treatment-and control-group design. *Human Resource Development Quarterly, 19*(1), 35–53. doi:10.1002/hrdq.1224

Gagné, R. M. (1962). Military training and principles of learning. *The American Psychologist, 17*(2), 83–91. doi:10.1037/h0048613

Gale, B. T. (1980). Can more capital buy higher productivity? *Harvard Business Review, 58*(4), 78–86.

Garavaglia, P. L. (1993). How to ensure transfer of training. *Training & Development, 47*(10), 63–69.

Garavan, T. N. (1997). Training, development, education and learning: Different or the same? *Journal of European Industrial Training, 21*(2), 39–50. doi:10.1108/03090599710161711

Garvin, D. (1993). Building a learning organization. *Harvard Business Review, 71*(4), 78–91. PMID:10127041

Garvin, D. A., Edmondson, A. C., & Gino, F. (2008). Is yours a learning organization? *Harvard Business Review, 86*(3), 109–134. PMID:18411968

Gephart, M. A., Marsick, V. J., Van Buren, M. E., & Spiro, M. S. (1996). Learning organizations come alive. *Training & Development, 50*, 56–66.

Ghiselli, E. E., & Brown, C. W. (1948). *Personnel and industrial psychology.* McGraw-Hill.

Goldstein, I. L. (1974). *Training: Program development and evaluation.* Brooks/ Cole.

Graham, J. W. (1991). Servant-leadership in organizations: Inspirational and moral. *The Leadership Quarterly, 2*(2), 105–119. doi:10.1016/1048-9843(91)90025-W

Gredler, M. E. (2012). Understanding Vygotsky for the classroom: Is it too late? *Educational Psychology Review, 24*(1), 113–131. doi:10.100710648-011-9183-6

Griego, O. V., Geroy, G. D., & Wright, P. C. (2000). Predictors of learning organizations: A human resource development practitioner's perspective. *The Learning Organization, 7*(1), 5–12. doi:10.1108/09696470010313632

Hall, R., & Andriani, P. (2000). Analyzing intangible resources and managing knowledge in a supply chain context. In *Knowledge creation* (pp. 231–257). Palgrave Macmillan. doi:10.1007/978-1-349-62753-0_9

Halsell, M. B. (2014). *Examining employees' perceptions of energy conservation behaviors in office settings.* [Doctoral dissertation, University of Arkansas]. https://scholarworks.uark.edu/cgi/viewcontent.cgi?article=3604&context=etd&httpsredir=1&referer=

Hamlin, R. G. (2002). In support of evidence- based management and research-informed HRD through HRD professional partnerships: An empirical and comparative study. *Human Resource Development International, 5*(4), 467–491. doi:10.1080/13678860210122643

Hardy, J. H. III, Day, E. A., & Steele, L. M. (2019). Interrelationships among self-regulated learning processes: Toward a dynamic process-based model of self-regulated learning. *Journal of Management, 45*(8), 3146–3177. doi:10.1177/0149206318780440

Hatch, M. J. (1993). The dynamics of organizational culture. *Academy of Management Review, 18*(4), 657–693. doi:10.2307/258594

Hatch, N. W., & Dyer, J. H. (2004). Human capital and learning as source of sustainable competitive advantage. *Strategic Management Journal, 25*(12), 1155–1178. doi:10.1002mj.421

Herzberg, F. (1966). Work and the nature of man. *WORLD (Oakland, Calif.).*

Horniman, A. B. (2004). Leading: A performing learning art. In M. Goldsmith, H. J. Morgan, & A. J. Ogg (Eds.), *Leading organizational learning: Harnessing the power of knowledge*. Jossey-Bass.

Hoskisson, R. E., Hitt, M. A., Ireland, R. D., & Harrison, J. S. (2008). *Competing for advantage* (2nd ed.). South-Western.

House, R. J. (1977). A 1976 theory of charismatic leadership. In J. G. Hunt & L. L. Larson (Eds.), *Leadership: The cutting edge* (pp. 189–273). Southern Illinois University Press.

Hughes, C. (2010). "People as technology" conceptual model: Towards a new value creation paradigm for strategic human resource development. *Human Resource Development Review*, *9*(1), 48–71. doi:10.1177/1534484309353561

Hughes, C. (2012). *Valuing people and technology in the workplace: A competitive advantage framework*. IGI Global. doi:10.4018/978-1-4666-0240-3

Hughes, C. (2016). *Diversity intelligence: Integrating diversity intelligence alongside intellectual, emotional, and cultural intelligence for leadership and career development*. Palgrave MacMillan Publications. doi:10.1057/978-1-137-52683-0

Hughes, C. (2018). *Workforce inter-personnel diversity: The power to influence human productivity and career development*. Springer International Publishing.

Hughes, C. (2019). *Ethical and legal issues in human resource development: Evolving roles and emerging trends*. Springer International Publishing. doi:10.1007/978-3-319-99528-1

Hughes, C. (Ed.). (2020). *Strategies for attracting, maintaining, and balancing a mature workforce*. IGI Global. doi:10.4018/978-1-7998-2277-6

Hughes, C. (2021). The changing learning technological landscape for trainers in the wake of COVID-19. *Advances in Developing Human Resources*, *23*(1), 66–74. doi:10.1177/1523422320972108

Hughes, C., & Gosney, M. (Eds.). (2016). *Bridging the scholar-practitioner gap in Human Resource Development*. IGI Global. doi:10.4018/978-1-4666-9998-4

Hughes, C., Wang, J., Zheng, W., & McLean, L. (2010). Implementation concerns of scholar-practitioners: A pilot study of the link between research and practice. *International Journal of Asian Business and Information Management, 1*(2), 32–46. doi:10.4018/jabim.2010040104

Huysman, M. (2000). An organizational learning approach to the learning organization. *European Journal of Work and Organizational Psychology, 9*(2), 133–145. doi:10.1080/135943200397905

Irving, P. G., & Meyer, J. P. (1995). On using direct measures of met expectations: A methodological note. *Journal of Management, 21*(6), 1159–1176. doi:10.1177/014920639502100608

Isaac, M., & Elrick, J. (2021). How COVID-19 may alleviate the multiple marginalization of racialized migrant workers. *Ethnic and Racial Studies, 44*(5), 851–863. doi:10.1080/01419870.2020.1842900

Isaacson, W. (2011). *Steve Jobs*. Simon and Schuster.

Jang, S., & Ardichvili, A. (2020). Examining the link between corporate social responsibility and human resources: Implications for HRD research and practice. *Human Resource Development Review, 19*(2), 183–211. doi:10.1177/1534484320912044

Johnson, R. E. (1975). Meaning in complex learning. *Review of Educational Research, 45*(3), 425–459. doi:10.3102/00346543045003425

Kadlec, M. (2020). Game changing legislation: NCAA forced to revise name, image, and likeness compensation rules. *Nova Law Review, 45*, 227–267.

Kanfer, R., Frese, M., & Johnson, R. E. (2017). Motivation related to work: A century of progress. *The Journal of Applied Psychology, 102*(3), 338–355. doi:10.1037/apl0000133 PMID:28150980

Kelman, H. C. (1961). Processes of opinion change. *Public Opinion Quarterly, 25*(1), 57–78. doi:10.1086/266996

Kheirandish, M. (2014). Measuring the personal and organizational goals alignment: Developing a practical model. *Research Journal of Recent Sciences, 3*(2), 125–132.

Kieser, A., & Leiner, L. (2012). Collaborate with practitioners: But beware of collaborative research. *Journal of Management Inquiry, 21*(1), 14–28. doi:10.1177/1056492611411923

Kincheloe, J. (1999). *How do we tell the workers? The socioeconomic foundations of work and vocational education*. Westview Press.

Koopmans, M. (2014). Change, self-organization and the search for causality in educational research and practice. *Complicity: An International Journal of Complexity in Education*, *11*(1), 20–40. doi:10.29173/cmplct19523

Kontoghiorghes, C., Awbre, S. M., & Feurig, P. L. (2005). Examining the relationship between learning organization characteristics and change adaptation, innovation, and organizational performance. *Human Resource Development Quarterly*, *16*(2), 185–212. doi:10.1002/hrdq.1133

Kostromina, S. (2013). Academic skills as a basis for self-organization of human activity. *Procedia: Social and Behavioral Sciences*, *86*, 543–550. doi:10.1016/j.sbspro.2013.08.611

Kraiger, K., & Ford, J. K. (2007). The expanding role of workplace training: Themes and trends influencing training research and practice. In L. L. Koppes (Ed.), *Historical perspectives in industrial and organizational psychology*. Psychology Press.

Kupritz, V. W. (2002). The relative impact of workplace design on training transfer. *Human Resource Development Quarterly*, *13*(4), 427–447. doi:10.1002/hrdq.1042

Kyriakopoulos, G. (2012). Half a century of management by objectives (MBO): A review. *African Journal of Business Management*, *5*(6), 1772–1786.

Latham, G. P., & Locke, E. A. (1991). Self- regulation through goal setting. *Organizational Behavior and Human Decision Processes*, *50*(2), 212–247. doi:10.1016/0749-5978(91)90021-K

Lawler, E. E. III. (2000). *Rewarding excellence: Pay strategies for the new economy*. Jossey-Bass Publishers.

Lee, D. M. S., & Allen, T. J. (1982). Integrating new technical staff: Implications for acquiring new technology. *Management Science*, *28*(12), 1405–1420. doi:10.1287/mnsc.28.12.1405

Leifer, M. S., & Newstron, J. W. (1980). Solving the transfer of training problems. *Training and Development Journal*, (August), 42–46.

Lepper, M. R., Greene, D., & Nisbett, R. E. (1973). Undermining children's intrinsic interest with extrinsic reward: A test of the "over justification" hypothesis. *Journal of Personality and Social Psychology*, *28*(1), 129–137. doi:10.1037/h0035519

Levinson, H. (1970). Management by whose objectives? *Harvard Business Review*, *48*(4), 125–134. PMID:12545927

Levitt, B., & March, J. G. (1988). Organizational learning. *Annual Review of Sociology*, *14*(1), 319–340. doi:10.1146/annurev.so.14.080188.001535

Lewin, K. (1946). Action research and minority problems. *The Journal of Social Issues*, *2*(4), 34–46. doi:10.1111/j.1540-4560.1946.tb02295.x

Likert, R. (1961). *New patterns of management*. McGraw-Hill.

Likert, R. (1967). *The human organization*. McGraw-Hill.

Lin, M., Wu, X., & Li, X. (2022). Who are the empowered employees: Those with high work performance or high ethical behavior? *Journal of Business Ethics*, 1–17. doi:10.100710551-022-05232-9 PMID:35540176

Litwin, G. H., & Stringer, R. A. Jr. (1968). *Motivation and organizational climate*. Division of Research, Harvard Business School.

Liu, C. H., & Matthews, R. (2005). Vygotsky's philosophy: Constructivism and its criticisms examined. *International Education Journal*, *6*(3), 386–399.

Liu, X., Greenbaum, R. L., Allen, D., & Zhang, Z. (2022). A Newcomer socialization perspective on the proliferation of unethical conduct in organizations: The influences of peer coaching practices and newcomers' goal orientations. *Journal of Business Ethics*, *176*(1), 73–88. doi:10.100710551-020-04730-y

Locke, E. A. (1969). Purpose without consciousness: A contradiction. *Psychological Reports*, *25*(3), 991–1009. doi:10.2466/pr0.1969.25.3.991

Lovallo, D., & Kahneman, D. (2003). Delusions of success: How optimism undermines executives' decision. *Harvard Business Review*, *81*, 56–63. PMID:12858711

Luebker, J. (2021). *A focused evaluation of sales employees' ethics training and its effect on the diffusion of ethics in a financial organization*. [Doctoral dissertation, University of Arkansas]. https://scholarworks.uark.edu/cgi/viewcontent.cgi?article=58 17&context=etd

Luhn, A. (2016). The learning organization. *Creative and Knowledge Society*, *6*(1), 1–13. doi:10.1515/cks-2016-0005

Marsick, V. J., & Watkins, K. E. (1994). The learning organization: An integrative vision for HRD. *Human Resource Development Quarterly*, *5*(4), 353–360. doi:10.1002/hrdq.3920050406

Martin, H. J. (2010). Workplace climate and peer support as determinants of training transfer. *Human Resource Development Quarterly*, *19*(1), 87–104. doi:10.1002/hrdq.20038

Martinez, M. E. (2010). *Learning and cognition: The design of the mind*. Pearson.

Martinez, A. (2019). The right to be an asshole: The need for increased first amendment public employment protections in the age of social media. *The American University Journal of Gender, Social Policy & the Law*, *27*(2), 1–35.

Masadeh, M. (2012). Training, education, development and learning: What is the difference? *European Scientific Journal*, *8*(10), 62–68. doi:10.19044/esj.2012.v8n10p%25p

Maslow, A. (1987). *Motivation and personality* (3rd ed.). Harper & Row.

McClelland, D. C. (1961). *The achieving society*. Free Press. doi:10.1037/14359-000

McGregor, D. (2006). *The human side of enterprise, annotated edition*. The McGraw-Hill Companies, Inc.

Mintzberg, H. (1998). Covert leadership: Notes on managing professionals. Knowledge workers respond to inspiration, not supervision. *Harvard Business Review*, *76*(6), 140–147. PMID:10187244

Mitchell, T. (1974). Expectancy models of job satisfaction, occupational preference and effort: A theoretical, methodological, and empirical appraisal. *Psychological Bulletin*, *81*(12), 1053–1077. doi:10.1037/h0037495

Mittelstadt, B. (2019). Principles alone cannot guarantee ethical AI. *Nature Machine Intelligence, 1*(11), 501–507. doi:10.103842256-019-0114-4

Mohrman, S., Gibson, C., & Mohrman, A. (2001). Doing research that is useful to practice: A model and empirical exploration. *Academy of Management Journal, 44*(2), 357–375. doi:10.2307/3069461

Moran, J. W., & Brightman, B. K. (2000). Leading organizational change. *Journal of Workplace Learning: Employee Counseling Today, 12*(2), 66–74. doi:10.1108/13665620010316226

Morrison, E. W. (2023). Employee voice and silence: Taking stock a decade later. *Annual Review of Organizational Psychology and Organizational Behavior, 10*(1), 79–107. doi:10.1146/annurev-orgpsych-120920-054654

Muchinsky, P. M. (2004). When the psychometrics of test development meets organizational realities: A conceptual framework for organizational change, examples and recommendations. *Personnel Psychology, 57*(1), 179–205. doi:10.1111/j.1744-6570.2004.tb02488.x

Münsterberg, H. (1913). *Psychology and industrial efficiency.* Houghton Mifflin., doi:10.1037/10855-000

Murphy, K. R. (1989). Is the relationship between cognitive ability and job performance stable over time? *Human Performance, 2*(3), 183–200. doi:10.120715327043hup0203_3

Mutamba, C. (2017). The inter-relationship of organizational learning, learning organizations, virtual technology, and virtual communities of practice. *New Horizons in Adult Education and Human Resource Development, 29*(3), 4–14. doi:10.1002/nha3.20186

Myers, C. S. (1925). *Industrial psychology.* The People's Institute Publishing Company.

Neisser, U. (1967). *Cognitive psychology.* Appleton-Century- Crofts.

Newbold, C., & Pharoah, N. (2009). What it means to be a learning organization. *Strategic HR Review, 8*(3), 12–16. doi:10.1108/14754390910946521

News Staff. (2022). Most of Axon's ethics board resigns to protest drone plans. *Gov Tech.* https://www.govtech.com/biz/most-of-axons-ethics-board-resigns-to-protest-drone-plans

O'Brien, T. (2021). Consider ramifications of NCAA's new transfer rules. *College Athletics and the Law*, *18*(3), 8–8. doi:10.1002/catl.30882

Odiorne, G. S. (1965). *Management by objectives: A system of managerial leadership*. Pitman Publishing.

Odor, H. O. (2018). A literature review on organizational learning and learning organizations. *International Journal of Economics & Management Sciences*, *07*(01). doi:10.4172/2162-6359.1000494

Örtenblad, A. (2001). On differences between organizational learning and learning organization. *The Learning Organization*, *8*(3), 125–133. doi:10.1108/09696470110391211

Örtenblad, A. (2018). What does "learning organization" mean? *The Learning Organization*, *25*(3), 150–158. doi:10.1108/TLO-02-2018-0016

Osborne, R., & Wittrock, M. (1985). The generative learning model and its implications for science education. *Studies in Science Education*, *12*(1), 59–87. doi:10.1080/03057268508559923

Ormond, J. E. (1999). *Human learning* (3rd ed.). Prentice-Hall Inc.

Paarlberg, L. E., & Perry, J. L. (2007). Values management: Aligning employee values and organization goals. *American Review of Public Administration*, *37*(4), 387–408. doi:10.1177/0275074006297238

Pareek, U. (1989). Motivational analysis of organizations-climate (MAO-C). In Pfeiffer, J.W. (Ed.), The 1989 annual: Developing human resources (pp. 161–18). Pfeiffer & Company.

Park, S., Jeong, S., & Chai, D. S. (2021). Remote e-workers' psychological well-being and career development in the era of COVID-19: Challenges, success factors, and the roles of HRD professionals. *Advances in Developing Human Resources*, *23*(3), 222–236. doi:10.1177/15234223211017849

Pass, G. (2019). The humanistic roots of organization development-a reclamation? *e-Organisations & People*, *26*(1), 44-54.

Patton, M. Q. (2012). *Essentials of utilization-focused evaluation*. Sage.

Pavlov, I. P. (1927). *Conditioned reflexes*. Routledge and Kegan Paul.

Peng, H., & Wei, F. (2020). How and when does leader behavioral integrity influence employee voice? The roles of team independence climate and corporate ethical values. *Journal of Business Ethics*, *166*(3), 505–521. doi:10.100710551-019-04114-x

Penrose, E. T. (1959). *The theory of the growth of the firm*. Wiley.

Pettigrew, A. M. (1979). On studying organizational culture. *Administrative Science Quarterly*, *24*(4), 570–581. doi:10.2307/2392363

Pfeffer, J. (1992). *Managing with power: Politics and influence in organizations*. Harvard Business School Press.

Pfeffer, J. (1994). *Competitive advantage through people: Unleashing the power of the workforce*. Harvard Business School Press. doi:10.2307/41165742

Pfeffer, J. (1998). *The human equation. Building profits by putting people first*. Harvard Business School.

Pfeffer, J., & Sutton, R. I. (2006). Evidence-based management. *Harvard Business Review*, *84*(1), 62–75. PMID:16447370

Piaget, J. (1959). *The language and thought of the child*. Routledge.

Piaget, J. (1970). *Structuralism*. Basic Books.

Pineo, R. (2020). Immigration crisis: The United States under President Donald J. Trump. *Journal of Developing Societies*, *36*(1), 7–40. doi:10.1177/0169796X19896905

Plakhotnik, M. (2014). Organizational culture and HRD: The roots, the landscape, and the future. In N. E. Chalofsky, T. S. Rocco, L. M. and Morris (eds). Handbook of human resource development (pp. 80-93). John Wiley & Sons, Inc.

Plakhotnik, M. S., & Rocco, T. S. (2011). What do we know, how much, and why it matters: Organizational culture and AHRD research 1994-2009. *Human Resource Development Review*, *10*(1), 74–100. doi:10.1177/1534484310388992

Porter, L. W., & Steers, R. M. (1973). Organizational, work, and personal factors in employee turnover and absenteeism. *Journal of Management*, *80*, 151–176.

Ramlall, S. (2004). A review of employee motivation theories and their implications for employee retention within organizations. *The Journal of American Academy of Business, Cambridge, 5*(1/2), 52–63.

Rana, S., Ardichvili, A., & Polesello, D. (2016). Promoting self-directed learning in a learning organization: Tools and practices. *European Journal of Training and Development, 40*(7), 470–489. doi:10.1108/EJTD-10-2015-0076

Robbins, S. (2019). A misdirected principle with a catch: Explicability for AI. *Minds and Machines, 29*(4), 495–514. doi:10.100711023-019-09509-3

Robbins, S., & Judge, T. (2011). *Organizational behavior* (14th ed.). Prentice Hall.

Roth, W. F. (2009). Is management by objectives obsolete? *Global Business and Organizational Excellence, 28*(4), 36–43. doi:10.1002/joe.20266

Rousseau, D. M. (2006). Presidential address: Is there such a thing as "evidence-based management"? *Academy of Management Review, 31*(2), 256–269. doi:10.5465/amr.2006.20208679

Rumbles, S., & Rees, G. (2013). Continuous changes, organizational burnout and the implications for HRD. *Industrial and Commercial Training, 45*(4), 236–242. doi:10.1108/00197851311323538

Rynes, S. L., Bartunek, J. M., & Daft, R. L. (2001). Across the great divide: Knowledge creation and transfer between practitioners and academics. *Academy of Management Journal, 44*(2), 340–355. doi:10.2307/3069460

Sackett, D. L. (1997). Evidence-based medicine. *Seminars in Perinatology, 21*(1), 3–5. doi:10.1016/S0146-0005(97)80013-4 PMID:9190027

Saenz, R., & Sparks, C. (2020). *The inequities of job loss and recovery amid the COVID-19 pandemic.* Carsey School of Public Policy | UNH. https://carsey.unh.edu/publication/inequities-job-loss-recovery-amid-COVID-pandemic

Sarbanes, P. (2002, July). Sarbanes-Oxley act of 2002. In *The Public Company Accounting Reform and Investor Protection Act* (Vol. 55). US Congress.

Schein, E. H. (1983). The role of the founder in creating organizational culture. *Organizational Dynamics, 12*(1), 13–28. doi:10.1016/0090-2616(83)90023-2

Schein, E. H. (1988). Organizational socialization and the profession of management. *Sloan Management Review, 30*(1), 53–65.

Schifter, D., & Fosnot, C. T. (1993). *Reconstructing mathematics education: Stories of teachers meeting the challenge of reform.* Teachers College.

Senge, P. (1990). *The fifth discipline: The art and practice of the learning organization.* Doubleday.

Silberman, M. (1998). *Active training* (2nd ed.). Jossey-Bass/Pfeiffer.

Sitzmann, T., & Ely, K. (2011). A meta-analysis of self-regulated learning in work-related training and educational attainment: What we know and where we need to go. *Psychological Bulletin, 137*(3), 421–442. doi:10.1037/a0022777 PMID:21401218

Sitzmann, T., Brown, K. G., Casper, W. J., Ely, K., & Zimmerman, R. D. (2008). A review and meta-analysis of the nomological network of trainee reactions. *The Journal of Applied Psychology, 93*(2), 280–295. doi:10.1037/0021-9010.93.2.280 PMID:18361632

Skinner, B. F. (1953). *Science and human behavior.* Macmillan.

Skinner, B. F. (1957). *Verbal learning.* Appleton-Century-Crofts., doi:10.1037/11256-000

Slotte, V., Tynjälä, P., & Hytönen, T. (2004). How do HRD practitioners describe learning at work? *Human Resource Development International, 7*(4), 481–499. doi:10.1080/1367886042000245978

Smith, F. (1975). *Comprehension and learning.* Holt, Rinehart & Winston.

Stentoft, J., Olhager, J., Heikkilä, J., & Thoms, L. (2016). Manufacturing backshoring: A systematic literature review. *Operations Management Research, 9*(3), 53–61. doi:10.100712063-016-0111-2

Stewart, T. A. (1997). *Intellectual capital: The new wealth of organizations.* Doubleday.

Sun, H. (2003). Conceptual clarifications for 'organizational learning', 'learning organization' and 'a learning organization'. *Human Resource Development International, 6*(2), 153–166. doi:10.1080/13678860110086465

Tannenbaum, S. I. (1997). Enhancing continuous learning: Diagnostic findings from multiple companies. *Human Resource Management, 36*(4), 437–452. doi:10.1002/(SICI)1099-050X(199724)36:4<437::AID-HRM7>3.0.CO;2-W

Taylor, F. W. (1911). *The principles of scientific management.* Harper & Row.

Thoene, M. A., & Buszko, A. (2014). Quantitative model of tacit knowledge estimation for pharmaceutical industry. *The Engineering Economist, 25*(1), 40–46.

Thompson, C., & Gregory, J. B. (2012). Managing millennials: A framework for improving attraction, motivation, and retention. *The Psychologist Manager Journal, 15*(4), 237–246. doi:10.1080/10887156.2012.730444

Thorndike, E. L. (1911). *Animal intelligence*. Macmillan.

Tiffin, J. (1942). *Industrial psychology*. Prentice-Hall., doi:10.1037/11230-000

Tolman, E. C. (1938). The determiners of behavior at a choice point. *Psychological Review, 45*(1), 1–41. doi:10.1037/h0062733

Trevino, L. K. (1986). Ethical decision making in organizations: A person-situation interactionist model. *Academy of Management Review, 11*(3), 601–617. doi:10.2307/258313

Trevino, L. K., & Brown, M. E. (2004). Managing to be ethical: Debunking five business ethics myths. *The Academy of Management Executive, 18*(2), 69–81. doi:10.5465/ame.2004.13837400

Trice, H. M., & Beyer, J. M. (1986a). Charisma and its routinization in two social movement organizations. In B. M. Staw & L. L. Cummings (Eds.), *Research in organizational behavior* (Vol. 8, pp. 113–164). JAI Press.

Trice, H. M., & Beyer, J. M. (1986b). Cultural leadership in organizations. *Organization Science, 2*(2), 149–169. doi:10.1287/orsc.2.2.149

Van de Ven, A. H., & Johnson, P. E. (2006). Knowledge for theory and practice. *Academy of Management Review, 31*(4), 802–821. doi:10.5465/amr.2006.22527385

Vergano, D. (2011, February 17). Watson dominated at 'Jeopardy!- but what else can it do? *USA Today*, p. 2D.

Viteles, M. S. (1932). *Industrial psychology*. Norton.

Voss, J. (1978). Cognition and instruction: Toward a cognitive theory of learning. In A. Lesgold, J. Pellegrino, S. Fokkema, & R. Glaser (Eds.), *Cognitive psychology and instruction* (pp. 13–23). Plenum. doi:10.1007/978-1-4684-2535-2_3

Vroom, V. H. (1964). *Work and motivation*. John Wiley & Sons, Inc.

Vroom, V. H. (1995). *Work and motivation*. Jossey-Bass.

Vygotsky, L. (1978). Interaction between learning and development. *Readings On the Development of Children, 23*(3), 34–41.

Vygotsky, L. S. (1987). *The collected works of L.S. Vygotsky* (R. W. Rieber & A. S. Carton, (Eds). Plenum Press.

Wang, M. (2011). Integrating organizational, social, and individual perspectives in Web 2.0-based workplace e-learning. *Information Systems Frontiers, 13*, 191–205. doi:10.1007/s10796-009-9191-y

Watkins, K., & Marsick, V. (1993). *Sculpting the learning organization: Lessons in the art and science of systemic change*. Jossey-Bass.

Watson, J. B. (1913). Psychology as the behaviorist sees it. *Psychological Review, 20*(2), 157–177. doi:10.1037/h0074428

Weber, M. (1947). The theory of social and economic organization (Henderson, A. M., & Parsons, T. (Trans. Eds.)). The Free Press.

Weiner, B. (1985). An attributional theory of achievement motivation and emotion. *Psychological Review, 92*(4), 548–573. doi:10.1037/0033-295X.92.4.548 PMID:3903815

Whitman, M. (2010). *The power of many: Values for success in business and in life*. Three Rivers Press.

Wittrock, M. C. (1978). The cognitive movement in instruction. *Educational Psychologist, 15*(1), 15–29. doi:10.1080/00461527809529192

Wittrock, M. C. (1989). Generative processes of comprehension. *Educational Psychologist, 24*(4), 345–376. doi:10.120715326985ep2404_2

Womack, J. P., & Jones, D. T. (1996). *Lean thinking*. Simon & Schuster.

Xu, Z., Elomri, A., Kerbache, L., & El Omri, A. (2020). Impacts of COVID-19 on global supply chains: Facts and perspectives. *IEEE Engineering Management Review, 48*(3), 153–166. doi:10.1109/EMR.2020.3018420

Yarberry, S., & Sims, C. (2021). The impact of COVID-19-prompted virtual/remote work environments on employees' career development: Social learning theory, belongingness, and self-empowerment. *Advances in Developing Human Resources, 23*(3), 237–252. doi:10.1177/15234223211017850

Yorks, L., Abel, A. L., & Rotatori, D. (2022). *Strategic human resource development in practice: Leveraging talent for sustained performance in the digital age of AI.* Springer Nature. doi:10.1007/978-3-030-95775-9

Zamarro, G., & Prados, M. J. (2021). Gender differences in couples' division of childcare, work and mental health during COVID-19. *Review of Economics of the Household, 19*(1), 11–40. doi:10.100711150-020-09534-7 PMID:33488316

Zimmerman, B. J. (2002). Becoming a self-regulated learner: An overview. *Theory into Practice, 41*(2), 64–70. doi:10.120715430421tip4102_2

Chapter 9
Hughes's Human Resource Development (HRD) Value Creation Model

ABSTRACT

This chapter describes the seven-point Hughes human resource development (HRD) value creation model. The seven-point Hughes HRD value creation model is multidisciplinary. This model is both theoretical and operational. This model provides a theoretical framework for further research and practical applications of management practices, training practices, and HRD philosophy and strategies within organizations. Users of this model should keep ethics foremost in their minds as they seek to integrate people and technology in the workplace. This chapter centers around convincing managers and leaders to change their thought processes about how they perceive their employees' value within the workplace.

INTRODUCTION

Each organization must identify its dominant philosophical perspective and adjust its OD initiatives, as needed, to ensure alignment of goals and strategies. People and technology have to be complementary to each other for organizations to optimize their competitiveness in the marketplace. The biggest change in the model is that the OD initiatives became the last point in the model. Usually, stakeholders introduce the OD initiatives without

DOI: 10.4018/978-1-6684-5321-6.ch009

understanding their employees or technology value and something goes awry. *Hughes's HRD Value Creation Model* attempts to be a guide for organizations to follow through its people and technology towards success.

BACKGROUND

Sackett and Mullen (1993) described four reasons why evaluation should be completed:

1) to make decisions about the future use of a training program or technique (e.g., continue, modify, or eliminate); 2) to make decisions about individual trainees (e.g., certify as competent, provide additional training, etc.); 3) to contribute to a scientific understanding of the training process; or 4) for political or public relations purposes (e.g., documenting success may increase the training function's credibility and visibility within an organization). (p.619).

Effective evaluation increases credibility and visibility of the training function (Brinkerhoff, 1987; Bushnell, 1990; Galvin, 1983; Goldstein, 1980; Kirkpatrick, 1967, 1987, 1994, 1996; Warr et al., 1970). All four of these items are relevant to *Hughes's HRD Value Creation Model*, thus organizations should consider conducting evaluations to determine if there are areas for improvement through use of the model.

HUGHES'S HRD VALUE CREATION MODEL

The seven-point *Hughes's HRD Value Creation Model* was derived from Hughes's high performance manufacturing industry experiences. The model extends Hughes's (2010) PT conceptual model. Aguinis and Kraiger (2009) suggested that there is "[a]n important challenge for the practice of training… to integrate the training function with employee selection, performance, management, rewards, and other human resource practices (Aguinis, 2009; Aguinis & Pierce, 2008; Cascio & Aguinis, 2005)" (p.467). This model provides a theoretical framework for further research and practical applications of management practices, training practices (Cascio, 2019), and HRD philosophy and strategies within organizations. This chapter describes the seven-point *Hughes HRD Value Creation Model* (See Figure 1) and seeks to inspire transformation and examination of ways to develop measures for the values.

Figure 1. Hughes's HRD Value Creation Model
Note: This model was printed with permission of Diversity Intelligence® (DQ), LLC copyright 2022

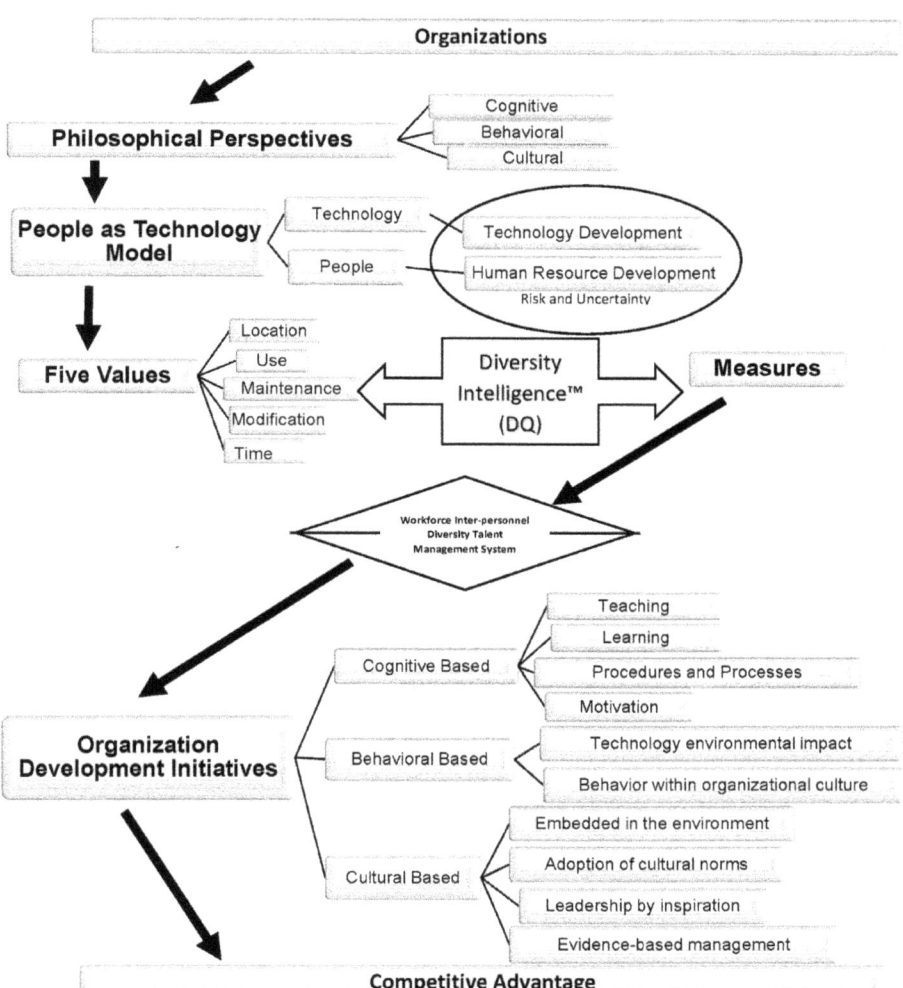

To understand this model, one must understand the purpose of organizations. Organizations compete in the marketplace for revenue (Carrig & Wright, 2006; Hamel & Prahalad, 1994; Hoskisson et al., 2008; Pfeffer, 1994; Porter, 1980; Schein, 1988; Welch, 2005; Womack & Jones, 1996). To attain revenue, organizations must meet customer demands using competitive advantage (Hoskisson et al., 2008; Porter, 1980).

The Seven Points

The first point of the model shows the three philosophical perspectives within which organizations operate. The philosophical perspectives are cognitive, behavioral, and cultural. The cognitive, behavioral and cultural philosophical perspective can be categorized as:

- *Thinking:* Cognitive
- *Doing:* Behavioral
- *Cultural Context:* Cultural

These philosophical perspectives are found in all organizations and the cognitive, behavioral, and cultural debate can be a limiting factor in the success of organizations. Some organizations may not even recognize that the cognitive, behavioral, and cultural philosophical dynamic is occurring and how they are limiting their ability to win against current and future competition. Organization leaders should begin to question: How do organizations thrive within their dominant philosophical context? If they are understood to operate from the cognitive philosophical perspective, is this understood by all employees and not an issue that prevents interaction across organizational units? According to Wittrock (1978) "Attribution of failure to lack of effort, rather than to luck or to lack of ability, leads to the inference that effort should be increased to attain success in school" (p. 20). How much effort is needed from the organizations and employees to be successful? How do organization leaders leverage the ability to locate, use, maintain, modify, and keep technology and people relevant for their organization's prosperity? Is there a philosophical perspective mismatch within organizations with regards to people and technology development? Organizations often operate from one dominant philosophical perspective that supports their strategy for performance but can include a combination of the philosophical perspectives.

The second point of the *Hughes HRD Value Creation Model* is the PT conceptual model (Hughes, 2010). The PT model contains the five values that relate people to technology and explains how people and technology relate to each other within the workplace. The PT model suggests that both technology and people have location, use, maintenance, modification, and time value to the organization. It suggests that managers and leaders should think of people positively and similarly to how they positively view technology within the workplace.

Some managers and leaders struggle as they attempt to supervise or lead people (Drucker, 2008; Kotter, 1996; Parker et al., 2020; Strebel, 1996). Otherwise, publishers and authors of leadership books and consultants who provide leadership training would be non-existent. Most research studies center on how to convince employees to change their behavior, this book centers around convincing managers and leaders to change their thought processes about how they perceive their employees' value within the workplace. They will know they have succeeded by their employees' improved actions or performances. The PT model provides ways that leaders can objectively evaluate opportunities of equivalence that exist between people and technology. All organizations should develop both its people and technology. Technology and Human Resource Development are two fields that can help organizations create value from integrating people and technology development.

Point three of the model involves the five values that relate people to technology within the workplace. The five values location, use, maintenance, modification, and time. The values are distinct, but they do not exist independent of one another. They represent the multidimensionality of technology and people. If these values can be quantified to the extent that organizations can see their people value as clearly as they see their technology value, they will help create a competitive advantage for the organization.

Point four describes diversity intelligence® (DQ) (Hughes, 2016) and how it can be used by leaders to understand all employees in the workplace. Diversity intelligent leaders will have the capability the knowledge and understanding of workplace protected class laws and categories; the workforce education and training needed to lead all employees; and an understanding of their own perception of their behavior towards all employees whom they lead. DQ bridges the gap between the five values and the ability to measure the five values within all employees.

Diversity intelligence® was derived from within my research agenda on valuing people and technology in the workplace. Diversity intelligence® was needed by leaders in my research to bridge the gap between the five values of people and technology. Diversity intelligent leaders will have the capability to lead all employees because they will have the knowledge and understanding of workplace protected class laws and categories; the workforce education and training needed to lead all employees; and an understanding of their own perception of their behavior towards all employees whom they lead. Diversity intelligence® integrated within organizational systems makes it unique and provides a reimagining diversity, equity, inclusion, and belonging efforts within organizations.

Point five describes ways that measurable five values can be integrated into the organization so that the organization can leverage its competitive advantage. They can be measured individually or collectively to yield a competitive advantage for the organization. For example, time value can be measured in length of time in position, seniority of an employee with the organization; it can also be measured along with use value with regards to efficiency of employee performance. Technology's location value can be measured in terms of capital expense to store and/or purchase the technology. There is no specified formula for the measures because each organization will be able to determine how the values are represented within their organization. Researchers, professionals, and practitioners can develop new measures. One example from Hughes (2012) of how this model can be applicable is to correlate the funding of military troops during war time versus during peace time. The measurements would center on military hardware investment versus soldier benefits. How is funding based on the location value of the troops during war vs. peace? What is the use benefit for military spending during a war as opposed to when not a war? What is the maintenance cost for troops and their technologies while at war vs. peace? What is the modification value of the GI bill while at war vs. peace? What is the time value of troops when at war than during peace time? The organization should be stronger as its people understand their value and perform at levels that enhance their productivity to the organization.

Point six of the *Hughes HRD Value Creation Model* is the workforce inter-personnel diversity talent management system (Hughes, 2018). This talent management system does not leave out employee potential as some studies of talent management suggests has been done (Cascio & Collings, 2022). With diversity intelligent leaders who are capable of leading and valuing all employees, workforce inter-personnel diversity can be recognized and used to manage all talent within organizations. No employee will be left out because they are different.

Point seven of the model addresses some of the different organization development (OD) initiatives that organizations introduce to develop technology and people within the workplace. These OD initiatives are where the organization should attempt to align their strategies with the philosophical perspectives of the organization. The model provides examples of types of initiatives that are appropriate within each philosophical perspective. Organization leaders should determine OD initiatives that contribute to their competitive advantage. Some OD initiatives, when they dissipate after much fanfare and limited results, are referred to as fads. These OD initiatives should be sustainable.

Most OD initiatives are well-intended and well-designed, yet problems arise when the employees who are asked to implement these OD initiatives do not know why the initiatives have been introduced or what they are being asked to do or change (Hughes, 2012). Most OD initiatives involve some type of major or minor change for the employee or even the culture of the organization. Research on cultural change (Bolman & Deal, 2008) suggested that it takes three to five years to change a culture. Some organizations want their OD initiatives to be effective almost immediately.

This model suggests that all OD initiatives should be understood from the philosophical perspective within which the organization operates. The new OD initiative's philosophical perspective may actually be at odds with the philosophical perspective of the organization. Once the philosophical perspective is understood, employees should be made aware of what is expected from them during the change. Clarifying employees' expectations may lead to less resistance and better implementation of the new initiative (Orr, 1996; Strebel, 1996; van den Heuvel et al., 2013, 2020). This *Hughes HRD Value Creation Model* framework is a starting point from which organizations can leverage their most valuable assets, people and technology.

Banks (2009) identified eight critical human performance issues in the US. They are included in Table 1 with information on how they relate to the five values.

These issues must be resolved for human performance to improve in the US. The *Hughes HRD Value Creation Model* offers an opportunity to solve some of the issues described here. The *Hughes HRD Value Creation Model* adds to the literature and is available for empirical studies to be developed. The model focuses on human resource development and technology development to

leverage all organizational resources. It suggests methods for organizations to adapt to change and ethically deal with employee concerns. It also allows organizations to investigate the inter-personnel diversity of its employees. Inter-personnel diversity recognizes that there are unique characteristics of each employee. Leveraging inter-personnel diversity allows organizational leaders to build stronger teams and provide training aligned with the needs of individual employees using improved talent management strategies (Hughes, 2018). Applying *Hughes's HRD Value Creation Model* to each employee provides a way to clearly distinguish the ways that the employees are inter-personally different. HRD professionals and practitioners should become proficient at leading change initiatives (Beckhard & Harris, 1987;

Table 1. Critical Human Performance Issues and Hughes's HRD Value Creation Model

Critical Human Performance Issues in the US	Hughes's HRD Value Creation Model
1. Expanding empirical research to address issues of hedonism	Points 1 and 7
2. Training, developing, inspiring and motivating employees	Point 3
3. The lack of consistent, testable models of human performance improvement	The entire model
4. Lack of focus on individual performers to achieve performance improvement goals	Point 6
5. Communicating and measuring value of human performance	Point 5
6. Managing and leveraging resources to reduce resource constraints	Point 4
7. Adaptability to change	Points 4, 6, and 7
8. Ethical implications for human performance.	Points 4, 5, 6, and 7

Biech, 2004; Burkhardt & Brass, 1990; Cummings & Worley, 2005; Kotter, 1996; Olmosk, 1972; Rumbles & Rees, 2013; Salas et al., 2012). If HRD professionals and practitioners use the *Hughes HRD Value Creation Model*, they will have a tool to help them develop an understanding of people and technology in the workplace and lead the change initiatives.

ISSUES, CONTROVERSIES, PROBLEMS

There are millions of unfulfilled people working in jobs or careers. These people include nurses, doctors, leaders, educators, public servants, and many other careers who touch the lives of others who need them the most. Despite being unfulfilled, these workers must be ethical in their performance on the job. Unfulfilled workers must feel valued to perform at their peak. If they do not feel valued, then their performance toward customers often reflects the lack of moral and ethical fulfillment. It is disheartening to think about, but there are so many people who impact the lives of others who are unfulfilled in what they are doing. It is out of this need that this book is so important. There are manufacturing workers who are producing food to feed millions who are unfulfilled. There are doctors making decisions on medications and treatments for patients who are unfulfilled. There are teachers who are impacting the futures of millions of children who are unfulfilled and feel less than valued in what they do. There are police officers and other public servants who are called to serve who are unfulfilled and end up taking out their frustrations on innocent citizens. Organizations must take a step back and evaluate how they truly value workers. The effect of how employees are treated on the job is astronomical, not just financially but also ethically. The COVID-19 pandemic has shown society where many of the unethical flaws are in the workplace. We have seen workers die, on the job, because their employers failed to protect their health during the COVID-19 pandemic. Their employers' moral or ethical standards did not rise to the level necessary to accommodate, sustain, and protect the health of their workers. Many organizations challenged the Occupational Safety and Health Administration's (OSHA) laws to the Supreme Court of America to not allow sick workers to be protected on the job during the COVID-19 pandemic. Until all of society and organizations realize that all humans want to be valued as a simple part of their existence, we will continue to have unfulfilled workers in the workplace and throughout society.

Solutions and Recommendations

Applying the *Hughes's HRD Value Creation Model* can help organizations identify unfulfilled workers and allow leaders to assist those workers as they seek to identify ways to help them feel valued at work. This model could provide a way for HRD scholars, professionals, and practitioners to leverage the oft forgotten career development pillar. It will also allow them to strengthen the organization development and training and development pillars. Integrating HRD with the business strategy using *Hughes's HRD Value Creation Model* can only enhance HRD's roll in employee and organizational success. There is room for growth within SHRD. *Hughes's HRD Value Creation Model* is one tool to assist HRD researchers, practitioners, and professionals to affect change and growth within their organizations.

Hughes's HRD Value Creation Model has introduced the cognitive, behavioral, and cultural philosophical perspectives to organizations. These philosophical perspectives have not been introduced in the organization theory or cultural theory literature in this context. These philosophical perspectives are frameworks within which operational cultures of organizations can be improved to better develop people and technology.

Cognitive Philosophical Perspective

The cognitive philosophical perspective has not been front and center in organization research. Smircich (1983) supported the work of Pondy and Boje (1975, 1981) by stating that:

The major practical consequence of conceiving of organizations as socially sustained cognitive enterprises is the emphasis on mind and thought. Organization members are seen as thinking as well as behaving. This is hardly a startling view, and yet much organization research ignores the place of the human mind. (p. 350)

The cognitive philosophical perspective was not used and examined in many organizations because employees were not expected to think for themselves. A societal cultural shift occurred when knowledge management (Alavi & Leidner, 2001; Ayestarán et al., 2022; Bollinger & Smith, 2001; Carlisle, 2002; De Long & Fahey, 2000; Gold et al., 2001; Ruggles, 1998) and critical thinking skills (Braun, 2004; Ennis, 1962, 1989; McPeck, 1990) were demanded of leaders and employees within organizations. Schein (1990) noted that the deepest "level of culture will be the cognitive in that the perceptions, language, and thought processes that a group comes to share will be the ultimate causal determinant of feelings, attitudes, espoused values, and overt behavior" (p. 111). The strength of the cognitive philosophical perspective is dependent on the minds of employees and how employees work together using their minds to improve organizational performance.

Behavioral Philosophical Perspective

The behavioral philosophical perspective has been the dominant philosophical perspective in most organizations because employee behavior is easy to see and measure. Understanding the employee behavior from a cognitive or cultural philosophical perspective has not been easy to understand. The speed at which organizations compete forced them to try and control the behavior of employees by limiting employee input to physical action as opposed to analytical thought or expressing of feelings. The behavioral philosophical perspective has also allowed organizations to replace employees with machines/technology because their focus in only on outputs. While the behavioral philosophical perspective remains dominant, there is room for change where both human behavior and technology strengths can be leveraged. Optimizing the value of people within organizations can remove some barriers.

Cultural Philosophical Perspective

Trice and Beyer (1984) introduced the concepts of cultural rites that are manifested to produce expressive social consequences. Their six rites (rites of passage, degradation, enhancement, renewal, conflict reduction and integration all have application within the context of *Hughes's Five Values* (See Table 2).

Table 2. Comparing Hughes's five values of people and technology development to six cultural rites and their manifest, expressive social consequences

Hughes (2010) Five Values of People and Technology Development	Trice and Beyer (1984, p. 657) Six Cultural Rites	Manifest, Expressive Social Consequences (Trice & Beyer, 1984, p.657)
Location, Use, Maintenance Modification, Time	Rites of Passage	Facilitate transition of persons into social roles and statuses that are new for them
Modification, Time	Rites of Degradation	Dissolve social identities and their power
Maintenance, Modification	Rites of Enhancement	Enhance social identities and their power
Maintenance, Modification	Rites of Renewal	Refurbish social structures and improve their functioning
Location, Use, Maintenance Modification, Time	Rites of Conflict	Reduce conflict and aggression
Location	Rites of Integration	Encourage and revive common feelings that bind members together and commit them to a social system

Location, use, modification, maintenance, and time value all relate to rites of passage because employees could be transitioned into new roles and experiences. Employees may be relocated within the organization so that they can better use all their KSAs. They may receive new training and development opportunities that allow them to transition to new roles they may have self-developed skills recognized by the organization through promotion. Most organizations want employees to remain with the organization for a long time.

Modification and time value relate to rites of degradation because self-developed skills may not be valued by the organization. Some employees may experience a feeling of degradation if their accomplishments are not recognized. Time value may be related to rites of degradation when employees who have seniority are demoted or passed over for promotion because they do not use their KSAs or do not have the necessary KSAs despite their time with the organization.

Maintenance and modification value relate to both rites of enhancement and rites of renewal. Employees may experience rites of enhancement through an increase in social identity and power within the workplace when their KSAs are developed by the organization and through personal efforts. They may experience rites of renewal when they continuously develop their KSAs internally and externally. Location, use, maintenance, modification, and time value most closely relate to rites of conflict. Employees may be frustrated when not placed on the right job or in the right location. They can become discouraged when not allowed to use their KSAs. They may experience conflict when they feel that their time with and organization is not rewarded. Maintenance value can lead to conflict if employees feel that they are not well-trained or do not receive access to needed training.

Organization leaders may require socialization interventions as they attempt to execute *Hughes's HRD Value Creation Model* in ways needed to better integrate people and technology. Socialization is needed for employees to acquire core values. Rites and rituals help employees to maintain the existing value system and can also help facilitate organizational changes (Wiener, 1982, 1988). The displacement of employees with technology is an example of when employees may feel degraded (Beyer & Trice, 1987). Employees being called nonessential is another example.

Enhanced Skills of HRD Researchers and Professionals

The *Hughes HRD Value Creation Model* holds promise for addressing the cognitive, behavioral, and cultural philosophical perspectives of organizations. Storberg-Walker (2005) noted the following:

HRD is about how people work together in organizational contexts, co-creating the processes, practices, norms, standards, and environment of the organization. Embedded within these processes lie three different types of capital, or value creation drivers: individual knowledge, skills, and attitudes (e.g., human capital); social relationships (e.g., social capital); and organizational systems (e.g., structural capital). Each of these three have the potential to create value for both the organization and the individual and knowing how HRD changes or mediates the relationships between the three is critical to understanding how value is created in organizational contexts. (p. 329)

The *Hughes HRD Value Creation Model* addresses human, social and structural capital that Storberg-Walker discussed. It provides a method of identifying how HRD changes and/or mediated the relationship between human, social, and structural capital through the cognitive, behavioral, and cultural philosophical perspectives of the model (Hughes, 2012). The *Hughes HRD Value Creation Model* create value through:

1. The cognitive philosophical perspective & human capital: four independent variable constructs: teaching, learning, procedures and processes, and motivation.
2. The behavioral philosophical perspective & social capital: two independent variable constructs: technology's environmental impact and employee behavior within organizational culture.
3. The cultural philosophical perspective & structural capital: four independent variable constructs: embedded in the environment, adoption of culture norms, leadership by inspiration, and evidence-based management (Hughes, 2012).

Aligning the *Hughes's HRD Value Creation Model* with organization design from the cognitive, behavioral and/or cultural philosophical perspectives can lead to better management, leadership, and HRD practice within organizations. The value creation model also aligns with systems theory of HRD.

FUTURE RESEARCH DIRECTIONS

Measurement and research techniques are often limited to higher education researchers as opposed to professionals and practitioners in the workplace; however, to understand what is happening in organizations, organization leaders, HRD practitioners and professionals must use valid and reliable research techniques. Conducting a quasi- experiment is better for an organization with limited resources, lots of constraints, and lower risk in making an incorrect decision (Werner & DeSimone, 2012). Schein (2010) suggested that

instead of OD we need a new concept that will help the manager with four basic issues: 1) The management of complexity 2) The management of diversity 3) The management of interdependence and integration 4) The management of perpetual change.

Hughes's HRD Value Creation Model offers a new concept to incorporate OD into a system that helps leaders and managers with these four basic issues. To what extent are these four issues examined in the workplace and to what extent are quasi-experiments used to conduct research within organizations?

There is also a perception that HRD professionals and practitioners do not evaluate their training and OD programs because they do not want to fail and lose their jobs. This is an ethical dilemma for HRD professionals and practitioners. Does this not pose a bigger problem for the organization? If HRD is failing and it is not known prior to employees failing at their job tasks due to improper training, does not the organization fail as well? What is HRD professionals' and practitioners' role with regards to the ethics of developing employees? Do HRD professionals even have a code of ethics within their workplace with regards to their impact on employees in the workplace and if not, should they have one? Most professional organizations such as ATD, SHRM, and AHRD have codes of ethics for their members but how does that translate back to each members' job? Is it ethical for HRD professionals and practitioners to cause employees to lose their jobs because of their inability to properly train employees? Improving and instituting objective, ethical professional research policies within organizations may help to increase the performance level of organization and HRD leaders. Russ-Eft and Hatcher (2003) argued for a global HRD code of ethics and Russ-Eft (2018) and Werner (2022) continues to advocate for ethics among HRD scholars, practitioners, and professionals. HRD leaders who are afraid to evaluate their own performance send a negative message throughout the organization. Is the focus on solving the problem or on looking good within one's job? Having a code of ethics within each organization where employee development is valued may increase employee morale (Hughes, 2012).

People in the workplace will be more diverse than ever and not just in their thinking. Some managers and leaders prefer to focus on the diversity of thought and ignore their responsibility of addressing the needs of their protected class employees (Hughes & Brown, 2018). Ignoring and marginalizing employees must stop immediately if organizations intend to compete in the marketplace that will be made up of majority minorities. DQ has been added to the *Hughes HRD Value Creation Model* so that leaders can see how their lack of DQ impacts how they value employees and limits their ability to manage their talent effectively. Without DQ, leaders cannot fully embrace workforce inter-personnel diversity (Hughes, 2018) and the strength that it brings to their talent management strategies. Using workforce inter-personnel diversity as a talent management system as the model suggests, will allow managers and leaders to include every employee, appropriately, within their OD initiatives.

The worldwide, COVID-19 pandemic has exacerbated many of the existing trends in human resource and technology development. The explosive nature of the disruption has highlighted known problems that will be highlighted throughout this book. Emerging research can examine the focus of targeted training. The *Hughes HRD Value Creation Model* can be used to help target training to specific employees with respect to the technological innovations of the organization. Research targeted to assessment of current needs of employees may serve the organization better than targeted training. Organization leaders may already have in-house talent needed. The willingness to think differently may produce results that may cost the organization only the amount of time it takes to align people to their strengths (Hughes, 2012). Studying the established PT model (Hughes, 2010) and the *Hughes HRD Value Creation Model* may lead to extensive research opportunities.

Many employees look for positions that are meaningful or satisfying to them. Meaningful and satisfying are defined by the amount of autonomy, complexity, and connection between effort and reward that employees find in the position (Gladwell, 2009). Whitman (2010) described Power of Many as how an organization utilizes communication and networking powers of modern technology to do things that otherwise would be impossible. She suggested using technology not only to save costs and improve efficiencies but also to engage the energy, ideas, and goodness of people, their desire to team up with others who share their interests, and work together to make lives better. Power of Many demands a style of leadership that emphasizes communication and openness. When faced with difficult decisions, the Power of Many requires everybody to consider the question: What is the right thing to do?

Management intent should be to integrate people and technology in the workplace.

Some additional areas for future research are to:

1. Explore ways to examine ethical structures of organizing employee knowledge.
2. Explore ways examine ethical and technological structures of imparting knowledge to employees.
3. Examine the ethical implications of developing low skilled workers using *Hughes's HRD Value Creation Model.* How can organizations benefit from better developing essential workers to help accomplish organizational goals?

4. Determine if there are HRD value statements and do they align with corporate value statements?
5. Determine if *Hughes's HRD Value Creation Model* help HRD professionals, practitioners, and scholars think in a disciplined way about the "hardware" –physical well-being and human capacity and the "software" – skills, information, etc.... of the workers.
6. Examine how computer technology including online education and social media (Lee & Lan, 2007; Wang, 2011) effect the maintenance and modification value of employees.
7. Examine how HRD and technology development changes and/or mediates the relationship between human, social, and structural capital through the cognitive, behavioral, and cultural philosophical perspectives of the model.
8. Wlodkowski and Ginsberg (1995) suggested that culturally responsive teaching could convert learning institutions into change agents to provide social and economic improvement. Researchers can look at culturally responsive teaching in relation to Rogers' (1995) diffusion of innovation theory. To what extent can a university or organization as change agent be used as a communication channel to improve social and economic situations of all stakeholders? How does the organization improve equity for stakeholders?
9. Examine how codes of ethics influence how HRD professionals and practitioners develop people within organizations.

CONCLUSION

Institutional or organizational transformation means "*planning* alterations in core elements of the institutions: authority, goals, decision-making practices and policies" (Fox, 2008, p. 83). Transformational change must also change organizational culture, customs, norms, outdated procedures, communication styles, and reward structures. The enormity of transformational change can pose a daunting picture for organizational leaders who know that their organization needs to transform. *Hughes's HRD Value Creation Model* can assist with transformational change. Organizations can begin by determining its dominant philosophical perspective; they can then come to terms with the concept of PT.

Smircich (1983) noted that "leadership can best be understood as the management of meaning and the shaping of interpretations". Management intent should be explained to employees so the employees can follow their leaders' guidance to achieve or exceed established goals (Peters, 1978; Smircich & Morgan, 1982). The *Hughes HRD Value Creation Model* is proposed to ethically improve the development, effectiveness, welfare, and success of people. The focus of this book is to help produce highly trained and educated workers who are managers of complex and interactive technologies involving machines, computers, and information systems.

Once HRD scholars, professionals, and practitioners understand the concepts in this book, they can ensure that their OD initiatives for change align with their philosophical perspectives with regards to people and technology. Organizations continue to try and find the competitive advantage through people, equipment, processes, training, and communication (Banks, 1995); however, people and technology are complementary to each other and can be understood through application of *Hughes's HRD Value Creation Model*. There are limitations to science and technology as there are limitations to people (Lama, 1999) and there are limitations to the model.

With all endeavors, there is risk and uncertainty, therefore risk and uncertainty are added to the model around both technology and human resource development. There are also ethical considerations with both technology development and human resource development. To accomplish any of the goals within organizations, employees and leaders take risks, face uncertainties, and face ethical dilemmas. The *Hughes HRD Value Creation Model* is a tool that they can use to help them consider the risks, evaluate the uncertainties, and make better decisions when encountering ethical dilemmas.

The existing challenges in the management of people and technology within the global workplace require modern thoughts as well as innovative technology. *Hughes's HRD Value Creation Model* provides an opportunity for more advanced thought in the workplace concerning the potential to leverage people and technology. There are many advantages from viewing people in ethical ways similar to technology as society enters into Industry 5.0. Some of the benefits from Hughes (2012) include:

1. An end to debate regarding the value of people versus technology in the workplace.
2. An ability to leverage the combined strength of the blend of people and technology in the workplace.
3. Better team development and alignment based on the values that people possess.

4. Improved morale as people better understands their value to the organization.
5. Clearer organizational design and change strategies to organizational values.
6. Management intent better aligned with people capacity.
7. Integration of HRD into succession planning rather than replacement planning.
8. HRD intervention into retention strategies.
9. Ability to truly "structure" interviews that are in alignment with people values that are being sought by the organization.
10. Ability to provide specific feedback that is aligned with the value characteristics of the employee.
11. Training and education that is truly tied to the needs of the organization's people resources. Hopefully, people with the desire to teach, willingness to teach, and a teachable point of view will prevail.
12. Diversity intelligent leaders who value all employees' contributions to the organizations' goals.
13. A workplace inter-personnel diversity talent management system that involves all employees.
14. A workplace environment where employee well-being and ethical treatment is supported.
15. Stronger people asset management tied to the balance sheet.

COVID-19 ETHICAL IMPACT MINI CASE STUDY

When workers were sent home during the onset of the COVID-19 worldwide pandemic, there was no choice but to focus on trainees as many workers had to be trained to use new technologies. The impact of the COVID-19 pandemic exposed the magnitude of workers who had been left behind by technological innovations. The learning cannot be left behind when applying new learning technologies. Some learners without access to technology resources were left behind during the COVID-19 pandemic, but many had already been left behind prior to the COVID-19 pandemic. New and more empirical research is needed to improve the value of people and technology. Examination of how the focus away from the training instructor to the focus on the trainee is needed. Some questions to consider:

1. How has trainees' ability to learn using all available materials and resources with the right training strategy and system been effective?
2. In what way(s) can learning be left behind through the introduction of new technologies?

REFERENCES

Aguinis, H. (2009). *Performance management* (2nd ed.). Pearson Prentice Hall.

Aguinis, H., & Kraiger, K. (2009). Benefits of training and development for individuals and teams, organizations, and society. *Annual Review of Psychology, 60*(1), 451–474. doi:10.1146/annurev.psych.60.110707.163505 PMID:18976113

Aguinis, H., & Pierce, C. A. (2008). Enhancing the relevance of organizational behavior by embracing performance management research. *Journal of Organizational Behavior, 29*(1), 139–145. doi:10.1002/job.493

Alavi, A., & Leidner, D. (2001). Review: Knowledge management and knowledge management systems: Conceptual foundations and research issues. *Management Information Systems Quarterly, 25*(1), 107–136. doi:10.2307/3250961

Ayestarán, S., Gómez, D., Martínez-Moreno, E., Lira, E. M., & Costa, S. D. (2022). A model of knowledge-sharing for the 21st century organizations. *Journal of Work and Organizational Psychology, 38*(3), 175–187. doi:10.5093/jwop2022a21

Banks, C. H. (1995). *Finding the competitive advantage through people, equipment, processes, training, and communication* [Unpublished master's degree project, North Carolina State University].

Banks, C. H. (2009). Critical human performance issues in the United States. In V. C. X. Wang & K. P. King (Eds.), *Human performance models revealed in the global context* (pp. 63–80). Information Age Publishing.

Bassi, L., Cheney, S., & Lewis, E. (1998). Trends in workplace learning: Supply and demand in interesting times. *Training & Development, 52*(11), 51–75.

Beckhard, R., & Harris, R. T. (1987). *Organizational transitions: Managing complex change* (2nd ed.). Addison-Wesley Publishing Company.

Betz, F. (1993). *Strategic technology management*. McGraw-Hill.

Beyer, J. M., & Trice, H. M. (1987). How an organization's rites reveal its culture. *Organizational Dynamics*, *8*(3), 5–24. doi:10.1016/0090-2616(87)90041-6

Biech, E. (2007). *Thriving through change*. ASTD Press.

Bollinger, A. S., & Smith, R. D. (2001). Managing organizational knowledge as a strategic asset. *Journal of Knowledge Management*, *5*(1), 8–18. doi:10.1108/13673270110384365

Bolman, L. G., & Deal, T. E. (2008). *Reframing organizations: Artistry, choice, and leadership* (4th ed.). Jossey-Bass.

Braun, N. M. (2004). Critical thinking in the business curriculum. *Journal of Education for Business*, *79*(4), 232–236. doi:10.1080/08832323.2020.1 2088718

Brinkerhoff, R. O. (1987). *Achieving results from training*. Jossey-Bass.

Burkhardt, M. E., & Brass, D. J. (1990). Changing patterns or patterns of change: The effects of a change in technology on social network structure and power. *Administrative Science Quarterly*, *35*(1), 104–127. doi:10.2307/2393552

Bushnell, D. S. (1990). Input, process, output: A model for evaluating training. *Training and Development Journal*, *44*(3), 41–43.

Carlisle, L. W. (2002). Knowledge management and training: The value of collaboration. *Performance Improvement*, *41*(4), 37–43. doi:10.1002/pfi.4140410407

Carrig, K., & Wright, P. M. (2006). *Building profit through building people: Making your work force the strongest link in the value-profit chain*. Society for Human Resource Management.

Cascio, W. F. (2019). Training trends: Macro, micro, and policy issues. *Human Resource Management Review*, *29*(2), 284–297. doi:10.1016/j.hrmr.2017.11.001

Cascio, W. F., & Aguinis, H. (2005). *Applied psychology in human resource management* (6th ed.). Pearson Prentice Hall.

Cascio, W. F., & Collings, D. G. (2022). Potential: The forgotten factor in talent management research. In D. Collings, V. Vaiman, and H. Scullion (Eds.) Talent management: A decade of developments (pp. 65-84), Emerald Publishing Limited. doi:10.1108/978-1-80117-834-120221004

Cummings, T. G., & Worley, C. G. (2005). Organizational development and change (8th ed.). South-Western/Thomson.

De Long, D. W., & Fahey, L. (2000). Diagnosing cultural barriers to knowledge management. *The Academy of Management Executive*, *14*(4), 113–127. doi:10.5465/ame.2000.3979820

Drucker, P. F. (2008). *Management* (rev. ed.). HarperCollins.

Ennis, R. H. (1962). A concept of critical thinking. *Harvard Educational Review*, *32*(1), 81–111.

Ennis, R. H. (1989). Critical thinking and subject specificity. *Educational Researcher*, *18*(3), 4–10. doi:10.3102/0013189X018003004

Fox, M. F. (2008). Institutional transformation and the advancement of women faculty: The case of academic science and engineering. In J. C. Smart (Ed.), *Higher education: Handbook of theory and research* (Vol. 23, pp. 73–103). Springer., doi:10.1007/978-1-4020-6959-8_3

Galvin, J. C. (1983). What trainers can learn from educators about evaluating management training. *Training and Development Journal*, *37*(8), 52–57.

Gladwell, M. (2009). *What the dog saw: And other adventures*. Little, Brown and Company.

Gold, A. H., Malhotra, A., & Segars, A. H. (2001). Knowledge management: An organizational capabilities perspective. *Journal of Management Information Systems*, *18*(1), 185–214. doi:10.1080/07421222.2001.11045669

Goldstein, I. L. (1980). Training in work organizations. *Annual Review of Psychology*, *31*(1), 229–272. doi:10.1146/annurev.ps.31.020180.001305

Hamel, G., & Prahalad, C. K. (1994). *Competing for the future*. Harvard Business School Press.

Hoskisson, R. E., Hitt, M. A., Ireland, R. D., & Harrison, J. S. (2008). *Competing for advantage* (2nd ed.). South-Western.

Hughes, C. (2010). "People as technology" conceptual model: Towards a new value creation paradigm for strategic human resource development. *Human Resource Development Review*, 9(1), 48–71. doi:10.1177/1534484309353561

Hughes, C. (2012). *Valuing people and technology in the workplace: A competitive advantage framework.* IGI Global. doi:10.4018/978-1-4666-0240-3

Hughes, C. (2016). *Diversity intelligence: Integrating diversity intelligence alongside intellectual, emotional, and cultural intelligence for leadership and career development.* Palgrave MacMillan Publications. doi:10.1057/978-1-137-52683-0

Hughes, C. (2018). *Workforce inter-personnel diversity: The power to influence human productivity and career development.* Springer International Publishing.

Hughes, C., & Brown, L. (2018). Exploring leaders' discriminatory, passive-aggressive behavior toward protected class employees using diversity intelligence. *Advances in Developing Human Resources*, 20(3), 263–284. doi:10.1177/1523422318778002

Kirkpatrick, D. L. (1967). Evaluation. In R. L. Craig & L. R. Bittle (Eds.), *Training and development handbook* (pp. 87–112). McGraw-Hill.

Kirkpatrick, D. L. (1987). Evaluation. In R. L. Craig (Ed.), *Training and development handbook* (3rd ed., pp. 301–319). McGraw-Hill.

Kirkpatrick, D. L. (1994). *Evaluating training programs: The four levels.* Berrett-Koehler.

Kirkpatrick, D. L. (1996). Great ideas revisited: Re-visiting Kirkpatrick's four-level model. *Training and Development Journal*, 50(1), 54–57.

Lama, D. (1999). *Ethics for the new millennium.* Riverhead Books.

Lee, M. R., & Lan, Y. (2007). From Web 2.0 to conversational knowledge management: Towards collaborative intelligence. *Journal of Entrepreneurship Research*, 2(2), 47–62.

McPeck, J. E. (1990). Critical thinking and subject specificity: A reply to Ennis. *Educational Researcher*, 19(4), 10–12. doi:10.3102/0013189X019004010

Olmosk, K. E. (1972). Seven pure strategies of change. In J. W. Pfeiffer & J. E. Jones (Eds.), *The 1972 annual handbook for group facilitators.* Pfeiffer & Company.

Orr, J. E. (1996). *Talking about machines. An ethnography of a modern job.* ILR Press/Cornell University Press.

Parker, S. K., Knight, C., & Keller, A. (2020). Remote managers are having trust issues. *Harvard Business Review*, *30*, 6–20.

Peters, T. J. (1978). Symbols, patterns and settings: An optimistic case for getting things done. *Organizational Dynamics*, *7*(2), 3–23. doi:10.1016/0090-2616(78)90035-9

Pfeffer, J. (1994). *Competitive advantage through people: Unleashing the power of the workforce.* Harvard Business School Press. doi:10.2307/41165742

Pondy, L. R., & Boje, D. M. (1975). *Bringing mind back in: Paradigm development as a frontier problem in organization theory.* Paper presented at the Annual Meetings of the American Sociological Association, San Francisco, CA.

Pondy, L. R., & Boje, D. M. (1981). Bringing mind back in. In Evan, W. (Ed.), Frontiers in organization and management (pp. 83–101). Praeger.

Porter, M. (1980). *Competitive strategy.* Free Press.

Rogers, E. M. (1995). *Diffusion of innovations* (4th ed.). The Free Press.

Ruggles, R. (1998). The state of the notion: Knowledge management in practice. *California Management Review*, *40*(3), 80–89. doi:10.2307/41165944

Russ-Eft, D. (2018). Second time around: AHRD standards on ethics and integrity. *Human Resource Development Review*, *17*(2), 123–127. doi:10.1177/1534484318772123

Russ-Eft, D., & Hatcher, T. (2003). The issue of international values and beliefs: The debate for a global HRD code of ethics. *Advances in Developing Human Resources*, *5*(3), 296–307. doi:10.1177/1523422303254670

Sackett, P. R., & Mullen, E. J. (1993). Beyond formal experimental design: Towards an expanded view of the training evaluation process. *Personnel Psychology*, *46*(3), 613–615. doi:10.1111/j.1744-6570.1993.tb00887.x

Salas, E., Tannenbaum, S. I., Kraiger, K., & Smith-Jentsch, K. A. (2012). The science of training and development in organizations: What matters in practice. *Psychological Science in the Public Interest*, *13*(2), 74–101. doi:10.1177/1529100612436661 PMID:26173283

Schein, E. H. (1988). Organizational socialization and the profession of management. *Sloan Management Review*, *30*(1), 53–65.

Schein, E. H. (1990). Organizational culture. *The American Psychologist*, *45*(2), 109–119. doi:10.1037/0003-066X.45.2.109

Smircich, L. (1983). Concepts of culture and organizational analysis. *Administrative Science Quarterly*, *28*(3), 339–358. doi:10.2307/2392246

Smircich, L., & Morgan, G. (1982). Leadership: The management of meaning. *The Journal of Applied Behavioral Science*, *18*(3), 257–273. doi:10.1177/002188638201800303 PMID:10260212

Storberg-Walker, J. (2005). Towards a theory of human capital transformation through human resource development. In M. L. Morris & F. M. Nafukho (Eds.), *2005 Academy of Human Resource Development Annual Research Conference Proceeding,* (pp. 323-330). Academy of Human Resource Development.

Strebel, P. (1996). Why do employees resist change? *Harvard Business Review*, *74*(3), 86–92.

Swanson, R. A. (2007). Theory framework for applied disciplines: Boundaries, contributing, core, useful, novel, and irrelevant components. *Human Resource Development Review*, *6*(3), 321–339. doi:10.1177/1534484307303770

Trice, H. M., & Beyer, J. M. (1984). Studying organizational cultures through rites and ceremonials. *Academy of Management Review*, *9*(4), 653–669. doi:10.2307/258488

van den Heuvel, M., Demerouti, E., Bakker, A. B., Hetland, J., & Schaufeli, W. B. (2020). How do employees adapt to organizational change? The role of meaning-making and work engagement. *The Spanish Journal of Psychology*, *23*(e56), 1–16. doi:10.1017/SJP.2020.55 PMID:33345770

van den Heuvel, M., Demerouti, E., Bakker, A. B., & Schaufeli, W. B. (2013). Adapting to change: The value of change information and meaning-making. *Journal of Vocational Behavior*, *83*(1), 11–21. doi:10.1016/j.jvb.2013.02.004

Wang, M. (2011). Integrating organizational, social, and individual perspectives in Web 2.0-based workplace e-learning. *Information Systems Frontiers*, *13*(2), 191–205. doi:10.100710796-009-9191-y

Warr, P., Bird, M., & Rackham, N. (1970). *Evaluation of management training*. Gower Press.

Welch, J. (2005). *Winning*. HarperCollins.

Werner, J. M. (2022). Academic integrity and human resource development: Being and doing. *Human Resource Development Review*, *21*(2), 249–257. doi:10.1177/15344843221078505

Werner, J. M., & DeSimone, R. L. (2012). *Human resource development* (6th ed.). South-Western.

Whitman, M. (2010). *The power of many: Values for success in business and in life*. Three Rivers Press.

Wiener, Y. (1982). Commitment in organizations: A normative view. *Academy of Management Review*, *7*(3), 418–428. doi:10.2307/257334

Wiener, Y. (1988). Forms of value systems: A focus on organizational effectiveness and cultural change and maintenance. *Academy of Management Review*, *13*, 534–545.

Wittrock, M. C. (1978). The cognitive movement in instruction. *Educational Psychologist*, *13*(1), 15–29. doi:10.1080/00461527809529192

Wlodkowski, R. J., & Ginsberg, M. B. (1995). *Diversity and motivation: Culturally responsive teaching*. Jossey-Bass.

Womack, J. P., & Jones, D. T. (1996). *Lean thinking*. Simon & Schuster.

Compilation of References

Funding the development and manufacturing of COVID-19 vaccines. *The Center for Policy Impact in Global Health., Duke Global Working Paper Series*, (20), 1-26.

Abazi-Bexheti, L. (2008). Development of a learning content management system. *WSEAS Transactions on Information Science and Applications*, *5*(6), 1001–1010.

Abdeen, A. M., & Haight, G. T. (2002). A fresh look at economic value added: Empirical study of the fortune five-hundred companies. [JABR]. *Journal of Applied Business Research*, *18*(2), 27–36.

Abiddin, N. Z., Ismail, A., & Nasreen, A. (2021). The role of organizational and individual factors in predicting training transfer: A conceptual model. *Review of International Geographical Education Online*, *11*(8), 24–35.

Acemoglu, D., & Restrepo, P. (2019). Automation and new tasks: How technology displaces and reinstates labor. *The Journal of Economic Perspectives*, *33*(2), 3–30. doi:10.1257/jep.33.2.3

Acemoglu, D., & Restrepo, P. (2020). Robots and jobs: Evidence from US labor markets. *Journal of Political Economy*, *128*(6), 2188–2244. doi:10.1086/705716

Adams, J. S. (1963). Toward an understanding of inequity. *Journal of Abnormal and Social Psychology*, *67*(5), 422–436. doi:10.1037/h0040968 PMID:14081885

Adams, J. S. (1965). Inequity in social exchange. *Advances in Experimental Social Psychology*, *2*, 267–299. doi:10.1016/S0065-2601(08)60108-2

Agarwal, R., Grassl, W., & Pahl, J. (2012). Meta-SWOT: Introducing a new strategic planning tool. *The Journal of Business Strategy*, *33*(2), 12–21. doi:10.1108/02756661211206708

Agrawal, S., De Smet, A., Lacroix, S., & Reich, A. (2020). *To emerge stronger from the COVID-19 crisis, companies should start reskilling their workforces now. McKinsey Insights*. Issue May.

Aguinis, H., & Kraiger, K. (2009). Benefits of training and development for individuals and teams, organizations, and society. *Annual Review of Psychology*, *60*, 451–474. doi:. psych.60.110707.163505 doi:10.1146/annurev

Aguinis, H. (2009). *Performance management* (2nd ed.). Pearson Prentice Hall.

Aguinis, H., & Kraiger, K. (2009). Benefits of training and development for individuals and teams, organizations, and society. *Annual Review of Psychology*, *60*(1), 451–474. doi:10.1146/annurev.psych.60.110707.163505 PMID:18976113

Aguinis, H., & Pierce, C. A. (2008). Enhancing the relevance of organizational behavior by embracing performance management research. *Journal of Organizational Behavior*, *29*(1), 139–145. doi:10.1002/job.493

Alagaraja, M. (2013). Mobilizing organizational alignment through strategic human resource development. *Human Resource Development International*, *16*(1), 74–93. doi:10.1080/136788 68.2012.740794

Alassaf, N., Harfoushi, O., Obiedat, R., & Hammouri, T. (2014). Learning management systems and content management system: Definitions and characteristics. *Life Science Journal*, *11*(12), 39–41.

Alavi, M., & Leidner, D. E. (2001). Review: Knowledge management and knowledge management systems: Conceptual foundations and research issues. *Management Information Systems Quarterly*, *25*(1), 107–136. doi:10.2307/3250961

Alder, G. S., & Gilbert, J. (2006). Achieving ethics and fairness in hiring: Going beyond the law. *Journal of Business Ethics*, *68*(4), 449–464. doi:10.100710551-006-9039-z

Aliaga, O. A. (2001). Academy of HRD 2001 Conference Proceedings (pp. 805-812). Academy of Human Resource Development.

Alipour, J. V., Fadinger, H., & Schymik, J. (2021). My home is my castle–The benefits of working from home during a pandemic crisis. *Journal of Public Economics*, *196*(104373), 1–11. doi:10.1016/j.jpubeco.2021.104373

Allen, J. M. (2022). *Fostering wisdom at work*. Routledge. doi:10.4324/9781003018759

Allen, J., Bracey, P., Aguilar, M., & Zimmerman, T. (2019). Supporting workforce wisdom in a global economy. In C. Hughes (Ed.), *Handbook of research on attracting, maintaining, and balancing a mature workforce*. IGI Global.

Amankwah-Amoah, J., Khan, Z., & Wood, G. (2021). COVID-19 and business failures: The paradoxes of experience, scale, and scope for theory and practice. *European Management Journal*, *39*(2), 179–184. doi:10.1016/j.emj.2020.09.002

Ambrosini, V., & Bowman, C. (2009). What are dynamic capabilities and are they a useful construct in strategic management? *International Journal of Management Reviews*, *11*(1), 29–49. doi:10.1111/j.1468-2370.2008.00251.x

Anand, V., Glick, W. H., & Manz, C. C. (2002). Thriving on the knowledge of outsiders: Tapping organizational social capital. *The Academy of Management Executive*, *19*(1), 87–101. doi:10.5465/ame.2002.6640198

Anderson, V. (2022). Human resource development, professions and precarious workers. In P. Holland, T. Bartram, T. Garavan, & K. Grant (Eds.), *The Emerald handbook of work, workplaces and disruptive issues in HRM* (pp. 277–301). Emerald Publishing Limited. doi:10.1108/978-1-80071-779-420221028

Andoh, R. P. K., Owusu, E. A., Annan-Prah, E. C., & Boampong, G. N. (2022). Training value, employee internal states and training transfer: Examining the web of relationships. *The Learning Organization*, *29*(6), 674–691. doi:10.1108/TLO-09-2022-0100

Antonacopoulou, E. P. (2001). The paradoxical nature of the relationship between training and learning. *Journal of Management Studies*, *38*(3), 327–350. doi:10.1111/1467-6486.00239

Aragón-Sánchez, A., Barba-Aragón, I., & Sanz-Valle, R. (2003). Effects of training on business results. *International Journal of Human Resource Management*, *14*(6), 956–980. doi:10.1080/0958519032000106164

Argote, L., & Hora, M. (2017). Organizational learning and management of technology. *Production and Operations Management*, *26*(4), 579–590. doi:10.1111/poms.12667

Argote, L., & Miron-Spektor, E. (2011). Organizational learning: From experience to knowledge. *Organization Science*, *22*(5), 1123–1137. https://www.jstor.org/stable/41303106. doi:10.1287/orsc.1100.0621

Argyris, C. (1985). Making knowledge more relevant to practice: Maps for action. In Lawler, E. E. III, Mohrman, A. M., Mohrman, S. A., Led- ford, G. E. Jr, & Cummings, T. G. (Eds.), Doing research that is useful for theory and practice (pp. 29–125). Jossey-Bass.

Argyris, C. (1985). Making knowledge more relevant to practice: Maps for action. In E. E. Lawler (Ed.), *Doing research that is useful for theory and practice* (pp. 29–125). Jossey-Bass.

Argyris, C., & Schön, D. (1978). *Organizational learning*. Addison-Wesley.

Arora, A., & Gambardella, A. (2005). The globalization of the software industry: Perspectives and opportunities for developed and developing countries. *Innovation Policy and the Economy*, *5*, 1–32. doi:10.1086/ipe.5.25056169

Arrieta, A. B., Díaz-Rodríguez, N., Del Ser, J., Bennetot, A., Tabik, S., Barbado, A., Garcia, S., Gil-Lopez, S., Molina, D., Benjamins, R., Chatila, R., & Herrera, F. (2020). Explainable artificial intelligence (XAI): Concepts, taxonomies, opportunities and challenges toward responsible AI. *Information Fusion*, *58*, 82–115. doi:10.1016/j.inffus.2019.12.012

Arthur, J. B. (1994). Effects of human resource systems on manufacturing performance and turnover. *Academy of Management Journal*, *37*(3), 670–687. doi:10.2307/256705

Ash, M. K. (1981). *Mary Kay*. Harper and Row.

Attard-Frost, B., De los Ríos, A. & Walters, D.R. (2022). The ethics of AI business practices: A review of 47 AI ethics guidelines. *AI Ethics*, 1-18. doi:10.1007/s43681-022-00156-6

Ausubel, D. (1963). *The psychology of meaningful verbal learning*. Holt, Rinehart & Winston.

Ausubel, D. P. (1960). The use of advance organizers in the learning and retention of meaningful verbal material. *Journal of Educational Psychology*, *51*(5), 267–272. doi:10.1037/h0046669

Ausubel, D. P. (1978). In defense of advance organizers: A reply to the critics. *Review of Educational Research*, *48*(2), 251–257. doi:10.3102/00346543048002251

Ausubel, D. P., & Youseff, M. (1963). Role of discriminability in meaningful parallel learning. *Journal of Educational Psychology*, *54*(6), 331–336. doi:10.1037/h0042767

Avery, D. R. (2011). Support for diversity in organizations: A theoretical exploration of its origins and offshoots. *Organizational Psychology Review*, *1*(3), 239–256. doi:10.1177/2041386611402115

Awais Bhatti, M., Ali, S., Mohd Isa, M. F., & Mohamed Battour, M. (2014). Training transfer and transfer motivation: The influence of individual, environmental, situational, training design, and affective reaction factors. *Performance Improvement Quarterly*, *27*(1), 51–82. doi:10.1002/piq.21165

Ayestarán, S., Gómez, D., Martínez-Moreno, E., Lira, E. M., & Costa, S. D. (2022). A model of knowledge-sharing for the 21st century organizations. *Journal of Work and Organizational Psychology*, *38*(3), 175–187. doi:10.5093/jwop2022a21

Babbage, C. (1835). *On the economy of machinery and manufacturers*. Frank Cass & Co.

Badawy, M. K. (1995). *Developing managerial skills in engineers and scientists: Succeeding as a technical manager* (2nd ed.). Van Nostrand Reinhold.

Baena-Díez, J. M., Barroso, M., Cordeiro-Coelho, S. I., Díaz, J. L., & Grau, M. (2020). Impact of COVID-19 outbreak by income: Hitting hardest the most deprived. *Journal of Public Health*, *42*(4), 698–703. doi:10.1093/pubmed/fdaa136 PMID:32776102

Baird, L., & Meshoulam, I. (1988). Managing two fits of strategic human resource management. *Academy of Management Review*, *13*(1), 116–128. doi:10.2307/258359

Baker, S. (2008a, September 8). Management by the numbers. *Business Week*, pp. 32-36.

Baker, S. (2008b). *The numerati*. Houghton Mifflin.

Balcazar, F., Hopkins, B. L., & Suarez, Y. (1985). A critical, objective review of performance feedback. *Journal of Organizational Behavior Management*, *7*(3-4), 65–89. doi:10.1300/J075v07n03_05

Baldi, F., & Trigeorgis, L. (2020). Valuing human capital career development: A real options approach. *Journal of Intellectual Capital*, *21*(5), 781–807. doi:10.1108/JIC-06-2019-0134

Baldwin, T. T., & Ford, J. K. (1988). Transfer of training: A review and directions for future research. *Personnel Psychology*, *41*(1), 63–105. doi:10.1111/j.1744-6570.1988.tb00632.x

Balzer, W. K., Doherty, M. E., & O'Connor, R. Jr. (1989). Effects of cognitive feedback on performance. *Psychological Bulletin, 106*(3), 410–433. doi:10.1037/0033-2909.106.3.410

Bandura, A. (1977). Self-efficacy: Toward a unifying theory of behavioral change. *Psychological Review, 84*(2), 191–215. doi:10.1037/0033-295X.84.2.191 PMID:847061

Bandura, A. (1986). *Social foundations of thought and action: A social cognitive theory.* Prentice Hall.

Bandura, A., Ross, D., & Ross, S. A. (1961). Transmission of aggression through imitation of aggressive models. *Journal of Abnormal and Social Psychology, 63*(3), 575–582. doi:10.1037/h0045925 PMID:13864605

Banks, C. H. (2002). A descriptive analysis of the perceived effectiveness of Virginia Tech's faculty development institute. *Dissertation Abstracts International, 64*(08). (UMI No. 3102585)

Banks, C. H. (2002). A descriptive analysis of the perceived effectiveness of Virginia Tech's faculty development institute. *Dissertation Abstracts International, 64*(8). (UMI No. 3102585)

Banks, C. H., & Nafukho, F. M. (2008). Career transitions across and within organizations: Implications for human resource development. In T.M. Chermack & J. Storberg-Walker (Eds.), *2008 Academy of Human Resource Development Annual Research Conference Proceedings,* (pp. 1096- 1102). Academy of Human Resource Development.

Banks, C. H., & Nafukho, F. M. (2008). Career transitions across and within organizations: implications for human resource development. In T.M. Chermack & J. Storberg-Walker (Eds.), *2008 Academy of Human Resource Development Annual Research Conference Proceedings,* (pp. 1096- 1102). Bowling Green, OH: Academy of Human Resource Development.

Banks, C. G., & Murphy, K. R. (1985). Toward narrowing the research-practice gap in performance appraisal. *Personnel Psychology, 38*(2), 335–345. doi:10.1111/j.1744-6570.1985.tb00551.x

Banks, C. H. (1995). *Finding the competitive advantage through people, equipment, processes, training, and communication* [Unpublished master's degree project, North Carolina State University].

Banks, C. H. (2006). Career planning: Toward an inclusive model. In M. Karsten (Ed.), *Gender, race and ethnicity in the workplace* (Vol. 3, pp. 99–116). Greenwood Publishing Group, Inc.

Banks, C. H. (2009). Critical human performance issues in the United States. In V. C. X. Wang & K. P. King (Eds.), *Human performance models revealed in the global context* (pp. 63–80). Information Age Publishing.

Baptiste, I. (2001). Educating lone wolves: Pedagogical implications of human capital theory. *Adult Education Quarterly, 51*(3), 184–201. doi:10.1177/074171360105100302

Barnard, C. (1938). *The functions of the executive.* Harvard University Press.

Bartunek, J. M., & Rynes, S. L. (2014). Academics and practitioners are alike and unlike: The paradoxes of academic-practitioner relationships. *Journal of Management*, *40*(5), 1181–1201. doi:10.1177/0149206314529160

Bass, B. M. (1988). The inspirational process of leadership. *Journal of Management Development*, *7*(5), 21–31. doi:10.1108/eb051688

Bass, B. M. (1999). Two decades of research and development in transformational leadership. *European Journal of Work and Organizational Psychology*, *8*(1), 9–32. doi:10.1080/135943299398410

Bass, B. M., & Vaughn, J. A. (1966). *Training in industry: The management of learning*. Brooks/Cole.

Bassi, L., Cheney, S., & Lewis, E. (1998). Trends in workplace learning: Supply and demand in interesting times. *Training & Development*, *52*(11), 51–75.

Baumgartel, H., & Jeanpeiere, F. (1972). Applying new knowledge in the back home setting: A study of Indian managers' adoptive efforts. *The Journal of Applied Behavioral Science*, *8*(6), 674–694. doi:10.1177/002188637200800603

Bazzoli, A., & Probst, T. M. (2023). Vulnerable workers in insecure jobs: A critical meta-synthesis of qualitative findings. *Applied Psychology*, *72*(1), 85–105. doi:10.1111/apps.12415

Becker, B. E. (Ed.), *The HR scorecard: Linking people, strategy, and practice* (pp. 1–26). Harvard Business School.

Becker, B. E., Huselid, M. A., & Beatty, R. W. (2009). *The differentiated workforce: Transforming talent into strategic impact*. Harvard Business Press.

Becker, B. E., Huselid, M., & Ulrich, D. (2001). *HR as a strategic partner: The measurement challenge*.

Becker, G. S. (1962). Investment in human capital: A theoretical analysis. *Journal of Political Economy*, *70*(5, Part 2), 9–49. doi:10.1086/258724

Becker, G. S. (1964). *Human capital: A theoretical and empirical analysis, with special reference to education* (3rd ed.). University of Chicago Press.

Becker, G. S. (1993). *Human capital: A theoretical and empirical analysis, with special reference to education* (3rd ed.). University of Chicago Press. doi:10.7208/chicago/9780226041223.001.0001

Becker, K., & Bish, A. (2021). A framework for understanding the role of unlearning in onboarding. *Human Resource Management Review*, *31*(1), 1–13. doi:10.1016/j.hrmr.2019.100730

Beckhard, R., & Harris, R. T. (1987). *Organizational transitions: Managing complex change* (2nd ed.). Addison-Wesley Publishing Company.

Beer, M. (2001). Why management research findings are unimplementable: An action science perspective. *Reflections: The SoL Journal*, *2*(3), 58–65. doi:10.1162/152417301570383

Beer, M., & Spector, B. (1989). Corporate wide transformations in human resource management. In R. E. Walton & P. R. Lawrence (Eds.), *Human resource management: Trends and Challenges*. Harvard University School Press.

Belasco, J. A., & Stayer, R. C. (1993). *Flight of the buffalo: Soaring to excellence, learning to let employees lead*. Warner Books, Inc.

Bell, B. S., Tannenbaum, S. I., Ford, J. K., Noe, R. A., & Kraiger, K. (2017). 100 years of training and development research: What we know and where we should go. *The Journal of Applied Psychology*, *102*(3), 305–323. https://psycnet.apa.org/doi/10.1037/apl0000142. doi:10.1037/apl0000142 PMID:28125262

Bem, D. J. (1972). Self-perception theory. In L. Berkowitz (Ed.), Vol. 6, pp. 1–62). Advances in experimental and social psychology. Academic Press.

Bennett, E. E. (2022). Leveraging technology to design and deliver human resource development. In P. Holland, T. Bartram, T. Garavan, and K. Grant (Eds.). The Emerald handbook of work, workplaces and disruptive issues in HRM (pp. 261-276), Emerald Publishing Limited. doi:10.1108/978-1-80071-779-420221026

Bennett, E. E. (2014). How an intranet provides opportunities for learning organizational culture: Implications for virtual HRD. *Advances in Developing Human Resources*, *16*(3), 296–319. doi:10.1177/1523422314532093

Benson, G. S., Feingold, D., & Mohrman, S. A. (2004). You paid for the skills, now keep them: Tuition reimbursement and voluntary turnover. *Academy of Management Journal*, *47*(3), 315–331. doi:10.2307/20159584

Berger, N. O., Kehrhahn, M. T., & Summerville, M. (2004). Research to practice: Throwing a rope across the divide. *Human Resource Development International*, *7*(3), 403–409. doi:10.1080/1367886042000246003

Bernardin, H. J., & Buckley, M. R. (1981). Strategies in rater training. *Academy of Management Review*, *6*(2), 205–212.

Bernardin, H. J., Buckley, M. R., Tyler, C. L., & Weise, D. S. (2000). A reconsideration of strategies in rater training. *Research in Personnel and Human Resources Management*, *18*, 221–274.

Bernardin, H. J., & Villanova, P. (1986). Performance appraisal. In E. A. Locke (Ed.), *Generalizing from laboratory to field settings* (pp. 43–62). Lexington Books.

Betz, F. (1993). *Strategic technology management*. McGraw-Hill.

Beu, D. S., Buckley, M. R., & Harvey, M. G. (2003). Ethical decision–making: A multidimensional construct. *Business Ethics (Oxford, England)*, *12*(1), 88–107. doi:10.1111/1467-8608.00308

Beyer, J. M., & Trice, H. M. (1987). How an organization's rites reveal its culture. *Organizational Dynamics*, *8*(3), 5–24. doi:10.1016/0090-2616(87)90041-6

Bhattacharya, M., & Wright, P. M. (2005). Managing human assets in an uncertain world: Applying real world options theory to HRM. *International Journal of Human Resource Management, 16*(6), 929–948. doi:10.1080/09585190500120574

Biech, E. (2007). *Thriving through change.* ASTD Press.

Bingham, K., Gewin, A., Hu, C., Thomas, K., & Yanchus, N. (2005). The roles of protégé race, gender, and proactive socialization attempts on peer monitoring. *Advances in Developing Human Resources, 7*(4), 540–555. doi:10.1177/1523422305279681

Birati, A., & Tziner, A. (2000). Cost-benefit analysis of organizational interventions: The case of downsizing. *Journal of Business and Psychology, 15*(2), 277–286. doi:10.1023/A:1007894018069

Birkel, H. S., & Hartmann, E. (2020). Internet of Things–the future of managing supply chain risks. *Supply Chain Management, 25*(5), 535–548. doi:10.1108/SCM-09-2019-0356

Bittencourt, V. L., Alves, A. C., & Leão, C. P. (2019). Lean thinking contributions for industry 4.0: A systematic literature review. *IFAC-PapersOnLine, 52*(13), 904–909. doi:10.1016/j.ifacol.2019.11.310

Black, S. E., & Lynch, L. M. (1996). Human-capital investments and productivity. *The American Economic Review, 86*(2), 263–267.

Bliese, P. D., Edwards, J. R., & Sonnentag, S. (2017). Stress and well-being at work: A century of empirical trends reflecting theoretical and societal influences. *The Journal of Applied Psychology, 102*(3), 389–402. doi:10.1037/apl0000109 PMID:28125263

Bloom, B. (1968). Learning for mastery. *Evaluation Comment, 1*(2), 1–12.

Bloom, B. (1974). Time and learning. *The American Psychologist, 29*(9), 682–688. doi:10.1037/h0037632

Bloom, N., Davis, S. J., & Zhestkova, Y. (2021, May). Covid-19 shifted patent applications toward technologies that support working from home. *AEA Papers and Proceedings. American Economic Association, 111*, 263–266. doi:10.1257/pandp.20211057

Blume, B. D., Ford, J. K., Baldwin, T. T., & Huang, J. L. (2010). Transfer of training: A meta-analytic review. *Journal of Management, 36*(4), 1065–1105. doi:10.1177/0149206309352880

Blume, B. D., Ford, J. K., Surface, E. A., & Olenick, J. (2019). A dynamic model of training transfer. *Human Resource Management Review, 29*(2), 270–283. doi:10.1016/j.hrmr.2017.11.004

Blumenfeld, S., Anderson, G., & Hooper, V. (2020). Covid-19 and employee surveillance. *New Zealand Journal of Employment Relations, 45*(2), 42–56. doi:10.24135/nzjer.v45i2.28

Blundell, R., Dearden, L., Meghir, C., & Sianesi, B. (1999). Human capital investment: The returns from education and training to the individual, the firm and the economy. *Fiscal Studies, 20*(1), 1–23. doi:10.1111/j.1475-5890.1999.tb00001.x

Böhm-Bawerk, E. V., Hilferding, R., & Sweezy, P. M. (1984). *Karl Marx and the close of his system*. Orion Editions.

Bolander, P., Werr, A., & Asplund, K. (2017). The practice of talent management: A framework and typology. *Personnel Review*, *46*(8), 1523–1551. doi:10.1108/PR-02-2016-0037

Bollinger, A. S., & Smith, R. D. (2001). Managing organizational knowledge as a strategic asset. *Journal of Knowledge Management*, *5*(1), 8–18. doi:10.1108/13673270110384365

Bolman, L. G., & Deal, T. E. (2008). *Reframing organizations: Artistry, choice, and leadership* (4th ed.). Jossey-Bass.

Bossert, S., Dwyer, D., Rowan, B., & Lee, G. (1982). The instructional management role of the principal. *Educational Administration Quarterly*, *18*(3), 34–64. doi:10.1177/0013161X82018003004

Bossidy, L. (2001). The job no CEO should delegate. *Harvard Business Review*, *79*(3), 46–49. PMID:11246923

Boswell, W. (2006). Aligning employees with the organization's strategic objectives: Out of 'line of sight', out of mind. *International Journal of Human Resource Management*, *17*(9), 1489–1511. doi:10.1080/09585190600878071

Boudreaux, M. A. (2001). *Career development: What is its role in human resource development?*

Bowden, G. T. (1947). The adaptive capacity of workers. *Harvard Business Review*, *25*, 527–542.

Brache, A. P. (2002). *How organizations work: Taking a holistic approach to enterprise health*. John Wiley & Sons, Inc.

Brakman, S., Garretsen, H., & van Witteloostuijn, A. (2021). Robots do not get the coronavirus: The COVID-19 pandemic and the international division of labor. *Journal of International Business Studies*, *52*(6), 1215–1224. doi:10.105741267-021-00410-9 PMID:33758437

Brandenburg, D. C., & Ellinger, A. D. (2003). The future: Just-in-time learning expectations and potential implications for human resource development. *Advances in Developing Human Resources*, *5*(3), 308–320. doi:10.1177/1523422303254629

Brass, D. J., & Burkhardt, M. E. (1993). Potential power and power use: An investigation of structure and behavior. *Academy of Management Journal*, *36*(3), 441–470. doi:10.2307/256588

Braun, N. M. (2004). Critical thinking in the business curriculum. *Journal of Education for Business*, *79*(4), 232–236. doi:10.1080/08832323.2020.12088718

Brinkerhoff, R. O. (1987). *Achieving results from training*. Jossey-Bass.

Browell, S. (2000). Staff development and professional education: A cooperative model. *Journal of Workplace Learning: Employee Counseling Today*, *12*(2), 57–65. doi:10.1108/13665620010316208

Bruner, J. S., Goodnow, J. J., & Austin, G. A. (1956). *A study of thinking*. Wiley.

Bruning, R. H., Schrawg, J., & Norby, M. M. (2011). *Cognitive psychology and instruction* (5th ed.). Pearson.

Brynjolfsson, E., Horton, J. J., Ozimek, A., Rock, D., Sharma, G., & Tu, H. Y. (2020). *COVID-19 and remote work: An early look at US data* (No. w27344). National Bureau of Economic Research.

Brynjolfsson, E., Horton, J. J., Ozimek, A., Rock, D., Sharma, G., & Tu Ye, H. Y. (2020). *COVID-19 and remote work: An early look at US data* (No. w27344). National Bureau of Economic Research.

Brynjolfsson, E., & McAfee, A. (2011). *Race against the machine: How the digital revolution is accelerating innovation, driving productivity, and irreversibly transforming employment and the economy.* Digital Frontier Press.

Buchholz, R. A. (1977). The belief structure of managers relative to work concepts measured by a factor analytic model. *Personnel Psychology*, *30*(4), 567–587. doi:10.1111/j.1744-6570.1977.tb02328.x

Buch, K. (1992). How does downsizing affect employee involvement? *Journal for Quality and Participation*, *15*, 74–77.

Bunch, K. J. (2007). Training failure as a consequence of organizational culture. *Human Resource Development Review*, *6*(2), 142–163. doi:10.1177/1534484307299273

Burack, E. H. (1999). Bridging research to corpo- rate application. In L. Larwood & U. E. Gattiker (Eds.), *Impact analysis: How reach can enter application and make a difference* (pp. 17–46). Erlbaum.

Burack, E. H. (1999). Bridging research to corporate application. In L. Larwood & U. E. Gattiker (Eds.), *Impact analysis: How reach can enter application and make a difference* (pp. 17–46). Erlbaum.

Burke, L. A., & Hutchins, H. M. (2007). Training transfer: An integrative literature review. *Human Resource Development Review*, *6*(3), 263–296. doi:10.1177/1534484307303035

Burke, L. A., & Hutchins, H. M. (2008). A study of best practices in training transfer and proposed model of transfer. *Human Resource Development Quarterly*, *19*(2), 107–128. doi:10.1002/hrdq.1230

Burkhardt, M. E., & Brass, D. J. (1990). Changing patterns or patterns of change: The effects of a change in technology on social network structure and power. *Administrative Science Quarterly*, *35*(1), 104–127. doi:10.2307/2393552

Burnes, B., & Cooke, B. (2012). The past, present and future of organization development: Taking the long view. *Human Relations*, *65*(11), 1395–1429. doi:10.1177/0018726712450058

Bushnell, D. S. (1990). Input, process, output: A model for evaluating training. *Training and Development Journal*, *44*(3), 41–43.

Bush, P. D. (1987). The theory of institutional change. *Journal of Economic Issues*, *21*(3), 1075–1116. doi:10.1080/00213624.1987.11504697

Byrd, M. Y. (2016). The enlightened revelation: Toward a spirit-centered, socially just workplace. *New Directions for Adult and Continuing Education*, *152*(152), 85–94. doi:10.1002/ace.20215

Caffarella, R. S. (1993). Self-directed learning. *New Directions for Adult and Continuing Education*, *1993*(57), 25–35. doi:10.1002/ace.36719935705

Caldwell, C., & Peters, R. (2018). New employee onboarding – psychological contracts and ethical perspectives. *Journal of Management Development*, *37*(1), 27–39. doi:10.1108/JMD-10-2016-0202

Camerer, C., & Vepsalainen, A. (1988). The economic efficiency of corporate culture. *Strategic Management Journal*, *9*(Special Issue), 115–126. doi:10.1002mj.4250090712

Cameron, K. S. (1994). Strategies for successful organizational downsizing. *Human Resource Management*, *33*(2), 189–211. doi:10.1002/hrm.3930330204

Campbell, J. P. (1990). Modeling the performance prediction problem in industrial and organizational psychology. In M. D. Dunnette & L. M. Hough (EDs.), Handbook of industrial and organizational psychology (2nd ed., Vol. 1, pp. 687–732). Consulting Psychologists Press.

Campbell, J. P. (1990). Modeling the performance prediction problem in industrial and organizational psychology. In M. D. Dunnette & L. M. Hough (Eds.), *Handbook of industrial and organizational psychology* (2nd ed., Vol. 1, pp. 687–732). Consulting Psychologists Press.

Caplow, T. (1954). *The sociology of work*. McGraw-Hill Book Company.

Carlisle, L. W. (2002). Knowledge management and training: The value of collaboration. *Performance Improvement*, *41*(4), 37–43. doi:10.1002/pfi.4140410407

Carolan, T. F., Hutchins, S. D., Wickens, C. D., & Cumming, J. M. (2014). Costs and benefits of more learner freedom: Meta-analyses of exploratory and learner control training methods. *Human Factors*, *56*(5), 999–1014. doi:10.1177/0018720813517710 PMID:25141602

Carrig, K., & Wright, P. M. (2006). *Building profit through building people: Making your work force the strongest link in the value-profit chain*. Society for Human Resource Management.

Carrig, K., & Wright, P. M. (2006). *Building profit through building people: Making your workforce the strongest link in the value-profit chain*. Society for Human Resource Management.

Carrig, K., & Wright, P. M. (2006). *Building profit through building people: Making your work-force the strongest link in the value-profit chain*. Society for Human Resource Management.

Carr, N. G. (2003). IT doesn't matter. *Harvard Business Review*, *81*(5), 41–49. PMID:12747161

Cascio, W. F., & Collings, D. G. (2022). Potential: The forgotten factor in talent management research. In D. Collings, V. Vaiman, and H. Scullion (Eds.) Talent management: A decade of developments (pp. 65-84), Emerald Publishing Limited. doi:10.1108/978-1-80117-834-120221004

Cascio, W. F. (2019). Training trends: Macro, micro, and policy issues. *Human Resource Management Review*, *29*(2), 284–297. doi:10.1016/j.hrmr.2017.11.001

Cascio, W. F., & Aguinis, H. (2005). *Applied psychology in human resource management* (6th ed.). Pearson Prentice Hall.

Caselli, M., & Fracasso, A. (2022). COVID-19 and technology. In K. F. Zimmermann (Ed.), *Handbook of labor, human resources and population economics*. Springer., doi:10.1007/978-3-319-57365-6_331-1

Chalutz Ben-Gal, H. (2022). Person–skill fit: Why a new form of employee fit is required. *Academy of Management Perspectives*. doi:10.5465/amp.2022-0024

Champy, J., & Hammer, M. (1993). *Reengineering the corporation*. HarperBusiness.

Chatman, J. A., & Cha, S. E. (2003). Leading by leveraging culture. *California Management Review*, *45*(4), 20–34. doi:10.2307/41166186

Chatman, J. A., & Jehn, K. A. (1991). Assessing the relationship between industry characteristics and organizational culture: How different can you be? *Academy of Management Journal*, *37*(3), 522–553. doi:10.2307/256699

Chaumont, F. (2014). *Does corporate culture have a positive impact on motivation?* [Doctoral dissertation, Dublin Business School].

Cheng, L., Varshney, K. R., & Liu, H. (2021). Socially responsible ai algorithms: Issues, purposes, and challenges. *Journal of Artificial Intelligence Research*, *71*, 1137–1181. doi:10.1613/jair.1.12814

Chen, S., & Dodd, J. L. (1997). Economic value added (EVA™): An empirical examination of a new corporate performance measure. *Journal of Managerial Issues*, *9*(3), 318–333.

Chiaburu, D. S., & Lindsay, D. R. (2008). Can do or will do? The importance of self-efficacy and instrumentality for training transfer. *Human Resource Development International*, *11*(2), 199–206. doi:10.1080/13678860801933004

Choi, M. (2011). Employees' attitudes toward organizational change: A literature review. *Human Resource Management*, *50*(4), 479–500. doi:10.1002/hrm.20434

Chomsky, N., & Skinner, B. F. (1959). A review of B. F. Skinner's "verbal behavior.". *Language*, *35*(1), 26–58. doi:10.2307/411334

Christensen, K. E., & Staines, G. L. (1990). Flextime: A viable solution to work/family conflict? *Journal of Family Issues*, *11*(4), 455–476. doi:10.1177/019251390011004007

Chua, C. K. (2020). The global rise of 3D printing during the COVID-19 pandemic. *Nature Reviews. Materials*, *5*(9), 637–639. doi:10.103841578-020-00234-3 PMID:35194517

Chu, Q., Correa, R., Henry, T. L., McGregor, K. A., Stoklosa, H., Robinson, L., Jha, S., Annamalai, A., Hsu, B. S., Gupta, R., Patton, D. U., Moreno-Walton, L. A., Butts, C., Chai, C., & Kuy, S. (2020). Reallocating ventilators during the coronavirus disease 2019 pandemic: Is it ethical? *Surgery*, *168*(3), 388–391. doi:10.1016/j.surg.2020.04.044 PMID:32616345

Cimarolli, V. R., Bryant, N. S., Falzarano, F., & Stone, R. (2022). Job resignation in nursing homes during the COVID-19 pandemic: The role of quality of employer communication. *Journal of Applied Gerontology*, *41*(1), 12–21. doi:10.1177/07334648211040509 PMID:34428936

Clark, N. (2004). HRD and the challenges of assessing learning in the workplace. *International Journal of Training and Development*, *8*(2), 140–156. doi:10.1111/j.1468-2419.2004.00203.x

Clay, J. (2006). The deep difference between labor and use-value. *Science and Society*, *70*(3), 375–378. doi:10.1521iso.70.3.375

Cleveland, J. N., & Murphy, K. R. (1992). Analyzing performance appraisal as goal-directed behavior. *Research in Personnel and Human Resources Management*, *10*, 121–185.

Cohen, E., & Nycz, M. (2006). Learning objects and e-learning: An informing science perspective. *Interdisciplinary Journal of E-Learning and Learning Objects*, *2*(1), 23–34. doi:10.28945/399

Cohen, E., & Shampine, S. (2022, May 11). Immigration shortfall may be a headwind for labor supply. *Economic Bulletin*, 1–4.

Colbert, A., Yee, N., & George, G. (2016). The digital workforce and the workplace of the future. *Academy of Management Journal*, *59*(3), 731–739. doi:10.5465/amj.2016.4003

Collins, J. A., Greer, J. E., Kumar, V. S., McCalla, G. I., Meagher, P., & Tkatch, R. (1997). Inspectable user models for just-in-time workplace training. In A. Jameson, C. Paris, & C. Tasso (Eds.), *User Modeling: Proceedings of the Sixth International Conference UM97* (pp. 327-337). Springer Wien. 10.1007/978-3-7091-2670-7_33

Collins, J. (2001). *Good to great*. HarperCollins.

Collins, J., & Porras, J. (1994). *Built to last*. HarperBusiness.

Como, R., Hambley, L., & Domene, J. (2021). An exploration of work-life wellness and remote work during and beyond COVID-19. *Canadian Journal of Career Development*, *20*(1), 46–56.

Conley, Q., Lutz, H. S., & Miller, C. L. (2017). The flipped training model: Six steps for getting employees to flip out over training. *Performance Improvement*, *56*(5), 18–31. doi:10.1002/pfi.21692

Cook, I. (2021, September 15). Who is driving the Great Resignation? *Harvard Business Review*. https://hbr.org/2021/09/who-is-driving-the-great-resignation

Coughlan, R. (2005). Codes, values and justifications in the ethical decision-making process. *Journal of Business Ethics*, *59*(1–2), 45–53. doi:10.100710551-005-3409-9

Cowen, T. (2011). *The great stagnation: How America ate all the low-hanging fruit of modern history, got sick, and will(eventually) feel better*. Penguin Group Publishing.

Crampton, S. M., Hodge, J. W., Mishra, J. M., & Price, S. (1995). Stress and stress management. *S.A.M. Advanced Management Journal*, *60*(3), 10–29.

Crane, B., & Hartwell, C. J. (2018). Developing employees' mental complexity: Transformational leadership as a catalyst in employee development. *Human Resource Development Review, 17*(3), 234–257. doi:10.1177/1534484318781439

Cummings, T. G., & Worley, C. G. (2005). Organizational development and change (8th ed.). South-Western/Thomson.

Cyert, R. M., Dill, W. R., & March, J. G. (1958). The role of expectations in business decision making. *Administrative Science Quarterly, 3*(3), 307–340. doi:10.2307/2390716

Cyert, R. M., & March, J. G. (1963). *A behavioral theory of the firm*. Prentice Hall.

D'Netto, B., & Sohal, A. (1999). Human resource practices and workforce diversity: An empirical assessment. *International Journal of Manpower, 20*(8), 530–547. doi:10.1108/01437729910302723

Dalziel, M. M., & Schoonover, S. C. (1988). *Changing ways: A practical tool for implementing change within organizations*. AMACOM.

Damanpour, F. (1991). Organizational innovation: A meta-analysis of effects of determinants and moderators. *Academy of Management Journal, 34*(3), 555–590. doi:10.2307/256406

Danquah, J. K., Crocco, O. S., Mahmud, Q. M., Rehan, M., & Rizvi, L. J. (2023). Connecting concepts: Bridging the gap between capacity development and human resource development. *Human Resource Development International*, 1–18. doi:10.1080/13678868.2022.2108992

Davis, L., & North, D. (1970). Institutional change and American economic growth: A first step to-wards a theory of institutional innovation. *The Journal of Economic History, 30*(1), 131–149. doi:10.1017/S0022050700078633

Day, D. V., & Sulsky, L. M. (1995). Effects of frame-of-reference training and information configuration on memory organization and rating accuracy. *The Journal of Applied Psychology, 80*(1), 158–167. doi:10.1037/0021-9010.80.1.158

De Clercq, D., Dayan, M., & Ng, P. Y. (2023). When performance demands enable change: How employees can overcome emotional dissonance and organizational underappreciation. *European Management Journal*, 1–11. doi:10.1016/j.emj.2023.02.004

De Long, D. W., & Fahey, L. (2000). Diagnosing cultural barriers to knowledge management. *The Academy of Management Executive, 14*(4), 113–127. doi:10.5465/ame.2000.3979820

Deal, T., & Kennedy, A. (1984). *Corporate cultures*. Addison-Wesley.

Delery, J. E. (1998). Issues of fit in strategic human resource management: Implications for research. *Human Resource Management Review, 8*(3), 289–309. doi:10.1016/S1053-4822(98)90006-7

Deming, W. E. (1982). *Out of the crisis*. MIT Center for Advanced Engineering Study.

Deng, X., Joshi, K. D., & Galliers, R. D. (2016). The duality of empowerment and marginalization in microtask crowdsourcing. *Management Information Systems Quarterly, 40*(2), 279–302. doi:10.25300/MISQ/2016/40.2.01

DeNisi, A. S., & Murphy, K. R. (2017). Performance appraisal and performance management: 100 years of progress? *The Journal of Applied Psychology*, *102*(3), 421–433. doi:10.1037/apl0000085 PMID:28125265

Denison, D. R. (1996). What is the difference between organizational culture and organizational climate? A native's point of view on a decade of paradigm wars. *Academy of Management Review*, *21*(3), 619–654. doi:10.2307/258997

Dewey, J. (1910). *How we think*. D. C. Heath & Co., doi:10.1037/10903-000

Di Vesta, F. J. (1974). Cognitive structures and symbolic processes. *Teachers College Record*, *75*(3), 357–370. doi:10.1177/016146817407500302

DiBella, A. J. (1995). Developing learning organizations: A matter of perspective. *Academy of Management Journal*, *38*, 287–290.

Disselkamp, L. (2007). *Working the clock: How to win the race for productivity and profits with workforce management technology*. The Oaklea Press.

Disselkamp, L. (2009). *No boundaries: How to use time and labor management technology to win the race for profits and productivity*. John Wiley & Sons, Inc.

Dohmann, C. W. (1970). Teachers' perception toward innovations and change. *UMI Dissertation Services, 70*(25), 019. (University Microfilms No, 70-25, 019)

Donahoe, E., & Metzger, M. M. (2019). Artificial intelligence and human rights. *Journal of Democracy*, *30*(2), 115–126. doi:10.1353/jod.2019.0029

Driskell, J. E., Johnston, J. H., & Salas, E. (2001). Does stress training generalize to novel settings? *Human Factors*, *43*(1), 99–110. doi:10.1518/001872001775992471 PMID:11474766

Drouin, M., O'Connor, K. W., Schmidt, G. B., & Miller, D. A. (2015). Facebook fired: Legal perspectives and young adults' opinions on the use of social media in hiring and firing decisions. *Computers in Human Behavior*, *46*, 123–128. doi:10.1016/j.chb.2015.01.011

Drucker, P. F. (1954). *The practice of management*. Harper.

Drucker, P. F. (1969). *The age of discontinuity*. Butterworth-Heinemann.

Drucker, P. F. (1992). *Managing for the future*. Butterworth Heinemann.

Drucker, P. F. (1994). The age of social transformation. *Atlantic Monthly*, *274*(5), 53–80.

Drucker, P. F. (1999). Knowledge-worker productivity: The biggest challenge. *California Management Review*, *41*(2), 79–94. doi:10.2307/41165987

Drucker, P. F. (2002). *Managing in the next society*. Saint Martin's Press.

Drucker, P. F. (2008). *Management* (rev. ed.). HarperCollins.

Dwivedi, Y. K., Hughes, L., Ismagilova, E., Aarts, G., Coombs, C., Crick, T., & Williams, M. D. (2021). Artificial Intelligence (AI): Multidisciplinary perspectives on emerging challenges, opportunities, and agenda for research, practice and policy. *International Journal of Information Management, 57*, 101994

Eby, L. T., & Buch, K. (1998). The impact of adopting an ethical approach to employee dismissal during corporate restructuring. *Journal of Business Ethics, 17*(12), 1253–1264. doi:10.1023/A:1005758628414

Edmans, A., Gabaix, X., & Jenter, D. (2017). Executive compensation: A survey of theory and evidence. The Handbook of the Economics of Corporate Governance, 1, 383-539.

Egan, T. M. (2001). *Organization development: An examination of definitions and dependent variables.* Human Resource Development Research Center, University of Minnesota.

Egan, T. M. (2002). Organization development: An examination of definitions and dependent variables. *Organization Development Journal, 20*(2), 59–70.

Ege, T., Esen, A., & Aşik Dizdar, Ö. (2017). Organizational learning and learning organizations: An integrative framework. *International Journal of Management Economics & Business / Uluslararasi Yönetim Iktisat ve Isletme Dergisi, 13*(2), 439–460. doi:10.17130/ijmeb.2017228693

Eitel-Porter, R. (2021). Beyond the promise: Implementing ethical AI. *AI and Ethics, 1*(1), 73–80. doi:10.100743681-020-00011-6

Ennis, R. H. (1962). A concept of critical thinking. *Harvard Educational Review, 32*(1), 81–111.

Ennis, R. H. (1989). Critical thinking and subject specificity. *Educational Researcher, 18*(3), 4–10. doi:10.3102/0013189X018003004

Erickson, T. (2008). Plugged. In *The generation Y guide to thriving at work.* Harvard Business School Press.

Ericson, M. (2006). Strategic HRD and the relational self. *Human Resource Development Quarterly, 17*(2), 223–229. doi:10.1002/hrdq.1170

Espedal, B. (2005). Management development: Using internal or external resources in developing core competence. *Human Resource Development Review, 4*(2), 136–158. doi:10.1177/1534484305276217

Ezra, M., & Deckman, M. (1996). Balancing work and family responsibilities: Flextime and childcare in the federal government. *Public Administration Review, 56*(2), 174–179. doi:10.2307/977205

Fang, B. (2023). Bridging the gap between research and practice of engagement: Toward a collaborative human resource development. *Advances in Developing Human Resources, 0*(0), 1–21. doi:10.1177/15234223231156627

Fenwick, T. (2008). Workplace learning: Emerging trends and new perspectives. *New Directions for Adult and Continuing Education, 2008*(119), 17–26. doi:10.1002/ace.302

Figueroa, R. A. (1999). Modelling the value of location in Regina using GIS and spatial auto correlation statistics. *Assessment Journal, 6*(6), 29–37.

Fisher, S. R., & White, M. A. (2000). Downsizing in a learning organization: Are there hidden costs? *Academy of Management Review, 25*(1), 244–251. doi:10.2307/259273

Floridi, L., & Chiriatti, M. (2020). GPT-3: Its nature, scope, limits, and consequences. *Minds and Machines, 30*(4), 681–694. doi:10.100711023-020-09548-1

Folger, R., & Greenberg, J. (1985). Procedural justice: An interpretive analysis of personnel systems. *Research in Personnel and Human Resources Management, 3*, 141–183.

Ford, M. (2009). *The lights in the tunnel: Automation, accelerating technology and the economy of the future.* Acculant Publishing.

Formica, S., & Sfodera, F. (2022). The great resignation and quiet quitting paradigm shifts: An overview of current situation and future research directions. *Journal of Hospitality Marketing & Management, 31*(8), 899–907. doi:10.1080/19368623.2022.2136601

Formosa, P., & Ryan, M. (2021). Making moral machines: Why we need artificial moral agents. *AI & Society, 36*(3), 839–851. doi:10.100700146-020-01089-6

Fosnot, C. T., & Perry, R. S. (1996). Constructivism: A psychological theory of learning. *Constructivism: Theory, Perspectives, and Practice, 2*(1), 8–33.

Fox, A. (1974). *Beyond contract: Work, power, and trust relations.* Faber.

Fox, M. F. (2008). Institutional transformation and the advancement of women faculty: The case of academic science and engineering. In J. C. Smart (Ed.), *Higher education: Handbook of theory and research* (Vol. 23, pp. 73–103). Springer., doi:10.1007/978-1-4020-6959-8_3

Fox, R. (2001). Constructivism examined. *Oxford Review of Education, 27*(1), 23–35. doi:10.1080/03054980125310

Fraser, J. A. (2001). *White-collar sweatshop.* W. W. Norton & Co.

Freedman, S. M. (1978). Some determinants of compensation decisions. *Academy of Management Journal, 21*(3), 397–409. doi:10.2307/255722 PMID:10246525

Freidman, M. (1970, September 13). The social responsibility of business is to increase its profits. *The New York Times Magazine*, 32-33.

Friedland, W. H. (1964). For a sociological concept of charisma. *Social Forces, 43*(1), 18–26. doi:10.2307/2575961

Friedman, M. (1970, September 13). The social responsibility of business is to increase its profits. *The New York Times Magazine.*

Friedman, M. (1994). *Money mischief: Episodes in monetary history.* Harcourt Brace.

Friedman, T. L., & Mandelbaum, M. (2011). *That used to be us: How America fell behind in the world it invented and how we can come back.* Farrar, Strauss, and Giroux.

Fried, Y., & Ferris, G. R. (1987). The validity of the job characteristics model: A review and meta-analysis. *Personnel Psychology, 40*(2), 287–322. doi:10.1111/j.1744-6570.1987.tb00605.x

Frisque, D. A., & Kolb, J. A. (2008). The effects of an ethics training program on attitude, knowledge, and transfer of training of office professionals: A treatment-and control-group design. *Human Resource Development Quarterly, 19*(1), 35–53. doi:10.1002/hrdq.1224

Fromm, E. (1989). *Marx's concept of man.* The Continuum Publishing Company.

Fulkerson, J. R., & Schuler, R. S. (1992). Managing worldwide diversity at Pepsi-Cola International. In S. E. Jackson (Ed.), *Diversity in the workplace: Human resources initiatives, society for industrial and organisational psychology (The Professional Practice Series).* Guildford Press.

Gagné, R. M. (1962). Military training and principles of learning. *The American Psychologist, 17*(2), 83–91. doi:10.1037/h0048613

Galbraith, J. R., & Lawler, E. E. (1993). *Organizing for the future: The new logic for managing complex organizations.* Jossey-Bass.

Gale, B. T. (1980). Can more capital buy higher productivity? *Harvard Business Review, 58*(4), 78–86.

Gallimore, P., Fletcher, M., & Carter, M. (1996). Modelling the influence of location on value. *Journal of Property Valuation Investment, 14*(1), 6–19. doi:10.1108/14635789610107444

Gall, M. D., Gall, J. P., & Borg, W. R. (2007). *Educational research: An introduction* (8th ed.). Pearson.

Galvin, J. C. (1983). What trainers can learn from educators about evaluating management training. *Training and Development Journal, 37*(8), 52–57.

Garavaglia, P. L. (1993). How to ensure transfer of training. *Training & Development, 47*(10), 63–69.

Garavan, T. N. (1991). Strategic human resource development. *Journal of European Industrial Training, 15*(1), 17–30. doi:10.1108/EUM0000000000219

Garavan, T. N. (1997). Training, development, education and learning: Different or the same? *Journal of European Industrial Training, 21*(2), 39–50. doi:10.1108/03090599710161711

Garavan, T. N. (2007). A strategic perspective on human resource development. *Advances in Developing Human Resources, 9*(1), 11–30. doi:10.1177/1523422306294492

Garavan, T. N., Costine, P., & Heraty, N. (1995). The emergence of strategic human resource development. *Journal of European Industrial Training, 19*(10), 4–10. doi:10.1108/03090599510095816

Garavan, T. N., Shanahan, V., Carbery, R., & Watson, S. (2016). Strategic human resource development: Towards a conceptual framework to understand its contribution to dynamic capabilities. *Human Resource Development International*, *19*(4), 289–306. doi:10.1080/1367 8868.2016.1169765

Garrison, D. R. (1997). Self-directed learning: Toward a comprehensive model. *Adult Education Quarterly*, *48*(1), 18–33. doi:10.1177/074171369704800103

Garvin, D. (1993). Building a learning organization. *Harvard Business Review*, *71*(4), 78–91. PMID:10127041

Garvin, D. A., Edmondson, A. C., & Gino, F. (2008). Is yours a learning organization? *Harvard Business Review*, *86*(3), 109–134. PMID:18411968

Gelfand, M. J., Nishii, L. H., Raver, J. L., & Schneider, B. (2005). Discrimination in organizations: An organizational-level systems perspective. In R. L. Dipboye & A. Colella (Eds.), *Discrimination at work: The psychological and organizational bases* (pp. 117–144). Psychology Press.

George, G., Sleeth, R., & Siders, M. (1999). Organizing culture: Leader roles, behaviors, and reinforcement mechanisms. *Journal of Business and Psychology*, *13*(4), 545–560. doi:10.1023/A:1022923005165

Gephart, M. A., Marsick, V. J., Van Buren, M. E., & Spiro, M. S. (1996). Learning organizations come alive. *Training & Development*, *50*, 56–66.

Ghiselli, E. E., & Brown, C. W. (1948). *Personnel and industrial psychology*. McGraw-Hill.

Gilley, J. W., & Maycunich, A. (2000). *Organizational learning, performance, and change: An introduction to strategic human resource development*. Perseus Publishing.

Gilley, J., & Eggland, S. A. (1989). *Principle of human resource development*. Perseus.

Githens, R. P., Dirani, K., Gitonga, J., & Teng, Y. T. (2008). Technology-related research in HRD publications: An analysis of content and metaperspectives from 2000 to 2006. *Human Resource Development Quarterly*, *19*(3), 191–215. doi:10.1002/hrdq.1236

Gladwell, M. (2009). *What the dog saw: And other adventures*. Little, Brown and Company.

Glynn, M. A., & D'Aunno, T. (2023). An intellectual history of institutional theory: Looking back to move forward. *The Academy of Management Annals*, *17*(1), 301–330. doi:10.5465/annals.2020.0341

Goffman, E. (1959). *The presentation of self in everyday life*. Doubleday.

Gold, A. H., Malhotra, A., & Segars, A. H. (2001). Knowledge management: An organizational capabilities perspective. *Journal of Management Information Systems*, *18*(1), 185–214. doi:10.1080/07421222.2001.11045669

Goldstein, I. L. (1974). *Training: Program development and evaluation*. Brooks/ Cole.

Goldstein, I. L. (1980). Training in work organizations. *Annual Review of Psychology*, *31*(1), 229–272. doi:10.1146/annurev.ps.31.020180.001305

Gordon, G., & DiTomaso, N. (1992). Predicting corporate performance from organizational culture. *Journal of Management Studies*, *29*(6), 783–798. doi:10.1111/j.1467-6486.1992.tb00689.x

Gordon, J. S. (2020). Building moral robots: Ethical pitfalls and challenges. *Science and Engineering Ethics*, *26*(1), 141–157. doi:10.100711948-019-00084-5 PMID:30701408

Gotsis, G., & Grimani, K. (2016). Diversity as an aspect of effective leadership: Integrating and moving forward. *Leadership and Organization Development Journal*, *37*(2), 241–264. doi:10.1108/LODJ-06-2014-0107

Gowler, D. (1969). Determinants of the supply of labour to the firm. *Journal of Management Studies*, *6*(1), 73–95. doi:10.1111/j.1467-6486.1969.tb00582.x

Graham, J. W. (1991). Servant-leadership in organizations: Inspirational and moral. *The Leadership Quarterly*, *2*(2), 105–119. doi:10.1016/1048-9843(91)90025-W

Gredler, M. E. (2009). *Learning and instruction: Theory into practice* (6thed.). Pearson Education, Inc.

Gredler, M. E. (2009). *Learning and instruction: Theory into practice* (6th ed.). Pearson Education, Inc.

Gredler, M. E. (2012). Understanding Vygotsky for the classroom: Is it too late? *Educational Psychology Review*, *24*(1), 113–131. doi:10.100710648-011-9183-6

Griego, O. V., Geroy, G. D., & Wright, P. C. (2000). Predictors of learning organizations: A human resource development practitioner's perspective. *The Learning Organization*, *7*(1), 5–12. doi:10.1108/09696470010313632

Grieves, J. (2003). Strategic Human Resource Development. *Sage (Atlanta, Ga.)*.

Grossman, R., & Salas, E. (2011). The transfer of training: What really matters. *International Journal of Training and Development*, *15*(2), 103–120. doi:10.1111/j.1468-2419.2011.00373.x

Guion, R. (1973). A note on organizational climate. *Organizational Behavior and Human Performance*, *9*(1), 120–125. doi:10.1016/0030-5073(73)90041-X

Hackman, J. R., & Oldham, G. R. (1974). The job diagnostic survey: An instrument for the diagnosis of jobs and the evaluation of job redesign projects. *Catalog of Selected Documents in Psychology*, *4*, 148.

Hackman, J. R., & Oldham, G. R. (1975). Development of the job diagnostic survey. *The Journal of Applied Psychology*, *60*(2), 159–170. doi:10.1037/h0076546

Hall, D. T. (1990). Telecommuting and the management of work-home boundaries. In *Paradigms revised: The annual review of communications in society-1989* (pp. 177–208). Institute for Information Studies.

Hall, D. T., & Richter, J. (1988). Balancing work life and home life: What can organizations do to help? *The Academy of Management Executive, 3*(3), 213–223. doi:10.5465/ame.1988.4277258

Halloran, J. D. (1967). *Attitude formation and change*. Leicester University Press.

Hall, R. E., & Jones, C. I. (1999). Why do some countries produce so much more output per worker than others? *The Quarterly Journal of Economics, 114*(1), 83–116. doi:10.1162/003355399555954

Hall, R., & Andriani, P. (2000). Analyzing intangible resources and managing knowledge in a supply chain context. In *Knowledge creation* (pp. 231–257). Palgrave Macmillan. doi:10.1007/978-1-349-62753-0_9

Halsell, M. B. (2014). *Examining employees' perceptions of energy conservation behaviors in office settings*. [Doctoral dissertation, University of Arkansas]. https://scholarworks.uark.edu/cgi/viewcontent.cgi?article=3604&context=etd&httpsredir=1&referer=

Hamel, G., & Prahalad, C. K. (1994). *Competing for the future*. Harvard Business School Press.

Hamlin, R. G. (2002). In support of evidence- based management and research-informed HRD through HRD professional partnerships: An empirical and comparative study. *Human Resource Development International, 5*(4), 467–491. doi:10.1080/13678860210122643

Hamlin, R. G., Ellinger, A. D., & Beattie, R. S. (2009). Toward a profession of coaching? A definitional examination of 'coaching', 'organization development', and 'human resource development'. *International Journal of Evidence Based Coaching and Mentoring, 7*(1), 13–38.

Hamouche, S., & Chabani, Z. (2021). COVID-19 and the new forms of employment relationship: Implications and insights for human resource development. *Industrial and Commercial Training, 53*(4), 366–379. doi:10.1108/ICT-11-2020-0112

Hamrick, D. C., & MacMillan, I. C. (1984). SMR forum: Asset parsimony- Managing assets to manage profits. *Sloan Management Review, 25*(2), 67–74.

Hanna, D. P. (1988). *Designing organizations for high performance*. Addison- Wesley.

Hardy, J. H. III, Day, E. A., & Steele, L. M. (2019). Interrelationships among self-regulated learning processes: Toward a dynamic process-based model of self-regulated learning. *Journal of Management, 45*(8), 3146–3177. doi:10.1177/0149206318780440

Harris, M. M. (1994). Rater motivation in the performance appraisal context: A theoretical framework. *Journal of Management, 20*(4), 737–756. doi:10.1016/0149-2063(94)90028-0

Harrison, R. (1993). Developing people – for whose bottom line? In R. Harrison (Ed.), *Human resource management. Issues and strategies* (pp. 299–329). Addison-Wesley.

Harrison, R. (1997). *Employee development*. Institute of Personal and Development.

Hartman, L. P. (2001). Technology and ethics: Privacy in the workplace. *Business and Society Review, 106*(1), 1–27. doi:10.1111/0045-3609.00099

Hartman, L. P., & Bucci, G. (2004). The economic and ethical implications of new technology on privacy in the workplace. *Business and Society Review*, *102*(1), 1–24. doi:10.1111/0045-3609.00021

Hatala, J.-P., & Gumm, J. C. (2006). Managing organizational cultural influences during the implementation of competency-based training. *Advances in Developing Human Resources*, *8*(2), 229–246. doi:10.1177/1523422305286154

Hatch, M. J. (1993). The dynamics of organizational culture. *Academy of Management Review*, *18*(4), 657–693. doi:10.2307/258594

Hatch, N. W., & Dyer, J. H. (2004). Human capital and learning as source of sustainable competitive advantage. *Strategic Management Journal*, *25*(12), 1155–1178. doi:10.1002mj.421

Hax, A. C., & Majluf, N. S. (1996). *The strategy concept and process: A pragmatic approach* (2nd ed.). Prentice Hall.

Hayes, K. H. (2000). *Managing career transitions: Your career as a work in progress* (2nd ed.). Prentice Hall.

Heck, R. H., Larsen, T. J., & Marcoulides, G. A. (1990). Instructional leadership and school achievement: Validation of a causal model. *Educational Administration Quarterly*, *26*(2), 94–125. doi:10.1177/0013161X90026002002

Heilinger, J.-C. (2022). The ethics of AI ethics. A constructive critique. *Philosophy & Technology*, *35*(3), 61. doi:10.100713347-022-00557-9

Heinrich, T., & Witko, C. (2021). Technology-induced job loss and the prioritization of economic problems in the mass public. *The Review of Policy Research*, *38*(2), 164–179. doi:10.1111/ropr.12418

Hellriegel, D., & Slocum, J. W. Jr. (1974). Organizational climate: Measures, research, and contingencies. *Academy of Management Journal*, *17*(2), 255–280. doi:10.2307/254979

Heneson, M. E., Morris, L. L., & Fitz-Gibbon, C. T. (1978). How to measure attitudes. *Sage (Atlanta, Ga.)*.

Henriksen, A., & Bechmann, A. (2020). Building truths in AI: Making predictive algorithms doable in healthcare. *Information Communication and Society*, *23*(6), 802–816. doi:10.1080/1369118X.2020.1751866

Herzberg, F. (1966). Work and the nature of man. *WORLD (Oakland, Calif.)*.

High, J. C. (1991). Achieving excellence through people, technology, and teamwork. In NAECBSS (Ed.), People and technology in the workplace. The National Academies Press.

Hijal-Moghrabi, I., Sabharwal, M., & Berman, E. M. (2017). The importance of ethical environment to organizational performance in employment at will states. *Administration & Society*, *49*(9), 1346–1374. doi:10.1177/0095399715581043

Hinings, C. R., & Greenwood, R. (2002). Disconnects and consequences in organization theory? *Administrative Science Quarterly*, *47*, 411–421. doi:10.2307/3094844

Hirschi, A., Freund, P. A., & Herrmann, A. (2014). The career engagement scale: Development and validation of a measure of proactive career behaviors. *Journal of Career Assessment*, *22*(4), 575–594. doi:10.1177/1069072713514813

Hogan, W. T. (1987). *Minimills and integrated mills: A comparison of steelmaking in the United States*. Heath.

Holland, J. L. (1973). *Making vocational choices: A theory of careers*. Prentice-Hall.

Hollis, E. (2003). Southwest Airlines: Employee education takes flight. *Chief Learning Officer Magazine, 3*.

Hom, P. W., Lee, T. W., Shaw, J. D., & Hausknecht, J. P. (2017). One hundred years of employee turnover theory and research. *The Journal of Applied Psychology*, *102*(3), 530–545. doi:10.1037/apl0000103 PMID:28125259

Horniman, A. B. (2004). Leading: A performing learning art. In M. Goldsmith, H. J. Morgan, & A. J. Ogg (Eds.), *Leading organizational learning: Harnessing the power of knowledge*. Jossey-Bass.

Hoskisson, R. E., Hitt, M. A., Ireland, R. D., & Harrison, J. S. (2008). *Competing for advantage* (2nd ed.). South-Western.

Hounshell, D. A. (1984). *From the American system to mass production, 1800-1932: The development of manufacturing technology in the United States*. Johns Hopkins University Press. doi:10.56021/9780801829758

House, R. J. (1977). A 1976 theory of charismatic leadership. In J. G. Hunt & L. L. Larson (Eds.), *Leadership: The cutting edge* (pp. 189–273). Southern Illinois University Press.

Howe, D. C., Chauhan, R. S., Soderberg, A. T., & Buckley, M. R. (2021). Paradigm shifts caused by the COVID-19 pandemic. *Organizational Dynamics*, *50*(4), 100804. doi:10.1016/j.orgdyn.2020.100804 PMID:33191959

Hughes, C., & Stephens, D. M. (2012). Leveraging workforce diversity through a career development paradigm shift. In C. L. Scott and M. Y. Byrd (Eds.) Handbook of research on workforce diversity in a global society: Technologies and concepts, (pp. 262-272). IGI Global. doi:10.4018/978-1-4666-1812-1.ch015

Hughes, C., Gosney, M. W., & Sims, C. M. (2019a). Influencing people and technology using human resource development (HRD) philosophy. In Advanced Methodologies and Technologies in Business Operations and Management (pp. 854-866). IGI Global.

Hughes, C. (2010). People as technology conceptual model: Towards a new value creation paradigm for strategic human resource development. *Human Resource Development Review*, *9*(1), 48–71. doi:10.1177/1534484309353561

Hughes, C. (2012). *Valuing people and technology in the workplace: A competitive advantage framework*. IGI Global. doi:10.4018/978-1-4666-0240-3

Hughes, C. (2014). *American Black women and interpersonal leadership styles*. Sense Publishers. doi:10.1007/978-94-6209-878-7

Hughes, C. (2016). *Diversity intelligence: Integrating diversity intelligence alongside intellectual, emotional, and cultural intelligence for leadership and career development*. Palgrave MacMillan Publications. doi:10.1057/978-1-137-52683-0

Hughes, C. (2018). *Workforce inter-personnel diversity: The power to influence human productivity and career development*. Springer International Publishing.

Hughes, C. (2019). *Ethical and legal issues in human resource development: Evolving roles and emerging trends*. Springer International Publishing. doi:10.1007/978-3-319-99528-1

Hughes, C. (2021). The changing learning technological landscape for trainers in the wake of COVID-19. *Advances in Developing Human Resources*, *23*(1), 66–74. doi:10.1177/1523422320972108

Hughes, C. (Ed.). (2020). *Strategies for attracting, maintaining, and balancing a mature workforce*. IGI Global. doi:10.4018/978-1-7998-2277-6

Hughes, C., & Brown, L. (2018). Exploring leaders' discriminatory, passive-aggressive behavior toward protected class employees using diversity intelligence. *Advances in Developing Human Resources*, *20*(3), 263–284. doi:10.1177/1523422318778002

Hughes, C., & Byrd, M. (2015). *Managing human resource development programs: Current issues and evolving trends*. Palgrave Macmillan Publications. doi:10.1057/9781137492197

Hughes, C., & Gosney, M. (Eds.). (2016). *Bridging the scholar-practitioner gap in Human Resource Development*. IGI Global. doi:10.4018/978-1-4666-9998-4

Hughes, C., & Gosney, M. W. (2012). People, technology and human resource development (HRD) philosophy. In V. C. X. Wang (Ed.), *Encyclopedia of e-leadership, counseling and training* (pp. 759–771). IGI Global. doi:10.4018/978-1-61350-068-2.ch055

Hughes, C., & Niu, Y. (2021c). Responding to career development uncertainties and successfully navigating career journeys. *Advances in Developing Human Resources*, *23*(3), 267–272. doi:10.1177/15234223211017852

Hughes, C., & Niu, Y. (Eds.). (. (2021a). How COVID-19 is shifting career reality: Ways to navigate career journeys. *Advances in Developing Human Resources*, *23*(3). doi:10.1177/15234223211017847

Hughes, C., Robert, L., Frady, K., & Arroyos, A. (2019). *Managing technology and middle and low skilled employees: Advances for economic regeneration*. Emerald Publishing. doi:10.1108/9781789730777

Hughes, C., Wang, J., Zheng, W., & McLean, L. (2010). Implementation concerns scholar-practitioners: A pilot study of the link between research and practice. *International Journal of Asian Business and Information Management*, *1*(2), 32–46. doi:10.4018/jabim.2010040104

Hunter, L., Bernhardt, A., Hughes, K., & Skuratowicz, E. (2001). It's not just the ATMs: Technology, firm strategies, jobs, and earnings in retail banking. *Industrial & Labor Relations Review*, *54*(2A), 402–424. doi:10.1177/001979390105400222

Huselid, M. A. (1995). The impact of human resource management practices on turnover, productivity, and corporate financial performance. *Academy of Management Journal*, *38*(3), 635–872. doi:10.2307/256741

Huselid, M. A., Jackson, S. E., & Schuler, R. S. (1997). Technical and strategic human resource management effectiveness as determinants of firm performance. *Academy of Management Journal*, *40*(1), 171–188. doi:10.2307/257025

Huysman, M. (2000). An organizational learning approach to the learning organization. *European Journal of Work and Organizational Psychology*, *9*(2), 133–145. doi:10.1080/135943200397905

Irving, P. G., & Meyer, J. P. (1995). On using direct measures of met expectations: A methodological note. *Journal of Management*, *21*(6), 1159–1176. doi:10.1177/014920639502100608

Isaac, M., & Elrick, J. (2021). How COVID-19 may alleviate the multiple marginalization of racialized migrant workers. *Ethnic and Racial Studies*, *44*(5), 851–863. doi:10.1080/01419870.2020.1842900

Isaacson, L. E., & Brown, D. (1997). *Career information, career counseling, and career development* (6th ed.). Allyn & Bacon.

Isaacson, W. (2011). *Steve Jobs*. Simon and Schuster.

Ismail, J. (2001). The design of an e-learning system: Beyond the hype. *The Internet and Higher Education*, *4*(3-4), 329–336. doi:10.1016/S1096-7516(01)00069-0

Jacobs, R. (1989). Systems theory applied to hu- man resource development. In D. B. Gradous (Ed.), *Systems theory applied to human resource development* (pp. 27–60). American Society for Training and Development.

Jacobs, R. L. (2003). *Structured on-the-job training: Unleashing employee expertise in the Workplace* (2nd ed.). Berrett-Koehler.

Jago, A. G., & Vroom, V. H. (1978). Predicting leader behavior from a measure of behavioral intent. *Academy of Management Journal*, *21*, 715–721. doi:10.2307/255711

James, L., & Jones, A. (1974). Organizational climate: A review of theory and research. *Psychological Bulletin*, *18*(12), 1096–1112. doi:10.1037/h0037511

Jandl, C., Zafari, S., Taurer, F., Hartner-Tiefenthaler, M., & Schlund, S. (2023). Location-based monitoring in production environments: Does transparency help to increase the acceptance of monitoring? *Production & Manufacturing Research, 11*(1), 1–20. doi:10.1080/21693277.2022 .2160387

Jang, S., & Ardichvili, A. (2020). Examining the link between corporate social responsibility and human resources: Implications for HRD research and practice. *Human Resource Development Review, 19*(2), 183–211. doi:10.1177/1534484320912044

Jaspers, K. (1951). The way to wisdom. (trans. Manheim R.). Yale.

Jasson, C. C., & Govender, C. M. (2017). Measuring return on investment and risk in training–A business training evaluation model for managers and leaders. *Acta Commercii, 17*(1), 1–9. doi:10.4102/ac.v17i1.401

Jayne, M., & Dipboye, R. (2004). Leveraging diversity to improve business performance: Research findings and recommendations for organizations. *Human Resource Management, 43*(4), 409–424. doi:10.1002/hrm.20033

Jecker, N. S., & Atuire, C. A. (2021). What's yours is ours: Waiving intellectual property protections for COVID-19 vaccines. *Journal of Medical Ethics, 47*(9), 595–598. doi:10.1136/ medethics-2021-107555 PMID:34233956

Jecker, N. S., Wightman, A. G., & Diekema, D. S. (2021). Vaccine ethics: An ethical framework for global distribution of COVID-19 vaccines. *Journal of Medical Ethics, 47*(5), 308–317. doi:10.1136/medethics-2020-107036 PMID:33593876

Jenkins, J. J. (1974). Remember that old theory of memory? Well, forget it! *The American Psychologist, 25*(11), 785–795. doi:10.1037/h0037399

Jimoh, L. A., & Kee, D. M. H. (2022). Talent management: The way out of poor task performance. *Industrial and Commercial Training, 54*(4), 623–636. doi:10.1108/ICT-03-2022-0016

Jiskrova, G. K. (2022). Impact of COVID-19 pandemic on the workforce: From psychological distress to the Great Resignation. *Journal of Epidemiology and Community Health, 76*(6), 525–526. doi:10.1136/jech-2022-218826 PMID:35296522

Jobin, A., Ienca, M., & Vayena, E. (2019). The global landscape of AI ethics guidelines. *Nature Machine Intelligence, 1*(9), 389–399. doi:10.103842256-019-0088-2

Johnson, R. E. (1975). Meaning in complex learning. *Review of Educational Research, 45*(3), 425–459. doi:10.3102/00346543045003425

Jones, A. P., & James, L. R. (1979). Psychological climate: Dimensions and relationships of individual and aggregated work environment perceptions. *Organizational Behavior and Human Performance, 23*(2), 201–250. doi:10.1016/0030-5073(79)90056-4

Jo, S. J., & Park, S. (2016). Critical review on power in organization: Empowerment in human resource development. *European Journal of Training and Development*, *40*(6), 390–406. doi:10.1108/EJTD-01-2016-0005

Jovanovic, J., Gasevic, D., Brooks, C., Devedzic, V., Hatala, M., Eap, T., & Richards, G. (2007). Using semantic web technologies to analyze learning content. *IEEE Internet Computing*, *11*(5), 45–53. doi:10.1109/MIC.2007.116

Judge, T. A., Weiss, H. M., Kammeyer-Mueller, J. D., & Hulin, C. L. (2017). Job attitudes, job satisfaction, and job affect: A century of continuity and of change. *The Journal of Applied Psychology*, *102*(3), 356–374. doi:10.1037/apl0000181 PMID:28125260

Jundt, D. K., Shoss, M. K., & Huang, J. L. (2015). Individual adaptive performance in organizations: A review. *Journal of Organizational Behavior*, *36*(S1), S53–S71. doi:10.1002/job.1955

Juran, J. M. (1989). *Juran on leadership for quality*. The Free Press.

Kadlec, M. (2020). Game changing legislation: NCAA forced to revise name, image, and likeness compensation rules. *Nova Law Review*, *45*, 227–267.

Kahn, W. A. (1990). Psychological conditions of personal engagement and disengagement at work. *Academy of Management Journal*, *33*(4), 692–724. doi:10.2307/256287

Kajjumba, G. W., Nagitta, O. P., Osra, F. A., & Mkansi, M. (2020). Offshoring-outsourcing and onshoring tradeoffs: The impact of coronavirus on global supply chain. In *Outsourcing and offshoring*. IntechOpen. doi:10.5772/intechopen.95281

Kalimeri, K., & Tjostheim, I. (2020, July). Artificial intelligence and concerns about the future: A case study in Norway. In *International Conference on Human-Computer Interaction* (pp. 273-284). Springer. 10.1007/978-3-030-50344-4_20

Kandula, S. R. (2001). *Strategic human resource development*. Prentice-Hall of India Private Limited.

Kanfer, R., Frese, M., & Johnson, R. E. (2017). Motivation related to work: A century of progress. *The Journal of Applied Psychology*, *102*(3), 338–355. doi:10.1037/apl0000133 PMID:28150980

Kaplan, J. (2021). The psychologist who coined the phrase 'Great Resignation' reveals how he saw it coming and where he sees it going. 'Who we are as an employee and as a worker is very central to who we are.' *Insider*. www.businessinsider.com/why-everyone-is-quitting-great-resignationpsychologist-pandemic-rethink-life-2021-10

Karakas, F., & Manisaligil, A. (2012). Reorienting self-directed learning for the creative digital era. *European Journal of Training and Development*, *36*(7), 712–731. doi:10.1108/03090591211255557

Karsten, M. F., & Igou, F. (2005). Career planning: A model for a diverse workforce. *Refereed Proceedings of the North American Management Society track at the 2005 Midwest Business Administration Association Conference*. MBAA.

Kaye, B. (1997). *Up is not the only way*. Davies-Black.

Kelly, E., & Dobbin, F. (1998). How affirmative action became diversity management: Employer response to antidiscrimination laws, 1961 to 1996. *The American Behavioral Scientist, 41*(7), 960–984. doi:10.1177/0002764298041007008

Kelman, H. C. (1961). Processes of opinion change. *Public Opinion Quarterly, 25*(1), 57–78. doi:10.1086/266996

Kerno, S., & Kuznia, K. (2007). Modern career navigation: Preparing for success despite uncertainties. *Industrial Engineering (American Institute of Industrial Engineers), 39*(10), 31–33.

Kerr, C., Farrukh, C., Phaal, R., & Probert, D. (2013). Key principles for developing industrially relevant strategic technology management toolkits. *Technological Forecasting and Social Change, 80*(6), 1050–1070. doi:10.1016/j.techfore.2012.09.006

Kheirandish, M. (2014). Measuring the personal and organizational goals alignment: Developing a practical model. *Research Journal of Recent Sciences, 3*(2), 125–132.

Kieser, A., & Leiner, L. (2012). Collaborate with practitioners: But beware of collaborative research. *Journal of Management Inquiry, 21*(1), 14–28. doi:10.1177/1056492611411923

Kiesler, C. A., Collins, B. E., & Miller, N. (1969). *Attitude change*. John Wiley & Sons, Inc.

Kim, J., & Park, C. Y. (2020). Education, skill training, and lifelong learning in the era of technological revolution. *ADB Economics Working Paper Series*, (606), 1-15.

Kim, P. T. (2018). Big Data and artificial intelligence: New challenges for workplace equality. *University of Louisville Law Review, 57*, 313–328.

Kim, S. (2022). Working with robots: Human resource development considerations in human–robot interaction. *Human Resource Development Review, 21*(1), 48–74. doi:10.1177/15344843211068810

Kincheloe, J. (1999). *How do we tell the workers? The socioeconomic foundations of work and vocational education*. Westview Press.

Kirkpatrick, D. L. (1967). Evaluation. In R. L. Craig & L. R. Bittle (Eds.), *Training and development handbook* (pp. 87–112). McGraw-Hill.

Kirkpatrick, D. L. (1994). *Evaluating training programs: The four levels*. Berrett-Koehler.

Kirkpatrick, D. L. (1996). Great ideas revisited: Re-visiting Kirkpatrick's four-level model. *Training and Development Journal, 50*(1), 54–57.

Kiron, D. (2022). AI can change how you measure-and how you manage. *MIT Sloan Management Review, 63*(3), 24–28.

Kirton, M. J., & Mulligan, G. (1973). Correlates of managers' attitudes toward change. *The Journal of Applied Psychology, 58*(1), 101–107. doi:10.1037/h0035425

Klingenberg, C. O., Borges, M. A. V., & do Vale Antunes Jr, J. A. (2022). Industry 4.0: What makes it a revolution? A historical framework to understand the phenomenon. *Technology in Society*, *70*, 1–6. doi:10.1016/j.techsoc.2022.102009

Kluger, A. N., & DeNisi, A. (1996). The effects of feedback interventions on performance: A historical review, a meta-analysis, and a preliminary feedback intervention theory. *Psychological Bulletin*, *119*(2), 254–284. doi:10.1037/0033-2909.119.2.254

Kohn, A. (1993). Why incentive plans cannot work. *Harvard Business Review*, *71*(5), 54–63.

Kohn, M. L. (1981). Personality, occupation, and social stratification: A frame of reference. In D. J. Treiman & R. V. Robinson (Eds.), *Research in social stratification and mobility* (Vol. 1, pp. 267–297). JAI Press.

Kolbjørnsrud, V., Amico, R., & Thomas, R. J. (2016). How artificial intelligence will redefine management. *Harvard Business Review*, *2*(1), 3–10.

Konopka, Z. J. (2018). Prepare your organization for adaptive learning. *TD Magazine*, *72*(5), 20–22.

Konrad, A. (2006). Leveraging workplace diversity in organizations. *Organizational Management Journal*, *3*(3), 194–189. doi:10.1057/omj.2006.18

Kontoghiorghes, C. (2004). Reconceptualizing the learning transfer conceptual framework: Empirical validation of a new systemic model. *International Journal of Training and Development*, *8*(3), 210–221. doi:10.1111/j.1360-3736.2004.00209.x

Kontoghiorghes, C., Awbre, S. M., & Feurig, P. L. (2005). Examining the relationship between learning organization characteristics and change adaptation, innovation, and organizational performance. *Human Resource Development Quarterly*, *16*(2), 185–212. doi:10.1002/hrdq.1133

Koopmans, M. (2014). Change, self-organization and the search for causality in educational research and practice. *Complicity: An International Journal of Complexity in Education*, *11*(1), 20–40. doi:10.29173/cmplct19523

Kostromina, S. (2013). Academic skills as a basis for self-organization of human activity. *Procedia: Social and Behavioral Sciences*, *86*, 543–550. doi:10.1016/j.sbspro.2013.08.611

Kotter, J., & Heskett, J. (1992). *Corporate culture and performance*. Free Press.

Koy, D. J., Briggs, S., & Grenig, J. (1987). State court disparity on employment-at-will. *Personnel Psychology*, *40*(3), 565–577. doi:10.1111/j.1744-6570.1987.tb00615.x

Kozlowski, S. W. J., Chao, G. T., Smith, E. M., & Hedlund, J. (1993). Organizational downsizing: Strategies, interventions, and research implications. *International Review of Industrial and Organizational Psychology*, *6*, 263–332.

Kozlowski, S. W. J., & Salas, E. (Eds.). (2010). *Learning, training, and development in organizations*. Routledge.

Kraiger, K., & Ford, J. K. (2007). The expanding role of workplace training: Themes and trends influencing training research and practice. In L. L. Koppes (Ed.), *Historical perspectives in industrial and organizational psychology*. Psychology Press.

Kucharska, W., & Rebelo, T. (2022). Knowledge sharing and knowledge hiding in light of the mistakes acceptance component of learning culture- knowledge culture and human capital implications. *The Learning Organization*, *29*(6), 635–655. doi:10.1108/TLO-03-2022-0032

Kuchinke, K. P. (1995). Managing learning for performance. *Human Resource Development Quarterly*, *6*(3), 307–316. doi:10.1002/hrdq.3920060309

Kuchinke, K. P. (2000). Debates over the nature of HRD: An institutional theory perspective. *Human Resource Development International*, *3*(3), 279–283. doi:10.1080/13678860050128474

K. P. Kuchinke (Ed.). system levels. InK. P. Kuchinke (Ed.), *Proceedings of the* 1999 *AHRD Conference* (pp. 602-610). Academy of Human Resource Development.

Kuchinke, P. K. (1999). Philosophical foundations of human resource development. *Annual Meeting of the Association for Career and Technical Education*. ACTE.

Küçük, B. A. (2022). Understanding the employee job satisfaction depending on manager's fair treatment: The role of cynicism towards the organization and co-worker support. *European Review of Applied Psychology*, *72*(6), 1–21. doi:10.1016/j.erap.2022.100795

Kuenzi, M., Mayer, D. M., & Greenbaum, R. L. (2020). Creating an ethical organizational environment: The relationship between ethical leadership, ethical organizational climate, and unethical behavior. *Personnel Psychology*, *73*(1), 43–71. doi:10.1111/peps.12356

Kunneman, D. E., Key, J. P., & Sleezer, C. M. (2000). Management training activities and training needs within selected business and industry organizations in Oklahoma. *Journal of Career and Technical Education*, *16*(2), 51–56. doi:10.21061/jcte.v16i2.551

Kupritz, V. W. (2002). The relative impact of workplace design on training transfer. *Human Resource Development Quarterly*, *13*(4), 427–447. doi:10.1002/hrdq.1042

Kyriakopoulos, G. (2012). Half a century of management by objectives (MBO): A review. *African Journal of Business Management*, *5*(6), 1772–1786.

Laffey, J. G., Chikhani, M., Bates, D. G., & Hardman, J. G. (2020). Supporting more than one patient with a single mechanical ventilator: Useful last resort or unjustifiable risk? *British Journal of Anaesthesia*, *125*(3), 247–250. doi:10.1016/j.bja.2020.05.029 PMID:32536443

Lama, D. (1999). *Ethics for the new millennium*. Riverhead Books.

Lang, M., Bernier, A., & Knoppers, B. M. (2021). AI in cardiovascular imaging: "Unexplainable" legal and ethical challenges? *The Canadian Journal of Cardiology*, *38*(2), 225–233. doi:10.1016/j.cjca.2021.10.009 PMID:34737036

Larson, D., & Chang, V. (2016). A review and future direction of agile, business intelligence, analytics and data science. *International Journal of Information Management*, *36*(5), 700–710. doi:10.1016/j.ijinfomgt.2016.04.013

Latham, G. P., & Locke, E. A. (1991). Self- regulation through goal setting. *Organizational Behavior and Human Decision Processes*, *50*(2), 212–247. doi:10.1016/0749-5978(91)90021-K

Latkovikja, M. T., & Popovskab, M. B. (2020, June). How millennials, Gen z, and technology are changing the workplace design. In *Proceedings of the 6th International Workshop on Socio-Technical Perspective in IS Development (STPIS 2020)*. CEUR.

Lawler, E. E. III. (2000). *Rewarding excellence: Pay strategies for the new economy*. Jossey-Bass Publishers.

Lawler, E. E. III. (2003). *Treat people right! How organizations and individuals can propel each other into a virtuous spiral of success*. Jossey-Bass.

Lee, C. H., & Bruvold, N. T. (2003). Creating value for employees: Investment in employee development. *International Journal of Human Resource Management*, *14*(6), 981–1000. doi:10.1080/0958519032000106173

Lee, D. M. S., & Allen, T. J. (1982). Integrating new technical staff: Implications for acquiring new technology. *Management Science*, *28*(12), 1405–1420. doi:10.1287/mnsc.28.12.1405

Lee, M. (2003). *HRD in a complex world*. Routledge.

Lee, M. R., & Lan, Y. (2007). From Web 2.0 to conversational knowledge management: Towards collaborative intelligence. *Journal of Entrepreneurship Research*, *2*(2), 47–62.

Leibowitz, Z. B., Farren, C., & Kaye, B. L. (1986). *Designing career development systems*. Jossey-Bass.

Leifer, M. S., & Newstron, J. W. (1980). Solving the transfer of training problems. *Training and Development Journal*, (August), 42–46.

Leng, J., Sha, W., Wang, B., Zheng, P., Zhuang, C., Liu, Q., Wuest, T., Mourtzis, D., & Wang, L. (2022). Industry 5.0: Prospect and retrospect. *Journal of Manufacturing Systems*, *65*, 279–295. doi:10.1016/j.jmsy.2022.09.017

Lepak, D. P., & Snell, S. A. (1999). The human resource architecture: Toward a theory of human capital allocation and development. *Academy of Management Review*, *24*(1), 31–48. doi:10.2307/259035

Lepak, D. P., & Snell, S. A. (2002). Examining the human resource architecture: The relationships among human capital, employment, and human resource configurations. *Journal of Management*, *28*(4), 517–543. doi:10.1177/014920630202800403

Lepper, M. R., Greene, D., & Nisbett, R. E. (1973). Undermining children's intrinsic interest with extrinsic reward: A test of the "over justification" hypothesis. *Journal of Personality and Social Psychology*, *28*(1), 129–137. doi:10.1037/h0035519

Leventhal, G. S., & Whiteside, H. D. (1973). Equity and the use of reward to elicit high performance. *Journal of Personality and Social Psychology*, *25*(1), 75–83. doi:10.1037/h0034276

Levinson, H. (1970). Management by whose objectives? *Harvard Business Review*, *48*(4), 125–134. PMID:12545927

Levitt, B., & March, J. G. (1988). Organizational learning. *Annual Review of Sociology*, *14*(1), 319–340. doi:10.1146/annurev.so.14.080188.001535

Levy, F., & Murnane, R. J. (2005). *The new division of labor: How computers are creating the next job market*. Princeton University Press.

Lewin, K. (1946). Action research and minority problems. *The Journal of Social Issues*, *2*(4), 34–46. doi:10.1111/j.1540-4560.1946.tb02295.x

Lewin, K. (1993). Investing in technical and vocational education: A review of the evidence. *The Vocational Aspect of Education*, *45*(3), 217–227. doi:10.1080/0305787930450303

Li, J. (2013). Web-based technology and the changing landscape of HRD. *Human Resource Development International*, *16*(3), 247–250. doi:10.1080/13678868.2013.799401

Likert, R. (1961). *New patterns of management*. McGraw-Hill.

Likert, R. (1967). *The human organization*. McGraw-Hill.

Lin, M., Wu, X., & Li, X. (2022). Who are the empowered employees: Those with high work performance or high ethical behavior? *Journal of Business Ethics*, 1–17. doi:10.100710551-022-05232-9 PMID:35540176

Litwin, G. H., & Stringer, R. A. (1968). *Motivation and organizational climate*. Harvard Business School, Division of Research.

Liu, C. H., & Matthews, R. (2005). Vygotsky's philosophy: Constructivism and its criticisms examined. *International Education Journal*, *6*(3), 386–399.

Liu, X., Greenbaum, R. L., Allen, D., & Zhang, Z. (2022). A Newcomer socialization perspective on the proliferation of unethical conduct in organizations: The influences of peer coaching practices and newcomers' goal orientations. *Journal of Business Ethics*, *176*(1), 73–88. doi:10.100710551-020-04730-y

Liu, Z. R. (2014). Perspectives on organizational learning and learning organization. *Applied Mechanics and Materials*, *644*(650), 5917–5920. doi:10.4028/www.scientific.net/AMM.644-650.5917

Liyanage, J. P., & Kumar, U. (2003). Towards a value-based view on operations and maintenance performance management. *Journal of Quality in Maintenance Engineering, 9*(4), 333–350. doi:10.1108/13552510310503213

Loch, K. D., Conger, S., & Oz, E. (1998). Ownership, privacy and monitoring in the workplace: A debate on technology and ethics. *Journal of Business Ethics, 17*(6), 653–663.

Locke, E. A. (1969). Purpose without consciousness: A contradiction. *Psychological Reports, 25*(3), 991–1009. doi:10.2466/pr0.1969.25.3.991

Loden, M., & Rosener, J. B. (1991). *Workforce America! Managing employee diversity as a VITAL resource.* Business One Irwin.

Loewenberg, A. (2015). Child care teachers: Underpaid and underappreciated. *New America*: https://www.newamerica.org/educationpolicy/edcentral/child-c are-workers/

Loi, R., Lam, L. W., & Chan, K. W. (2012). Coping with job insecurity: The role of procedural justice, ethical leadership and power distance orientation. *Journal of Business Ethics, 108*(3), 361–372. doi:10.100710551-011-1095-3

London, M., & Diamante, T. (2002). Technology-focused expansive professionals: Developing continuous learning in the high-technology sector. *Human Resource Development Review, 1*(4), 500–524. doi:10.1177/1534484302238438

Lord, J. D. (2022). Quiet quitting is a new name for an old method of industrial action. *The Conversation.* https://usir.salford.ac.uk/id/eprint/65022/1/quiet-quitting-is-a-

Lovallo, D., & Kahneman, D. (2003). Delusions of success: How optimism undermines executives' decision. *Harvard Business Review, 81*, 56–63. PMID:12858711

Loyarte-López, E. & García-Olaizola, I. (2022). Machine learning based method for deciding internal value of talent. *Applied Artificial Intelligence, 36*(1), 1-19, doi:10.1080/08839514.20 22.2151160

Luan, Y., Zhao, K., Wang, Z., & Hu, F. (2022). Exploring the antecedents of unethical pro-organizational behavior (UPB): A meta-analysis. *Journal of Business Ethics.* doi:10.100710551-022-05269-w

Luebker, J. (2021). *A focused evaluation of sales employees' ethics training and its effect on the diffusion of ethics in a financial organization.* [Doctoral dissertation, University of Arkansas]. https://scholarworks.uark.edu/cgi/viewcontent.cgi?article=58 17&context=etd

Luhn, A. (2016). The learning organization. *Creative and Knowledge Society, 6*(1), 1–13. doi:10.1515/cks-2016-0005

Lund, B. D., & Wang, T. (2023). Chatting about ChatGPT: How may AI and GPT impact academia and libraries? *Library Hi Tech News*, *1-4*. doi:10.1108/LHTN-01-2023-0009

Lundgren, H., & Poell, R. F. (2022). How do HRD professionals and business managers interact in organizing HRD activities? *Human Resource Development Quarterly*, 1–23. doi:10.1002/hrdq.21485

Lusk, J. L., & Chandra, R. (2021). Farmer and farm worker illnesses and deaths from COVID-19 and impacts on agricultural output. *PLOS ONE, 16*(4), e0250621

Mackenzie, K. D. (1986). *Organizational design: The organizational audit and analysis technology.* Ablex Publishing Corporation.

Maidique, M. A., & Hayes, R. H. (1984). The art of high-technology management. *Sloan Management Review*, *25*(2), 17–31.

Makarius, E. E., & Srinivasan, M. (2017). Addressing skills mismatch: Utilizing talent supply chain management to enhance collaboration between companies and talent suppliers. *Business Horizons*, *60*(4), 495–505. doi:10.1016/j.bushor.2017.03.007

Malos, S. (1998). Current legal issues in performance appraisal. In J. Smither (Ed.), Performance appraisal: State of the art in practice (pp. 49–94). Jossey-Bass Publisher.

Malos, S. (1998). Current legal issues in performance appraisal. In J. Smither (Ed.), *Performance appraisal: State of the art in practice* (pp. 49–94). Jossey-Bass Publisher.

Mangham, I. L., & Overington, M. A. (1983). Dramatism and the theatrical metaphor: Really playing at critical distances. In G. Morgan (Ed.), *Beyond method: Social research strategies* (pp. 219–233). Sage.

Mankin, D. A. (2001). A model for human resource development. *Human Resource Development International*, *4*(1), 65–85. doi:10.1080/13678860121714

March, J., & Simon, H. (1959). *Organizations.* Wiley and Sons.

Marcoulides, G. A., & Heck, R. H. (1993). Organizational culture and performance: Proposing and testing a model. *Organization Science*, *4*(2), 209–225. doi:10.1287/orsc.4.2.209

Marques, J. (2007). Diversity as a win-win strategy. *Management Services*, *51*(1), 22–24.

Marsick, V. J., & Watkins, K. E. (1994). The learning organization: An integrative vision for HRD. *Human Resource Development Quarterly*, *5*(4), 353–360. doi:10.1002/hrdq.3920050406

Martelli, J. (1998). Training for new technology: Midwest steel company. In Rothwell, W. (Ed.), Linking HRD programs with organizational strategy (pp. 85–96). ASTD.

Martelli, J. (1998). *Training for new technology: Midwest steel company.* ASTD.

Martinez, A. (2019). The right to be an asshole: The need for increased first amendment public employment protections in the age of social media. *The American University Journal of Gender, Social Policy & the Law*, *27*(2), 1–35.

Martinez, M. E. (2010). *Learning and cognition: The design of the mind*. Pearson.

Martin, H. J. (2010). Workplace climate and peer support as determinants of training transfer. *Human Resource Development Quarterly*, *19*(1), 87–104. doi:10.1002/hrdq.20038

Martin, K., & Freeman, R. E. (2003). Some problems with employee monitoring. *Journal of Business Ethics*, *43*(4), 353–361. doi:10.1023/A:1023014112461

Marx, K. (1906). *Capital* (Vol. 1). Kerr.

Masadeh, M. (2012). Training, education, development and learning: What is the difference? *European Scientific Journal*, *8*(10), 62–68. doi:10.19044/esj.2012.v8n10p%25p

Maslow, A. (1987). *Motivation and personality* (3rd ed.). Harper & Row.

May, D. R., Gilson, R. L., & Harter, L. (2004). The psychological conditions of meaningfulness, safety, and availability and the engagement of the human spirit at work. *Journal of Occupational and Organizational Psychology*, *77*(1), 11–37. doi:10.1348/096317904322915892

McClelland, D. C. (1961). *The achieving society*. Free Press. doi:10.1037/14359-000

McGregor, D. (2006). *The human side of enterprise, annotated edition*. The McGraw-Hill Companies, Inc.

McLagan, P. (1989). *Models for HRD practice*. American Society for Training and Development.

McLean, G. N. (2006). *Organization development*. Berrett-Koehler.

McLean, G. N., & McLean, L. D. (2001). If we can't define HRD in one country, how can we define it in an international context? *Human Resource Development International*, *4*(3), 313–326. doi:10.1080/13678860110059339

McPeck, J. E. (1990). Critical thinking and subject specificity: A reply to Ennis. *Educational Researcher*, *19*(4), 10–12. doi:10.3102/0013189X019004010

McWhorter, R. R. (2014). A synthesis of new perspectives on Virtual HRD. *Advances in Developing Human Resources*, *16*(3), 391–401. doi:10.1177/1523422314532126

Melin, A. & Egkolfopoulou, M. (2021). Employees are quitting instead of giving up working from home. *Bloomberg Wealth*. www.bloomberg.com/news/articles/2021-06-01/return-to-officee mployees-are-quitting-instead-of-giving-up-work-from-home

Mero, N. P., & Motowidlo, S. J. (1995). Effects of rater accountability on the accuracy and the favorability of performance ratings. *The Journal of Applied Psychology*, *80*(4), 517–524. doi:10.1037/0021-9010.80.4.517

Meyers, C. (2004). Institutional culture and individual behavior: Creating an ethical environment. *Science and Engineering Ethics*, *10*(2), 269–276. doi:10.100711948-004-0022-8 PMID:15152852

Meyers, M. C., & van Woerkom, M. (2014). The influence of underlying philosophies on talent management: Theory, implications for practice, and research agenda. *Journal of World Business*, *49*(2), 192–203. doi:10.1016/j.jwb.2013.11.003

Meyers, M. C., van Woerkom, M., & Dries, N. (2013). Talent – Innate or acquired? Theoretical considerations and their implications for talent management. *Human Resource Management Review*, *23*(4), 305–321. doi:10.1016/j.hrmr.2013.05.003

Meyers, M. C., van Woerkom, M., Paauwe, J., & Dries, N. (2020). HR managers' talent philosophies: Prevalence and relationships with perceived talent management practices. *International Journal of Human Resource Management*, *31*(4), 562–588. doi:10.1080/09585192.2019.1579747

Miller, G. A. (1956). The magical number seven, plus-or-minus two: Some limits on our capacity for processing information. *Psychological Review*, *63*(2), 81–97. doi:10.1037/h0043158 PMID:13310704

Mintzberg, H. (1998). Covert leadership: Notes on managing professionals. Knowledge workers respond to inspiration, not supervision. *Harvard Business Review*, *76*(6), 140–147. PMID:10187244

Mital, A., & Pennathur, A. (2004). Advanced technologies and humans in manufacturing workplaces: An interdependent relationship. *International Journal of Industrial Ergonomics*, *33*(4), 295–313. doi:10.1016/j.ergon.2003.10.002

Mitchell, T. (1974). Expectancy models of job satisfaction, occupational preference and effort: A theoretical, methodological, and empirical appraisal. *Psychological Bulletin*, *81*(12), 1053–1077. doi:10.1037/h0037495

Mittelstadt, B. (2019). Principles alone cannot guarantee ethical AI. *Nature Machine Intelligence*, *1*(11), 501–507. doi:10.103842256-019-0114-4

Mohrman, S., Gibson, C., & Mohrman, A. (2001). Doing research that is useful to practice: A model and empirical exploration. *Academy of Management Journal*, *44*(2), 357–375. doi:10.2307/3069461

Montesino, M. U. (2002). Strategic alignment of training, transfer-enhancing behaviors, and training usage: A post training study. *Human Resource Development Quarterly*, *13*(1), 89–108. doi:10.1002/hrdq.1015

Moran, J. W., & Brightman, B. K. (2000). Leading organizational change. *Journal of Workplace Learning: Employee Counseling Today*, *12*(2), 66–74. doi:10.1108/13665620010316226

Morgan, J. (2017). *The employee experience advantage: How to win the war for talent by giving employees the workspaces they want, the tools they need, and a culture they can celebrate*. John Wiley & Sons.

Morgan, J. (2019). Will we work in twenty-first century capitalism? A critique of the fourth industrial revolution literature. Economy and Society, 48(3), 371–398

Morgan, J. M., & Liker, J. K. (2020). *The Toyota product development system: integrating people, process, and technology*. Productivity press.

Morgeson, F. P., & Campion, M. A. (1997). Social and cognitive sources of potential inaccuracy in job analysis. *The Journal of Applied Psychology, 82*(5), 627–655. doi:10.1037/0021-9010.82.5.627

Morkunas, V. J., Paschen, J., & Boon, E. (2019). How blockchain technologies impact your business model. *Business Horizons, 62*(3), 295–306. doi:10.1016/j.bushor.2019.01.009

Morrison, A. M. (1992). *The new leaders: Guide- lines on leadership diversity in America*. Jossey-Bass Publishers.

Morrison, E. W. (2023). Employee voice and silence: Taking stock a decade later. *Annual Review of Organizational Psychology and Organizational Behavior, 10*(1), 79–107. doi:10.1146/annurev-orgpsych-120920-054654

Muchinsky, P. M. (2004). When the psychometrics of test development meets organizational realities: A conceptual framework for organizational change, examples and recommendations. *Personnel Psychology, 57*(1), 179–205. doi:10.1111/j.1744-6570.2004.tb02488.x

Muhl, C. J. (2001). The employment-at-will doctrine: Three major exceptions. Monthly Labor Review, 124, 3-11..

Muir, C. P., Sherf, E. N., & Liu, J. T. (2022). It's not only what you do, but why you do it: How managerial motives influence employees' fairness judgments. *The Journal of Applied Psychology, 107*(4), 581–603. doi:10.1037/apl0000898 PMID:34197139

Müller, V. C. (2020). Ethics of artificial intelligence and robotics. In E. N. Zalta (Ed.), *The Stanford encyclopedia of philosophy*.

Munck, B. (2001). Changing a culture of face time. *Harvard Business Review, 79*(10), 125–131.

Munn, L. (2022). The uselessness of AI ethics. *AI and Ethics,* 1-9. doi:022-00209-w doi:10.1007/s43681

Münsterberg, H. (1913). *Psychology and industrial efficiency*. Houghton Mifflin., doi:10.1037/10855-000

Murphy, K. R. (1989). Is the relationship between cognitive ability and job performance stable over time? *Human Performance, 2*(3), 183–200. doi:10.120715327043hup0203_3

Murphy, K. R. (2008). Explaining the weak relationship between job performance and ratings of job performance. *Industrial and Organizational Psychology: Perspectives on Science and Practice, 1*(2), 148–160. doi:10.1111/j.1754-9434.2008.00030.x

Murphy, K. R., & Cleveland, J. N. (1991). *Performance appraisal: An organizational perspective*. Allyn & Bacon.

Murray, A., Rhymer, J. E. N., & Sirmon, D. G. (2021). Humans and technology: Forms of conjoined agency in organizations. *Academy of Management Review*, *46*(3), 552–571. doi:10.5465/amr.2019.0186

Mutamba, C. (2017). The inter-relationship of organizational learning, learning organizations, virtual technology, and virtual communities of practice. *New Horizons in Adult Education and Human Resource Development*, *29*(3), 4–14. doi:10.1002/nha3.20186

Myers, C. S. (1925). *Industrial psychology*. The People's Institute Publishing Company.

Nadler, L., & Wiggs, G. (1986). *Managing human resource development: A Practical guide*. Jossey-Bass.

Nakajima, S. (1988). *Introduction to total productive maintenance*. Productivity Press.

National Academy of Engineering and Commission on Behavioral and Social Sciences and Education (NAECBSS). (1991). *People and technology in the workplace*. The National Academies Press.

Neisser, U. (1967). *Cognitive psychology*. Appleton-Century-Crofts.

Neumark, D., & Shirley, P. (2022). Myth or measurement: What does the new minimum wage research say about minimum wages and job loss in the United States? Industrial Relations, 61(4), 384–417.

Newbold, C., & Pharoah, N. (2009). What it means to be a learning organization. *Strategic HR Review*, *8*(3), 12–16. doi:10.1108/14754390910946521

News Staff. (2022). Most of Axon's ethics board resigns to protest drone plans. *Gov Tech*. https://www.govtech.com/biz/most-of-axons-ethics-board-resigns-to-protest-drone-plans

Nicholson, N., & Johns, G. (1985). The absence culture and the psychological contract—Who's in control of absence? *Academy of Management Review*, *10*, 397–407.

O'Brien, T. (2021). Consider ramifications of NCAA's new transfer rules. *College Athletics and the Law*, *18*(3), 8–8. doi:10.1002/catl.30882

O'Reilly, C. A. III, Chatman, J., & Caldwell, D. F. (1991). People and organizational culture: A profile comparison approach to assessing person- organization fit. *Academy of Management Journal*, *34*(3), 487–516. doi:10.2307/256404

Odiorne, G. S. (1965). *Management by objectives: A system of managerial leadership*. Pitman Publishing.

Odor, H. O. (2018). A literature review on organizational learning and learning organizations. *International Journal of Economics & Management Sciences*, *07*(01). doi:10.4172/2162-6359.1000494

Oh, E. G., & Huang, W. D. (2018). A review of technology research in HRD from design-based research perspective. *Human Resource Development Review*, *17*(3), 258–276. doi:10.1177/1534484318784798

Olmosk, K. E. (1972). Seven pure strategies of change. In J. W. Pfeiffer & J. E. Jones (Eds.), *The 1972 annual handbook for group facilitators*. Pfeiffer & Company.

Olson, G. P. (2002). Organizing for the future. In J. L. Pierce & J. W. Newstrom (Eds.), *The manager's bookshelf: A mosaic of contemporary views* (6th ed.). Prentice Hall.

O'Reilly III, C. A., Doerr, B., Caldwell, D. F., & Chatman, J. A. (2014). Narcissistic CEOs and executive compensation. The Leadership Quarterly, 25(2), 218–231.

Ormond, J. E. (1999). *Human learning* (3rd ed.). Prentice-Hall Inc.

Orr, J. E. (1996). *Talking about machines. An ethnography of a modern job*. ILR.

Örtenblad, A. (2001). On differences between organizational learning and learning organization. *The Learning Organization*, *8*(3), 125–133. doi:10.1108/09696470110391211

Örtenblad, A. (2018). What does "learning organization" mean? *The Learning Organization*, *25*(3), 150–158. doi:10.1108/TLO-02-2018-0016

Osborne, R., & Wittrock, M. (1985). The generative learning model and its implications for science education. *Studies in Science Education*, *12*(1), 59–87. doi:10.1080/03057268508559923

Ouchi, W. (1981). *Theory Z*. Addison-Wesley.

Owens, R. (1987). *Organizational behavior in education*. Prentice-Hall.

Paarlberg, L. E., & Perry, J. L. (2007). Values management: Aligning employee values and organization goals. *American Review of Public Administration*, *37*(4), 387–408. doi:10.1177/0275074006297238

Pareek, U. (1989). Motivational analysis of organizations-climate (MAO-C). In Pfeiffer, J.W. (Ed.), The 1989 annual: Developing human resources (pp. 161–18). Pfeiffer & Company.

Park, C. S. (2006). Reply. *Science and Society*, *70*(3), 379–380. doi:10.1521iso.70.3.379

Parker, S. K., Knight, C., & Keller, A. (2020). Remote managers are having trust issues. *Harvard Business Review*, *30*, 6–20.

Park, S., Jeong, S., & Chai, D. S. (2021). Remote e-workers' psychological well-being and career development in the era of COVID-19: Challenges, success factors, and the roles of HRD professionals. *Advances in Developing Human Resources*, *23*(3), 222–236. doi:10.1177/15234223211017849

Pascale, R., & Athos, A. (1981). *The art of Japanese management*. Simon &Schuster. doi:10.1016/0007-6813(81)90032-X

Pass, G. (2019). The humanistic roots of organization development-a reclamation? *e-Organisations & People, 26*(1), 44-54.

Patton, M. Q. (2012). *Essentials of utilization-focused evaluation.* Sage.

Pavlov, I. P. (1927). *Conditioned reflexes.* Routledge and Kegan Paul.

Peng, H., & Wei, F. (2020). How and when does leader behavioral integrity influence employee voice? The roles of team independence climate and corporate ethical values. *Journal of Business Ethics, 166*(3), 505–521. doi:10.100710551-019-04114-x

Penrose, E. T. (1959). *The theory of the growth of the firm.* Wiley.

Pereira, V., Hadjielias, E., Christofi, M., & Vrontis, D. (2023). A systematic literature review on the impact of artificial intelligence on workplace outcomes: A multi-process perspective. *Human Resource Management Review, 33*(1), 1-22. doi:10.1016/j.hrmr.2021.100857

Perry, B. L., Aronson, B., & Pescosolido, B. A. (2021). Pandemic precarity: COVID-19 is exposing and exacerbating inequalities in the American heartland. *Proceedings of the National Academy of Sciences, 118*(8), e2020685118

Peters, T. J. (1978). Symbols, patterns and settings: An optimistic case for getting things done. *Organizational Dynamics, 7*(2), 3–23. doi:10.1016/0090-2616(78)90035-9

Pettigrew, A. M. (1979). On studying organizational culture. *Administrative Science Quarterly, 24*(4), 570–581. doi:10.2307/2392363

Pfau, B. N., & Kay, I. T. (2002). *The human capital edge: 21 people management practices your company must implement (or avoid) to maximize shareholder value.* McGraw-Hill.

Pfau, B. N., & Kay, I. T. (2002). *The human capital edge: 21 people management practices your company must implement (or avoid) to maximize shareholder value.* McGraw-Hill.

Pfeffer, J. (1994). *Competitive advantage through people: Unleashing the power of the workforce.* Harvard Business School Press.

Pfeffer, J. (1992). *Managing with power.* Harvard Business School Press.

Pfeffer, J. (1992). *Managing with power: Politics and influence in organizations.* Harvard Business School Press.

Pfeffer, J. (1994). *Competitive advantage through people: Unleashing the power of the workforce.* Harvard Business School Press. doi:10.2307/41165742

Pfeffer, J. (1998). *The human equation. Building profits by putting people first.* Harvard Business School.

Pfeffer, J. (1998). *The human equation: Building profits by putting people first.* Harvard Business School Press.

Pfeffer, J., & Sutton, R. I. (2006). Evidence-based management. *Harvard Business Review, 84*(1), 62–75. PMID:16447370

Phaal, R., Kerr, C., Oughton, D., & Probert, D. (2012). Towards a modular toolkit for strategic technology management. *International Journal of Technology Intelligence and Planning*, *8*(2), 161–181. doi:10.1504/IJTIP.2012.048475

Pham, Q., Madhavan, R., Righetti, L., Smart, W., & Chatila, R. (2018). The impact of robotics and automation on working conditions and employment [ethical, legal, and societal issues]. *IEEE Robotics & Automation Magazine*, *25*(2). https://doi.org/10.1109/mra.2018.2822058

Phillips, J. J. (2003). *Return on investment in training and performance improvement programs* (2nd ed.). Elsevier Science.

Phillips, J. J. (2003). *Return on investment in training and performance improvement programs* (2nd ed.). Elsevier Science.

Piaget, J. (1959). *The language and thought of the child*. Routledge.

Piaget, J. (1970). *Structuralism*. Basic Books.

Pineo, R. (2020). Immigration crisis: The United States under President Donald J. Trump. *Journal of Developing Societies*, *36*(1), 7–40. doi:10.1177/0169796X19896905

Pitts, D. (2006). Modeling the impact of diversity management. *Review of Public Personnel Administration*, *26*(3), 245–268. doi:10.1177/0734371X05278491

Plakhotnik, M. (2014). Organizational culture and HRD: The roots, the landscape, and the future. In N. E. Chalofsky, T. S. Rocco, L. M. and Morris (eds). Handbook of human resource development (pp. 80-93). John Wiley & Sons, Inc.

Plakhotnik, M. S., & Rocco, T. S. (2011). What do we know, how much, and why it matters: Organizational culture and AHRD research 1994-2009. *Human Resource Development Review*, *10*(1), 74–100. doi:10.1177/1534484310388992

Ployhart, R. E., Nyberg, A. J., Reilly, G., & Maltarich, M. A. (2014). *Human capital is dead*. Ployhart, R. E., Nyberg, A. J., Reilly, G., & Maltarich, M. A. (2014, February). long live human capital resources! *Journal of Management*, *40*(2), 371–398. doi:10.1177/0149206313512152

Ployhart, R. E., & Moliterno, T. P. (2011). Emergence of the human capital resource: A multilevel model. *Academy of Management Review*, *36*(1), 127–150. doi:10.5465/amr.2009.0318

Ployhart, R. E., Schmitt, N., & Tippins, N. T. (2017). Solving the Supreme Problem: 100 years of selection and recruitment at the Journal of Applied Psychology. *The Journal of Applied Psychology*, *102*(3), 291–304. doi:10.1037/apl0000081 PMID:28125261

Pokrovskaia, N. N., Gildingersh, M. G., & Gornykh, E. V. (2018, July). Reengineering of corporate management in the innovative context and professional competencies of a reengineer. In *2018 Third International Conference on Human Factors in Complex Technical Systems and Environments (ERGO) s and Environments (ERGO)* (pp. 32-35). IEEE.

Pondy, L. R., & Boje, D. M. (1975). *Bringing mind back in: Paradigm development as a frontier problem in organization theory.* Paper presented at the Annual Meetings of the American Sociological Association, San Francisco, CA.

Pondy, L. R., & Boje, D. M. (1981). Bringing mind back in. In Evan, W. (Ed.), Frontiers in organization and management (pp. 83–101). Praeger.

Porter, L. W., & Lawler, E. E. (1968). *Managerial attitudes and performance.* Richard D. Irwin, Inc.

Porter, L. W., & Steers, R. M. (1973). Organizational, work, and personal factors in employee turnover and absenteeism. *Journal of Management, 80,* 151–176.

Porter, L. W., & Steers, R. M. (1973). Organizational, work, and personal factors in employee turnover and absenteeism. *Psychological Bulletin, 80*(2), 151–176. doi:10.1037/h0034829

Porter, M. (1980). *Competitive strategy.* Free Press.

Porter, M. (2001). Strategy and the Internet. *Harvard Business Review, 79*(3), 62–78. PMID:11246925

Potnuru, R. K. G., & Sahoo, C. K. (2016). HRD interventions, employee competencies and organizational effectiveness: An empirical study. *European Journal of Training and Development, 40*(5), 345–365. doi:10.1108/EJTD-02-2016-0008

Powell, G. N., & Butterfield, D. A. (1994). Race, gender and the glass ceiling: An empirical study of actual promotions to top management. Paper presented at the *annual meeting of the Academy of Management.* Emerald Insight.

Prause, D., & Mujtaba, B. G. (2015). Conflict management practices for diverse workplaces. *Journal of Business Studies Quarterly, 6*(3), 13-22.

Prusak, L., & Cohen, D. (2001). How to invest in social capital. *Harvard Business Review, 79*(6), 86–93. PMID:11408980

Qureshi, S., Briggs, R. O., & Hlupic, V. (2006). Value creation from intellectual capital: Convergence of knowledge management and collaboration in the intellectual bandwidth model. *Group Decision and Negotiation, 15*(3), 197–220. doi:10.100710726-006-9018-x

Qwaider, W. Q. (2017). Information security and learning content management system (LCMS). *International Journal of Advanced Computer Science & Applications, 8*(11). https://doi.org/10.14569/IJACSA.2017.081174

Rainey, G. W. Jr, & Wolf, L. (1981). Flex-time: Short-term benefits; long-term...? *Public Administration Review, 41*(1), 52–63. doi:10.2307/975724

Rajecki, B. (2022). Go digital: How technology can mitigate the effects of the workforce shortage. *McKnight's Long-Term Care News, 43*(3), 14-15.

Ramlall, S. (2004). A review of employee motivation theories and their implications for employee retention within organizations. *Journal of American Academy of Business, Cambridge, 5*(1/2), 52–63.

Ramlall, S. (2004). A review of employee motivation theories and their implications for employee retention within organizations. *The Journal of American Academy of Business, Cambridge, 5*(1/2), 52–63.

Ramsey, M. (1986). *The super supervisor.* Positive Presentations, Inc.

Rana, S., Ardichvili, A., & Polesello, D. (2016). Promoting self-directed learning in a learning organization: Tools and practices. *European Journal of Training and Development, 40*(7), 470–489. doi:10.1108/EJTD-10-2015-0076

Ransbotham, S., Kiron, D., Gerbert, P., & Reeves, M. (2017). Reshaping business with artificial intelligence: Closing the gap between ambition and action. MIT Sloan Management Review, 59(1), 1–17.

Rego, A., Souto, S., & Cunha, M. P. (2009). Does the need to belong moderate the relationship between perceptions of spirit of camaraderie and employees' happiness? *Journal of Occupational Health Psychology, 14*(2), 148–164. doi:10.1037/a0014767

Reich, R. B. (1992). The work of nations: Preparing ourselves for 21st century capitalism (Rev. ed.). Vintage Books.

Reich, R. B. (2010). *Aftershock: The next economy and America's future.* Alfred A. Knopf.

Righetti, L., Madhavan, R., & Chatila, R. (2019). Unintended consequences of biased robotic and artificial intelligence systems [ethical, legal, and societal issues]. *IEEE Robotics & Automation Magazine, 26*(3), 11–13. https://doi.org/10.1109/MRA.2019.2926996

Ringo, T., & McDonald, R. (2008). *Unlocking the DNA of the adaptable workforce: The global human capital study.* IBM Global Services.

Ritti, R., & Funkhouser, G. (1982). *The ropes to skip and the ropes to know.* Grid.

Robbins, S. (2019). A misdirected principle with a catch: Explicability for AI. *Minds and Machines, 29*(4), 495–514. doi:10.100711023-019-09509-3

Robbins, S., & Judge, T. (2011). *Organizational behavior* (14th ed.). Prentice Hall.

RobertR.Kentish-BarnesN.BoyerA.LaurentA.AzoulayE.ReignierJ. (2020). Ethical dilemmas due to the Covid-19 pandemic. Annals of Intensive Care, 10(1), 1–9.

Robles, M. M. (2012). Executive perceptions of the top 10 soft skills needed in today's workplace. *Business Communication Quarterly, 75*(4), 453–465. doi:10.1177/1080569912460400

Roche, C., Wall, P.J. & Lewis, D. (2022). Ethics and diversity in artificial intelligence policies, strategies and initiatives. *AI Ethics,* 1-21. doi:10.1007/s43681-022-00218-9

Rogers, E. M. (2003). *Diffusion of innovations* (5th ed.). The Free Press.

Romani, L., Holck, L., & Risberg, A. (2018). Benevolent discrimination: Explaining how human resources professionals can be blind to the harm of diversity initiatives. *Organization*, *26*(3), 371–390. doi:10.1177/1350508418812585

Rosenberg, N. (1972). *Technology and American economic growth*. M. E. Sharp.

Roth, W. F. (2009). Is management by objectives obsolete? *Global Business and Organizational Excellence*, *28*(4), 36–43. doi:10.1002/joe.20266

Rothwell, W., & Kazanas, H. (1991). *Strategic human resource planning and management.* Prentice-Hall.

Rousseau, D. M. (2006). Presidential address: Is there such a thing as "evidence-based management"? *Academy of Management Review*, *31*(2), 256–269. doi:10.5465/amr.2006.20208679

Ruggles, R. (1998). The state of the notion: Knowledge management in practice. *California Management Review*, *40*(3), 80–89. doi:10.2307/41165944

Ruiner, C., Debbing, C. E., Hagemann, V., Schaper, M., Klumpp, M., & Hesenius, M. (2023). Job demands and resources when using technologies at work-development of a digital work typology. *Employee Relations: The International Journal, 45*(1), 190–208. doi:10.1108/er-11-2021-0468

Rumbles, S., & Rees, G. (2013). Continuous changes, organizational burnout and the implications for HRD. *Industrial and Commercial Training, 45*(4), 236–242. doi:10.1108/00197851311323538

Ruona, W. E. A., & Roth, G. (Eds.). (2000). Philosophical foundations of human resource development practice. Advance in Developing Human Resources, 2(3), 49-73.

Ruona, W. E., & Lynham, S. A. (2004). A philosophical framework for thought and practice in human resource development. *Human Resource Development International*, *7*(2), 151–164. doi:10.1080/13678860310001630665

Russ-Eft, D. (2018). Second time around: AHRD standards on ethics and integrity. *Human Resource Development Review*, *17*(2), 123–127. doi:10.1177/1534484318772123

Russ-Eft, D., & Hatcher, T. (2003). The issue of international values and beliefs: The debate for a global HRD code of ethics. *Advances in Developing Human Resources*, *5*(3), 296–307. doi:10.1177/1523422303254670

Rynes, S. L., Bartunek, J. M., & Daft, R. L. (2001). Across the great divide: Knowledge creation and transfer between practitioners and academics. *Academy of Management Journal*, *44*, 340–355. doi:10.2307/3069460

Sabol, A., & Sverer, F. (2017). A review of the economic value-added literature and application. *UTMS Journal of Economics (Skopje)*, *8*(1), 19–27.

Sackett, P. R., Lievens, F., Van Iddekinge, C. H., & Kuncel, N. R. (2017). Individual differences and their measurement: A review of 100 years of research. *Journal of Applied Psychology, 102*(3), 254–273. doi:10.1037/apl0000151

Sackett, D. L. (1997). Evidence-based medicine. *Seminars in Perinatology, 21*(1), 3–5. doi:10.1016/S0146-0005(97)80013-4 PMID:9190027

Sackett, P. R., & Mullen, E. J. (1993). Beyond formal experimental design: Towards an expanded view of the training evaluation process. *Personnel Psychology, 46*(3), 613–615. doi:10.1111/j.1744-6570.1993.tb00887.x

Saenz, R., & Sparks, C. (2020). *The inequities of job loss and recovery amid the COVID-19 pandemic.* Carsey School of Public Policy | UNH. https://carsey.unh.edu/publication/inequities-job-loss-recovery-amid-COVID-pandemic

Salas, E., Tannenbaum, S. I., Kraiger, K., & Smith-Jentsch, K. A. (2012). The science of training and development in organizations: What matters in practice. *Psychological Science in the Public Interest, 13*(2), 74–101. doi:10.1177/1529100612436661 PMID:26173283

Sambataro, M. (2000, April). Just-in-time learning. *Computerworld.* http://www.computerworld.com/news/2002/ story/0,11280.44312,00.html

Sarbanes, P. (2002, July). Sarbanes-Oxley act of 2002. In *The Public Company Accounting Reform and Investor Protection Act* (Vol. 55). US Congress.

Sari, D. Y. (2022). The study of learning organization models: A literature review. *Journal Research of Social, Science, Economics, and Management, 2*(02), 188–202. doi:10.36418/jrssem.v2i2.251

Saulnier, C., & Frank, L. (2019). Unappreciated and underpaid: Early Childhood Educators in Nova Scotia. Canadian Centere for Policy Alternatives–Nova Scotia Office. https://www. policyalternatives. ca/publications/reports/early-childhood-educators-ns.

Saxena, A. (2014). Workforce diversity: A key to improve productivity. *Procedia Economics and Finance, 11*, 76–85. doi:10.1016/S2212-5671(14)00178-6

SCANS. (1991). What work requires of schools. *A SCANS report for America 2000.* Washington, DC: U.S. Department of Labor, The Secretary's Commission on Achieving Necessary Skills (SCANS).

Schein, E. H. (2010). Organization development: Science, technology or philosophy? In Coghlan D., Shani A. B. (Rami) (eds). Fundamentals of organization development (Vol. 1, pp. 91-100). Sage.

Schein, E. (1990). Organizational culture. *The American Psychologist, 45*(2), 109–119. doi:10.1037/0003-066X.45.2.109

Schein, E. H. (1975). How career anchors hold executives to their career paths. *Personnel, 52*, 11–24.

Schein, E. H. (1983). The role of the founder in creating organizational culture. *Organizational Dynamics*, *12*(1), 13–28. doi:10.1016/0090-2616(83)90023-2

Schein, E. H. (1984). Coming to a new awareness of organizational culture. *Sloan Management Review*, *25*(2), 3–16.

Schein, E. H. (1988). Organizational socialization and the profession of management. *Sloan Management Review*, *30*(1), 53–65.

Schifter, D., & Fosnot, C. T. (1993). *Reconstructing mathematics education: Stories of teachers meeting the challenge of reform*. Teachers College.

Schleicher, D. J., Hansen, S. D., & Fox, K. E. (2011). Job attitudes and work values. In S. Zedeck (Ed.), APA handbook of industrial and organizational psychology, Vol. 3. Maintaining, expanding, and contracting the organization (pp. 137–189). American Psychological Association. doi:10.1037/12171-004

Schmidt, F., Hunter, J., & Outerbridge, A. (1986). Impact of job experience and ability on job knowledge, work sample performance, and supervisory ratings of job performance. *The Journal of Applied Psychology*, *71*(3), 432–439. doi:10.1037/0021-9010.71.3.432

Schneider, B. (1975). Organizational climate: An essay. *Personnel Psychology*, *28*(4), 447–479. doi:10.1111/j.1744-6570.1975.tb01386.x

Schneider, B., González-Romá, V., Ostroff, C., & West, M. A. (2017). Organizational climate and culture: Reflections on the history of the constructs in the Journal of Applied Psychology. *The Journal of Applied Psychology*, *102*(3), 468–482. doi:10.1037/apl0000090 PMID:28125256

Schneider, B., & Reiehers, A. E. (1983). On the etiology of climates. *Personnel Psychology*, *36*(1), 19–40. doi:10.1111/j.1744-6570.1983.tb00500.x

Schor, J. (1991). *The overworked American: The unexpected decline of leisure*. Basic Books.

Schreiber, C. T., Price, K. F., & Morrison, A. (1993). Workplace diversity and the glass ceiling: Practices, barriers, possibilities. *Human Resource Planning*, *16*(2), 51–69.

Schuler, R. S., Dowling, P. J., Smart, J. P., & Huber, V. L. (1992). *Human resource management in Australia* (2nd ed.). Harper Educational Publishers.

Schultz, T. W. (1961). Investment in human capital. *The American Economic Review*, *51*(1), 1–17.

Scott, D., & Markham, S. (1982). Absenteeism control methods: A survey of practices and results. *The Personnel Administrator*, *27*(6), 73–84.

Scott, W. R. (1987). The adolescence of institutional theory. *Administrative Science Quarterly*, *32*(4), 493–511. doi:10.2307/2392880

Scott, W. R. (2004). Institutional theory. In G. Ritzer (Ed.), *Encyclopedia of social theory* (pp. 408–414). Sage.

Selznick, P. (1949). *TVA and the grass roots: A study of politics and organization.* University of California Press.

Senge, P. (1990). *The fifth discipline: The art and practice of the learning organization.* Doubleday.

Senge, P. M. (1990). *The fifth discipline: the art and practice of the learning organizations.* Doubleday.

Serenko, A. (2022). The great resignation: The great knowledge exodus or the onset of the great knowledge revolution? Journal of Knowledge Management. Advance online publication. doi:10.1108/JKM-12-2021-0920

Servan-Schreiber. J.-J. (1967). The American challenge. Atheneum Publishers.

Sharma, A. K., & Kumar, S. (2010). Economic value added (EVA)-literature review and relevant issues. *International Journal of Economics and Finance, 2*(2), 200–220. doi:10.5539/ijef.v2n2p200

Sheaffer, Z., Carmeli, A., Steiner-Revivo, M., & Zionit, S. (2009). Downsizing strategies and organizational performance: A longitudinal study. *Management Decision, 47*(6), 950–974. doi:10.1108/00251740910966677

Shen, J., Chanda, A., D'netto, B., & Monga, M. (2009). Managing diversity through human resource management: An international perspective and conceptual framework. *International Journal of Human Resource Management, 20*(2), 235–251. doi:10.1080/09585190802670516

Short, D. C. (Host). (2022). HRD and philosophy [Audio podcast episode]. In *Human Resource Development Masterclass.* Academy of Human Resource Development. https://www.ahrd.org/general/custom.asp?page=HRD-Masterclass-Podcast-Series

Short, D. (2006). Closing the gap between research and practice in HRD. *Human Resource Development Quarterly, 17*(3), 343–350. doi:10.1002/ hrdq.1178

Short, D. C. (2013). Designing a 3D virtual HRD environment from a scholar-practitioner perspective. *Advances in Developing Human Resources, 15*(3), 270–283. doi:10.1177/1523422313487838

Short, D. C., Sherlock, J. J., & Sugrue, B. (2004). Time to recognize those who link research and practice. *Human Resource Development Quarterly, 15*(3), 259–262. doi:10.1002/hrdq.1102

Shukla, P., Wilson, H.J., Alter, A. and Lavieri, D. (2017). Machine reengineering: Robots and people working smarter together. *Strategy & Leadership, 45*(6), 50-54. doi:10.1108/SL-09-2017-0089

Siegmann, K. A. (2020). From clapping for essential workers to revaluing them. Global Labour Column, (339), 1-2.

Silberman, M. (1998). *Active training* (2nd ed.). Jossey-Bass/Pfeiffer.

Simonite, T. (2020). How decades of offshoring led to a mask shortage in a pandemic. *Wired.* https://www.wired.com/story/decades-offshoring-led-mask-shortage-pandemic/

Sim, S. H., & Endrenyi, J. (1988). Optimal preventive maintenance with repair. *IEEE Transactions on Reliability*, *37*(1), 92–96. doi:10.1109/24.3721

Singh, R. K., Agrawal, S., & Modgil, S. (2021). Developing human capital 4.0 in emerging economies: An industry 4.0 perspective. *International Journal of Manpower*, *43*(2), 286–309. doi:10.1108/IJM-03-2021-0159

Sitzmann, T., Brown, K. G., Casper, W. J., Ely, K., & Zimmerman, R. D. (2008). A review and meta-analysis of the nomological network of trainee reactions. *The Journal of Applied Psychology*, *93*(2), 280–295. doi:10.1037/0021-9010.93.2.280 PMID:18361632

Sitzmann, T., & Ely, K. (2011). A meta-analysis of self-regulated learning in work-related training and educational attainment: What we know and where we need to go. *Psychological Bulletin*, *137*(3), 421–442. doi:10.1037/a0022777 PMID:21401218

Skinner, B. F. (1953). *Science and human behavior*. Macmillan.

Skinner, B. F. (1957). *Verbal learning*. Appleton-Century-Crofts., doi:10.1037/11256-000

Sliter, M. T., & Boyd, E. M. (2014). Two (or three) is not equal to one: Multiple jobholding as a neglected topic in organizational research. Journal of Organizational Behavior, 35(7), 1042–1046.

Slotte, V., Tynjälä, P., & Hytönen, T. (2004). How do HRD practitioners describe learning at work? *Human Resource Development International*, *7*(4), 481–499. doi:10.1080/1367886042000245978

Smircich, L. (1983). Concepts of culture and organizational analysis. *Administrative Science Quarterly*, *28*(3), 339–358. doi:10.2307/2392246

Smircich, L., & Morgan, G. (1982). Leadership: The management of meaning. *The Journal of Applied Behavioral Science*, *18*(3), 257–273. doi:10.1177/002188638201800303 PMID:10260212

Smith, F. (1975). *Comprehension and learning*. Holt, Rinehart & Winston.

Snell, S. A., & Dean, J. W. (1992). Integrated manufacturing and human resource management: A human capital perspective. *Academy of Management Journal*, *35*(3), 467–504. doi:10.2307/256484

Somers, M. J. (2001). Ethical codes of conduct and organizational context: A study of the relationship between codes of conduct, employee behavior and organizational values. *Journal of Business Ethics*, *30*(2), 185–195. doi:10.1023/A:1006457810654

Spring, M., Faulconbridge, J., & Sarwar, A. (2022). How information technology automates and augments processes: Insights from artificial-intelligence-based systems in professional service operations. *Journal of Operations Management, 68*(6-7), 592–618. doi:10.1002/joom.1215

Stahl, B. C., Schroeder, D., & Rodrigues, R. (2023). The ethics of artificial intelligence: A conclusion. In Springerbriefs in research and innovation governance (pp. 107–111). SpringerBriefs in Research and Innovation Governance. https://doi.org/10.1007/978-3-031-17040-9_9.

Stahl, B. C., Schroeder, D., & Rodrigues, R. (2023). Unfair and illegal discrimination. In *Springerbriefs in research and innovation governance* (pp. 9–23). Springer Briefs in Research and Innovation Governance. doi:10.1007/978-3-031-17040-9_2

Staw, B. M. (1980). The consequences of turnover. *Journal of Occupational Behaviour, 1*, 253–273.

Steele, T. (2018). Toxicity in the work environment: Retaining staff members of color at a predominantly White institution. *The College Student Affairs Journal, 36*(1), 109–123. doi:10.1353/csj.2018.0007

Steers, R. M., Mowday, R. T., & Shapiro, D. L. (2004). The future of work motivation theory. Academy of Management Review, 29(3), 379–387.

Steers, R. M., Mowday, R. T., & Shapiro, D. L. (2004). The future of work motivation theory. *Academy of Management Review, 29*(3), 379–387. doi:10.2307/20159049

Steers, R. M., & Porter, L. W. (1979). *Motivation and work behavior* (2nd ed.). McGraw-Hill.

Steers, R. M., & Rhodes, S. R. (1978). Major influences on employee attendance: A process model. *The Journal of Applied Psychology, 63*(4), 391–407. doi:10.1037/0021-9010.63.4.391

Stentoft, J., Olhager, J., Heikkilä, J., & Thoms, L. (2016). Manufacturing backshoring: A systematic literature review. *Operations Management Research, 9*(3), 53–61. doi:10.100712063-016-0111-2

Stewart, C., Wall, A., & Marciniec, S. (2016, July). Mixed signals: Do college graduates have the soft skills that employers want? In Competition forum (Vol. 14, p. 276). American Society for Competitiveness.

Stewart, T. A. (1999). Intellectual capital: The new wealth of organizations. Doubleday. Swanson, R. A. (1982). Industrial training. In W. H. Mitzel (Ed.), 5th encyclopedia of educational research (pp. 864-870). Macmillan.

Stewart, T. A. (1997). *Intellectual capital: The new wealth of organizations*. Doubleday.

Storberg-Walker, J. (2005). Towards a theory of human capital transformation through human resource development. In M. L. Morris & F. M. Nafukho (Eds.), *2005 Academy of Human Resource Development Annual Research Conference Proceeding,* (pp. 323-330). Academy of Human Resource Development.

Strebel, P. (1996). Why do employees resist change? *Harvard Business Review, 74*(3), 86–92.

Sull, D., Sull, C., & Zweig, B. (2022). Toxic culture is driving the great resignation. MIT Sloan Management Review, 63(2), 1–9.

Sultana, A., Sharma, R., Hossain, M. M., Bhattacharya, S., & Purohit, N. (2020). Burnout among healthcare providers during COVID-19: Challenges and evidence-based interventions. *Indian Journal of Medical Ethics, 5*(4), 308–311. doi:10.20529/IJME.2020.73 PMID:34018959

Sun, H. C. (2003). Conceptual clarifications for 'organizational learning', 'learning organization' and 'a learning organization'. *Human Resource Development International*, *6*(2), 153–166. doi:10.1080/13678860110086465

Super, D. (2002). A life-span, life-space approach to career development. In D. Brown & L. Brooks (Eds.), *Career choice and development* (2nd ed.). Jossey-Bass. doi:10.1016/0001-8791(80)90056-1

Sutton, R. I. (2001). The weird rules of creativity. *Harvard Business Review*, *79*(8), 94–103. PMID:11550634

Swamy, M. R. K. (2004). Does non-inclusion of intangible asset values lead to distortion of financial statements and mislead judicious financial decision making? Focus on environmental accounting and estimation of knowledge capital values. *Journal of Financial Management and Analysis*, *17*(1), 77–91.

Swanson, R. A. (1999). The foundations of performance improvement and implications for practice. In R. Torraco (Ed.), *Performance improvement theory and practice: Advances in developing human resources* (pp. 1–25). Sage. doi:10.1177/152342239900100102

Swanson, R. A. (2001). Human resource development and its underlying theory. *Human Resource Development International*, *4*(3), 299–312. doi:10.1080/13678860110059311

Swanson, R. A. (2001). The discipline of human resource development. In R. A. Swanson & E. F. Holton (Eds.), *Foundations of human re- source development* (pp. 88–100). Berrett-Koehler Publishers.

Swanson, R. A. (2007). Theory framework for applied disciplines: Boundaries, contributing, core, useful, novel, and irrelevant components. *Human Resource Development Review*, *6*(3), 321–339. doi:10.1177/1534484307303770

Swanson, R. A., & Holton, E. F. (2001). *Foundation of human resource development*. Berrett-Koehler Publishers.

Swanson, R. A., & Holton, E. F. III. (2009). *Foundations of human resource development* (2nd ed.). Berrett-Koehler Publishers, Inc.

Swanson, R. A., & Torraco, R. J. (1994). Technical training's challenges and goals. *Technical & Skills Training*, *5*(7), 18–22.

Sweetland, S. R. (1996). Human capital theory: Foundations of a field of inquiry. *Review of Educational Research*, *66*(3), 341–359. doi:10.3102/00346543066003341

Tagiuri, R., & Litwin, G. H. (Eds.). (1968). *Organizational climate: Exploration of a concept*. Harvard Business School, Division of Research.

Tannenbaum, S. I. (1997). Enhancing continuous learning: Diagnostic findings from multiple companies. *Human Resource Management*, *36*(4), 437–452. doi:10.1002/(SICI)1099-050X(199724)36:4<437::AID-HRM7>3.0.CO;2-W

Tarrant, K., & Nagasawa, M. (2020). New York Early care and education survey: Understanding the impact of COVID-19 on New York early childhood system. https://educate.bankstreet.edu/sc/2/

Taylor, F. W. (1911). *The principles of scientific management.* Harper & Row.

Taylor, J. R., & Van Every, E. J. (2000). *The emergent organization: Communication as its site and surface.* Erlbaum.

Taylor, P. J. (1974). Sickness absence: Factors and misconceptions. *Journal of the Royal College of Physicians, 8,* 315–334. PMID:4841341

Thériault, M., Des Rosiers, F., Villeneuve, P., & Kestens, Y. (2003). Modelling interactions of location with specific value of housing at- tributes. *Property Management, 21*(1), 25–62. doi:10.1108/02637470310464472

Thoben, K. D., Wiesner, S., & Wuest, T. (2017). "Industrie 4.0" and smart manufacturing-a review of research issues and application examples. *International Journal of Automotive Technology, 11*(1), 4–16. doi:10.20965/ijat.2017.p0004

Thoene, M. A., & Buszko, A. (2014). Quantitative model of tacit knowledge estimation for pharmaceutical industry. *The Engineering Economist, 25*(1), 40–46.

Thomas, K. M. (2008). *Diversity resistance in organizations.* Lawrence Erlbaum.

Thompson, C., & Gregory, J. B. (2012). Managing millennials: A framework for improving attraction, motivation, and retention. *The Psychologist Manager Journal, 15*(4), 237–246. doi:10.1080/10887156.2012.730444

Thompson, G. L. (1968). Optimal maintenance policy and sale date of a machine. *Management Science, 14*(9), 543–550. doi:10.1287/mnsc.14.9.543

Thorndike, E. L. (1898). Animal intelligence: An experimental study of the associate processes in animals. *Psychological Review Monograph Supplement, 2*(4), 1–8. doi:10.1037/10780-000

Thorndike, E. L. (1911). *Animal intelligence.* Macmillan.

Tolman, E. C. (1932). *Purposive behavior in animals and men.* Century.

Tolman, E. C. (1938). The determiners of behavior at a choice point. *Psychological Review, 45*(1), 1–41. doi:10.1037/h0062733

Torraco, R. J. (2000). The relationship of learning and performance improvement at different system levels. *Performance Improvement Quarterly, 13*(1), 60–83. doi:10.1111/j.1937-8327.2000.tb00157.

Trevino, L. K. (1986). Ethical decision making in organizations: A person-situation interactionist model. *Academy of Management Review, 11*(3), 601–617. doi:10.2307/258313

Trevino, L. K., & Brown, M. E. (2004). Managing to be ethical: Debunking five business ethics myths. *The Academy of Management Executive, 18*(2), 69–81. doi:10.5465/ame.2004.13837400

Triana, M. D. C., Gu, P., Chapa, O., Richard, O., & Colella, A. (2021). Sixty years of discrimination and diversity research in human resource management: A review with suggestions for future research directions. *Human Resource Management*, *60*(1), 145–204. doi:10.1002/hrm.22052

Trice, H. M., & Beyer, J. M. (1984). Studying organizational cultures through rites and ceremonials. *Academy of Management Review*, *9*(4), 653–669. doi:10.2307/258488

Trice, H. M., & Beyer, J. M. (1986a). Charisma and its routinization in two social movement organizations. In B. M. Staw & L. L. Cummings (Eds.), *Research in organizational behavior* (Vol. 8, pp. 113–164). JAI Press.

Trice, H. M., & Beyer, J. M. (1986b). Cultural leadership in organizations. *Organization Science*, *2*(2), 149–169. doi:10.1287/orsc.2.2.149

Tripathi, A., & Dhir, S. (2022). HRD interventions, learning agility and organizational innovation: A PLS-SEM modelling approach. *The International Journal of Organizational Analysis*. doi:10.1108/IJOA-12-2021-3064

Trumbo, D. A. (1958). *An analysis of attitudes toward change among the employees of an insurance company*. [Unpublished Doctoral dissertation, Michigan State University].

Trumbo, D. A. (1961). Individual and group correlates of attitudes toward work-related change. *The Journal of Applied Psychology*, *45*(5), 338–344. doi:10.1037/h0040464

Tseng, C. C., & McLean, G. N. (2008). Strategic HRD practices as key factors in organizational learning. *Journal of European Industrial Training*, *32*(6), 418–432. https://doi.org/10.1108/03090590810886544

Turale, S., Meechamnan, C., & Kunaviktikul, W. (2020). Challenging times: Ethics, nursing and the COVID-19 pandemic. International Nursing Review, 67(2), 164–167.

Tushman, M. L., & Anderson, P. (1986). Technological discontinuities and organizational environments. *Administrative Science Quarterly*, *31*(3), 439–465. doi:10.2307/2392832

Tziner, A., Murphy, K. R., Cleveland, J. N., & Roberts-Thompson, G. P. (2001). Relationships between attitudes toward organizations and performance appraisal systems and rating behavior. *International Journal of Selection and Assessment*, *9*(3), 226–239. doi:10.1111/1468-2389.00176

Upadhyay, A. K., & Khandelwal, K. (2019). Artificial intelligence-based training learning from application. *Development and Learning in Organizations*, *33*(2), 20–23. doi:10.1108/DLO-05-2018-0058

Van Barneveld, K., Quinlan, M., Kriesler, P., Junor, A., Baum, F., Chowdhury, A., Junankar, P. N., Clibborn, S., Flanagan, F., Wright, C. F., Friel, S., Halevi, J., & Rainnie, A. (2020). The COVID-19 pandemic: Lessons on building more equal and sustainable societies. *The Economic and Labour Relations Review, 31*(2), 133-157.

Van de Ven, A. H., & Johnson, P. E. (2006). Knowledge for theory and practice. *Academy of Management Review*, *31*(4), 802–821. doi:10.5465/ AMR.2006.22527385 van den Heuvel, M., Demerouti, E., Bakker, A. B., Hetland, J., & Schaufeli, W. B. (2020). How do employees adapt to organizational change? The role of meaning-making and work engagement. *The Spanish Journal of Psychology*, *23*(e56), 1–16. doi:10.1017/SJP.2020.55 PMID:33345770

van den Heuvel, M., Demerouti, E., Bakker, A. B., & Schaufeli, W. B. (2013). Adapting to change: The value of change information and meaning-making. *Journal of Vocational Behavior*, *83*(1), 11–21. doi:10.1016/j.jvb.2013.02.004

van Hoek, R., & Dobrzykowski, D. (2021). Towards more balanced sourcing strategies–are supply chain risks caused by the COVID-19 pandemic driving reshoring considerations? *Supply Chain Management*, *26*(6), 689–701. doi:10.1108/SCM-09-2020-0498

Vardi, Y. (1980). Organizational career mobility: An integrative model. *Academy of Management Review*, *5*(3), 341–355. doi:10.2307/257109

Venkatraman, N., & Henderson, J. C. (1998). Real strategies for virtual organizing. *Sloan Management Review*, *34*(2), 73–87.

Vergano, D. (2011, February 17). Watson dominated at 'Jeopardy!- but what else can it do? *USA Today*, p. 2D.

Vergne, J. P. (2020). Decentralized vs. distributed organization: Blockchain, machine learning and the future of the digital platform. *Organization Theory, 1*(4), 1-26.

Vial, G. (2019). Understanding digital transformation: A review and a research agenda. *The Journal of Strategic Information Systems*, *28*(2), 118–144. doi:10.1016/j.jsis.2019.01.003

Vince, R. (2003). The future practice of HRD. *Human Resource Development International*, *6*(4), 559–563. doi:10.1080/13678860310001630656

Viswesvaran, C. (2001). Assessment of individual job performance: A review of the past century and a look ahead. In N. Anderson, D. S. Ones, H. K. Sinangil, & C. Viswesvaran (Eds.), *Handbook of industrial, work and organizational psychology* (Vol. 1, pp. 110–126). Sage. doi:10.4135/9781848608320.n7

Voss, J. (1978). Cognition and instruction: Toward a cognitive theory of learning. In A. Lesgold, J. Pellegrino, S. Fokkema, & R. Glaser (Eds.), *Cognitive psychology and instruction* (pp. 13–23). Plenum. doi:10.1007/978-1-4684-2535-2_3

Vrontis, D., Christofi, M., Pereira, V., Tarba, S., Makrides, A., & Trichina, E. (2022). Artificial intelligence, robotics, advanced technologies and human resource management: A systematic review. *International Journal of Human Resource Management*, *33*(6), 1237–1266.

Vroom, V. H. (1964). *Work and motivation*. John Wiley & Sons, Inc.

Vroom, V. H. (1973). A new look at managerial decision making. *Organizational Dynamics*, *1*(4), 66–80. doi:10.1016/S0090-2616(73)80024-5

Vroom, V. H. (2003). Educating managers for decision making and leadership. *Management Decision, 41*(10), 968–978. doi:10.1108/00251740310509490

Vroom, V. H., & MacCrimmon, K. R. (1968). Toward a stochastic model of managerial careers. *Administrative Science Quarterly, 13*(1), 26–46. doi:10.2307/2391260

Vygotsky, L. S. (1979). Consciousness as a problem in the psychology of behavior. *Soviet Psychology, 176*(4), 3-35. (Original work published 1924).

Vygotsky, L. (1978). Interaction between learning and development. *Readings On the Development of Children, 23*(3), 34–41.

Vygotsky, L. S. (1987). *The collected works of L.S. Vygotsky* (R. W. Rieber & A. S. Carton, (Eds). Plenum Press.

Wadors, P. (2016, August 10). Diversity efforts fall short unless employees feel that they belong. *Harvard Business Review*. Retrieved from https://hbr.org/2016/08/ diversity-efforts-fall-short-unless-employees-feel-that-they-belong

Waldfogel, J. (1999). The impact of the family and medical leave act. *Journal of Policy Analysis and Management, 18*(2), 281–302. doi:10.1002/(SICI)1520-6688(199921)18:2<281::AID-PAM5>3.0.CO;2-J

WaltenburgM. A.VictoroffT.RoseC. E.ButterfieldM.JervisR. H.FedakK. M.HoneinM. A. (2020). Update: COVID-19 among workers in meat and poultry processing facilities—United States, April–May 2020. Morbidity and Mortality Weekly Report, 69(27), 887.

Wang, M. (2011). Integrating organizational, social, and individual perspectives in Web 2.0-based workplace e-learning. Information Systems Frontiers, 13, 191–205.

Wang, G. G., Dou, Z., & Li, N. (2002). A systems approach to measuring return on investment for HRD interventions. *Human Resource Development Quarterly, 13*(2), 203–224. doi:10.1002/hrdq.1024

Wang, M. (2011). Integrating organizational, social, and individual perspectives in Web 2.0-based workplace e-learning. *Information Systems Frontiers, 13*(2), 191–205. doi:10.100710796-009-9191-y

Warr, P., Bird, M., & Rackham, N. (1970). *Evaluation of management training.* Gower Press.

Watkins, K., & Marsick, V. (1993). *Sculpting the learning organization: Lessons in the art and science of systemic change.* Jossey-Bass.

Watson, J. B. (1913). Psychology as the behaviorist sees it. *Psychological Review, 20*(2), 157–177. doi:10.1037/h0074428

Way, S. A., & Johnson, D. E. (2005). Theorizing about the impact of strategic human resource management. *Human Resource Management Review, 15*(1), 1–19. doi:10.1016/j.hrmr.2005.01.004

Weber, M. (1947). The theory of social and economic organization (Henderson, A. M., & Parsons, T. (Trans. Eds.)). The Free Press.

Weber, M. (1964). *The theory of social and eco- nomic organization*. Free Press.

Weick, K. E., Sutcliffe, K. M., & Obstfeld, D. (2005). Organizing and the process of sensemaking. *Organization Science*, *16*(4), 409–421. doi:10.1287/orsc.1050.0133

Weiner, B. (1972). *Theories of motivation: From mechanism to cognition*. Markham.

Weiner, B. (1985). An attributional theory of achievement motivation and emotion. *Psychological Review*, *92*(4), 548–573. doi:10.1037/0033-295X.92.4.548 PMID:3903815

Weintraub, R. S., & Martineau, J. W. (2002, June). The just-in-time imperative. *Training and Development Journal*, 51–57.

Welch, J. (2005). *Winning*. HarperCollins.

Wen, L., Maani, S. A., & Dong, Z. (2023). Educational job mismatch, job satisfaction, on-the-job training, and employee quit behaviour: A dynamic analytical approach. *Applied Economics*, 1-22. doi:10.1080/00036846.2022.2161990

Wenstop, F., & Myrmel, A. (2006). Structuring organizational value statements. *Management Research News*, *29*(11), 673–683. doi:10.1108/01409170610715990

Werner, J. M. (2022). Academic integrity and human resource development: Being and doing. *Human Resource Development Review*, *21*(2), 249–257. doi:10.1177/15344843221078505

Werner, J. M., & DeSimone, R. L. (2012). *Human resource development* (6th ed.). South-Western.

White, D. B., & Lo, B. (2020). A framework for rationing ventilators and critical care beds during the COVID-19 pandemic. Journal of the American Medical Association, 323(18).

White, E. M., Wetle, T. F., Reddy, A., & Baier, R. R. (2021). Front-line nursing home staff experiences during the COVID-19 pandemic. Journal of the American Medical Directors Association, 22(1), 199–203.

Whitman, M. (2010). *The power of many: Values for success in business and in life*. Three Rivers Press.

Wiener, Y. (1982). Commitment in organizations: A normative view. *Academy of Management Review*, *7*(3), 418–428. doi:10.2307/257334

Wiener, Y. (1988). Forms of value systems: A focus on organizational effectiveness and cultural change and maintenance. *Academy of Management Review*, *13*, 534–545.

Wiley, C. (1997). What motivates employees ac- cording to over 40 years of motivation surveys. *International Journal of Manpower*, *18*(3), 263–280. doi:10.1108/01437729710169373

Wilkins, A. L., & Ouchi, W. G. (1983). Efficient cultures: Exploring the relationship between culture and organizational performance. *Administrative Science Quarterly*, *28*(3), 468–481. doi:10.2307/2392253

Wilson, C. (2012). Retaining good people through a focus on talent and purpose: Proper inductions make employees feel as though they truly belong. Human Resource Management International Digest, 20(2), 29–31.

Wilson, H. T. (2004). Use value and substantive rationality in the work of Marx and Weber. *Journal of Classical Sociology*, *4*(1), 4–30. doi:10.1177/1468795X04040650

Wilson, J., & Daugherty, P. (2019). Creating the symbiotic AI workforce of the future. *MIT Sloan Management Review*, *61*(1), 1–4. https://www.proquest.com/scholarly-journals/creating-symbiotic-ai-workforce-future/docview/2315489026/se-2

Wilson, M., Robertson, P., Cruickshank, P., & Gkatzia, D. (2022). Opportunities and risks in the use of AI in career development practice. *Journal of the National Institute for Career Education and Counselling*, *48*(1), 48–57. doi:10.20856/jnicec.4807

Wittrock, M. C. (1978). The cognitive movement in instruction. *Educational Psychologist*, *15*(1), 15–29. doi:10.1080/00461527809529192

Wittrock, M. C. (1989). Generative processes of comprehension. *Educational Psychologist*, *24*(4), 345–376. doi:10.120715326985ep2404_2

Wlodkowski, R. J., & Ginsberg, M. B. (1995). *Diversity and motivation: Culturally responsive teaching*. Jossey-Bass.

Woehr, D. J., & Huffcutt, A. I. (1994). Rater training for performance appraisal: A quantitative review. *Journal of Occupational and Organizational Psychology*, *67*(3), 189–205. doi:10.1111/j.2044-8325.1994.tb00562.x

Womack, J. P., & Jones, D. T. (1996). *Lean thinking*. Simon & Schuster.

World Economic Forum. (2020). *The future of jobs report 2020*. Geneva.

Wright, P. M., & McMahan, G. C. (1992). Theoretical perspectives for strategic human resource management. *Journal of Management*, *18*(2), 295–320. doi:10.1177/014920639201800205

Wright, V. A., Vaughan, B. W., Laurent, T., Lopez, R., Brooksbank, C., & Schneider, M. V. (2010). Bioinformatics training: Selecting an appropriate learning content management system—an example from the European Bioinformatics Institute. *Briefings in Bioinformatics*, *11*(6), 552–562. https://doi.org/10.1093/bib/bbq023

Xu, Z., Elomri, A., Kerbache, L., & El Omri, A. (2020). Impacts of COVID-19 on global supply chains: Facts and perspectives. *IEEE Engineering Management Review*, *48*(3), 153–166. doi:10.1109/EMR.2020.3018420

Yamey G. Schäferhoff M. Pate M. Chawla M. Ranson K. Hatchett R. Wilder R.

Yarberry, S., & Sims, C. (2021). The impact of COVID-19-prompted virtual/remote work environments on employees' career development: Social learning theory, belongingness, and self-empowerment. *Advances in Developing Human Resources, 23*(3), 237–252. doi:10.1177/15234223211017850

Yildiz, R. O., & Esmer, S. (2023). Talent management strategies and functions: A systematic review. *Industrial and Commercial Training, 55*(1), 93–111. doi:10.1108/ICT-01-2022-0007

Yorks, L., Abel, A. L., & Rotatori, D. (2022). Using data and analytics for improved HRD performance in the age of digital technologies. In *Strategic human resource development in practice: Leveraging talent for sustained performance in the digital age of AI* (pp. 81-92). Springer International Publishing.

Yorks, L. (2005). Nothing so practical as a good theory. *Human Resource Development Review, 4*(2), 111–113. doi:10.1177/1534484305276176

Yorks, L., Abel, A. L., & Rotatori, D. (2022). *Strategic human resource development in practice: Leveraging talent for sustained performance in the digital age of AI.* Springer Nature. doi:10.1007/978-3-030-95775-9

Yorks, L., Abel, A. L., & Rotatori, D. (2022). Using data and analytics for improved HRD performance in the age of digital technologies. In *Strategic human resource development in practice: Leveraging talent for sustained performance in the digital age of AI* (pp. 81–92). Springer International Publishing. doi:10.1007/978-3-030-95775-9_5

Young, S. S., & Choi, J. N. (2014). Do organizations spend wisely on employees? Effects of training and development investments on learning and innovation in organizations. *Journal of Organizational Behavior, 35*(3), 393–412. doi:10.1002/job.1897 PMID:25598576

Yu, W., & Wang, Z. (2022). Dual influencing paths of time pressure on employee creativity. *International Journal of Stress Management,* 1–12. doi:10.1037tr0000267

Zakaria, F. (2010, November). Restoring the American dream. *Time, 176*(18), 30–35.

Zaleznik, A. (2004). Managers and leaders: Are they different? *Harvard Business Review, 82*(1), 1–11. PMID:14723179

Zamarro, G., & Prados, M. J. (2021). Gender differences in couples' division of childcare, work and mental health during COVID-19. *Review of Economics of the Household, 19*(1), 11–40. doi:10.100711150-020-09534-7 PMID:33488316

Zenger, J., & Folkman, J. (2022, August 31). Quiet quitting is about bad bosses, not bad employees. *Harvard Business Review.* https://hbr.org/2022/08/quiet-quittingis-about-bad-bosses-not-bad-employees

Zhang, R., Kang, H., Jiang, Z., & Niu, X. (2023). How does workplace ostracism hurt employee creativity? Thriving at work as a mediator and organization-based self-esteem as a moderator. *Applied Psychology, 72*(1), 211–230. doi:10.1111/apps.12374

Zimmerman, B. J. (2002). Becoming a self-regulated learner: An overview. *Theory into Practice*, *41*(2), 64–70. doi:10.120715430421tip4102_2

Zsidisin, G. A. (2003). A grounded definition of supply risk. *Journal of Purchasing and Supply Management*, 9(5-6), 217–224.

Related References

To continue our tradition of advancing information science and technology research, we have compiled a list of recommended IGI Global readings. These references will provide additional information and guidance to further enrich your knowledge and assist you with your own research and future publications.

Abdul Razak, R., & Mansor, N. A. (2021). Instagram Influencers in Social Media-Induced Tourism: Rethinking Tourist Trust Towards Tourism Destination. In M. Dinis, L. Bonixe, S. Lamy, & Z. Breda (Eds.), *Impact of New Media in Tourism* (pp. 135-144). IGI Global. https://doi.org/10.4018/978-1-7998-7095-1.ch009

Abir, T., & Khan, M. Y. (2022). Importance of ICT Advancement and Culture of Adaptation in the Tourism and Hospitality Industry for Developing Countries. In C. Ramos, S. Quinteiro, & A. Gonçalves (Eds.), *ICT as Innovator Between Tourism and Culture* (pp. 30–41). IGI Global. https://doi.org/10.4018/978-1-7998-8165-0.ch003

Abtahi, M. S., Behboudi, L., & Hasanabad, H. M. (2017). Factors Affecting Internet Advertising Adoption in Ad Agencies. *International Journal of Innovation in the Digital Economy*, 8(4), 18–29. doi:10.4018/IJIDE.2017100102

Afenyo-Agbe, E., & Mensah, I. (2022). Principles, Benefits, and Barriers to Community-Based Tourism: Implications for Management. In I. Mensah & E. Afenyo-Agbe (Eds.), *Prospects and Challenges of Community-Based Tourism and Changing Demographics* (pp. 1–29). IGI Global. doi:10.4018/978-1-7998-7335-8.ch001

Agbo, V. M. (2022). Distributive Justice Issues in Community-Based Tourism. In I. Mensah & E. Afenyo-Agbe (Eds.), *Prospects and Challenges of Community-Based Tourism and Changing Demographics* (pp. 107–129). IGI Global. https://doi.org/10.4018/978-1-7998-7335-8.ch005

Agrawal, S. (2017). The Impact of Emerging Technologies and Social Media on Different Business(es): Marketing and Management. In O. Rishi & A. Sharma (Eds.), *Maximizing Business Performance and Efficiency Through Intelligent Systems* (pp. 37–49). Hershey, PA: IGI Global. doi:10.4018/978-1-5225-2234-8.ch002

Ahmad, A., & Johari, S. (2022). Georgetown as a Gastronomy Tourism Destination: Visitor Awareness Towards Revisit Intention of Nasi Kandar Restaurant. In M. Valeri (Ed.), *New Governance and Management in Touristic Destinations* (pp. 71–83). IGI Global. https://doi.org/10.4018/978-1-6684-3889-3.ch005

Alkhatib, G., & Bayouq, S. T. (2021). A TAM-Based Model of Technological Factors Affecting Use of E-Tourism. *International Journal of Tourism and Hospitality Management in the Digital Age*, 5(2), 50–67. https://doi.org/10.4018/IJTHMDA.20210701.oa1

Altinay Ozdemir, M. (2021). Virtual Reality (VR) and Augmented Reality (AR) Technologies for Accessibility and Marketing in the Tourism Industry. In C. Eusébio, L. Teixeira, & M. Carneiro (Eds.), *ICT Tools and Applications for Accessible Tourism* (pp. 277-301). IGI Global. https://doi.org/10.4018/978-1-7998-6428-8.ch013

Anantharaman, R. N., Rajeswari, K. S., Angusamy, A., & Kuppusamy, J. (2017). Role of Self-Efficacy and Collective Efficacy as Moderators of Occupational Stress Among Software Development Professionals. *International Journal of Human Capital and Information Technology Professionals*, 8(2), 45–58. doi:10.4018/IJHCITP.2017040103

Aninze, F., El-Gohary, H., & Hussain, J. (2018). The Role of Microfinance to Empower Women: The Case of Developing Countries. *International Journal of Customer Relationship Marketing and Management*, 9(1), 54–78. doi:10.4018/IJCRMM.2018010104

Antosova, G., Sabogal-Salamanca, M., & Krizova, E. (2021). Human Capital in Tourism: A Practical Model of Endogenous and Exogenous Territorial Tourism Planning in Bahía Solano, Colombia. In V. Costa, A. Moura, & M. Mira (Eds.), *Handbook of Research on Human Capital and People Management in the Tourism Industry* (pp. 282–302). IGI Global. https://doi.org/10.4018/978-1-7998-4318-4.ch014

Arsenijević, O. M., Orčić, D., & Kastratović, E. (2017). Development of an Optimization Tool for Intangibles in SMEs: A Case Study from Serbia with a Pilot Research in the Prestige by Milka Company. In M. Vemić (Ed.), *Optimal Management Strategies in Small and Medium Enterprises* (pp. 320–347). Hershey, PA: IGI Global. doi:10.4018/978-1-5225-1949-2.ch015

Aryanto, V. D., Wismantoro, Y., & Widyatmoko, K. (2018). Implementing Eco-Innovation by Utilizing the Internet to Enhance Firm's Marketing Performance: Study of Green Batik Small and Medium Enterprises in Indonesia. *International Journal of E-Business Research*, *14*(1), 21–36. doi:10.4018/IJEBR.2018010102

Asero, V., & Billi, S. (2022). New Perspective of Networking in the DMO Model. In M. Valeri (Ed.), *New Governance and Management in Touristic Destinations* (pp. 105–118). IGI Global. https://doi.org/10.4018/978-1-6684-3889-3.ch007

Atiku, S. O., & Fields, Z. (2017). Multicultural Orientations for 21st Century Global Leadership. In N. Baporikar (Ed.), *Management Education for Global Leadership* (pp. 28–51). Hershey, PA: IGI Global. doi:10.4018/978-1-5225-1013-0.ch002

Atiku, S. O., & Fields, Z. (2018). Organisational Learning Dimensions and Talent Retention Strategies for the Service Industries. In N. Baporikar (Ed.), *Global Practices in Knowledge Management for Societal and Organizational Development* (pp. 358–381). Hershey, PA: IGI Global. doi:10.4018/978-1-5225-3009-1.ch017

Atsa'am, D. D., & Kuset Bodur, E. (2021). Pattern Mining on How Organizational Tenure Affects the Psychological Capital of Employees Within the Hospitality and Tourism Industry: Linking Employees' Organizational Tenure With PsyCap. *International Journal of Tourism and Hospitality Management in the Digital Age*, *5*(2), 17–28. https://doi.org/10.4018/IJTHMDA.2021070102

Ávila, L., & Teixeira, L. (2018). The Main Concepts Behind the Dematerialization of Business Processes. In M. Khosrow-Pour, D.B.A. (Ed.), Encyclopedia of Information Science and Technology, Fourth Edition (pp. 888-898). Hershey, PA: IGI Global. https://doi.org/ doi:10.4018/978-1-5225-2255-3.ch076

Ayorekire, J., Mugizi, F., Obua, J., & Ampaire, G. (2022). Community-Based Tourism and Local People's Perceptions Towards Conservation: The Case of Queen Elizabeth Conservation Area, Uganda. In I. Mensah & E. Afenyo-Agbe (Eds.), *Prospects and Challenges of Community-Based Tourism and Changing Demographics* (pp. 56–82). IGI Global. https://doi.org/10.4018/978-1-7998-7335-8.ch003

Baleiro, R. (2022). Tourist Literature and the Architecture of Travel in Olga Tokarczuk and Patti Smith. In R. Baleiro & R. Pereira (Eds.), *Global Perspectives on Literary Tourism and Film-Induced Tourism* (pp. 202-216). IGI Global. https://doi.org/10.4018/978-1-7998-8262-6.ch011

Barat, S. (2021). Looking at the Future of Medical Tourism in Asia. *International Journal of Tourism and Hospitality Management in the Digital Age*, 5(1), 19–33. https://doi.org/10.4018/IJTHMDA.2021010102

Barbosa, C. A., Magalhães, M., & Nunes, M. R. (2021). Travel Instagramability: A Way of Choosing a Destination? In M. Dinis, L. Bonixe, S. Lamy, & Z. Breda (Eds.), *Impact of New Media in Tourism* (pp. 173-190). IGI Global. https://doi.org/10.4018/978-1-7998-7095-1.ch011

Bari, M. W., & Khan, Q. (2021). Pakistan as a Destination of Religious Tourism. In E. Alaverdov & M. Bari (Eds.), *Global Development of Religious Tourism* (pp. 1-10). IGI Global. https://doi.org/10.4018/978-1-7998-5792-1.ch001

Bartens, Y., Chunpir, H. I., Schulte, F., & Voß, S. (2017). Business/IT Alignment in Two-Sided Markets: A COBIT 5 Analysis for Media Streaming Business Models. In S. De Haes & W. Van Grembergen (Eds.), *Strategic IT Governance and Alignment in Business Settings* (pp. 82–111). Hershey, PA: IGI Global. doi:10.4018/978-1-5225-0861-8.ch004

Bashayreh, A. M. (2018). Organizational Culture and Organizational Performance. In W. Lee & F. Sabetzadeh (Eds.), *Contemporary Knowledge and Systems Science* (pp. 50–69). Hershey, PA: IGI Global. doi:10.4018/978-1-5225-5655-8.ch003

Bechthold, L., Lude, M., & Prügl, R. (2021). Crisis Favors the Prepared Firm: How Organizational Ambidexterity Relates to Perceptions of Organizational Resilience. In A. Zehrer, G. Glowka, K. Schwaiger, & V. Ranacher-Lackner (Eds.), *Resiliency Models and Addressing Future Risks for Family Firms in the Tourism Industry* (pp. 178–205). IGI Global. https://doi.org/10.4018/978-1-7998-7352-5.ch008

Bedford, D. A. (2018). Sustainable Knowledge Management Strategies: Aligning Business Capabilities and Knowledge Management Goals. In N. Baporikar (Ed.), *Global Practices in Knowledge Management for Societal and Organizational Development* (pp. 46–73). Hershey, PA: IGI Global. doi:10.4018/978-1-5225-3009-1.ch003

Bekjanov, D., & Matyusupov, B. (2021). Influence of Innovative Processes in the Competitiveness of Tourist Destination. In J. Soares (Ed.), *Innovation and Entrepreneurial Opportunities in Community Tourism* (pp. 243–263). IGI Global. https://doi.org/10.4018/978-1-7998-4855-4.ch014

Bharwani, S., & Musunuri, D. (2018). Reflection as a Process From Theory to Practice. In M. Khosrow-Pour, D.B.A. (Ed.), Encyclopedia of Information Science and Technology, Fourth Edition (pp. 1529-1539). Hershey, PA: IGI Global. doi:10.4018/978-1-5225-2255-3.ch132

Bhatt, G. D., Wang, Z., & Rodger, J. A. (2017). Information Systems Capabilities and Their Effects on Competitive Advantages: A Study of Chinese Companies. *Information Resources Management Journal*, *30*(3), 41–57. doi:10.4018/IRMJ.2017070103

Bhushan, M., & Yadav, A. (2017). Concept of Cloud Computing in ESB. In R. Bhadoria, N. Chaudhari, G. Tomar, & S. Singh (Eds.), *Exploring Enterprise Service Bus in the Service-Oriented Architecture Paradigm* (pp. 116–127). Hershey, PA: IGI Global. doi:10.4018/978-1-5225-2157-0.ch008

Bhushan, S. (2017). System Dynamics Base-Model of Humanitarian Supply Chain (HSCM) in Disaster Prone Eco-Communities of India: A Discussion on Simulation and Scenario Results. *International Journal of System Dynamics Applications*, *6*(3), 20–37. doi:10.4018/IJSDA.2017070102

Binder, D., & Miller, J. W. (2021). A Generations' Perspective on Employer Branding in Tourism. In V. Costa, A. Moura, & M. Mira (Eds.), *Handbook of Research on Human Capital and People Management in the Tourism Industry* (pp. 152–174). IGI Global. https://doi.org/10.4018/978-1-7998-4318-4.ch008

Birch Freeman, A. A., Mensah, I., & Antwi, K. B. (2022). Smiling vs. Frowning Faces: Community Participation for Sustainable Tourism in Ghanaian Communities. In I. Mensah & E. Afenyo-Agbe (Eds.), *Prospects and Challenges of Community-Based Tourism and Changing Demographics* (pp. 83–106). IGI Global. https://doi.org/10.4018/978-1-7998-7335-8.ch004

Biswas, A., & De, A. K. (2017). On Development of a Fuzzy Stochastic Programming Model with Its Application to Business Management. In S. Trivedi, S. Dey, A. Kumar, & T. Panda (Eds.), *Handbook of Research on Advanced Data Mining Techniques and Applications for Business Intelligence* (pp. 353–378). Hershey, PA: IGI Global. doi:10.4018/978-1-5225-2031-3. ch021

Boragnio, A., & Faracce Macia, C. (2021). "Taking Care of Yourself at Home": Use of E-Commerce About Food and Care During the COVID-19 Pandemic in the City of Buenos Aires. In M. Korstanje (Ed.), *Socio-Economic Effects and Recovery Efforts for the Rental Industry: Post-COVID-19 Strategies* (pp. 45–71). IGI Global. https://doi.org/10.4018/978-1-7998-7287-0.ch003

Borges, V. D. (2021). Happiness: The Basis for Public Policy in Tourism. In A. Perinotto, V. Mayer, & J. Soares (Eds.), *Rebuilding and Restructuring the Tourism Industry: Infusion of Happiness and Quality of Life* (pp. 1–25). IGI Global. https://doi.org/10.4018/978-1-7998-7239-9.ch001

Bücker, J., & Ernste, K. (2018). Use of Brand Heroes in Strategic Reputation Management: The Case of Bacardi, Adidas, and Daimler. In A. Erdemir (Ed.), *Reputation Management Techniques in Public Relations* (pp. 126–150). Hershey, PA: IGI Global. doi:10.4018/978-1-5225-3619-2.ch007

Buluk Eşitti, B. (2021). COVID-19 and Alternative Tourism: New Destinations and New Tourism Products. In M. Demir, A. Dalgıç, & F. Ergen (Eds.), *Handbook of Research on the Impacts and Implications of COVID-19 on the Tourism Industry* (pp. 786–805). IGI Global. https://doi.org/10.4018/978-1-7998-8231-2.ch038

Bureš, V. (2018). Industry 4.0 From the Systems Engineering Perspective: Alternative Holistic Framework Development. In R. Brunet-Thornton & F. Martinez (Eds.), *Analyzing the Impacts of Industry 4.0 in Modern Business Environments* (pp. 199–223). Hershey, PA: IGI Global. doi:10.4018/978-1-5225-3468-6.ch011

Buzady, Z. (2017). Resolving the Magic Cube of Effective Case Teaching: Benchmarking Case Teaching Practices in Emerging Markets – Insights from the Central European University Business School, Hungary. In D. Latusek (Ed.), *Case Studies as a Teaching Tool in Management Education* (pp. 79–103). Hershey, PA: IGI Global. doi:10.4018/978-1-5225-0770-3.ch005

Camillo, A. (2021). *Legal Matters, Risk Management, and Risk Prevention: From Forming a Business to Legal Representation.* IGI Global. doi:10.4018/978-1-7998-4342-9.ch004

Căpusneanu, S., & Topor, D. I. (2018). Business Ethics and Cost Management in SMEs: Theories of Business Ethics and Cost Management Ethos. In I. Oncioiu (Ed.), *Ethics and Decision-Making for Sustainable Business Practices* (pp. 109–127). Hershey, PA: IGI Global. doi:10.4018/978-1-5225-3773-1.ch007

Chan, R. L., Mo, P. L., & Moon, K. K. (2018). Strategic and Tactical Measures in Managing Enterprise Risks: A Study of the Textile and Apparel Industry. In K. Strang, M. Korstanje, & N. Vajjhala (Eds.), *Research, Practices, and Innovations in Global Risk and Contingency Management* (pp. 1–19). Hershey, PA: IGI Global. doi:10.4018/978-1-5225-4754-9.ch001

Charlier, S. D., Burke-Smalley, L. A., & Fisher, S. L. (2018). Undergraduate Programs in the U.S: A Contextual and Content-Based Analysis. In J. Mendy (Ed.), *Teaching Human Resources and Organizational Behavior at the College Level* (pp. 26–57). Hershey, PA: IGI Global. doi:10.4018/978-1-5225-2820-3.ch002

Chumillas, J., Güell, M., & Quer, P. (2022). The Use of ICT in Tourist and Educational Literary Routes: The Role of the Guide. In C. Ramos, S. Quinteiro, & A. Gonçalves (Eds.), *ICT as Innovator Between Tourism and Culture* (pp. 15–29). IGI Global. https://doi.org/10.4018/978-1-7998-8165-0.ch002

Dahlberg, T., Kivijärvi, H., & Saarinen, T. (2017). IT Investment Consistency and Other Factors Influencing the Success of IT Performance. In S. De Haes & W. Van Grembergen (Eds.), *Strategic IT Governance and Alignment in Business Settings* (pp. 176–208). Hershey, PA: IGI Global. doi:10.4018/978-1-5225-0861-8.ch007

Damnjanović, A. M. (2017). Knowledge Management Optimization through IT and E-Business Utilization: A Qualitative Study on Serbian SMEs. In M. Vemić (Ed.), *Optimal Management Strategies in Small and Medium Enterprises* (pp. 249–267). Hershey, PA: IGI Global. doi:10.4018/978-1-5225-1949-2.ch012

Daneshpour, H. (2017). Integrating Sustainable Development into Project Portfolio Management through Application of Open Innovation. In M. Vemić (Ed.), *Optimal Management Strategies in Small and Medium Enterprises* (pp. 370–387). Hershey, PA: IGI Global. doi:10.4018/978-1-5225-1949-2.ch017

Daniel, A. D., & Reis de Castro, V. (2018). Entrepreneurship Education: How to Measure the Impact on Nascent Entrepreneurs. In A. Carrizo Moreira, J. Guilherme Leitão Dantas, & F. Manuel Valente (Eds.), *Nascent Entrepreneurship and Successful New Venture Creation* (pp. 85–110). Hershey, PA: IGI Global. doi:10.4018/978-1-5225-2936-1.ch004

David, R., Swami, B. N., & Tangirala, S. (2018). Ethics Impact on Knowledge Management in Organizational Development: A Case Study. In N. Baporikar (Ed.), *Global Practices in Knowledge Management for Societal and Organizational Development* (pp. 19–45). Hershey, PA: IGI Global. doi:10.4018/978-1-5225-3009-1.ch002

De Uña-Álvarez, E., & Villarino-Pérez, M. (2022). Fostering Ecocultural Resources, Identity, and Tourism in Inland Territories (Galicia, NW Spain). In G. Fernandes (Ed.), *Challenges and New Opportunities for Tourism in Inland Territories: Ecocultural Resources and Sustainable Initiatives* (pp. 1-16). IGI Global. https://doi.org/10.4018/978-1-7998-7339-6.ch001

Delias, P., & Lakiotaki, K. (2018). Discovering Process Horizontal Boundaries to Facilitate Process Comprehension. *International Journal of Operations Research and Information Systems*, *9*(2), 1–31. doi:10.4018/IJORIS.2018040101

Denholm, J., & Lee-Davies, L. (2018). Success Factors for Games in Business and Project Management. In *Enhancing Education and Training Initiatives Through Serious Games* (pp. 34–68). Hershey, PA: IGI Global. doi:10.4018/978-1-5225-3689-5.ch002

Deshpande, M. (2017). Best Practices in Management Institutions for Global Leadership: Policy Aspects. In N. Baporikar (Ed.), *Management Education for Global Leadership* (pp. 1–27). Hershey, PA: IGI Global. doi:10.4018/978-1-5225-1013-0.ch001

Deshpande, M. (2018). Policy Perspectives for SMEs Knowledge Management. In N. Baporikar (Ed.), *Knowledge Integration Strategies for Entrepreneurship and Sustainability* (pp. 23–46). Hershey, PA: IGI Global. doi:10.4018/978-1-5225-5115-7.ch002

Dezdar, S. (2017). ERP Implementation Projects in Asian Countries: A Comparative Study on Iran and China. *International Journal of Information Technology Project Management*, 8(3), 52–68. doi:10.4018/IJITPM.2017070104

Domingos, D., Respício, A., & Martinho, R. (2017). Reliability of IoT-Aware BPMN Healthcare Processes. In C. Reis & M. Maximiano (Eds.), *Internet of Things and Advanced Application in Healthcare* (pp. 214–248). Hershey, PA: IGI Global. doi:10.4018/978-1-5225-1820-4.ch008

Dosumu, O., Hussain, J., & El-Gohary, H. (2017). An Exploratory Study of the Impact of Government Policies on the Development of Small and Medium Enterprises in Developing Countries: The Case of Nigeria. *International Journal of Customer Relationship Marketing and Management*, 8(4), 51–62. doi:10.4018/IJCRMM.2017100104

Durst, S., Bruns, G., & Edvardsson, I. R. (2017). Retaining Knowledge in Smaller Building and Construction Firms. *International Journal of Knowledge and Systems Science*, 8(3), 1–12. doi:10.4018/IJKSS.2017070101

Edvardsson, I. R., & Durst, S. (2017). Outsourcing, Knowledge, and Learning: A Critical Review. *International Journal of Knowledge-Based Organizations*, 7(2), 13–26. doi:10.4018/IJKBO.2017040102

Edwards, J. S. (2018). Integrating Knowledge Management and Business Processes. In M. Khosrow-Pour, D.B.A. (Ed.), Encyclopedia of Information Science and Technology, Fourth Edition (pp. 5046-5055). Hershey, PA: IGI Global. doi:10.4018/978-1-5225-2255-3.ch437

Eichelberger, S., & Peters, M. (2021). Family Firm Management in Turbulent Times: Opportunities for Responsible Tourism. In A. Zehrer, G. Glowka, K. Schwaiger, & V. Ranacher-Lackner (Eds.), *Resiliency Models and Addressing Future Risks for Family Firms in the Tourism Industry* (pp. 103–124). IGI Global. https://doi.org/10.4018/978-1-7998-7352-5.ch005

Eide, D., Hjalager, A., & Hansen, M. (2022). Innovative Certifications in Adventure Tourism: Attributes and Diffusion. In R. Augusto Costa, F. Brandão, Z. Breda, & C. Costa (Eds.), *Planning and Managing the Experience Economy in Tourism* (pp. 161-175). IGI Global. https://doi.org/10.4018/978-1-7998-8775-1.ch009

Ejiogu, A. O. (2018). Economics of Farm Management. In *Agricultural Finance and Opportunities for Investment and Expansion* (pp. 56–72). Hershey, PA: IGI Global. doi:10.4018/978-1-5225-3059-6.ch003

Ekanem, I., & Abiade, G. E. (2018). Factors Influencing the Use of E-Commerce by Small Enterprises in Nigeria. *International Journal of ICT Research in Africa and the Middle East*, *7*(1), 37–53. doi:10.4018/IJICTRAME.2018010103

Ekanem, I., & Alrossais, L. A. (2017). Succession Challenges Facing Family Businesses in Saudi Arabia. In P. Zgheib (Ed.), *Entrepreneurship and Business Innovation in the Middle East* (pp. 122–146). Hershey, PA: IGI Global. doi:10.4018/978-1-5225-2066-5.ch007

El Faquih, L., & Fredj, M. (2017). Ontology-Based Framework for Quality in Configurable Process Models. *Journal of Electronic Commerce in Organizations*, *15*(2), 48–60. doi:10.4018/JECO.2017040104

Faisal, M. N., & Talib, F. (2017). Building Ambidextrous Supply Chains in SMEs: How to Tackle the Barriers? *International Journal of Information Systems and Supply Chain Management*, *10*(4), 80–100. doi:10.4018/IJISSCM.2017100105

Fernandes, T. M., Gomes, J., & Romão, M. (2017). Investments in E-Government: A Benefit Management Case Study. *International Journal of Electronic Government Research*, *13*(3), 1–17. doi:10.4018/IJEGR.2017070101

Figueira, L. M., Honrado, G. R., & Dionísio, M. S. (2021). Human Capital Management in the Tourism Industry in Portugal. In V. Costa, A. Moura, & M. Mira (Eds.), *Handbook of Research on Human Capital and People Management in the Tourism Industry* (pp. 1–19). IGI Global. doi:10.4018/978-1-7998-4318-4.ch001

Gao, S. S., Oreal, S., & Zhang, J. (2018). Contemporary Financial Risk Management Perceptions and Practices of Small-Sized Chinese Businesses. In I. Management Association (Ed.), Global Business Expansion: Concepts, Methodologies, Tools, and Applications (pp. 917-931). Hershey, PA: IGI Global. doi:10.4018/978-1-5225-5481-3.ch041

Garg, R., & Berning, S. C. (2017). Indigenous Chinese Management Philosophies: Key Concepts and Relevance for Modern Chinese Firms. In B. Christiansen & G. Koc (Eds.), *Transcontinental Strategies for Industrial Development and Economic Growth* (pp. 43–57). Hershey, PA: IGI Global. doi:10.4018/978-1-5225-2160-0.ch003

Gencer, Y. G. (2017). Supply Chain Management in Retailing Business. In U. Akkucuk (Ed.), *Ethics and Sustainability in Global Supply Chain Management* (pp. 197–210). Hershey, PA: IGI Global. doi:10.4018/978-1-5225-2036-8.ch011

Gera, R., Arora, S., & Malik, S. (2021). Emotional Labor in the Tourism Industry: Strategies, Antecedents, and Outcomes. In V. Costa, A. Moura, & M. Mira (Eds.), *Handbook of Research on Human Capital and People Management in the Tourism Industry* (pp. 73–91). IGI Global. https://doi.org/10.4018/978-1-7998-4318-4.ch004

Giacosa, E. (2018). The Increasing of the Regional Development Thanks to the Luxury Business Innovation. In L. Carvalho (Ed.), *Handbook of Research on Entrepreneurial Ecosystems and Social Dynamics in a Globalized World* (pp. 260–273). Hershey, PA: IGI Global. doi:10.4018/978-1-5225-3525-6.ch011

Glowka, G., Tusch, M., & Zehrer, A. (2021). The Risk Perception of Family Business Owner-Manager in the Tourism Industry: A Qualitative Comparison of the Intra-Firm Senior and Junior Generation. In A. Zehrer, G. Glowka, K. Schwaiger, & V. Ranacher-Lackner (Eds.), *Resiliency Models and Addressing Future Risks for Family Firms in the Tourism Industry* (pp. 126–153). IGI Global. https://doi.org/10.4018/978-1-7998-7352-5.ch006

Glykas, M., & George, J. (2017). Quality and Process Management Systems in the UAE Maritime Industry. *International Journal of Productivity Management and Assessment Technologies, 5*(1), 20–39. doi:10.4018/IJPMAT.2017010102

Glykas, M., Valiris, G., Kokkinaki, A., & Koutsoukou, Z. (2018). Banking Business Process Management Implementation. *International Journal of Productivity Management and Assessment Technologies, 6*(1), 50–69. doi:10.4018/IJPMAT.2018010104

Gomes, J., & Romão, M. (2017). The Balanced Scorecard: Keeping Updated and Aligned with Today's Business Trends. *International Journal of Productivity Management and Assessment Technologies, 5*(2), 1–15. doi:10.4018/IJPMAT.2017070101

Gomes, J., & Romão, M. (2017). Aligning Information Systems and Technology with Benefit Management and Balanced Scorecard. In S. De Haes & W. Van Grembergen (Eds.), *Strategic IT Governance and Alignment in Business Settings* (pp. 112–131). Hershey, PA: IGI Global. doi:10.4018/978-1-5225-0861-8.ch005

Goyal, A. (2021). Communicating and Building Destination Brands With New Media. In M. Dinis, L. Bonixe, S. Lamy, & Z. Breda (Eds.), *Impact of New Media in Tourism* (pp. 1-20). IGI Global. https://doi.org/10.4018/978-1-7998-7095-1.ch001

Grefen, P., & Turetken, O. (2017). Advanced Business Process Management in Networked E-Business Scenarios. *International Journal of E-Business Research, 13*(4), 70–104. doi:10.4018/IJEBR.2017100105

Guasca, M., Van Broeck, A. M., & Vanneste, D. (2021). Tourism and the Social Reintegration of Colombian Ex-Combatants. In J. da Silva, Z. Breda, & F. Carbone (Eds.), *Role and Impact of Tourism in Peacebuilding and Conflict Transformation* (pp. 66-86). IGI Global. https://doi.org/10.4018/978-1-7998-5053-3.ch005

Haider, A., & Saetang, S. (2017). Strategic IT Alignment in Service Sector. In S. Rozenes & Y. Cohen (Eds.), *Handbook of Research on Strategic Alliances and Value Co-Creation in the Service Industry* (pp. 231–258). Hershey, PA: IGI Global. doi:10.4018/978-1-5225-2084-9.ch012

Hajilari, A. B., Ghadaksaz, M., & Fasghandis, G. S. (2017). Assessing Organizational Readiness for Implementing ERP System Using Fuzzy Expert System Approach. *International Journal of Enterprise Information Systems*, *13*(1), 67–85. doi:10.4018/IJEIS.2017010105

Haldorai, A., Ramu, A., & Murugan, S. (2018). Social Aware Cognitive Radio Networks: Effectiveness of Social Networks as a Strategic Tool for Organizational Business Management. In H. Bansal, G. Shrivastava, G. Nguyen, & L. Stanciu (Eds.), *Social Network Analytics for Contemporary Business Organizations* (pp. 188–202). Hershey, PA: IGI Global. doi:10.4018/978-1-5225-5097-6.ch010

Hall, O. P. Jr. (2017). Social Media Driven Management Education. *International Journal of Knowledge-Based Organizations*, *7*(2), 43–59. doi:10.4018/IJKBO.2017040104

Hanifah, H., Halim, H. A., Ahmad, N. H., & Vafaei-Zadeh, A. (2017). Innovation Culture as a Mediator Between Specific Human Capital and Innovation Performance Among Bumiputera SMEs in Malaysia. In N. Ahmad, T. Ramayah, H. Halim, & S. Rahman (Eds.), *Handbook of Research on Small and Medium Enterprises in Developing Countries* (pp. 261–279). Hershey, PA: IGI Global. doi:10.4018/978-1-5225-2165-5.ch012

Hartlieb, S., & Silvius, G. (2017). Handling Uncertainty in Project Management and Business Development: Similarities and Differences. In Y. Raydugin (Ed.), *Handbook of Research on Leveraging Risk and Uncertainties for Effective Project Management* (pp. 337–362). Hershey, PA: IGI Global. doi:10.4018/978-1-5225-1790-0.ch016

Hass, K. B. (2017). Living on the Edge: Managing Project Complexity. In Y. Raydugin (Ed.), *Handbook of Research on Leveraging Risk and Uncertainties for Effective Project Management* (pp. 177–201). Hershey, PA: IGI Global. doi:10.4018/978-1-5225-1790-0.ch009

Hawking, P., & Carmine Sellitto, C. (2017). Developing an Effective Strategy for Organizational Business Intelligence. In M. Tavana (Ed.), *Enterprise Information Systems and the Digitalization of Business Functions* (pp. 222–237). Hershey, PA: IGI Global. doi:10.4018/978-1-5225-2382-6.ch010

Hawking, P., & Sellitto, C. (2017). A Fast-Moving Consumer Goods Company and Business Intelligence Strategy Development. *International Journal of Enterprise Information Systems*, *13*(2), 22–33. doi:10.4018/IJEIS.2017040102

Hawking, P., & Sellitto, C. (2017). Business Intelligence Strategy: Two Case Studies. *International Journal of Business Intelligence Research, 8*(2), 17–30. doi:10.4018/IJBIR.2017070102

Hee, W. J., Jalleh, G., Lai, H., & Lin, C. (2017). E-Commerce and IT Projects: Evaluation and Management Issues in Australian and Taiwanese Hospitals. *International Journal of Public Health Management and Ethics, 2*(1), 69–90. doi:10.4018/IJPHME.2017010104

Hernandez, A. A. (2018). Exploring the Factors to Green IT Adoption of SMEs in the Philippines. *Journal of Cases on Information Technology, 20*(2), 49–66. doi:10.4018/JCIT.2018040104

Hollman, A., Bickford, S., & Hollman, T. (2017). Cyber InSecurity: A Post-Mortem Attempt to Assess Cyber Problems from IT and Business Management Perspectives. *Journal of Cases on Information Technology, 19*(3), 42–70. doi:10.4018/JCIT.2017070104

Ibrahim, F., & Zainin, N. M. (2021). Exploring the Technological Impacts: The Case of Museums in Brunei Darussalam. *International Journal of Tourism and Hospitality Management in the Digital Age, 5*(1), 1–18. https://doi.org/10.4018/IJTHMDA.2021010101

Igbinakhase, I. (2017). Responsible and Sustainable Management Practices in Developing and Developed Business Environments. In Z. Fields (Ed.), *Collective Creativity for Responsible and Sustainable Business Practice* (pp. 180–207). Hershey, PA: IGI Global. doi:10.4018/978-1-5225-1823-5.ch010

Iwata, J. J., & Hoskins, R. G. (2017). Managing Indigenous Knowledge in Tanzania: A Business Perspective. In P. Jain & N. Mnjama (Eds.), *Managing Knowledge Resources and Records in Modern Organizations* (pp. 198–214). Hershey, PA: IGI Global. doi:10.4018/978-1-5225-1965-2.ch012

Jain, P. (2017). Ethical and Legal Issues in Knowledge Management Life-Cycle in Business. In P. Jain & N. Mnjama (Eds.), *Managing Knowledge Resources and Records in Modern Organizations* (pp. 82–101). Hershey, PA: IGI Global. doi:10.4018/978-1-5225-1965-2.ch006

James, S., & Hauli, E. (2017). Holistic Management Education at Tanzanian Rural Development Planning Institute. In N. Baporikar (Ed.), *Management Education for Global Leadership* (pp. 112–136). Hershey, PA: IGI Global. doi:10.4018/978-1-5225-1013-0.ch006

Janošková, M., Csikósová, A., & Čulková, K. (2018). Measurement of Company Performance as Part of Its Strategic Management. In R. Leon (Ed.), *Managerial Strategies for Business Sustainability During Turbulent Times* (pp. 309–335). Hershey, PA: IGI Global. doi:10.4018/978-1-5225-2716-9.ch017

Jean-Vasile, A., & Alecu, A. (2017). Theoretical and Practical Approaches in Understanding the Influences of Cost-Productivity-Profit Trinomial in Contemporary Enterprises. In A. Jean Vasile & D. Nicolò (Eds.), *Sustainable Entrepreneurship and Investments in the Green Economy* (pp. 28–62). Hershey, PA: IGI Global. doi:10.4018/978-1-5225-2075-7.ch002

Joia, L. A., & Correia, J. C. (2018). CIO Competencies From the IT Professional Perspective: Insights From Brazil. *Journal of Global Information Management*, *26*(2), 74–103. doi:10.4018/JGIM.2018040104

Juma, A., & Mzera, N. (2017). Knowledge Management and Records Management and Competitive Advantage in Business. In P. Jain & N. Mnjama (Eds.), *Managing Knowledge Resources and Records in Modern Organizations* (pp. 15–28). Hershey, PA: IGI Global. doi:10.4018/978-1-5225-1965-2.ch002

K., I., & A, V. (2018). Monitoring and Auditing in the Cloud. In K. Munir (Ed.), *Cloud Computing Technologies for Green Enterprises* (pp. 318-350). Hershey, PA: IGI Global. https://doi.org/ doi:10.4018/978-1-5225-3038-1.ch013

Kabra, G., Ghosh, V., & Ramesh, A. (2018). Enterprise Integrated Business Process Management and Business Intelligence Framework for Business Process Sustainability. In A. Paul, D. Bhattacharyya, & S. Anand (Eds.), *Green Initiatives for Business Sustainability and Value Creation* (pp. 228–238). Hershey, PA: IGI Global. doi:10.4018/978-1-5225-2662-9.ch010

Kaoud, M. (2017). Investigation of Customer Knowledge Management: A Case Study Research. *International Journal of Service Science, Management, Engineering, and Technology*, *8*(2), 12–22. doi:10.4018/IJSSMET.2017040102

Katuu, S. (2018). A Comparative Assessment of Enterprise Content Management Maturity Models. In N. Gwangwava & M. Mutingi (Eds.), *E-Manufacturing and E-Service Strategies in Contemporary Organizations* (pp. 93–118). Hershey, PA: IGI Global. doi:10.4018/978-1-5225-3628-4.ch005

Khan, M. Y., & Abir, T. (2022). The Role of Social Media Marketing in the Tourism and Hospitality Industry: A Conceptual Study on Bangladesh. In C. Ramos, S. Quinteiro, & A. Gonçalves (Eds.), *ICT as Innovator Between Tourism and Culture* (pp. 213–229). IGI Global. https://doi.org/10.4018/978-1-7998-8165-0.ch013

Kinnunen, S., Ylä-Kujala, A., Marttonen-Arola, S., Kärri, T., & Baglee, D. (2018). Internet of Things in Asset Management: Insights from Industrial Professionals and Academia. *International Journal of Service Science, Management, Engineering, and Technology*, *9*(2), 104–119. doi:10.4018/IJSSMET.2018040105

Klein, A. Z., Sabino de Freitas, A., Machado, L., Freitas, J. C. Jr, Graziola, P. G. Jr, & Schlemmer, E. (2017). Virtual Worlds Applications for Management Education. In L. Tomei (Ed.), *Exploring the New Era of Technology-Infused Education* (pp. 279–299). Hershey, PA: IGI Global. doi:10.4018/978-1-5225-1709-2.ch017

Kővári, E., Saleh, M., & Steinbachné Hajmásy, G. (2022). The Impact of Corporate Digital Responsibility (CDR) on Internal Stakeholders' Satisfaction in Hungarian Upscale Hotels. In M. Valeri (Ed.), *New Governance and Management in Touristic Destinations* (pp. 35–51). IGI Global. https://doi.org/10.4018/978-1-6684-3889-3.ch003

Kożuch, B., & Jabłoński, A. (2017). Adopting the Concept of Business Models in Public Management. In M. Lewandowski & B. Kożuch (Eds.), *Public Sector Entrepreneurship and the Integration of Innovative Business Models* (pp. 10–46). Hershey, PA: IGI Global. doi:10.4018/978-1-5225-2215-7.ch002

Kumar, J., Adhikary, A., & Jha, A. (2017). Small Active Investors' Perceptions and Preferences Towards Tax Saving Mutual Fund Schemes in Eastern India: An Empirical Note. *International Journal of Asian Business and Information Management*, *8*(2), 35–45. doi:10.4018/IJABIM.2017040103

Latusi, S., & Fissore, M. (2021). Pilgrimage Routes to Happiness: Comparing the Camino de Santiago and Via Francigena. In A. Perinotto, V. Mayer, & J. Soares (Eds.), *Rebuilding and Restructuring the Tourism Industry: Infusion of Happiness and Quality of Life* (pp. 157–182). IGI Global. https://doi.org/10.4018/978-1-7998-7239-9.ch008

Lavassani, K. M., & Movahedi, B. (2017). Applications Driven Information Systems: Beyond Networks toward Business Ecosystems. *International Journal of Innovation in the Digital Economy*, 8(1), 61–75. doi:10.4018/IJIDE.2017010104

Lazzareschi, V. H., & Brito, M. S. (2017). Strategic Information Management: Proposal of Business Project Model. In G. Jamil, A. Soares, & C. Pessoa (Eds.), *Handbook of Research on Information Management for Effective Logistics and Supply Chains* (pp. 59–88). Hershey, PA: IGI Global. doi:10.4018/978-1-5225-0973-8.ch004

Lechuga Sancho, M. P., & Martín Navarro, A. (2022). Evolution of the Literature on Social Responsibility in the Tourism Sector: A Systematic Literature Review. In G. Fernandes (Ed.), *Challenges and New Opportunities for Tourism in Inland Territories: Ecocultural Resources and Sustainable Initiatives* (pp. 169–186). IGI Global. https://doi.org/10.4018/978-1-7998-7339-6.ch010

Lederer, M., Kurz, M., & Lazarov, P. (2017). Usage and Suitability of Methods for Strategic Business Process Initiatives: A Multi Case Study Research. *International Journal of Productivity Management and Assessment Technologies*, 5(1), 40–51. doi:10.4018/IJPMAT.2017010103

Lee, I. (2017). A Social Enterprise Business Model and a Case Study of Pacific Community Ventures (PCV). In V. Potocan, M. Üngan, & Z. Nedelko (Eds.), *Handbook of Research on Managerial Solutions in Non-Profit Organizations* (pp. 182–204). Hershey, PA: IGI Global. doi:10.4018/978-1-5225-0731-4.ch009

Leon, L. A., Seal, K. C., Przasnyski, Z. H., & Wiedenman, I. (2017). Skills and Competencies Required for Jobs in Business Analytics: A Content Analysis of Job Advertisements Using Text Mining. *International Journal of Business Intelligence Research*, 8(1), 1–25. doi:10.4018/IJBIR.2017010101

Levy, C. L., & Elias, N. I. (2017). SOHO Users' Perceptions of Reliability and Continuity of Cloud-Based Services. In M. Moore (Ed.), *Cybersecurity Breaches and Issues Surrounding Online Threat Protection* (pp. 248–287). Hershey, PA: IGI Global. doi:10.4018/978-1-5225-1941-6.ch011

Levy, M. (2018). Change Management Serving Knowledge Management and Organizational Development: Reflections and Review. In N. Baporikar (Ed.), *Global Practices in Knowledge Management for Societal and Organizational Development* (pp. 256–270). Hershey, PA: IGI Global. doi:10.4018/978-1-5225-3009-1.ch012

Lewandowski, M. (2017). Public Organizations and Business Model Innovation: The Role of Public Service Design. In M. Lewandowski & B. Kożuch (Eds.), *Public Sector Entrepreneurship and the Integration of Innovative Business Models* (pp. 47–72). Hershey, PA: IGI Global. doi:10.4018/978-1-5225-2215-7.ch003

Lhannaoui, H., Kabbaj, M. I., & Bakkoury, Z. (2017). A Survey of Risk-Aware Business Process Modelling. *International Journal of Risk and Contingency Management*, 6(3), 14–26. doi:10.4018/IJRCM.2017070102

Li, J., Sun, W., Jiang, W., Yang, H., & Zhang, L. (2017). How the Nature of Exogenous Shocks and Crises Impact Company Performance?: The Effects of Industry Characteristics. *International Journal of Risk and Contingency Management*, 6(4), 40–55. doi:10.4018/IJRCM.2017100103

Lopez-Fernandez, M., Perez-Perez, M., Serrano-Bedia, A., & Cobo-Gonzalez, A. (2021). Small and Medium Tourism Enterprise Survival in Times of Crisis: "El Capricho de Gaudí. In D. Toubes & N. Araújo-Vila (Eds.), *Risk, Crisis, and Disaster Management in Small and Medium-Sized Tourism Enterprises* (pp. 103–129). IGI Global. doi:10.4018/978-1-7998-6996-2.ch005

Mahajan, A., Maidullah, S., & Hossain, M. R. (2022). Experience Toward Smart Tour Guide Apps in Travelling: An Analysis of Users' Reviews on Audio Odigos and Trip My Way. In R. Augusto Costa, F. Brandão, Z. Breda, & C. Costa (Eds.), *Planning and Managing the Experience Economy in Tourism* (pp. 255-273). IGI Global. https://doi.org/10.4018/978-1-7998-8775-1.ch014

Malega, P. (2017). Small and Medium Enterprises in the Slovak Republic: Status and Competitiveness of SMEs in the Global Markets and Possibilities of Optimization. In M. Vemić (Ed.), *Optimal Management Strategies in Small and Medium Enterprises* (pp. 102–124). Hershey, PA: IGI Global. doi:10.4018/978-1-5225-1949-2.ch006

Malewska, K. M. (2017). Intuition in Decision-Making on the Example of a Non-Profit Organization. In V. Potocan, M. Üngan, & Z. Nedelko (Eds.), *Handbook of Research on Managerial Solutions in Non-Profit Organizations* (pp. 378–399). Hershey, PA: IGI Global. doi:10.4018/978-1-5225-0731-4. ch018

Maroofi, F. (2017). Entrepreneurial Orientation and Organizational Learning Ability Analysis for Innovation and Firm Performance. In N. Baporikar (Ed.), *Innovation and Shifting Perspectives in Management Education* (pp. 144–165). Hershey, PA: IGI Global. doi:10.4018/978-1-5225-1019-2.ch007

Marques, M., Moleiro, D., Brito, T. M., & Marques, T. (2021). Customer Relationship Management as an Important Relationship Marketing Tool: The Case of the Hospitality Industry in Estoril Coast. In M. Dinis, L. Bonixe, S. Lamy, & Z. Breda (Eds.), Impact of New Media in Tourism (pp. 39-56). IGI Global. https://doi.org/ doi:10.4018/978-1-7998-7095-1.ch003

Martins, P. V., & Zacarias, M. (2017). A Web-based Tool for Business Process Improvement. *International Journal of Web Portals*, 9(2), 68–84. doi:10.4018/IJWP.2017070104

Matthies, B., & Coners, A. (2017). Exploring the Conceptual Nature of e-Business Projects. *Journal of Electronic Commerce in Organizations*, 15(3), 33–63. doi:10.4018/JECO.2017070103

Mayer, V. F., Fraga, C. C., & Silva, L. C. (2021). Contributions of Neurosciences to Studies of Well-Being in Tourism. In A. Perinotto, V. Mayer, & J. Soares (Eds.), *Rebuilding and Restructuring the Tourism Industry: Infusion of Happiness and Quality of Life* (pp. 108–128). IGI Global. https://doi. org/10.4018/978-1-7998-7239-9.ch006

McKee, J. (2018). Architecture as a Tool to Solve Business Planning Problems. In M. Khosrow-Pour, D.B.A. (Ed.), Encyclopedia of Information Science and Technology, Fourth Edition (pp. 573-586). Hershey, PA: IGI Global. doi:10.4018/978-1-5225-2255-3.ch050

McMurray, A. J., Cross, J., & Caponecchia, C. (2018). The Risk Management Profession in Australia: Business Continuity Plan Practices. In N. Bajgoric (Ed.), *Always-On Enterprise Information Systems for Modern Organizations* (pp. 112–129). Hershey, PA: IGI Global. doi:10.4018/978-1-5225-3704-5. ch006

Meddah, I. H., & Belkadi, K. (2018). Mining Patterns Using Business Process Management. In R. Hamou (Ed.), *Handbook of Research on Biomimicry in Information Retrieval and Knowledge Management* (pp. 78–89). Hershey, PA: IGI Global. doi:10.4018/978-1-5225-3004-6.ch005

Melian, A. G., & Camprubí, R. (2021). The Accessibility of Museum Websites: The Case of Barcelona. In C. Eusébio, L. Teixeira, & M. Carneiro (Eds.), *ICT Tools and Applications for Accessible Tourism* (pp. 234–255). IGI Global. https://doi.org/10.4018/978-1-7998-6428-8.ch011

Mendes, L. (2017). TQM and Knowledge Management: An Integrated Approach Towards Tacit Knowledge Management. In D. Jaziri-Bouagina & G. Jamil (Eds.), *Handbook of Research on Tacit Knowledge Management for Organizational Success* (pp. 236–263). Hershey, PA: IGI Global. doi:10.4018/978-1-5225-2394-9.ch009

Menezes, V. D., & Cavagnaro, E. (2021). Communicating Sustainable Initiatives in the Hotel Industry: The Case of the Hotel Jakarta Amsterdam. In F. Brandão, Z. Breda, R. Costa, & C. Costa (Eds.), *Handbook of Research on the Role of Tourism in Achieving Sustainable Development Goals* (pp. 224-234). IGI Global. https://doi.org/10.4018/978-1-7998-5691-7.ch013

Menezes, V. D., & Cavagnaro, E. (2021). Communicating Sustainable Initiatives in the Hotel Industry: The Case of the Hotel Jakarta Amsterdam. In F. Brandão, Z. Breda, R. Costa, & C. Costa (Eds.), *Handbook of Research on the Role of Tourism in Achieving Sustainable Development Goals* (pp. 224-234). IGI Global. https://doi.org/10.4018/978-1-7998-5691-7.ch013

Mitas, O., Bastiaansen, M., & Boode, W. (2022). If You're Happy, I'm Happy: Emotion Contagion at a Tourist Information Center. In R. Augusto Costa, F. Brandão, Z. Breda, & C. Costa (Eds.), *Planning and Managing the Experience Economy in Tourism* (pp. 122-140). IGI Global. https://doi.org/10.4018/978-1-7998-8775-1.ch007

Mnjama, N. M. (2017). Preservation of Recorded Information in Public and Private Sector Organizations. In P. Jain & N. Mnjama (Eds.), *Managing Knowledge Resources and Records in Modern Organizations* (pp. 149–167). Hershey, PA: IGI Global. doi:10.4018/978-1-5225-1965-2.ch009

Mokoqama, M., & Fields, Z. (2017). Principles of Responsible Management Education (PRME): Call for Responsible Management Education. In Z. Fields (Ed.), *Collective Creativity for Responsible and Sustainable Business Practice* (pp. 229–241). Hershey, PA: IGI Global. doi:10.4018/978-1-5225-1823-5.ch012

Monteiro, A., Lopes, S., & Carbone, F. (2021). Academic Mobility: Bridging Tourism and Peace Education. In J. da Silva, Z. Breda, & F. Carbone (Eds.), *Role and Impact of Tourism in Peacebuilding and Conflict Transformation* (pp. 275-301). IGI Global. https://doi.org/10.4018/978-1-7998-5053-3.ch016

Muniapan, B. (2017). Philosophy and Management: The Relevance of Vedanta in Management. In P. Ordóñez de Pablos (Ed.), *Managerial Strategies and Solutions for Business Success in Asia* (pp. 124–139). Hershey, PA: IGI Global. doi:10.4018/978-1-5225-1886-0.ch007

Murad, S. E., & Dowaji, S. (2017). Using Value-Based Approach for Managing Cloud-Based Services. In A. Turuk, B. Sahoo, & S. Addya (Eds.), *Resource Management and Efficiency in Cloud Computing Environments* (pp. 33–60). Hershey, PA: IGI Global. doi:10.4018/978-1-5225-1721-4.ch002

Mutahar, A. M., Daud, N. M., Thurasamy, R., Isaac, O., & Abdulsalam, R. (2018). The Mediating of Perceived Usefulness and Perceived Ease of Use: The Case of Mobile Banking in Yemen. *International Journal of Technology Diffusion*, *9*(2), 21–40. doi:10.4018/IJTD.2018040102

Naidoo, V. (2017). E-Learning and Management Education at African Universities. In N. Baporikar (Ed.), *Management Education for Global Leadership* (pp. 181–201). Hershey, PA: IGI Global. doi:10.4018/978-1-5225-1013-0.ch009

Naidoo, V., & Igbinakhase, I. (2018). Opportunities and Challenges of Knowledge Retention in SMEs. In N. Baporikar (Ed.), *Knowledge Integration Strategies for Entrepreneurship and Sustainability* (pp. 70–94). Hershey, PA: IGI Global. doi:10.4018/978-1-5225-5115-7.ch004

Naumov, N., & Costandachi, G. (2021). Creativity and Entrepreneurship: Gastronomic Tourism in Mexico. In J. Soares (Ed.), *Innovation and Entrepreneurial Opportunities in Community Tourism* (pp. 90–108). IGI Global. https://doi.org/10.4018/978-1-7998-4855-4.ch006

Nayak, S., & Prabhu, N. (2017). Paradigm Shift in Management Education: Need for a Cross Functional Perspective. In N. Baporikar (Ed.), *Management Education for Global Leadership* (pp. 241–255). Hershey, PA: IGI Global. doi:10.4018/978-1-5225-1013-0.ch012

Nedelko, Z., & Potocan, V. (2017). Management Solutions in Non-Profit Organizations: Case of Slovenia. In V. Potocan, M. Üngan, & Z. Nedelko (Eds.), *Handbook of Research on Managerial Solutions in Non-Profit Organizations* (pp. 1–22). Hershey, PA: IGI Global. doi:10.4018/978-1-5225-0731-4.ch001

Nedelko, Z., & Potocan, V. (2017). Priority of Management Tools Utilization among Managers: International Comparison. In V. Wang (Ed.), *Encyclopedia of Strategic Leadership and Management* (pp. 1083–1094). Hershey, PA: IGI Global. doi:10.4018/978-1-5225-1049-9.ch075

Nedelko, Z., Raudeliūnienė, J., & Črešnar, R. (2018). Knowledge Dynamics in Supply Chain Management. In N. Baporikar (Ed.), *Knowledge Integration Strategies for Entrepreneurship and Sustainability* (pp. 150–166). Hershey, PA: IGI Global. doi:10.4018/978-1-5225-5115-7.ch008

Nguyen, H. T., & Hipsher, S. A. (2018). Innovation and Creativity Used by Private Sector Firms in a Resources-Constrained Environment. In S. Hipsher (Ed.), *Examining the Private Sector's Role in Wealth Creation and Poverty Reduction* (pp. 219–238). Hershey, PA: IGI Global. doi:10.4018/978-1-5225-3117-3.ch010

Obicci, P. A. (2017). Risk Sharing in a Partnership. In *Risk Management Strategies in Public-Private Partnerships* (pp. 115–152). Hershey, PA: IGI Global. doi:10.4018/978-1-5225-2503-5.ch004

Obidallah, W. J., & Raahemi, B. (2017). Managing Changes in Service Oriented Virtual Organizations: A Structural and Procedural Framework to Facilitate the Process of Change. *Journal of Electronic Commerce in Organizations*, *15*(1), 59–83. doi:10.4018/JECO.2017010104

Ojo, O. (2017). Impact of Innovation on the Entrepreneurial Success in Selected Business Enterprises in South-West Nigeria. *International Journal of Innovation in the Digital Economy*, *8*(2), 29–38. doi:10.4018/IJIDE.2017040103

Okdinawati, L., Simatupang, T. M., & Sunitiyoso, Y. (2017). Multi-Agent Reinforcement Learning for Value Co-Creation of Collaborative Transportation Management (CTM). *International Journal of Information Systems and Supply Chain Management, 10*(3), 84–95. doi:10.4018/IJISSCM.2017070105

Olivera, V. A., & Carrillo, I. M. (2021). Organizational Culture: A Key Element for the Development of Mexican Micro and Small Tourist Companies. In J. Soares (Ed.), *Innovation and Entrepreneurial Opportunities in Community Tourism* (pp. 227–242). IGI Global. doi:10.4018/978-1-7998-4855-4.ch013

Ossorio, M. (2022). Corporate Museum Experiences in Enogastronomic Tourism. In R. Augusto Costa, F. Brandão, Z. Breda, & C. Costa (Eds.), Planning and Managing the Experience Economy in Tourism (pp. 107-121). IGI Global. https://doi.org/ doi:10.4018/978-1-7998-8775-1.ch006

Ossorio, M. (2022). Enogastronomic Tourism in Times of Pandemic. In G. Fernandes (Ed.), *Challenges and New Opportunities for Tourism in Inland Territories: Ecocultural Resources and Sustainable Initiatives* (pp. 241–255). IGI Global. https://doi.org/10.4018/978-1-7998-7339-6.ch014

Özekici, Y. K. (2022). ICT as an Acculturative Agent and Its Role in the Tourism Context: Introduction, Acculturation Theory, Progress of the Acculturation Theory in Extant Literature. In C. Ramos, S. Quinteiro, & A. Gonçalves (Eds.), *ICT as Innovator Between Tourism and Culture* (pp. 42–66). IGI Global. https://doi.org/10.4018/978-1-7998-8165-0.ch004

Pal, K. (2018). Building High Quality Big Data-Based Applications in Supply Chains. In A. Kumar & S. Saurav (Eds.), *Supply Chain Management Strategies and Risk Assessment in Retail Environments* (pp. 1–24). Hershey, PA: IGI Global. doi:10.4018/978-1-5225-3056-5.ch001

Palos-Sanchez, P. R., & Correia, M. B. (2018). Perspectives of the Adoption of Cloud Computing in the Tourism Sector. In J. Rodrigues, C. Ramos, P. Cardoso, & C. Henriques (Eds.), *Handbook of Research on Technological Developments for Cultural Heritage and eTourism Applications* (pp. 377–400). Hershey, PA: IGI Global. doi:10.4018/978-1-5225-2927-9.ch018

Papadopoulou, G. (2021). Promoting Gender Equality and Women Empowerment in the Tourism Sector. In F. Brandão, Z. Breda, R. Costa, & C. Costa (Eds.), Handbook of Research on the Role of Tourism in Achieving Sustainable Development Goals (pp. 152-174). IGI Global. https://doi.org/ doi:10.4018/978-1-7998-5691-7.ch009

Papp-Váry, Á. F., & Tóth, T. Z. (2022). Analysis of Budapest as a Film Tourism Destination. In R. Baleiro & R. Pereira (Eds.), *Global Perspectives on Literary Tourism and Film-Induced Tourism* (pp. 257-279). IGI Global. https://doi.org/10.4018/978-1-7998-8262-6.ch014

Patiño, B. E. (2017). New Generation Management by Convergence and Individual Identity: A Systemic and Human-Oriented Approach. In N. Baporikar (Ed.), *Innovation and Shifting Perspectives in Management Education* (pp. 119–143). Hershey, PA: IGI Global. doi:10.4018/978-1-5225-1019-2.ch006

Patro, C. S. (2021). Digital Tourism: Influence of E-Marketing Technology. In M. Dinis, L. Bonixe, S. Lamy, & Z. Breda (Eds.), *Impact of New Media in Tourism* (pp. 234-254). IGI Global. https://doi.org/10.4018/978-1-7998-7095-1.ch014

Pawliczek, A., & Rössler, M. (2017). Knowledge of Management Tools and Systems in SMEs: Knowledge Transfer in Management. In A. Bencsik (Ed.), *Knowledge Management Initiatives and Strategies in Small and Medium Enterprises* (pp. 180–203). Hershey, PA: IGI Global. doi:10.4018/978-1-5225-1642-2.ch009

Pejic-Bach, M., Omazic, M. A., Aleksic, A., & Zoroja, J. (2018). Knowledge-Based Decision Making: A Multi-Case Analysis. In R. Leon (Ed.), *Managerial Strategies for Business Sustainability During Turbulent Times* (pp. 160–184). Hershey, PA: IGI Global. doi:10.4018/978-1-5225-2716-9.ch009

Perano, M., Hysa, X., & Calabrese, M. (2018). Strategic Planning, Cultural Context, and Business Continuity Management: Business Cases in the City of Shkoder. In A. Presenza & L. Sheehan (Eds.), *Geopolitics and Strategic Management in the Global Economy* (pp. 57–77). Hershey, PA: IGI Global. doi:10.4018/978-1-5225-2673-5.ch004

Pereira, R., Mira da Silva, M., & Lapão, L. V. (2017). IT Governance Maturity Patterns in Portuguese Healthcare. In S. De Haes & W. Van Grembergen (Eds.), *Strategic IT Governance and Alignment in Business Settings* (pp. 24–52). Hershey, PA: IGI Global. doi:10.4018/978-1-5225-0861-8.ch002

Pérez-Uribe, R. I., Torres, D. A., Jurado, S. P., & Prada, D. M. (2018). Cloud Tools for the Development of Project Management in SMEs. In R. Perez-Uribe, C. Salcedo-Perez, & D. Ocampo-Guzman (Eds.), *Handbook of Research on Intrapreneurship and Organizational Sustainability in SMEs* (pp. 95–120). Hershey, PA: IGI Global. doi:10.4018/978-1-5225-3543-0.ch005

Petrisor, I., & Cozmiuc, D. (2017). Global Supply Chain Management Organization at Siemens in the Advent of Industry 4.0. In L. Saglietto & C. Cezanne (Eds.), *Global Intermediation and Logistics Service Providers* (pp. 123–142). Hershey, PA: IGI Global. doi:10.4018/978-1-5225-2133-4.ch007

Pierce, J. M., Velliaris, D. M., & Edwards, J. (2017). A Living Case Study: A Journey Not a Destination. In N. Silton (Ed.), *Exploring the Benefits of Creativity in Education, Media, and the Arts* (pp. 158–178). Hershey, PA: IGI Global. doi:10.4018/978-1-5225-0504-4.ch008

Pipia, S., & Pipia, S. (2021). Challenges of Religious Tourism in the Conflict Region: An Example of Jerusalem. In E. Alaverdov & M. Bari (Eds.), *Global Development of Religious Tourism* (pp. 135-148). IGI Global. https://doi.org/10.4018/978-1-7998-5792-1.ch009

Poulaki, P., Kritikos, A., Vasilakis, N., & Valeri, M. (2022). The Contribution of Female Creativity to the Development of Gastronomic Tourism in Greece: The Case of the Island of Naxos in the South Aegean Region. In M. Valeri (Ed.), *New Governance and Management in Touristic Destinations* (pp. 246–258). IGI Global. https://doi.org/10.4018/978-1-6684-3889-3.ch015

Radosavljevic, M., & Andjelkovic, A. (2017). Multi-Criteria Decision Making Approach for Choosing Business Process for the Improvement: Upgrading of the Six Sigma Methodology. In J. Stanković, P. Delias, S. Marinković, & S. Rochhia (Eds.), *Tools and Techniques for Economic Decision Analysis* (pp. 225–247). Hershey, PA: IGI Global. doi:10.4018/978-1-5225-0959-2.ch011

Radovic, V. M. (2017). Corporate Sustainability and Responsibility and Disaster Risk Reduction: A Serbian Overview. In M. Camilleri (Ed.), *CSR 2.0 and the New Era of Corporate Citizenship* (pp. 147–164). Hershey, PA: IGI Global. doi:10.4018/978-1-5225-1842-6.ch008

Raghunath, K. M., Devi, S. L., & Patro, C. S. (2018). Impact of Risk Assessment Models on Risk Factors: A Holistic Outlook. In K. Strang, M. Korstanje, & N. Vajjhala (Eds.), *Research, Practices, and Innovations in Global Risk and Contingency Management* (pp. 134–153). Hershey, PA: IGI Global. doi:10.4018/978-1-5225-4754-9.ch008

Raman, A., & Goyal, D. P. (2017). Extending IMPLEMENT Framework for Enterprise Information Systems Implementation to Information System Innovation. In M. Tavana (Ed.), *Enterprise Information Systems and the Digitalization of Business Functions* (pp. 137–177). Hershey, PA: IGI Global. doi:10.4018/978-1-5225-2382-6.ch007

Rao, Y., & Zhang, Y. (2017). The Construction and Development of Academic Library Digital Special Subject Databases. In L. Ruan, Q. Zhu, & Y. Ye (Eds.), *Academic Library Development and Administration in China* (pp. 163–183). Hershey, PA: IGI Global. doi:10.4018/978-1-5225-0550-1.ch010

Ravasan, A. Z., Mohammadi, M. M., & Hamidi, H. (2018). An Investigation Into the Critical Success Factors of Implementing Information Technology Service Management Frameworks. In K. Jakobs (Ed.), *Corporate and Global Standardization Initiatives in Contemporary Society* (pp. 200–218). Hershey, PA: IGI Global. doi:10.4018/978-1-5225-5320-5.ch009

Rezaie, S., Mirabedini, S. J., & Abtahi, A. (2018). Designing a Model for Implementation of Business Intelligence in the Banking Industry. *International Journal of Enterprise Information Systems*, *14*(1), 77–103. doi:10.4018/IJEIS.2018010105

Richards, V., Matthews, N., Williams, O. J., & Khan, Z. (2021). The Challenges of Accessible Tourism Information Systems for Tourists With Vision Impairment: Sensory Communications Beyond the Screen. In C. Eusébio, L. Teixeira, & M. Carneiro (Eds.), *ICT Tools and Applications for Accessible Tourism* (pp. 26–54). IGI Global. https://doi.org/10.4018/978-1-7998-6428-8.ch002

Rodrigues de Souza Neto, V., & Marques, O. (2021). Rural Tourism Fostering Welfare Through Sustainable Development: A Conceptual Approach. In A. Perinotto, V. Mayer, & J. Soares (Eds.), *Rebuilding and Restructuring the Tourism Industry: Infusion of Happiness and Quality of Life* (pp. 38–57). IGI Global. https://doi.org/10.4018/978-1-7998-7239-9.ch003

Romano, L., Grimaldi, R., & Colasuonno, F. S. (2017). Demand Management as a Success Factor in Project Portfolio Management. In L. Romano (Ed.), *Project Portfolio Management Strategies for Effective Organizational Operations* (pp. 202–219). Hershey, PA: IGI Global. doi:10.4018/978-1-5225-2151-8.ch008

Rubio-Escuderos, L., & García-Andreu, H. (2021). Competitiveness Factors of Accessible Tourism E-Travel Agencies. In C. Eusébio, L. Teixeira, & M. Carneiro (Eds.), *ICT Tools and Applications for Accessible Tourism* (pp. 196–217). IGI Global. https://doi.org/10.4018/978-1-7998-6428-8.ch009

Rucci, A. C., Porto, N., Darcy, S., & Becka, L. (2021). Smart and Accessible Cities?: Not Always – The Case for Accessible Tourism Initiatives in Buenos Aries and Sydney. In C. Eusébio, L. Teixeira, & M. Carneiro (Eds.), *ICT Tools and Applications for Accessible Tourism* (pp. 115–145). IGI Global. https://doi.org/10.4018/978-1-7998-6428-8.ch006

Ruhi, U. (2018). Towards an Interdisciplinary Socio-Technical Definition of Virtual Communities. In M. Khosrow-Pour, D.B.A. (Ed.), Encyclopedia of Information Science and Technology, Fourth Edition (pp. 4278-4295). Hershey, PA: IGI Global. doi:10.4018/978-1-5225-2255-3.ch371

Ryan, L., Catena, M., Ros, P., & Stephens, S. (2021). Designing Entrepreneurial Ecosystems to Support Resource Management in the Tourism Industry. In V. Costa, A. Moura, & M. Mira (Eds.), *Handbook of Research on Human Capital and People Management in the Tourism Industry* (pp. 265–281). IGI Global. https://doi.org/10.4018/978-1-7998-4318-4.ch013

Sabuncu, I. (2021). Understanding Tourist Perceptions and Expectations During Pandemic Through Social Media Big Data. In M. Demir, A. Dalgıç, & F. Ergen (Eds.), *Handbook of Research on the Impacts and Implications of COVID-19 on the Tourism Industry* (pp. 330–350). IGI Global. https://doi.org/10.4018/978-1-7998-8231-2.ch016

Safari, M. R., & Jiang, Q. (2018). The Theory and Practice of IT Governance Maturity and Strategies Alignment: Evidence From Banking Industry. *Journal of Global Information Management*, *26*(2), 127–146. doi:10.4018/JGIM.2018040106

Sahoo, J., Pati, B., & Mohanty, B. (2017). Knowledge Management as an Academic Discipline: An Assessment. In B. Gunjal (Ed.), *Managing Knowledge and Scholarly Assets in Academic Libraries* (pp. 99–126). Hershey, PA: IGI Global. doi:10.4018/978-1-5225-1741-2.ch005

Saini, D. (2017). Relevance of Teaching Values and Ethics in Management Education. In N. Baporikar (Ed.), *Management Education for Global Leadership* (pp. 90–111). Hershey, PA: IGI Global. doi:10.4018/978-1-5225-1013-0.ch005

Sambhanthan, A. (2017). Assessing and Benchmarking Sustainability in Organisations: An Integrated Conceptual Model. *International Journal of Systems and Service-Oriented Engineering*, 7(4), 22–43. doi:10.4018/IJSSOE.2017100102

Sambhanthan, A., & Potdar, V. (2017). A Study of the Parameters Impacting Sustainability in Information Technology Organizations. *International Journal of Knowledge-Based Organizations*, 7(3), 27–39. doi:10.4018/IJKBO.2017070103

Sánchez-Fernández, M. D., & Manríquez, M. R. (2018). The Entrepreneurial Spirit Based on Social Values: The Digital Generation. In P. Isaias & L. Carvalho (Eds.), *User Innovation and the Entrepreneurship Phenomenon in the Digital Economy* (pp. 173–193). Hershey, PA: IGI Global. doi:10.4018/978-1-5225-2826-5.ch009

Sanchez-Ruiz, L., & Blanco, B. (2017). Process Management for SMEs: Barriers, Enablers, and Benefits. In M. Vemić (Ed.), *Optimal Management Strategies in Small and Medium Enterprises* (pp. 293–319). Hershey, PA: IGI Global. doi:10.4018/978-1-5225-1949-2.ch014

Sanz, L. F., Gómez-Pérez, J., & Castillo-Martinez, A. (2018). Analysis of the European ICT Competence Frameworks. In V. Ahuja & S. Rathore (Eds.), *Multidisciplinary Perspectives on Human Capital and Information Technology Professionals* (pp. 225–245). Hershey, PA: IGI Global. doi:10.4018/978-1-5225-5297-0.ch012

Sarvepalli, A., & Godin, J. (2017). Business Process Management in the Classroom. *Journal of Cases on Information Technology*, 19(2), 17–28. doi:10.4018/JCIT.2017040102

Saxena, G. G., & Saxena, A. (2021). Host Community Role in Medical Tourism Development. In M. Singh & S. Kumaran (Eds.), *Growth of the Medical Tourism Industry and Its Impact on Society: Emerging Research and Opportunities* (pp. 105–127). IGI Global. https://doi.org/10.4018/978-1-7998-3427-4.ch006

Saygili, E. E., Ozturkoglu, Y., & Kocakulah, M. C. (2017). End Users' Perceptions of Critical Success Factors in ERP Applications. *International Journal of Enterprise Information Systems*, *13*(4), 58–75. doi:10.4018/IJEIS.2017100104

Saygili, E. E., & Saygili, A. T. (2017). Contemporary Issues in Enterprise Information Systems: A Critical Review of CSFs in ERP Implementations. In M. Tavana (Ed.), *Enterprise Information Systems and the Digitalization of Business Functions* (pp. 120–136). Hershey, PA: IGI Global. doi:10.4018/978-1-5225-2382-6.ch006

Schwaiger, K. M., & Zehrer, A. (2021). The COVID-19 Pandemic and Organizational Resilience in Hospitality Family Firms: A Qualitative Approach. In A. Zehrer, G. Glowka, K. Schwaiger, & V. Ranacher-Lackner (Eds.), *Resiliency Models and Addressing Future Risks for Family Firms in the Tourism Industry* (pp. 32–49). IGI Global. https://doi.org/10.4018/978-1-7998-7352-5.ch002

Scott, N., & Campos, A. C. (2022). Cognitive Science of Tourism Experiences. In R. Augusto Costa, F. Brandão, Z. Breda, & C. Costa (Eds.), Planning and Managing the Experience Economy in Tourism (pp. 1-21). IGI Global. https://doi.org/ doi:10.4018/978-1-7998-8775-1.ch001

Seidenstricker, S., & Antonino, A. (2018). Business Model Innovation-Oriented Technology Management for Emergent Technologies. In M. Khosrow-Pour, D.B.A. (Ed.), Encyclopedia of Information Science and Technology, Fourth Edition (pp. 4560-4569). Hershey, PA: IGI Global. doi:10.4018/978-1-5225-2255-3.ch396

Selvi, M. S. (2021). Changes in Tourism Sales and Marketing Post COVID-19. In M. Demir, A. Dalgıç, & F. Ergen (Eds.), *Handbook of Research on the Impacts and Implications of COVID-19 on the Tourism Industry* (pp. 437–460). IGI Global. doi:10.4018/978-1-7998-8231-2.ch021

Senaratne, S., & Gunarathne, A. D. (2017). Excellence Perspective for Management Education from a Global Accountants' Hub in Asia. In N. Baporikar (Ed.), *Management Education for Global Leadership* (pp. 158–180). Hershey, PA: IGI Global. doi:10.4018/978-1-5225-1013-0.ch008

Sensuse, D. I., & Cahyaningsih, E. (2018). Knowledge Management Models: A Summative Review. *International Journal of Information Systems in the Service Sector, 10*(1), 71–100. doi:10.4018/IJISSS.2018010105

Seth, M., Goyal, D., & Kiran, R. (2017). Diminution of Impediments in Implementation of Supply Chain Management Information System for Enhancing its Effectiveness in Indian Automobile Industry. *Journal of Global Information Management, 25*(3), 1–20. doi:10.4018/JGIM.2017070101

Seyal, A. H., & Rahman, M. N. (2017). Investigating Impact of Inter-Organizational Factors in Measuring ERP Systems Success: Bruneian Perspectives. In M. Tavana (Ed.), *Enterprise Information Systems and the Digitalization of Business Functions* (pp. 178–204). Hershey, PA: IGI Global. doi:10.4018/978-1-5225-2382-6.ch008

Shaqrah, A. A. (2018). Analyzing Business Intelligence Systems Based on 7s Model of McKinsey. *International Journal of Business Intelligence Research, 9*(1), 53–63. doi:10.4018/IJBIR.2018010104

Sharma, A. J. (2017). Enhancing Sustainability through Experiential Learning in Management Education. In N. Baporikar (Ed.), *Management Education for Global Leadership* (pp. 256–274). Hershey, PA: IGI Global. doi:10.4018/978-1-5225-1013-0.ch013

Shetty, K. P. (2017). Responsible Global Leadership: Ethical Challenges in Management Education. In N. Baporikar (Ed.), *Innovation and Shifting Perspectives in Management Education* (pp. 194–223). Hershey, PA: IGI Global. doi:10.4018/978-1-5225-1019-2.ch009

Sinthupundaja, J., & Kohda, Y. (2017). Effects of Corporate Social Responsibility and Creating Shared Value on Sustainability. *International Journal of Sustainable Entrepreneurship and Corporate Social Responsibility, 2*(1), 27–38. doi:10.4018/IJSECSR.2017010103

Škarica, I., & Hrgović, A. V. (2018). Implementation of Total Quality Management Principles in Public Health Institutes in the Republic of Croatia. *International Journal of Productivity Management and Assessment Technologies, 6*(1), 1–16. doi:10.4018/IJPMAT.2018010101

Skokic, V. (2021). How Small Hotel Owners Practice Resilience: Longitudinal Study Among Small Family Hotels in Croatia. In A. Zehrer, G. Glowka, K. Schwaiger, & V. Ranacher-Lackner (Eds.), *Resiliency Models and Addressing Future Risks for Family Firms in the Tourism Industry* (pp. 50–73). IGI Global. doi:10.4018/978-1-7998-7352-5.ch003

Smuts, H., Kotzé, P., Van der Merwe, A., & Loock, M. (2017). Framework for Managing Shared Knowledge in an Information Systems Outsourcing Context. *International Journal of Knowledge Management, 13*(4), 1–30. doi:10.4018/IJKM.2017100101

Sousa, M. J., Cruz, R., Dias, I., & Caracol, C. (2017). Information Management Systems in the Supply Chain. In G. Jamil, A. Soares, & C. Pessoa (Eds.), *Handbook of Research on Information Management for Effective Logistics and Supply Chains* (pp. 469–485). Hershey, PA: IGI Global. doi:10.4018/978-1-5225-0973-8.ch025

Spremic, M., Turulja, L., & Bajgoric, N. (2018). Two Approaches in Assessing Business Continuity Management Attitudes in the Organizational Context. In N. Bajgoric (Ed.), *Always-On Enterprise Information Systems for Modern Organizations* (pp. 159–183). Hershey, PA: IGI Global. doi:10.4018/978-1-5225-3704-5.ch008

Steenkamp, A. L. (2018). Some Insights in Computer Science and Information Technology. In *Examining the Changing Role of Supervision in Doctoral Research Projects: Emerging Research and Opportunities* (pp. 113–133). Hershey, PA: IGI Global. doi:10.4018/978-1-5225-2610-0.ch005

Stipanović, C., Rudan, E., & Zubović, V. (2022). Reaching the New Tourist Through Creativity: Sustainable Development Challenges in Croatian Coastal Towns. In M. Valeri (Ed.), *New Governance and Management in Touristic Destinations* (pp. 231–245). IGI Global. https://doi.org/10.4018/978-1-6684-3889-3.ch014

Tabach, A., & Croteau, A. (2017). Configurations of Information Technology Governance Practices and Business Unit Performance. *International Journal of IT/Business Alignment and Governance, 8*(2), 1–27. doi:10.4018/IJITBAG.2017070101

Talaue, G. M., & Iqbal, T. (2017). Assessment of e-Business Mode of Selected Private Universities in the Philippines and Pakistan. *International Journal of Online Marketing, 7*(4), 63–77. doi:10.4018/IJOM.2017100105

Tam, G. C. (2017). Project Manager Sustainability Competence. In *Managerial Strategies and Green Solutions for Project Sustainability* (pp. 178–207). Hershey, PA: IGI Global. doi:10.4018/978-1-5225-2371-0.ch008

Tambo, T. (2018). Fashion Retail Innovation: About Context, Antecedents, and Outcome in Technological Change Projects. In I. Management Association (Ed.), Fashion and Textiles: Breakthroughs in Research and Practice (pp. 233-260). Hershey, PA: IGI Global. https://doi.org/ doi:10.4018/978-1-5225-3432-7.ch010

Tantau, A. D., & Frățilă, L. C. (2018). Information and Management System for Renewable Energy Business. In *Entrepreneurship and Business Development in the Renewable Energy Sector* (pp. 200–244). Hershey, PA: IGI Global. doi:10.4018/978-1-5225-3625-3.ch006

Teixeira, N., Pardal, P. N., & Rafael, B. G. (2018). Internationalization, Financial Performance, and Organizational Challenges: A Success Case in Portugal. In L. Carvalho (Ed.), *Handbook of Research on Entrepreneurial Ecosystems and Social Dynamics in a Globalized World* (pp. 379–423). Hershey, PA: IGI Global. doi:10.4018/978-1-5225-3525-6.ch017

Teixeira, P., Teixeira, L., Eusébio, C., Silva, S., & Teixeira, A. (2021). The Impact of ICTs on Accessible Tourism: Evidence Based on a Systematic Literature Review. In C. Eusébio, L. Teixeira, & M. Carneiro (Eds.), *ICT Tools and Applications for Accessible Tourism* (pp. 1–25). IGI Global. doi:10.4018/978-1-7998-6428-8.ch001

Trad, A., & Kalpić, D. (2018). The Business Transformation Framework, Agile Project and Change Management. In M. Khosrow-Pour, D.B.A. (Ed.), Encyclopedia of Information Science and Technology, Fourth Edition (pp. 620-635). Hershey, PA: IGI Global. https://doi.org/ doi:10.4018/978-1-5225-2255-3.ch054

Trad, A., & Kalpić, D. (2018). The Business Transformation and Enterprise Architecture Framework: The Financial Engineering E-Risk Management and E-Law Integration. In B. Sergi, F. Fidanoski, M. Ziolo, & V. Naumovski (Eds.), *Regaining Global Stability After the Financial Crisis* (pp. 46–65). Hershey, PA: IGI Global. doi:10.4018/978-1-5225-4026-7.ch003

Trengereid, V. (2022). Conditions of Network Engagement: The Quest for a Common Good. In R. Augusto Costa, F. Brandão, Z. Breda, & C. Costa (Eds.), *Planning and Managing the Experience Economy in Tourism* (pp. 69-84). IGI Global. https://doi.org/10.4018/978-1-7998-8775-1.ch004

Turulja, L., & Bajgoric, N. (2018). Business Continuity and Information Systems: A Systematic Literature Review. In N. Bajgoric (Ed.), *Always-On Enterprise Information Systems for Modern Organizations* (pp. 60–87). Hershey, PA: IGI Global. doi:10.4018/978-1-5225-3704-5.ch004

Vargas-Hernández, J. G. (2017). Professional Integrity in Business Management Education. In N. Baporikar (Ed.), *Management Education for Global Leadership* (pp. 70–89). Hershey, PA: IGI Global. doi:10.4018/978-1-5225-1013-0.ch004

Varnacı Uzun, F. (2021). The Destination Preferences of Foreign Tourists During the COVID-19 Pandemic and Attitudes Towards: Marmaris, Turkey. In M. Demir, A. Dalgıç, & F. Ergen (Eds.), *Handbook of Research on the Impacts and Implications of COVID-19 on the Tourism Industry* (pp. 285–306). IGI Global. https://doi.org/10.4018/978-1-7998-8231-2.ch014

Vasista, T. G., & AlAbdullatif, A. M. (2017). Role of Electronic Customer Relationship Management in Demand Chain Management: A Predictive Analytic Approach. *International Journal of Information Systems and Supply Chain Management*, *10*(1), 53–67. doi:10.4018/IJISSCM.2017010104

Vieru, D., & Bourdeau, S. (2017). Survival in the Digital Era: A Digital Competence-Based Multi-Case Study in the Canadian SME Clothing Industry. *International Journal of Social and Organizational Dynamics in IT*, *6*(1), 17–34. doi:10.4018/IJSODIT.2017010102

Vijayan, G., & Kamarulzaman, N. H. (2017). An Introduction to Sustainable Supply Chain Management and Business Implications. In M. Khan, M. Hussain, & M. Ajmal (Eds.), *Green Supply Chain Management for Sustainable Business Practice* (pp. 27–50). Hershey, PA: IGI Global. doi:10.4018/978-1-5225-0635-5.ch002

Vlachvei, A., & Notta, O. (2017). Firm Competitiveness: Theories, Evidence, and Measurement. In A. Vlachvei, O. Notta, K. Karantininis, & N. Tsounis (Eds.), *Factors Affecting Firm Competitiveness and Performance in the Modern Business World* (pp. 1–42). Hershey, PA: IGI Global. doi:10.4018/978-1-5225-0843-4.ch001

Wang, C., Schofield, M., Li, X., & Ou, X. (2017). Do Chinese Students in Public and Private Higher Education Institutes Perform at Different Level in One of the Leadership Skills: Critical Thinking?: An Exploratory Comparison. In V. Wang (Ed.), *Encyclopedia of Strategic Leadership and Management* (pp. 160–181). Hershey, PA: IGI Global. doi:10.4018/978-1-5225-1049-9.ch013

Wang, J. (2017). Multi-Agent based Production Management Decision System Modelling for the Textile Enterprise. *Journal of Global Information Management*, *25*(4), 1–15. doi:10.4018/JGIM.2017100101

Wiedemann, A., & Gewald, H. (2017). Examining Cross-Domain Alignment: The Correlation of Business Strategy, IT Management, and IT Business Value. *International Journal of IT/Business Alignment and Governance*, *8*(1), 17–31. doi:10.4018/IJITBAG.2017010102

Wolf, R., & Thiel, M. (2018). Advancing Global Business Ethics in China: Reducing Poverty Through Human and Social Welfare. In S. Hipsher (Ed.), *Examining the Private Sector's Role in Wealth Creation and Poverty Reduction* (pp. 67–84). Hershey, PA: IGI Global. doi:10.4018/978-1-5225-3117-3.ch004

Yablonsky, S. (2018). Innovation Platforms: Data and Analytics Platforms. In *Multi-Sided Platforms (MSPs) and Sharing Strategies in the Digital Economy: Emerging Research and Opportunities* (pp. 72–95). Hershey, PA: IGI Global. doi:10.4018/978-1-5225-5457-8.ch003

Yaşar, B. (2021). The Impact of COVID-19 on Volatility of Tourism Stocks: Evidence From BIST Tourism Index. In M. Demir, A. Dalgıç, & F. Ergen (Eds.), *Handbook of Research on the Impacts and Implications of COVID-19 on the Tourism Industry* (pp. 23–44). IGI Global. https://doi.org/10.4018/978-1-7998-8231-2.ch002

Yusoff, A., Ahmad, N. H., & Halim, H. A. (2017). Agropreneurship among Gen Y in Malaysia: The Role of Academic Institutions. In N. Ahmad, T. Ramayah, H. Halim, & S. Rahman (Eds.), *Handbook of Research on Small and Medium Enterprises in Developing Countries* (pp. 23–47). Hershey, PA: IGI Global. doi:10.4018/978-1-5225-2165-5.ch002

Zacher, D., & Pechlaner, H. (2021). Resilience as an Opportunity Approach: Challenges and Perspectives for Private Sector Participation on a Community Level. In A. Zehrer, G. Glowka, K. Schwaiger, & V. Ranacher-Lackner (Eds.), *Resiliency Models and Addressing Future Risks for Family Firms in the Tourism Industry* (pp. 75–102). IGI Global. https://doi.org/10.4018/978-1-7998-7352-5.ch004

Zanin, F., Comuzzi, E., & Costantini, A. (2018). The Effect of Business Strategy and Stock Market Listing on the Use of Risk Assessment Tools. In *Management Control Systems in Complex Settings: Emerging Research and Opportunities* (pp. 145–168). Hershey, PA: IGI Global. doi:10.4018/978-1-5225-3987-2.ch007

Zgheib, P. W. (2017). Corporate Innovation and Intrapreneurship in the Middle East. In P. Zgheib (Ed.), *Entrepreneurship and Business Innovation in the Middle East* (pp. 37–56). Hershey, PA: IGI Global. doi:10.4018/978-1-5225-2066-5.ch003

About the Author

Claretha Hughes, Ph.D. Professor, teaches Human Resource Development at the University of Arkansas in Fayetteville, Arkansas. She has over 31 years of extensive professional experience in business and industry and continues to serve as a consultant to international, national, and state organizations. Her research interests include valuing people and technology in the workplace, technology development, diversity intelligence, learning technologies, and ethical and legal issues. She has published numerous articles in peer-reviewed journals and books and has authored or co-authored 15 books. She is a book proposal reviewer for SAGE, Emerald, IGI Global, and Palgrave Macmillan. She has completed a National Science Foundation Research in Formation of Engineers grant as a Co-PI. She is the 2021 recipient of the Academy of Human Resource Development's FORWARD Award, and the 2009 University Council of Workforce and Human Resource Education Outstanding Assistant Professor award. Dr. Hughes has a Ph.D. in Career & Technical Education from Virginia Tech, a MT degree in Textile Technology Management from NC State University, a BA in Chemistry from Clemson University, and an MBA from the Sam M. Walton College of Business at the University of Arkansas. She has publications in journals such as *Human Resource Development Review, Advances in Developing Human Resources, New Horizons in Adult Education and Human Resource Development, Human Resource Development International*, the *International Journal of Human Resource Development and Management,* and the *Journal of the North American Management Society.*

Index

Ingram Content Group UK Ltd.
Milton Keynes UK
UKHW030034250423
420723UK00007B/164